The **WHY** *of the*

BUY

The
WHY
of the

BUY

CONSUMER BEHAVIOR AND FASHION MARKETING

Patricia Mink Rath
INTERNATIONAL ACADEMY OF DESIGN AND TECHNOLOGY—CHICAGO

Stefani Bay
THE ILLINOIS INSTITUTE OF ART—CHICAGO

Richard Petrizzi
THE ILLINOIS INSTITUTE OF ART—CHICAGO

Penny Gill
PWG COMMUNICATIONS INC.—WHITE PLAINS, N.Y.

FAIRCHILD BOOKS, INC.
NEW YORK

Director of Sales and Acquisitions: Dana Meltzer-Berkowitz
Executive Editor: Olga T. Kontzias
Acquisitions Editor: Joseph Miranda
Senior Development Editor: Jennifer Crane
Development Editor: Laurie Gibson
Art Director: Adam B. Bohannon
Production Manager: Ginger Hillman
Associate Production Editor: Jessica Rozler
Photo Researcher: Justine Brennan, Erin Fitzsimmons
Copyeditor: Joanne Slike
Cover Design: Adam B. Bohannon
Text Design: Adam B. Bohannon
Page Composition: Westchester Book Group

Library of Congress Catalog Card Number: 2007935038
ISBN: 978-1-56367-456-3
GST R 133004424
Printed in the United States of America
CH08, TP08

CONTENTS

Extended Contents   vii
Preface   xiii
Acknowledgments   xviii
Introduction   xix

PART I: WE ARE ALL CONSUMERS
CHAPTER 1   Why Is Consumer Behavior Important to the Fields of Fashion and Design?   3
CHAPTER 2   Consumer Behavior, Marketing, and Fashion: A Working Relationship   29

PART II: INTERNAL FACTORS INFLUENCE FASHION CONSUMERS
CHAPTER 3   How Fashion Consumers Perceive, Learn, and Remember   55
CHAPTER 4   Motivation and the Fashion Consumer   77
CHAPTER 5   Attitude and the Fashion Consumer   103
CHAPTER 6   Personality and the Fashion Consumer   131

PART III: EXTERNAL FACTORS INFLUENCE FASHION CONSUMERS
CHAPTER 7   Age, Family, and Life Cycle Influences   161
CHAPTER 8   Social Influences on Fashion Consumers   187
CHAPTER 9   Demographics, Psychographics, and the Fashion Consumer   213

PART IV: HOW FASHION MARKETERS COMMUNICATE AND CONSUMERS DECIDE
CHAPTER 10   How Marketers Obtain and Use Consumer Information   251
CHAPTER 11   Decision Making   273
CHAPTER 12   How Fashion Consumers Buy   299
CHAPTER 13   The Use of Fashion Goods by Organizations   325
CHAPTER 14   Global Consumers of Fashion and Design   349

PART V: FASHION CONSUMERS AND RESPONSIBLE CITIZENSHIP
CHAPTER 15   Ethics and Social Responsibility   377
CHAPTER 16   The Role of Government   405

Glossary   431
Credits: 449
Index   453

EXTENDED CONTENTS

Preface   xiii
Acknowledgments   xviii
Introduction   xix

PART I: WE ARE ALL CONSUMERS

CHAPTER 1   Why Is Consumer Behavior Important to the Fields of Fashion and Design?   3
Fashion and Design Purchases Are Unique   5
How Marketing Influences the Purchase of Designed Goods   6
Coordinating Marketing Efforts   8
Recent Approaches to Marketing   9
Summary   23
Key Terms   24
Questions for Review   24
Activities   25
Mini-Projects   25
References   26
Additional Resources   26

CHAPTER 2   Consumer Behavior, Marketing, and Fashion: A Working Relationship   29
Marketplace Conditions   29
Value versus Cost   30
Buyer Requirements   32
Staying on Track   36
Approaching the Marketplace   41
Satisfying Customers   48
Summary   50
Key Terms   51
Questions for Review   51
Activities   51
Mini-Project   52
References   52
Additional Resources   53

PART II: INTERNAL FACTORS INFLUENCE FASHION CONSUMERS

CHAPTER 3   How Fashion Consumers Perceive, Learn, and Remember   57
How Stimuli Influence Our Five Senses   59
How We Perceive   62
How We Pay Attention   65
How We Process   67
How We Learn   68
How We Remember   72
Summary   75
Key Terms   75
Questions for Review   76
Activities   76
Mini-Project   77
References   77

CHAPTER 4   Motivation and the Fashion Consumer   79
Understanding Human Behavior   81
How Motivation Works   82
Motivation Is Complex   86
The Power of Motivation   90
Motivation and Design   97
Summary   97
Key Terms   98
Questions for Review   99
Activities   99
Mini-Projects   99
References   100
Additional Resources   100

CHAPTER 5   Attitude and the Fashion Consumer   103
What Is "Attitude"?   104
What Goes into Our Attitudes?   105
The Hierarchy of Effects   107
How Do Attitudes Serve Us?   112
What Influences Our Attitude Formation?   113
How Do Marketers Use Attitudes?   116
What is the Effect of Attitudes on Our Buying Behavior?   118
Summary   126
Key Terms   127

Questions for Review   127
Activities   128
Mini-Project   128
References   129

CHAPTER 6   Personality and the Fashion Consumer   131
What Is Personality?   132
Effect of Personality on the Fashion Consumer   132
Major Personality Theories   132
Products and Their Personalities   147
Summary   153
Key Terms   154
Questions for Review   154
Activities   155
Mini-Project   155
References   155

PART III: EXTERNAL FACTORS INFLUENCE FASHION CONSUMERS
CHAPTER 7   Age, Family, and Life Cycle Influences   161
The Changing Face of the American Consumer   161
Today's Family   172
Household Decision Making Today   178
Summary   182
Key Terms   182
Questions for Review   183
Activities   183
Mini-Projects   183
References   184
Additional Resources   184

CHAPTER 8   Social Influences on Fashion Consumers   187
Forces That Influence Behavior   187
Influences on Fashion and Design   190
Consumer Socialization Process   207
Summary   208
Key Terms   208
Questions for Review   208
Activities   209
Mini-Projects   209
References   209
Additional Resources   211

CHAPTER 9   Demographics, Psychographics, and the Fashion Consumer   213
What Are Demographics?   215
Examples of Typical Demographics   215
Values Driving Consumption   234
What Are Psychographics?   238
Geodemographic Measurements: An Example (PRIZM NE)   242
Summary   244
Key Terms   244
Questions for Review   245
Activities   245
Mini-Project   246
References   246
Additional Resources   248

PART IV: HOW FASHION MARKETERS COMMUNICATE AND CONSUMERS DECIDE

CHAPTER 10   How Marketers Obtain and Use Consumer Information   251
Conducting Market and Marketing Research   252
Putting Marketing Research to Work   262
Summary   268
Key Terms   268
Questions for Review   269
Activities   269
Mini-Project   270
References   270

CHAPTER 11   Decision Making   273
Making the Right Choice   275
Types of Decision Making   289
Consumer Effort Expended   292
Summary   294
Key Terms   294
Questions for Review   295
Activities   295
Mini-Project   295
References   296
Additional Resources   296

CHAPTER 12   How Fashion Consumers Buy   299
Changes in Fashion and Fashion Consumption   300

Retail Marketing of Fashion   305
Summary   318
Key Terms   319
Questions for Review   319
Activities   319
Mini-Project   320
References   320

CHAPTER 13   The Use of Fashion Goods by Organizations   325
Organizations   325
Outside Influences   332
Understanding the Market   333
Fashion Combinations   334
Summary   343
Key Terms   344
Questions for Review   344
Activities   345
Mini-Projects   345
References   345
Additional Resources   346

CHAPTER 14   Global Consumers of Fashion and Design   349
Are We All Alike?   349
Subcultural Differences Influence American Buying Habits   350
Fashion and Design as Unifying Forces   359
Summary   370
Key Terms   370
Questions for Review   371
Activities   371
Mini-Projects   371
References   372
Additional Resources   372

PART V: FASHION CONSUMERS AND RESPONSIBLE CITIZENSHIP
CHAPTER 15   Ethics and Social Responsibility   377
Defining Ethics   378
Consumer Theft   379
Counterfeiting   381
Business Ethics   384
Social Issues   392

Summary   397
Key Terms   398
Questions for Review   398
Activities   398
Mini-Project   399
References   400

CHAPTER 16   The Role of Government   405
Federal Agencies   406
Other Government Programs   424
Independent Agencies and Services   426
Summary   426
Key Terms   427
Questions for Review   428
Activities   428
Mini-Project   429
References   429

Glossary   431
Credits   449
Index   453

PREFACE

What makes people decide what to buy for their wardrobes and their homes? Consumer behavior can appear to be made up of a mysterious set of activities, sometimes not even recognized by consumers themselves as they make up their minds for or against purchasing a new outfit, pair of shoes, set of towels, or sofa. There are, however, certain internal and external influences and patterns of decision making that shed some light on the consumer decision-making process in fashion, and it is for that purpose that this text has been created.

This book was developed because no previous work existed expressly to meet the needs of college students as they explore the consumer buying process and the fashion industry. The text begins with an overview of why the study of consumer behavior is important and the relationship between consumers and marketers; continues by explaining the internal and external influences on fashion consumer decision-making; describes how fashion marketers communicate fashion messages; and concludes with a discussion of fashion consumers and responsible citizenship. To provide relevant industry examples of fashion interest to consumers, each chapter contains related Point of View and Special Focus sidebars as well as Key Terms, Questions for Review, Activities, and Mini-Projects.

Organization of this Text

Part I: We Are All Consumers

Chapter 1 explains why consumer behavior is important, and Chapter 2 points out the relationship between consumers and fashion marketers.

Part II: Internal Factors Influence Fashion Consumers

Chapter 3 describes how consumers perceive, learn and remember; Chapter 4 explains motivation in relation to consuming fashion goods; in Chapter 5 consumer attitudes are explored; while personality and the consumer are the topics of Chapter 6.

Part III: External Factors Influence Fashion Consumers

In Chapter 7, age, family, and life cycle influences are covered; Chapter 8 deals with the topic of social influences on consumers; while demographics and psychographics important in understanding consumer behavior in fashion are found in Chapter 9.

Part IV: How Fashion Marketers Communicate and Consumers Decide

Chapter 10 is concerned with marketing research, how marketers obtain and use consumer information; Chapter 11 points out how consumers reach buying decisions. Chapter 12 indicates when and where consumers purchase fashion goods; while Chapter 13 shows how businesses and other organizations make use of fashion products and information. The global aspects of fashion design and consumption are the topic of Chapter 14.

Part V: Fashion Consumers and Responsible Citizenship

Chapter 15 explains the importance of ethics and social responsibility in the marketing, purchase, and disposal of fashion goods. Chapter 16 describes the role of government across the fashion industry.

Text Features

In addition to its enthusiastic and engaging writing style, *The Why of the Buy* contains a number of features concerning consumer behavior and marketing strategies that arouse student attention and maintain interest. They are useful for further investigation, class discussion, individual reports, and team projects.

Summary and Review

Each of the 16 chapters includes the following features to reinforce and strengthen student comprehension of that chapter's consumer behavior concepts in an interesting way:

The Summary reviews the major chapter topics in a succinct, step-by-step manner.

The Key Terms list the most useful words in comprehending consumer behavior and in grasping the chapter emphasis. (Each term is fully defined both in the chapter and in the Glossary at the end of the text.)

The Review Questions cover the major points brought out in the chapter while the Activities provide an opportunity for students to connect the study of consuming to fashion marketing in a realistic setting. The Mini-Projects offer an opportunity to apply consumer behavior concepts in a fashion marketing situation.

Special Focus

Each chapter contains one or more Special Focus segments on relevant consumer behavior and fashion marketing topics. These features add timeliness and interest to the chapter content and make the material more meaningful to the student. Some examples are:

- Why up-branding is here to stay
- Fashion communicates across the globe
- Holiday shoppers are hunter-gatherers
- Focusing on the product, consumers reveal inner feelings

Point of View

The chapters feature one or more Point of View segments that describe a current concept or situation that fashion consumers and marketers are encountering in society today. These segments, too, add a slice of reality and offer insights into the fashion world that are intriguing to students. Some examples include:

- Fashion and semiotics: the hidden meaning of a style
- When shopping, men aren't like women
- J. C. Penney rolls out the red carpet for a new private brand
- Target communicates attitude through design

Let's Talk

Also contained within each chapter are several Let's Talk questions relating to the content just presented. These questions enable instructors and students to discuss, react to, and perhaps elaborate on the topics explained. Some examples are:

- How do you decide what to buy? Do you base your decisions on trends, practicality, brand name, or the suggestions of friends?
- For each of the last three fashion purchases you made, which of the three elements of the hierarchy of attitude was the greatest influence? Explain.
- Have you been asked recently to complete a survey using an attitude scale? Why do you think marketers seem to be using this type of survey more frequently?
- What products would you consider purchasing online? Are there any items you'd prefer to buy in a physical store? Why or why not?

Mini-Projects

To round off the end-of-chapter materials, each chapter contains one or two Mini-Projects which offer an opportunity to apply in a realistic fashion setting some of the concepts presented in the chapter. Examples include:

- Create a consumer profile and a corresponding brand personality
- Recalling a recent fashion purchase, identify the decision-making process

- Teaming with two other class members, identify a product or service each team member recently purchased using either routine, limited, or extensive decision making.
- Explain the effect of NAFTA and whether its expectations are being met

Glossary

The Glossary at the end of the text contains the key terms from each of the 16 chapters, plus their definitions. These terms enable students to understand communication within the consumer behavior and fashion communities and to put their words to use.

Instructor's Manual

An Instructor's Manual accompanying the *Why of the Buy* is available and contains chapter outlines, answers to review and discussion questions and mini-projects, plus a test bank and answers.

ACKNOWLEDGMENTS

Many people contributed to the creation and development of this text, among them representatives of the publisher, experts in the fashion and academic fields, and the families of the authors.

The authors are particularly grateful to Olga T. Kontzias, Executive Editor of Fairchild Books, who provided the original inspiration for the text, and who faithfully maintained her support and encouragement throughout its preparation. We also appreciate the contribution of Joseph Miranda, Acquisitions Editor, whose early recognition of the need for this work aided its genesis. And to the many other people in the Production and Marketing departments at Fairchild who made this work possible, the authors owe our gratitude. Among the people in the fashion and academic fields, the authors deeply appreciate the efforts of the following people for providing information and suggestions for the text, and, on occasion, for reading portions of the manuscript:

Kathy Embry, Dean, Design Studies, International Academy of Merchandising and Design, Chicago

Karen Janko, Program Director, Fashion Marketing and Management, Illinois Institute of Art, Chicago

Wilma Kozar, Program Director, Merchandising Management, IADT, Chicago

Alice McNeil, Director of Educational Resources, IADT, Chicago

Jacqueline Peterson, Senior Academic Director of Fashion Marketing, The Art Institute of Phoenix

Eric Rath, Ph.D., Associate Professor of History, University of Kansas, Lawrence

Margot Wallace, Professor of Marketing Communication, School of Media Arts, Columbia College, Chicago

Sidney Wasserman, D.S.W., retired Associate Professor, Smith College, Northampton, MA, and Lecturer, University of Bradford, Yorkshire, England

The students of Patricia Rath's Marketing and Consumer Behavior class (MK215), Fall 2006, IADT Chicago campus, who read and commented on many chapters of the original manuscript

Former students and valued friends who continue to inform and inspire: Nicholas Braggo, Gina Gesmond, Inese Apale, and Morgan Kiederlen

Colleagues (and valued friends) whose expertise and encouragement in wide-ranging collaborations have provided great knowledge as well as inspiration for this and other projects: Jules Abend and Cathy Callegari

The reviewers whom Fairchild Books enlisted to peer review the manuscript: Petra Barnes, Kansas State University, Dr. Joanne Leoni, Johnson & Wales University, and Joanne Offerman, the Fashion Institute of Technology

In addition, the authors recall with affection and admiration Fairchild's late acquisitions editor, Mary A. McGarry, the memory of whose dedication to the creation of state-of-the-art student learning materials remains with us to this day.

This work could not have come about without the support of our friends and families during its development. In particular, Patricia Mink Rath thanks her husband, Philip Balsamo, for his sustaining love, perceptive views, and inimitable sense of humor; and Penny Gill thanks her son, Justin Gill, and mother, Phoebe D. Gill, for their love, patience, understanding, and encouragement through the research and writing process; and Richard Petrizzi and Stefani Bay wish to thank Pat, Penny, and each other for the cooperative perseverance that brought this work to life.

INTRODUCTION

"I never thought I'd get married, but she swept away all my resolve, and now I want to buy her something—not gaudy and huge—but something she'd be happy to wear for a long time." This is how Michael Smyth expressed his feelings recently when shopping for an engagement ring at Buccellati jewelers in New York. He wasn't looking for the largest, most unusual, or costliest diamond; he was searching for a remembrance that his wife-to-be might treasure for years.[1]

Like Michael Smyth, we are all consumers, and we all have different reasons for buying. Maybe we just want a coat to keep us warm and dry; perhaps we're aiming to succeed in a job and so dress to look the part; or, like Mr. Smyth, we might be hoping to bring joy to someone we love. The purpose of this book is twofold: to examine our many reasons for buying and using fashion goods, and to recognize how fashion marketers use their understanding of consumer behavior to inform and persuade us to try their products.

Welcome, then, to the intriguing world of *consumer behavior*, the series of actions we go through in deciding to buy and use goods and services. The focus of this book is consumer behavior as it relates to *fashion goods*—that is, those items that are popular at a given time. Fashion goods include a variety of products such as apparel, cosmetics, furniture, home accessories—and diamond rings. Our focus also is on how the fashion industries use knowledge of consumer behavior to anticipate and satisfy our needs for those goods and services.

Notice that as Michael Smyth is contemplating his purchase, he is thinking about how his fiancée will feel about the ring and whether she will like it, not just for the time being but for years to come. In other words, his concern is with the benefits of the ring. *Consumer benefits* are the qualities that make people feel good about their purchases. We buy emotionally and justify logically. Consumer benefits can be both tangible—in this case the beauty and value of the diamond itself—or intangible, such as the delight his fiancée will feel when Michael presents the gift.

When people buy fashion goods, they are buying benefits—what the product will do for them. "Will the dark suit make me look slimmer?" "Does that bronzer make me look healthier?" "By driving that convertible, will I stand a chance with

---

[1] Rozhon, Tracie. "Competition Is Forever: The Net and Discount Retailers Change the Diamond Business." *New York Times*. February 9, 2005, pp. 1, 9.

that certain someone?" Of course, everyone's ideas of product benefits are different, but marketers have found that large groups of people may be looking for the same kinds of benefits and that their marketplace behavior is similar. Marketers identify these groups and organize them according to those similarities. Businesses, particularly fashion businesses, know that they cannot serve every customer equally well, so they have to decide which customers they can serve most efficiently and profitably. To do this, marketers use a process called *market segmentation*: dividing the total population into distinct groups seeking similar customer benefits and showing similar purchasing behaviors. In this way, fashion marketers can best work to meet customer needs.

There are many ways to identify customers who share similar behaviors. Furthermore, consumers are often grouped by gender, age, and geographic location—statistics that fashion marketers are concerned with in addition to consumer income. But obviously, not all fashion goods are intended for high-income consumers. For example, the mid-price retailer Gap recognized that many of its female customers were either too large or too short to fit into regular sizes, and so the company began offering plus and petite sizes. Market segmentation, then, allows fashion marketers to most accurately anticipate, identify, and respond to consumer fashion needs with the hope of keeping their customers and thus staying in business and improving their profits. Another example of how companies cater to specific market segments can be seen in the efforts of Saks, which opened a number of Club Libby Lu stores (both freestanding and inside other stores—and even a flagship location at Disneyland) to meet the demands of preteen girls who are intensely interested in fashion.[2]

As you can tell, marketers respond to consumer needs, because customers—as they decide what they will buy and use—are the reason for the existence of a business. However, any given business cannot serve everyone; therefore, by using strategies such as market segmentation, a business finds those customers it can best serve profitably. For example, Target understands that its customers want fashions—even designer names like Mossimo or Michael Graves—but at a very moderate price. Target needs to generate a profit in order to continue its business. Identifying customers' needs and focusing on the needs that a company can best serve while making a profit is the *marketing concept*. In the highly competitive fashion field, the most successful businesses pay close attention to the marketing concept—their very existence depends on it!

Today's fashion marketplace is global, and electronic technology such as the Internet permits consumers to express their needs and marketers to fulfill them, often instantaneously. Let's see how this is done. Our approach begins with a look at the

[2] Yerack, Becky. "Saks' Club Libby Lu on a Roll with Preteens." *Chicago Tribune.* February 15, 2005. Sec. 3, page 3.

relationship between consumers and the field of fashion, showing the contributions that consumers make to fashion and design. Next we explore the minds of consumers to observe how humans perceive and learn. We then look at what motivates consumers and how attitudes and values influence their selection and purchase of fashion goods. Our focus then shifts to examine how marketers' methods of persuasion work to influence consumer actions. As consumers we see ourselves a number of ways, and our self-perceptions can also influence our choice of the fashion goods.

The outside world can have an effect as well; factors such as family, age, and ethnicity also have an impact on our fashion purchases, as can our friends, social class, income, and lifestyle. Fashion marketers collect extensive information on consumer motivations and decisions in an effort to ensure their persuasion will lead to our ultimate satisfaction as consumers. Before buying, consumers can go through numerous decision-making steps, seeking information from sources such as stores, catalogs, the Internet, TV, and friends, among others. For some consumers, this search can be local; for others, it can be worldwide. Organizations (both private and governmental) have been created to help consumers in reaching buying decisions, and to protect consumers from potentially harmful products or business practices. These topics and more are what we will be exploring as we delve into the "why of the buy." Consumer behavior and fashion marketing are fascinating processes—let's see how they interact!

PART I

We Are All Consumers

Shopping has become an American pastime. Consumers buy both for need and for entertainment, as Part I describes.

Through learning as much as possible about consumers, fashion businesses can work to influence customer purchasing today and in the future. Chapter 1 lays the groundwork for *The Why of the Buy*, discussing what consumers want and how marketers can best serve them. Chapter 2 examines what consumers value, and the connection between companies and customers, followed by a description of how businesses gather consumer information, develop strategies, and create what they hope will be lasting marketing relationships with their customers.

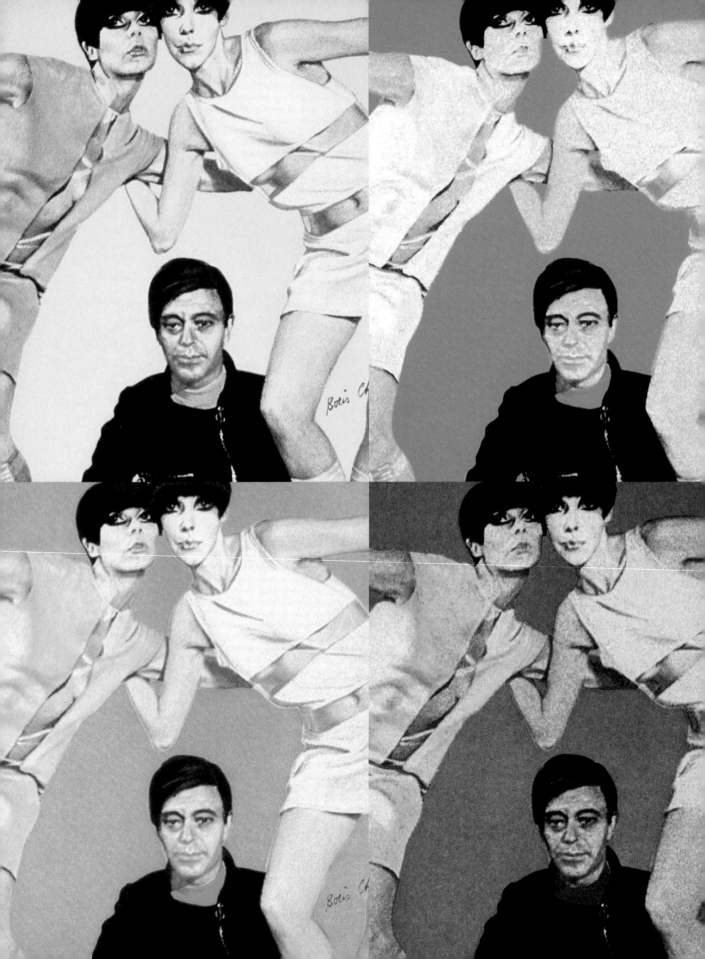

CHAPTER 1

Why Is Consumer Behavior Important to the Fields of Fashion and Design?

When the National Retail Federation held its 95th Annual Convention and Expo in New York City, the topics most important to those attending this event were as follows:

- Emerging consumer trends
- How to better serve customers' needs
- The effects of cultural attitudes on buying habits
- Customer-centric merchandising
- Techniques to improve shopper satisfaction[1]

Why? Because convention attendees were seeking the answer to the eternal marketing question—the one that's asked again and again by businesspeople every day: What do customers want, and how can we best serve them?

It's an important question—one that addresses the very essence of doing business

FIGURE 1.1. Would the recipient of this extravagant diamond necklace care if she knew it had been purchased for her at a store like Sam's Club, rather than at Cartier?

successfully. The more we learn about what people purchase and their behaviors before, during, and after those purchases, the more fascinating the issue becomes. Read these examples and you'll see what we mean.

Did you know that there are young men from the Democratic Republic of the Congo (formerly Zaire) known as *sapeurs*, who, although chronically unemployed and living in poverty, purchase and wear *haute couture* clothing, made in the finest ateliers in Paris? To possess these precious pieces, *sapeurs* do whatever it takes to make enough money to go to Paris and buy an *haute couture* ensemble. While in Paris, they display their outfits proudly until their money runs out, and then they return home triumphant, to begin the process again.[2]

Did you know that, outside of Asia, Mexico is the world's fourth largest consumer of a certain Japanese fast food invented after World War II by a man from Osaka, who was motivated by the sadness he felt watching the hungry citizens of his city line up for meager servings of food? It has little resemblance to the luscious Mexican cuisine, immortalized by novels such as *Like Water for Chocolate*, in which the zesty dishes awakened forbidden desires. Give up? It's instant ramen noodles, eaten with a plastic spoon from a Styrofoam cup.[3]

Did you know that during a recent holiday season, a well-known retailer offered an 82-carat diamond wreath necklace for $263,574 that could be purchased online? Was it Tiffany & Company, known for creating some of the most important pieces of diamond jewelry in the world? Was it Cartier, the jeweler that has serviced, among its many illustrious clients, the gem-worshipping maharajahs of India, the royals of Europe, and the industrialists of the United States? Not quite. It was Sam's Club, the warehouse division of Wal-Mart, the emperor of discounters.[4]

These stories all lead to one essential question: Why? Why do customers shop where they shop and buy what they buy? That's the central issue of this book—**consumer behavior**. We can define it as the actions and decision-making processes of buyers as they recognize their desire for a product or service and engage in the search, evaluation, purchase, use, and disposal of that particular commodity. Consumer behavior is the study of **consumption**: the using up of a resource by the person who has selected, adopted, used, discarded, and (hopefully) recycled it.

Fashion and Design Purchases Are Unique

When it comes to the selection of fashion-related goods, some very specific influences determine our buying behavior. Why? We use fashionable items primarily to make statements about ourselves, our tastes, our values, our identities, our aspirations—that is, the way we want others to see us. People seek different goods for different reasons. Some of us are drawn to items that bear the names of famous designers, some to pieces that are comfortable and affordable, some to items that reflect elements of good design.

What, exactly, is *design*? In his book *By Design*, author Ralph Caplan calls it "a process for making things right, for shaping what people need. We all live with designed objects that we love, hate, use, break, and don't know how to fix . . . we live in a designed world."[5] *Webster's New World Dictionary* defines it as "to plan and carry out, especially by artistic arrangement or in a skillful way; to make original plans for or outcome aimed at."[6] Our working definition of **design** is a hybrid: a creative process, driven by a need, which leads to an invention of some sort, be it practical or artistic, functional or simply attractive, devised to enhance life in some way.

To be sure, fashion has an important relationship to design of all kinds, because the concept of fashion pertains to more than just clothing. It includes automobiles, furniture, accessories, cuisine, appliances, lighting, bathroom fixtures, jewelry, music, graphics, photography, industrial products, paint colors, electronics, and so on. Simply stated, design covers a lot of ground.

The term **fashion** applies to anything that's of the moment and subject to change; it's anything that members of a population deem desirable and appropriate at a given time. During the past few years, many celebrities have

FIGURE 1.2. Pampered pups make great fashion statements.

turned their pampered pooches into chic fashion accessories. These doggy darlings have accompanied their famous owners to openings and galas, traveling in Louis Vuitton canine carriers, decked out in cashmere, sequins, and Burberry plaids. (Yes, we're talking about the pups!) Who knows what type of pet will be *de rigueur* by the time you read this book? But one thing is for sure: Celebrity dogs will eventually find themselves at home, playing fetch with their nannies, and fashion followers will be on the trail of something entirely different by then.

Fashion and design are both about tuning into the **zeitgeist,** the spirit of the times. To be fashionable or engage productively in the process of design, one must be extremely well read, well rounded, in tune with current aesthetics, politics, popular products, culture, art, architecture, business—everything occurring in the present, which comprises the zeitgeist. Developing awareness and sensitivity must be top priorities, because success in the worlds of fashion and design requires a person to be up-to-date and in sync with the moment, for the moment is the indicator of all that is important, valued, and wanted by customers (whether it be symbolic or functional, real or perceived).

How Marketing Influences the Purchase of Designed Goods

Suppose you want to develop your own fashion-related business in the future—a video production company, an online designer resale boutique, an interior design consulting service, an art gallery, a contemporary furniture showroom in a bustling mart center, and so forth. There are so many possibilities in the world of design, retailing, wholesaling, and consulting that the choices seem endless. How will you begin? How will you determine who your customers are? How will you connect with them, once you identify them? How will you decide what to offer them next season and the season after that? How will you get them to keep coming back to you and not go somewhere else the next time they go shopping?

> *Let's Talk*
> *If you opened a retail or service business of your own, how would you let consumers know about it? How would you get them to continue buying from you, rather than from a competitor?*

Certainly you need to have some kind of plan for the *marketing* of your idea—that is, getting the word out to the public that you exist and what it is that makes you unique. **Marketing** is a process that includes the communication of all information that sellers want to share with consumers, from the time a product or service is an idea through its purchase, use, evaluation, and disposal by the customer. Marketing covers a broad range of activities, from design, research, and test marketing to pricing, production, promotion, and distribution. And it doesn't stop there. Marketers must continuously evaluate and innovate, since no product or service can remain the same forever and still be desirable. Furthermore, marketers need to concentrate on maintaining relationships with customers while seeking to attract new ones. Coordinate these activities successfully and you can give your product or service a **competitive advantage**: the delivery of benefits that exceed those supplied by the competition, making your product or service the best choice for the customer and the most profitable for your organization. In other words, satisfy the customer, and you'll make money.

So, what are the actual areas of expertise that comprise marketing? Think of marketing as an umbrella term that covers several integrated activities, the basis of which we believe is the study of consumer behavior. Why? If you don't know what people think they need, you can't give them what they think they want. Finding out as much as you can about your customers also will help you successfully use other marketing components or areas a marketer must master, such as:

Advertising. Space that is paid for and used to communicate an organization's intended message

Branding. Creating identity and recognition for a product/service/company through the development and use of both visual symbols (color, letters, words) and intangibles (meanings, impressions) to build a brand's image and buyers' loyalty

Communications. Effectively sharing ideas to generate interest

Community involvement. Implementing the societal marketing concept (see Chapter 2)

Customer relationship building and maintenance. Continuous and regular interaction with customers in order to develop and maintain a bond with them

Direct marketing. Selling directly to the public via television, Internet, telephone, mail, and so on

Global marketing. Marketing to customers in foreign markets

Media planning. Selecting and purchasing advertising space that will reach the desired audience while staying within the organization's budget

Pricing strategies. Pricing to please customers and benefit stakeholders

Product development. Using innovative ideas to create new and better products

Professional selling. Personal communications that uncover customers' needs and assist them with buying decisions

Psychology and sociology. The studies of individual and group behavior

Public relations. Enhancing the image of a person, product, company, or service in the eyes of the customer

Sales promotion. Activities and efforts designed to increase sales in the immediate future

Supply chain management/distribution. The organizations associated with the manufacture and delivery and sale of a product/service

Table 1.1. Areas of Marketing

Coordinating Marketing Efforts

Consumer behavior is the aspect of marketing that propels it into action. The discovery and information processing inherent in consumers' actions before, during, and after they buy keeps marketers on their toes. Savvy marketers want to influence these processes and direct potential customers to their products and services through expert use and careful implementation of their particular marketing specialty. Obviously, communication is a key element if all departments are "to be on the same page." It makes sense that the advertising department should know what the sales promotion people are planning, so those plans can be included in current ads. Likewise, the sales associates need to know what promotions are either planned or under way so they can effectively encourage purchases and work to ensure good customer relationships. In other words, all of the cross-functional "team members" need to be in touch, via what is called an **integrated marketing system (IMS)**, the continuous, efficient sharing of information and ideas supplied by participants. The intended result of an IMS is organized and effective communication with the desired audience that includes employees, stakeholders, and, of course, targeted customers.

Here's what can happen without an IMS. A large department store is hosting a trunk show featuring the new evening wear collection of a well-known designer. In preparation, the sales associates in the second-floor *Designer Salon* sent advance notices to their best customers but did not request RSVPs. To make sure the event would be well attended, the store manager decided that it should be opened to the public, so an ad was placed in the Style section of the newspaper, where it appeared on the morning of the event. However, no one communicated to the associates on the first floor that the event had been opened to the public. Hence, when customers who'd seen the advertisement arrived and asked for directions to the event, they were told, "We're sorry, but this is a private showing for our special customers." Many left in a huff, filed complaints with the management, and said they would not return to the store unless they received formal apologies.

So, who benefits from an integrated marketing system? Just about everyone who's involved with the process of creating, producing, selling, and buying, since coordinated marketing informs and helps provide consistent information about a product or a service. Additionally, better marketing, which includes inviting and integrating feedback from customers and employees, results in products and services that are higher in quality and, therefore, higher in customer satisfaction. And isn't that the goal of the whole process? Without some kind of an IMS in place, the customer and the organization both lose.

FIGURE 1.3. The origin of buzz—how it all began.

Recent Approaches to Marketing

The fundamental purpose of marketing is to create goodwill, interest, excitement, and desire among prospective buyers. Marketers know that most people want to be in the know; they want to feel that they belong and, at the same time, that they're unique—a conflicting but common human condition we're all familiar with. The creation of **buzz**, the tongue wagging and ongoing chatter that's set in motion by marketers, particularly public relations and advertising experts, is a strategy being used more and more often to get the word out about new products. The theory is this: Everyone wants to participate in spreading the news about something exciting and avant-garde; people are flattered when they're part of the process. This results in wider exposure and greater momentum for the product, not to mention the positive feelings enjoyed by consumers when they believe they have "inside" information.

〉〉〉 SPECIAL FOCUS 1.1: BUILDING BUZZ ON CAMPUS 〈〈〈

Students help companies bring guerrilla marketing to campus.

During lunch at Boston University, five girls ogled a 6-foot-7 blond senior with a winning smile and high cool quotient as he approached their table. He was cute, they agreed. But equally intriguing was his pitch.

In an age when the college demographic is no longer easily reached by television, radio or newspapers—as TiVo, satellite radio, iPods and the Internet crowd out the traditional advertising venues—a microindustry of campus marketing has emerged. Niche firms have sprung up to act as recruiters of students, who then market products on campus for companies such as Microsoft, JetBlue Airways, The Cartoon Network and Victoria's Secret.

The students selected tend to be campus leaders with large social networks that can be tapped for marketing. Good looks and charm tend to follow. Many are specially trained, sometimes at corporate headquarters, Gossett said, as in the case with Microsoft. They are expected to devote about 10 to 15 hours a week talking up the products to friends, securing corporate sponsorship of campus events and lobbying student newspaper reporters to mention products in articles. They also must plaster bulletin boards with posters and chalk sidewalks—tactics known as "guerrilla marketing," which, marketing firms acknowledge, intentionally skirt the boundaries of campus rules.

College students are, however, a tough crowd for marketers. The generation's members not only tend to ignore traditional media—television, radio and newspapers—but, studies show, they are no more likely to click open an Internet ad than older adults are. They do, however, listen to one another.

The method is a blend of other emerging tactics: buzz marketing, in which people talk up a product to friends and family without necessarily revealing corporate representation, and street teams, young people who hand out stickers, fliers and products.

"I probably listened to Trevor more because he's a friend," said Kelsey Henager, a sophomore studying public relations. "Students come from your level, and you don't feel like they are just pushing a product on you—it's more like they're sharing their opinion."

〉〉〉 Source: Sarah Schweitzer, "Building a Buzz on Campus," *The Boston Globe*, October 24, 2005.

Hype is another device used by marketers to communicate a message; it's a set of activities put in motion before the actual appearance of a new product or service that helps create a supportive marketing environment and a spontaneously infectious kind of person-to-person image spinning. Then, when the product actually becomes available, consumers are eager to purchase it. Did you ever notice how, before a new movie opens, the starring actors seem to be everywhere—on late night TV, on morning talk shows, making caviar pies with celebrity chefs, endorsing products—in general being highly visible and chatty? Then, the next day at school or work, people ask, "Did you see J. Lo last night on _____? Her movie is coming out this Friday." This is marketing hype in action.

However, there are those who believe that buzz and hype are not really spontaneous at all but, rather, calculated, covert operations by marketing agents in disguise, and therefore, unethical. Some see devices such as these as nothing more than a way to get customers to spread promotional propaganda without knowing they've been recruited. Perhaps that's why the use of such methods is sometimes referred to as **guerilla marketing** (a term coined by Jay Conrad Levinson to describe unconventional marketing tactics designed to get maximum results from minimal resources), **ambush marketing** (placing unique marketing materials in venues that result in consumer and media attention), and **viral marketing** (passing a marketing message to others, much like passing a virus from one person to another). These techniques are part of what's called **WOM**, or **word-of-mouth marketing**, and are all based on the sharing habits of human beings.

❯❯❯ SPECIAL FOCUS 1.2: WHAT LOOKS LIKE GRAFFITI COULD REALLY BE AN AD ❮❮❮

The images are painted directly onto building walls in urban areas, graffiti-style. Wide-eyed kids, portrayed in a stylized, comic-book rendering, pose with a mysterious, hand-size gadget. One licks his like a lollipop. Another is playing paddleball with the thing.

What looks like artful vandalism, though, is really part of a guerrilla marketing campaign for Sony's PlayStation Portable, a device that can play games, music and movies.

In major cities such as San Francisco, Miami and New York, Sony has paid building owners to use wall space for the campaign, and the images have become a familiar sight. It's the latest effort by a big corporation to capitalize on the hot world of street art to reach an urban market that has learned to tune out traditional advertising.

Advertising Age critic Bob Garfield said that an increase in such edgy advertising campaigns, which attempt to create 'buzz about buzz,' are a sign that traditional advertising methods are failing.

"Marketers are desperate to find ways to reach people," Garfield said. "Especially young men, who are far too busy playing 'Grand Theft Auto' to notice, say, a 30-second TV commercial."

The increasingly blurred lines between street art, graffiti and marketing is leading to strange situations. One graffiti artist was detained by police in Chicago last summer after he was caught spray-painting over a paid graffiti ad for Axe deodorant.

Among artists who risk arrest to put up paintings and posters they hope will surprise, provoke or delight passersby, the co-opting of street art by corporate America is touchy issue. Patrick McNeil, a member of a three-person street-art collective called Faile, accused Sony of "trying to cash in on an art movement where they and the product they are selling don't belong" and derided Sony's painters as "an army of pimped-out artists."

But street artists who do corporate work to pay the bills say they are doing the same creative work they did before, just in a different medium.

For corporations, graffiti and street art can be a tempting way to get noticed. When *Time* magazine paid a graffiti artist to festoon a wall in the SoHo section of New York this summer, a local politician denounced it as underwriting the work of vandals. *Time* magazine Associate Publisher and Marketing Director Taylor Gray said the stunt was a success because it "cut through the clutter" of marketing messages to which New Yorkers are exposed every day.

Many street artists say they can intuitively grasp this strategy, even if it makes them cringe. For New York-based street artist Michael De Feo, the [Sony] PSP campaign seems to elicit a shrug. "Who are we to say they can't do it?" he said.

De Feo, a high school art teacher who spends his evenings decorating cities with cartoonish paintings and stencils of flowers and sharks, said the worst crime in Sony's PSP ad campaign is a lack of originality.

"People seem to get all bent out of shape with campaigns like this, when the fact remains that most of the public has the ability to tell good art from bad," he said.

De Feo does not rank the PSP campaign as good art. "I think it really lacks creativity," he said. "It's boring."

>>> Source: Mike Musgrove, "What Looks Like Graffiti Could Really Be an Ad," *Washington Post*, December 26, 2005, A01

Whatever your opinion about buzz and hype, it's clear that both were at work recently, prior to the actual appearance of clothing designer Stella McCartney's apparel line, created especially for well-known retailer H&M. Everyone in the fashion industry was talking about the potential risks and/or rewards of such a bold marketing strategy for weeks before it debuted. As you may know, the entire line sold out in less than a day—wow!

FIGURE 1.4. Was it conventional advertising or word-of-mouth marketing that resulted in this kind of response to the debut of Stella McCartney's collection for H&M?

Finding Your Audience

Consider the assortment of shoppers shown in Figure 1.4 waiting for H&M to open. They are all unique individuals, but they have at least one thing in common—the desire to buy clothing designed by Ms. McCartney. In that way, they share similar characteristics, and each one is displaying the same behavior: a willingness to wait in line to get what she desires, possibly to gain status and prestige. Thus, each woman in the picture is a member of a clearly delineated **market segment**, a homogeneous group of buyers displaying like needs, wants, values, and buying behaviors.

Consumer behavior experts provide marketers with the research they need to learn everything possible about the types of customers they want to attract. These market segments are then selected and combined into a **target market**, an incorporation of the likely groups of potential customers who share similar lifestyles and preferences, on which a company intends to focus its marketing efforts. (See Chapters 2, 7, 8, and 9 for additional segmentation information.) Without consumer research, which uncovers and keeps pace with the wants and needs of a diverse marketplace (and a target market in particular), organizations would still be using the old method of **mass marketing**, the mass distribution and mass promotion of the same product to all potential customers. It's dull, and that method is no longer an option. Today there is simply too much competition. Furthermore, customers do their own careful research in order to get the greatest benefit from each item they purchase. They want a reason to buy.

❯ ❯ ❯ SPECIAL FOCUS 1.3: FACEBOOK OPENS THE DOORS AND MEDIA FLOCKS IN ❮ ❮ ❮

Facebook users love to "poke" friends they have linked to on the site, an electronic way to tap their pals on the shoulder, even if they are miles away in a classroom or office. Now aficionados of the popular social-networking site will have just as much opportunity to do the same to advertisers and media outlets who want to vie for their attention and disposable income.

One day after Facebook unveiled a number of ad innovations, marketers are setting up shop on the site. CBS plans to promote the recent return of longstanding reality program *The Amazing Race*. CondéNet's Epicurious.com has a site offering a recipe for "beef stroganov" from the pages of *Gourmet* magazine . . . Facebook is in many ways going down a path used by MySpace, opening its collection of user-generated profile pages to marketers, who can now populate the social net with "personifications" of individual products and services. Facebook also unveiled a system that lets marketers spread promotional messages virally . . . A new program called Facebook Beacon provides a way for users to choose to share their activities with their friends on the social network. People who surf Blockbuster .com, for example, might send the titles of the movies they add to their queue on Blockbuster's website back to their friends on the Facebook website . . . Marketing observers have some concerns that Facebook users could be a little rattled when they find their activities on some applications, such as Facebook Beacon, communicated to a broad array of friends. But Sarah Chubb, president of CondéNet . . . said people are generally interested in talking about hobbies and passions, and so long as advertisers appeal to that dimension of consumer behavior, the ads and promotions could be more welcome.

>>> Source: Excerpted from "Facebook Opens the Doors and Media Flocks In," Brian Steinberg, www.AdAge.com, November 7, 2007

Consumers Can Be Inconsistent

Stella McCartney is currently a very popular designer, but no one knows what will happen in the future. Rudi Gernreich was also very popular at one time, but have you ever heard of him? Mr. Gernreich is considered by many to be one of the ten most influential designers of the twentieth century, having changed the face of modern fashion with his concept called "unisex" dressing (which was once considered crazy) and his invention of the soft, unstructured "no bra" bra.

When it comes to fashion-related and designed goods, people tend to be fickle, forget quickly, and for the most part, want novelty. Consumer behavior is therefore inconsistent and capricious. Inevitably, something more desirable will come along and dethrone what was previously at the top of everyone's most wanted list, because many purchasers of designed goods pay close attention to trends. A **trend** is a direction in which something is moving, be it a trend in global warming, population growth, real estate, politics, video games, kitchen appliances, textiles, and so on. Some trends last for many years, while others slow and decline rather quickly. Many consumers want to be up-to-date regarding trends; this awareness signals that they are knowledgeable about what's considered to be "the latest."

Buyers Often Stick Together

Consumers tend to accept or reject various goods in large numbers; buyers actually cast a "vote" in the marketplace regarding what they like and don't like, want and don't want, purchase or refuse to purchase. This "voting" of sorts has been referred to as the theory of **collective selection**, a process by which a mass of people formulate certain collective tastes reflected by the goods or services they choose, and their selections illustrate the beliefs and values of the group's social system. Only those goods most consistent with the sociocultural environment win.[7] Consumer researchers point to a collective buying behavior that's recently become the norm—the demand for luxury goods by shoppers at many income levels. These premium products and services were once considered out of reach by all but the very wealthy, but they are now purchased by many. That's because marketers recognized the collective desire for premium products, or at least for those that *appear* to be premium, and began offering upscale everything, from bottled water to in-home spas.

FIGURE 1.5. As many in the worlds of art and fashion know, fame is fleeting.

⟩ ⟩ ⟩ SPECIAL FOCUS 1.4: WHY UP-BRANDING IS HERE TO STAY ⟨ ⟨ ⟨

Just when you thought the luxury market couldn't get any more luxurious, there came the first-class-only airline, the designer pup and the $172,000 diamond-studded fountain pen.

It boggles the minds and wallets of all but a select few.

However, as the real luxury market moves into the stratosphere, it's leaving open a vast universe in which mass marketers can fulfill the neo-luxury desires of mass consumers. And these consuming masses have shown strong evidence they are ready, willing and able to pay premium prices for products and services that were once considered commodities.

Premium Becomes Commonplace

With basic water needs satisfied, for example, American consumers want Evian, Deja Blue, Glaceau or any bottled-water brand carried in Patagonia water pouches by athletes, movie stars and politicians.

Consumers may get hungry, but no basic burger will do: Nieman Ranch beef cooked on one of Frontgate's sleekest grills followed by a Tassimo espresso is the only way up-branders will go. Some even think they'll be loved far better if they use Olay Regenerist and Crest Vivid White and launder their Victoria Secrets in Whirlpool Duets.

Small Indulgences

On another level, given all the stresses of the world, there seems to be an increasing desire to "take care of me." People want a bit of luxury however they can get it. Starbucks, early on, recognized that while not everyone can afford to go to Tiffany's, they can enjoy the small indulgence of a grande nonfat latte. The coffee costs $5—a small price to pay to treat oneself well.

But while up-branding is definitely here to stay, it's a tricky thing to get right. . . . Consumers are becoming more aware. . . . Hence (nice up-market word), here a few rules of thumb for taking your brand up a few notches:

1. *Play from your brand's strength.* Offer a benefit that is legitimately better and different but aligned with what consumers already associate with your brand. Crest, for example, has always been associated with a beautiful, healthy smile. Its up-branded product, Crest Vivid White, builds on this well-known brand association by adding whiteness to the beautiful, healthy equation. The key to success, however, is to make it simple for people to understand what makes your product worthy of up-brand status at an up-brand price.

2. *Leverage design.* Sophisticated or elegant design is one of the fastest ways to communicate better quality. Consumers have been trained to factor in aesthetics when assessing value. The more attractive a product, the more valuable they perceive it to be. Just as with genuine luxury brands, one of the most telegraphic ways to signal an up-branded product is to make it look like one, not just function like one. The new Whirlpool Duet "fabric care system" offers enhanced laundering efficiency in an ultrasleek design. The elegantly proportioned Whirlpool Duet signals that laundry day can actually be a very pleasant experience.

3. *Consider limiting your distribution channels.* Limiting distribution can be a powerful way to signal an up-branded product or service. If you're everywhere, how special can you be? Häagen-Dazs ice cream became the

up-brand it is by starting out with limited distribution; for many years it was available only at gourmet shops and ice-cream boutiques. Apple took great care to create an all-Apple, all-the-time retail experience in which its customers could try out products and get Apple-friendly assistance. Stihl, the leading manufacturer of consumer power tools, has taken a similar up-brand tack by limiting availability of its products to local, customer-focused retailers. The environment in which a company decides to sell speaks volumes about the company it wishes to keep.

4. *Give your brand a "green" label.* Today green has gone mainstream, and consumers across many market segments are willing to pay more for products they believe will make a difference in the efforts to mitigate global warming. While Whole Foods, Patagonia, Aveda and the Body Shop were forerunners in this area, more conventional brands are taking up the cause, not just for the financial up-brand value but for the environmental value. GE, as part of its Ecomagination program, has developed a number of environment-friendly consumer products, from compact fluorescent lighting to SmartDispense dishwashers.

Up-branding is here to stay, but step back before you step up. Think about how your up-branded product will actually be different and more relevant—and why people should pay for the privilege you offer.

>>> Source: Allen Adamson, "Why Up-Branding Is Here to Stay," www.AdAge .com, May 28, 2007

Let's Talk
How do you decide what to buy? Do you base your decisions on current trends, on an item's usefulness and practicality, on the brand name, or on the suggestions of friends?

Culture Influences Buying Habits

One of the more fascinating aspects of the study of buying behavior is so firmly tied to a concept that it's critical to the understanding of consumer behavior. Culture is the compass that guides us and affects every observation and decision we make. **Culture** is composed of all the shared beliefs, values, and traditions learned and practiced by a group of people, rich or poor, educated or uneducated, whether they live close to one another or far apart, all of whom are focused on a common quest. A quest is a search, a pursuit, like that of the famous fictional character, Don Quixote, who spent his life

"Louise, everyone is wearing that this year ... don't be such a sheep to fashion."

FIGURE 1.6.

FIGURE 1.7. Like Don Quixote, the members of each culture share in the pursuit of a common goal which guides them and influences their decisions.

pursuing the impossible dream. Americans, no matter who we are, share the ongoing pursuit of freedom and independence, and our absolute commitment to it unites us as one culture. One of the ways we express this value is through the products and services we consume and, to be sure, we are among the most savvy and complex risk takers when it comes to making purchasing decisions.

In today's marketplace, information abounds, and all of it influences buying behavior. That's why the jobs of consumer researchers are both evolving and demanding. Clearly, one of the biggest challenges is staying a few steps ahead of purchasers. By studying psychology, sociology, history, economics, and the causes of change, and through constant, close observation, marketers can increase their knowledge and expertise, becoming both effective and efficient in determining what consumers are likely to want next.

What Will Customers Want Tomorrow?

Does this mean consumer behaviorists have to add fortune-telling to their résumés, in addition to all the other subjects they have to master? Not exactly, but they probably will be asked on occasion to draw conclusions from their findings and make some reliable predictions as to what's most likely to occur in the future. This is another tool that successful marketers use. It's called **forecasting**, a creative process used by industry professionals, which can be understood, practiced, and applied by those familiar with the applicable theories and tools.[8] (See Chapter 14 for information about trend forecasting services.)

Accurate forecasts are compiled using information from the past and present to calculate what's likely to happen in the future, and are crucial to the success of every business. Because we live in a time when change occurs with amazing speed, designers, product developers, analysts, and so on must explore all possible futures in order to establish directions for their companies. Consumer researchers play a crucial role in this effort. They systematically gather the kind of data that helps forecasters make informed predictions on subjects such as population shifts, cultural changes, attitude fluctuations, economic deviations, the emergence of new products and businesses, all of which may be significant to executives and planners who are plotting a company's future. Research and evaluation are essential elements in the study of consumer behavior; without them, there is no basis on which to strategically plan. And in business, planning precedes success.

But are forecasters always right in their determinations of what customers are likely to want? One example of what was deemed accurate and useable forecasting was applied to the creation of a retail chain, Forth & Towne, a specialty store division of Gap, Inc. Researchers had been carefully tracking the buying behavior of the baby boomer population for years and anticipating the tremendous cultural shift that would take place when the group reached middle age.

A *baby boomer* is someone born during a period of increased birth rates, such as those born in the United States during the period of economic prosperity after World War II, 1946 to 1964. Forecasters have predicted for decades that the mind-sets and buying habits of boomers would force marketers to employ new and different tactics, and clearly they were right. Boomers, 76 million of them, make up the single largest group in the United States today and spend approximately $2 trillion on goods and services each year. Over the next 30 years, their retail purchases will continue to increase, in addition to what they'll be spending on new homes, travel, and leisure activities.

Until recently, the fashion industry has largely ignored this group, especially women, opting to direct its marketing efforts almost exclusively at the young, whom designers prefer to dress. Part of our cultural belief system is that youth is synonymous with beauty, while aging makes people less attractive. Nevertheless, after assessing data supplied by researchers, Gap marketers decided it was the right time to focus on this huge market segment whose female members were hungry for chic and stylish clothing.

The opening of Forth & Towne made national headlines. All cultural indicators pointed to success, since in both planning and execution, Gap had utilized the most essential marketing activity: determining what customers want and giving it to them. (In addition to its numerous other definitions, marketing is also referred to as *problem solving*.)

However, the Forth & Towne stores performed poorly. Although the targeted group was (and is) a large one with a lot of money to spend, the eclectic tastes and diverse lifestyles of the segment were harder to pinpoint than anticipated. Plus, internal problems at Gap concerning executive shake-ups and financial difficulties, combined with the company's general confusion over the identification and implementation of marketing strategies, ultimately led to the closing of Forth & Towne, less than two years after its launch. (See Point of View 1.1.)

❯ ❯ ❯ POINT OF VIEW 1.1 ❮ ❮ ❮

The Opening

For the millions of American women over 35 who face the conundrum each morning of a closet full of clothes but nothing to wear, there is little solace to be found at the vast Palisades Center mall here. With nearly 300 stores and more than half of them aimed at teenage consumers, this temple of consumerism in Rockland County, about 25 miles north of Manhattan, is full of clothes, but for women of a certain age, many find little to buy.

The new Forth & Towne stores—4 more will be opened in malls in the Chicago area beginning next week, 5 more in 2006 and 20 in 2007—represent the first of several retail spin-offs being developed by fashion companies to cater to older customers.

❯❯❯ Source: Eric Wilson, "Gap's New Chain Store Aims at the Fashionably Mature Woman," New York Times, August 24, 2005. Retrieved on August 31, 2007, from www.nytimes.com/2005/08/24/business/24gap.html?_r=1&oref =slogin

The Closing

Time's run out on Gap's Forth & Towne.

Gap will close 19 Forth & Towne stores in 10 domestic markets by June.

Gap Inc. is shuttering the concept after an 18-month pilot proved the store brand, which was aimed at women over age 35, wouldn't deliver "an acceptable long-term return on investment."

❯❯❯ Source: Michael Barbaro, "Gap Closing Chain Aimed at Over-30s," New York Times, February 27, 2007. Retrieved on August 31, 2007, from www.nytimes .com/2007/02/27/business/27gap.html

Standing Out from the Rest

Let's examine the idea of marketing as problem solving. The customer has a dilemma and is looking for a solution. It's up to the marketer to offer one (or two, or more). For many years, it's been the job of marketers to help businesses position their products or services as the best remedies for customers' problems. **Positioning** is creating a certain perception or image about the product in the minds of consumers that differentiates it from the competition. In the world of kitchen design, appliances by Thermador and Viking have been positioned as such high-tech options that their ovens were referred to as "kitchen jewelry" by the *Dallas Morning News*. And because saving time is so important to so many people today, TurboChef, a prestige appliance manufacturer, offers a very pricey oven that cooks a 21-pound turkey in only 75 minutes.

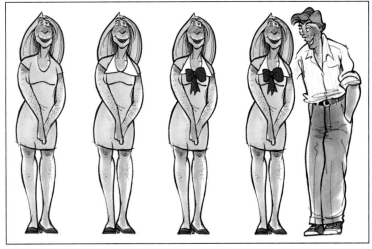

FIGURE 1.8. By differentiating a product (in this case, the dress), it often becomes more meaningful, and therefore, more desirable than competitive products.

But how are these three high-end appliance makers going to make sure consumers don't confuse their products? By using a marketing strategy known as **product differentiation**, the way companies attempt to make their products seem unique when compared to similar products by competitors.

Take blue jeans, for example. A lot has happened to this widely regarded symbol of the American worker. It certainly has evolved from its origins as the uniform of prospectors and cattle ranchers in the 1800s. For nearly four decades, blue jeans have taken over as *the uniform*, period. And what about the endless choice of styles, cuts, treatments, and embellishments? What is it that differentiates Levi's jeans from those by True Religion or Diesel, for which people pay anywhere from $19.95 to $595.00? Is it the actual quality of the denim, the finish, or the fit? Or is it something more illusive? Perhaps it has more to do with people's *ideas* about jeans and what jeans *symbolize*, more than their value as a physical product.

Marketers know that the meanings consumers attach to items are every bit as powerful (sometimes more so) as the actual contents or quality of the product itself. Of course, this is not to diminish the importance of high quality and fine design, but that may not be enough in today's competitive marketplace. The title of the 1981 best seller by marketing gurus Jack Ries and Al Trout says it all—marketing is "The Battle for Your Mind."

So, if the customer thinks she will be more satisfied . . . attractive . . . unique . . . special . . . desirable . . . wearing $250 jeans than in $50 jeans, and she has the means to make that purchase, then the marketers of those jeans have done their jobs.

What's in a Name?

When it comes to illusive qualities, nothing is more fascinating than consumers' attraction to certain brands. A **brand** is everything that is known and felt about a product or service or organization, from its recognizable name, logo, slogan, and packaging, to the power it holds in peoples' minds. You might say that we actually become emotionally attached to certain brands, and you'd be right. Think about Coke and Pepsi. You probably know people who will argue vehemently that one is better than the other, that the two drinks taste different, and that even if they were blindfolded, they could tell which one is which. Researchers have found, however, that blind taste tests show quite the opposite—most people can't really tell the difference, and they're less influenced by the actual taste and more influenced by the advertising, promotion, and affiliations the products have with certain celebrities and/or activities they enjoy.

Much of the time, consumers respond to a **brand image**, the deliberate, consistent way the company communicates a product's qualities and essence. Imagine you're traveling and want something to eat, but no place looks appealing. You see a sign indicating that a familiar fast-food spot is a short distance ahead. Even though you've never eaten at this particular location, you expect a friendly place with good food because the name and logo evoke positive feelings, based on your past experience. The creation of a positive brand image will draw targeted buyers to that particular brand and keep them coming back. That's a big part of successful marketing—developing **brand loyalty**, behavior exhibited by customers who have strong connections to their favorite brands; this includes purchasing a certain brand again and again. Are you loyal to a specific hair product, a certain brand of cologne or toothpaste? Do you tend to buy these items again and again? If so, you're brand loyal. When brand image and brand loyalty have both been achieved, the result is **brand equity**, a group of strong assets that include value, esteem, worth— all of the intangibles that help create satisfaction, retention, and demand in the marketplace.

Customers can become very attached to certain brands and refuse to buy others for a variety of reasons that range from emotional (their parents used it, their ex-boyfriend used it, it reminds them of a special evening) to rational (they prefer the taste, the price, the convenience, the use of natural ingredients). Whatever the reasons, the successfully integrated marketing system (from the product development phase through to the point of purchase and beyond) has created an image that satisfies the needs of the customer in ways that are more appealing than the efforts of competitors.

New Isn't Always Best

Numerous theories exist about people's relationships with designed goods. Some of these date back more than 100 years. Most of the time these theories, regardless of when they were developed, share one common "truth": the attraction of consumers to designed goods results from their curiosity about **innovation**, the belief that inherent in the object they desire is something that is new; however, it doesn't have to be new in actuality—it just has to be regarded as new by the person viewing it. People are naturally curious about what's new, but newness doesn't guarantee success. Adopting something new requires people to be willing to change their behavior in some way. That's where innovations become challenges—how much are customers willing to change? Of course, the answer depends on the individual; some consumers might be ready for a radical departure from what they're currently doing, using, wanting, purchasing, while others might not want their habits disrupted. Some people might be influenced by peers or celebrities and jump on the bandwagon right away; others might be extremely slow to respond to newness or reject an innovation, calling it silly or even potentially harmful. How do consumer researchers make sense of this?

> *Let's Talk*
> *How do you feel when you hear about something new like a phone, a celebrity clothing line, a great late-night spot? Are you curious or skeptical about "newness"? What is it that makes something not only new, but truly exciting?*

The following chapters address this issue with some practical and workable ideas. We will assist you, the student who is looking ahead to a productive career in the fashion or design fields, by enhancing your understanding of the principles of consumer behavior. We want to make sure you're able to both choose the methods that fit your business needs and use them effectively.

Summary

Consumer behavior is one of the far-reaching arms of *marketing*, a group of activities designed to persuade prospective buyers to choose one product, service, or company over others. Consumer behaviorists identify those who are most likely to need and want certain goods, be they designed objects, fashion-related products, or any consumable item. Designed goods have a special place in the minds of consumers; this is largely driven by a combination of two conflicting behaviors: wanting (then buying) what the rest of the crowd wants, and seeking (then purchasing) what's truly unique and innovative. To address this issue, marketers try to develop and impart to the purchaser a special set of characteristics and qualities that distinguishes a product, service, or company from those of competitors. There are various ways to accomplish this, some traditional and some less conventional. But regardless of the approach used, all marketers must listen to their customers and give them what they want.

Key Terms

Ambush marketing	Guerilla marketing
Brand	Hype
Brand equity	Innovation
Brand image	Integrated marketing system (IMS)
Brand loyalty	Market segment
Buzz	Marketing
Collective selection	Mass marketing
Competitive advantage	Positioning
Consumer behavior	Product differentiation
Consumption	Target market
Culture	Trend
Design	Viral marketing
Differentiation	Word-of-mouth marketing (WOM)
Fashion	Zeitgeist
Forecasting	

Questions for Review

1. What kinds of criteria do consumers of fashion and designed goods use when deciding whether to buy that they probably don't use when evaluating other types of products?

2. Explain the importance of the zeitgeist as it relates to fashion and designed goods. What is the current zeitgeist and what influences has it had on recent creations by your favorite designer?

3. Choose three components of marketing from the list on page 7 and explain how each might be implemented in the fashion and design arenas.

4. Cite and explain an instance in your own employment experience when an IMS was or was not in place. What were the results?

5. Clearly explain the importance of branding, brand image, and brand equity when it comes to the customer's selection of fashion and design-related goods. Give specific examples of brands you are familiar with that demonstrate successful branding.

Activities

1. People can be marketed as well as products. Identify a new designer in your field. List some of the marketing techniques that are being used to create interest in this person.

2. List three stores where you like to shop, and note the marketing efforts each store uses to get your business and develop loyalty.

3. Go online and find five answers to the question: "What is consumer behavior?" Are the responses all similar or did you find additional information not covered in this chapter? If so, make a note of your findings, and suggest them for class discussion.

4. Read the "soft" news sections of your favorite newspaper (for example, Style, Home, Gardening, etc.).Cite examples of public relations activities and sales promotions featured in these sections.

5. Subscribe to either of these free online newsletters: Retail News Today (www .retailforward.com/newsletter/sign_up.asp) or NRF Smart Brief (www.smart brief.com/nrf/)

6. Visit the Word of Mouth Marketing Association (WOMMA) Web site: www .womma.com. Look at the mission statement of this organization and learn how members view the potential word of mouth versus traditional marketing methods.

Mini-Projects

1. Hold an in-class panel discussion, and ask panelists what they look for when choosing designed goods that will be visible to others. What matters most to them? Uniqueness? Aesthetic appeal? The responses of peers? Why is this important to them? How would the discoveries made during this discussion help a marketer plan an effective branding strategy? Relate your findings to the class in a five-minute presentation.

2. Visit a retail store that sells designed goods, such as jewelry, clothing, appliances, or furniture. Identify a specific item, and the audience that is most likely being targeted, choosing from among the following age groups:

   18–25 years
   25–35 years
   35–49 years
   Over 50

Name a few innovative ways to modify the item so it would appeal to a completely different age group. Why do you feel these innovations will work? Relate your findings to the class in a five-minute presentation.

References

1. National Retail Federation News Release. Retrieved November 3, 2005, from www .nrf@smartbrief.com.
2. Edmund Sanders, "In Congo, Designer Cheek," *Los Angeles Times*, November 28, 2006, p. A1. Retrieved August 3, 2007, from www.latimes.com.
3. Marla Dickerson, "Steeped in a New Tradition," *Los Angeles Times*. Retrieved October 21, 2005, from www.latimes.com.
4. Michael Barbaro, "Ready, Aim, Shop," *New York Times*, November 19, 2005.
5. Ralph Caplan, *By Design* 2nd ed. (New York: Fairchild Publications, 2005).
6. *Webster's New World Dictionary of American English,* 3rd college ed. (New York: Simon and Shuster, 1988), 373.
7. George B. Sproles and Leslie D. Burns, *Changing Appearances: Understanding Dress in Contemporary Society* (New York: Fairchild Publications, 1994) 127–128.
8. Evelyn L. Brannon, *Fashion Forecasting,* 2nd ed. (New York: Fairchild Publications, 2005) 6.

Additional Resources

Adamson, Allen. "Why Up-Branding Is Here to Stay." www.AdAge.com. Retrieved on May 28, 2007.

Harrell, Gilbert D. *Marketing: Connecting with Customers.* 2nd ed. Upper Saddle River, NJ: Prentice Hall, 2002.

Horn, Marilyn J., and Lois M. Gurel. *The Second Skin: An Interdisciplinary Study of Clothing.* 3rd ed. Boston: Houghton Mifflin Company, 1975.

Khermouth, Gerry, and Jeff Green. "Buzz Marketing." *BusinessWeekonline.* Retrieved on July 30, 2001, from www.businessweek.com.

Kellogg, Ann T., Amy T. Peterson, Stefani Bay, and Natalie Swindell. *In An Influential Fashion: An Encyclopedia of Nineteenth and Twentieth Century Fashion Designers and Retailers Who Transformed Dress.* Westport, CT: Greenwood Press, 2002.

MacArthur, Kate. "Gap Inc. Pulls Plug on Forth & Towne." *New York Times.* Retrieved on February 26, 2007, from www.nytimes.com.

Musgrove, Mike. "What Looks Like Graffiti Could Really Be an Ad." *Washington Post.* Retrieved on December 26, 2005, from www.washingtonpost.com.

Popcorn, Faith. *The Popcorn Report.* New York: Doubleday, 1991.

Ries, Al, and Jack Trout. *Positioning: The Battle for Your Mind.* New York: McGraw-Hill, 2000.

Schweitzer, Sarah. "Building a Buzz on Campus." *The Boston Globe.* October 24, 2005.

Retrieved on October 27, 2005, from http://seattlepi.nwsource.com/business/ 246065_onenote27.html.

White, Sara. *The Complete Idiot's Guide to Marketing.* New York: Alpha Books, 2003.

Wilson, Eric. "Gap's New Chain Store Aims at the Fashionably Mature Woman." *New York Times.* Retrieved on August 24, 2005, from www.nytimes.com.

CHAPTER 2

Consumer Behavior, Marketing, and Fashion: A Working Relationship

Marketplace Conditions

As you learned in the first chapter, marketing is much more than just promoting a business, a product, or a service. Marketing includes a range of activities that span from the time a product or service is simply an idea, through its evaluation, purchase, use, and disposal by the customer. Businesses, and the marketers they employ, must integrate activities such as sales promotion, media planning, and community involvement (see Table 1.1 in Chapter 1 for a more comprehensive list) to increase their chances of success in the marketplace. However, they also need to understand marketplace conditions and be able to respond appropriately.

Buyer's Market versus Seller's Market

In a **buyer's market**, a market that has more sellers than buyers, an excess of supply over demand results in lower prices for consumers. This means that buyers can be more selective about their purchases because there are many sellers. In *A Wealth of Nations* (1776), economist Adam Smith suggested that competition among companies would help customers get the best products and prices; as a result, only the best would survive in the marketplace.[1] Because buyers have more clout in these situations, they can make more demands on companies during a buyer's market cycle. Most customers also value service and quality. It's been said that shoppers want quality merchandise and lots of options. They want things they can't find at other stores, unusual pieces that have friends asking, "Where did you find that?" And it all has to be wrapped up with a certain level of service.[2]

On the other hand, a **seller's market** has more buyers than sellers; increased demand and low supply result in higher prices. Simply stated, many people want a product, but a limited supply gives sellers an advantage so they can charge more.

Let's Talk
Can you list some products or services that you personally use and categorize the marketplace for them as either a buyer's or seller's market?

Value versus Cost

During the 2005 holiday season, the last one for department store Marshall Field's before it was absorbed into the Macy's chain, several ornaments and other products with the Field's name on them were available on eBay's Web site, including a $46 Christopher Radko clock priced at $199. All the items sold at inflated prices. Why? Because they were in demand due to the imminent end of Marshall Field's era.

What are some other reasons that consumers are willing to pay high prices or stand in long lines to buy something? When sellers add **value**, tangible or intangible attributes that improve the desirability of a product or service, to the buying experience, it increases the likelihood that customers will buy. A store's ambiance, helpful employees, or customer service that exceeds expectations all might add value to a buying experience. For example, Nordstrom provides customers with a superior level of service that's well regarded in the marketplace.

According to Peter Drucker (often referred to as the father of modern business management), "The aim of business is to create a customer."[3] When customers believe that an item has an attractive rate of return in terms of time, money, or some other benefit, then the value begins to outweigh the item's price.

FIGURE 2.1.

Calculating the Cost

Math has been used to identify, account for, and tabulate things throughout the centuries, but what part does it play in our discussion of the fashion business? Whether customers are buying products or services, it's important to keep a running total of potential benefits. Here's an equation that can help customers and marketers keep score. The equation **P/V = Cost**, where **P** = Price and **V** = Value, demonstrates that as the denominator (**V**) gets larger, the overall **perceived cost**, the balance between the benefits received and a competitor's comparable cost, appears smaller. Conversely, if the **V** (Value) decreases, then the overall perceived cost increases. When customers perceive that something has value, it's valuable. (See Chapter 3 for a discussion of perception.)

Examples: P (Price) / V (Value) = Perceived Cost

1. The *denominator* V (Value) increases, thereby reducing the Perceived cost. ↓
   A. $100 / 2 = $50 where P = $100, V = 2, then Perceived cost = $50
   B. $100 / 4 = $25 where P = $100, V = 4, then Perceived cost = $25
   C. $100 / 5 = $20 where P = $100, V = 5, then Perceived cost = $20

   Or

2. The *denominator* V (value) decreases, thereby increasing the Perceived cost. ↑
   A. $200 / 5 = $40 where P = $200, V = 5, then Perceived cost = $40
   B. $200 / 4 = $50 where P = $200, V = 4, then Perceived cost = $50
   C. $200 / 2 = $100 where P = $200, V = 2, then Perceived cost = $100

This exercise demonstrates a fundamental marketing idea: Identify what is valued by (important to) the customer, and then provide and communicate that characteristic. This will reduce the customer's perceived cost. Businesses of all types try to turn today's buyer into tomorrow's loyal customer by continuously searching for and implementing ways to add value to multiple parts of the shopping experience. If distinct value is not added to the transaction, that consumer may not buy a specific product, service, or brand initially, or in the future.

Buyer Requirements

Consumer researchers have discovered that more and more customers are demanding customized products and services. Writer Catherine Getches summed up this issue nicely in an article in the *Boston Globe*: "It's as if marketers want to make us feel like our shopping experience is as customized as our Starbucks concoction."[4]

Customization

Consumers can personalize phones, candy, breakfast cereal, clothing, and many other items with customized comments, colors, wrapping, or packaging. **Customization** is the integration of individual requirements into a product.

Obviously, there are various levels of customization. In 1996 Joseph Lampel, assistant professor, New York University, and Henry Mintzberg, professor, McGill University, noted a *continuum of customization strategies*. "In tailored customization, a product prototype is adapted to a customer's wishes, as a suit is tailored to a customer, but customization does not enter the design process. In pure customization, however, customization reaches all the way to the design, as custom jewelry is made to customer specifications."[5]

A business called PhotoStamps provides an example of the customization process. How does the company personalize/customize postage stamps? After a customer

FIGURE 2.2. Personalized Items

downloads an image or photograph via computer, the e-customization interface allows that person to zoom, move, and rotate the image, and then select one of ten border colors to match the image.[6] The result: a postage stamp with a personalized choice of an image or photo.

The customization trend appears to be growing, and there are an increasing number of customized or personalized products and services available in the marketplace. (See Special Focus 2.1.) Perhaps you've bought or seen coffee mugs or T-shirts with personalized photos, or heard about the dolls that are customized to look like the little girls who own them.

❯❯❯ SPECIAL FOCUS 2.1: BRAND BOGGLED ❮❮❮

Whatever happened to the generic aisle? It's not that I'm pining for plastic bags of puffed rice cereal, paper towels, or cotton swabs, but lately I wish choices at the grocery store were a little more black and white. When I was growing up most consumer decisions pitted brand against brand (or nonbrand). You drank Coca-Cola or you drank Pepsi. Very simple.

But these days, even if you want to practice brand loyalty, it's harder than ever. There are more and more specialized products lining store shelves—green tea infused, calcium enriched, Mega and Mini varieties, Diet with this or that, and Atkins friendly. It's as if marketers want to make us feel like our shopping experience is as customized as our Starbucks concoction. But as marketers try to spice it up, getting out of a convenience store isn't so convenient anymore.

Sure, one New Coke flopped in the '80s, but today there's Coke with Lemon, with Lime, with Splenda, Coke II or CO_2, Vanilla Coke, not to mention the diet and caffeine varieties. Once you decide between Minute Maid or Tropicana orange juice, brace yourself for permutations of pulp, vitamins, and styles for your heart, your kids, or your home. Chewing gum is probably the worst offender. At the National Confectioners Association trade show, more than 80 new gums were introduced as gum sales reached $3.3 billion last year. But if you're simply looking to buy the original flavor of, say, Trident, good luck. And yes, Viagra gum is on the way.

But what's next? Product personalization. I half-expect my face to appear on boxes of pasta or cans of tuna I might like. Cadbury Adams, the maker of M&Ms, has tapped into the trend. Sure, plain chocolate M&Ms are tasty. But now consumers can customize candies with personalized messages, colors, and even packaging.

The inundation of pseudo-personalized product lines comes at a strange time. Now that there are virtual googols of information at our fingertips to help us navigate, it's as if we need a search engine on our grocery cart. Madison

Avenue calls it brand or line extension—an apt name since it has extended our shopping experience.

According to an economic theory called the "The Long Tail," we have shifted from mass markets to niche markets thanks to the Internet. Popularized most recently by Chris Anderson of *Wired* magazine, The Long Tail refers to the huge demand for a deep catalog of alternatives. Unlimited selection is the new blockbuster. This explains the overwhelming success of Amazon and Netflix, which have proven that products that are in low demand or have low sales volume can collectively make up a market share that rivals or exceeds the limited number of current bestsellers and blockbusters.

According to Anderson (his book on the subject is due out soon), "The Long Tail is *about the economics of abundance—what happens when the bottlenecks that stand between supply and demand in our culture start to disappear and everything becomes available to everyone*."

People have been branding themselves and then extending their brand for years. Martha Kostrya changed her name, started a magazine called *Martha Stewart Living*, and spawned books, television shows, newspaper columns, and home products. But these days when extending your brand isn't enough, why not just extend your name? P. Diddy is changing his again—Sean Combs, then Puffy Combs, Puff Daddy, P. Diddy, and now just Diddy. And then there's Donald Trump, who doesn't just have a real estate company and a TV show, he has a magazine, a cologne, Trump University, and a blog.

Now that life has gone convenience store—you can get everything everywhere—I guess it will be easier for everyone to be indecisive. And if there are too many choices at bigger stores I can stick to smaller ones. You can practically subsist at 7-Eleven now that namesake cell phones and service are for sale there. In the meantime, I'm thinking about branding and extending myself. I thought my yellow LiveStrong bracelet was enough but now I see I can also let people know I'm all for "Anti-Bullying." Unless, of course, it's in the name of my brand.

>>> Source: Catherine Getches, "Brand Boggled," *Boston Globe*, September 1, 2005. Retrieved on August 31, 2007, from www.boston.com/news/globe/editorial_opinion/oped/articles/2005/09/01/brand_boggled/.

Let's Talk
What kind of personalized services or products do you request? Have you ever had your name or personal messages imprinted on any clothing?

In addition, homes are being built using "green products" (natural materials), new vehicles are purchased where specific upgrades are ordered and tracked via computers by customers, mail and package deliveries also include options of tracking them via computers, and phones and clothes are customized with colors and imprints. Ask your grandparents or parents what options they had at your age; you might be surprised by what they tell you.

The term *marketing customization* refers to the crafting of marketing campaigns and messages to address a particular market. If a marketing message is more focused, the response rate (the number of people who actually respond) is greater.

Finding the Answers

In order to effectively connect with the marketplace, how does a company find out what established or new customers value? A company uses **primary data,** original information that is collected firsthand (via personal interviews, focus groups, and surveys), as well as **secondary data,** information that has previously been collected from other studies or sources such as textbooks, magazines, the Internet, and other published materials, to learn about the buying habits of specific customer segments. This information provides a strong foundation for making solid business decisions. For example, has anyone ever stopped you in a shopping mall, identified him- or herself as a representative for a specific company, and then asked you a series of questions? If so, you participated in primary research. On the other hand, if you search the

+ Customized Value = Selling Advantage

FIGURE 2.3. Selling Advantage

Internet or go to the local library to collect specific data already compiled, you are reviewing secondary research.

Simply stated, value and customization are critical success factors for many businesses. Delivering value to the customer and personalizing it better than the competition while earning a profit can help one company to thrive while another company that doesn't excel at these activities might merely survive. How is the effectiveness of a company's efforts measured? Marketers need to measure the responses to their efforts (for example, computer pop-ups or banner ads, magazine ads, or surveys). To do this they use a method called **quantifying**, measuring and expressing a result as a number equivalent. By measuring responses in this manner, marketers can get a quick "snapshot" of the success of their efforts. An example of how you could quantify a response to a question:

Q: How good are your computer skills?
A: On a scale of 1 to 5, where 1 represents fear of the computer, 2.5 means average skills, and 5 is an expert, I am a 4.

This quantified response quickly gives the researcher valuable information.

Staying on Track

"Plan your work and work your plan" is a saying that has been around for decades. It's a reminder to take the time to create a **strategic marketing plan**, a road map that identifies a specific target market, the preferences of that market's members, and specific ways to connect with and keep them. This gives the businessperson an advantage over competitors who have not taken the time to plan for success. A key element to include in this planning process is the ability to adapt in an evolving marketplace.

Companies that cannot interpret changes and then adapt to them face the threat of serious losses. An example of the importance of adaptability can be seen in the following: During the 2005 annual conference of the Association of National Advertisers in Phoenix,

FIGURE 2.4. Change is inevitable.

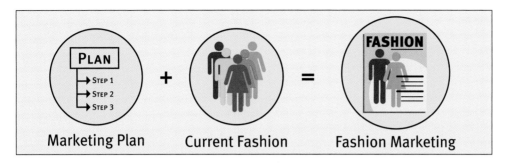

FIGURE 2.5. The Relationship between Marketing and Fashion

Arizona, more than 900 executives discussed the rapid and often bewildering changes rippling across the marketing and media landscape and noted that none of the parties involved in any brand-building effort could be exactly sure what the market or media realities would look like six months down the road.[7]

Fashionable Solutions

Yes, we've read about the changes that evolution has brought since the times of dinosaurs and cavemen, and you have probably witnessed multiple fashion changes in the last 12 years, but what do these have in common? Change, especially fashion-related, does not take a vacation. The term "fashion" was defined in Chapter 1 as anything that's popular at the moment and subject to change; it's anything that members of a population deem desirable and appropriate at a given time, and includes clothes, vehicles, furniture, appliances, electronics, and so on. So, fashion solutions respond to rapid marketplace changes. "It seems that each year what we're seeing in the women's fashion luxury market has been a migration from one category to the next," said Marshal Cohen, chief retail analyst for The NPD Group, a market research firm in Port Washington, New York. "A few years ago it was shoes, and then it was jeans. The reign of the handbag began in 2005. Shoppers' infatuation with handbags has lent that category significant clout, to the point where retailers and industry analysts say that bags have supplanted shoes, jeans, and even jewelry as consumers' choice signifier of affluence, social standing, and hipness."

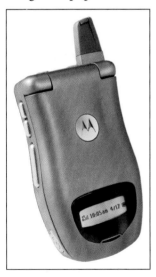

FIGURE 2.6. Pininfarina Limited Edition Motorola i833

What encourages fashion-minded buyers to buy? Hiring celebrities to endorse brands is one of the most time-honored tactics in consumer marketing. During the second season of *Desperate Housewives*, almost every cast member was in an ad, some for more than one marketer, in a rush reminiscent of the ardor to use the actors from other popular shows like *Friends* and *Sex and the City*. (See Special Focus 2.2.) And in an earlier effort to target design-sensitive buyers, Motorola partnered with Italian design firm Pininfarina (the company behind such iconic cars as Ferrari and Maserati) on the design of Motorola's i830 cell phone. (See figure 2.6 on page 37.) The result was the special edition i833, complete with an "industrial" look. The main attraction was the phone's resemblance to a 1950s-era Ferrari. The titanium-colored hoodlike ornament, the top half of the phone, the wood coloring, and exposed bolt screws on the interior were intended for those with fond memories (or those who *wished* they had fond memories) of the car. The carlike housing of the handset also featured a lens that gave customers a peek under the "hood" of the phone; it also featured a gas tank-shaped audio jack cover and a grill-like bottom connector cover.

❭ ❭ ❭ SPECIAL FOCUS 2.2: "HOUSEWIVES" IS A BIG HIT ON MADISON AVE., TOO ❬ ❬ ❬

Madison Avenue seems to believe that desperate housewives can sell disparate housewares. Advertisers and agencies seeking endorsers for campaigns are making belles of the ball of the actresses appearing on the hit ABC series *Desperate Housewives*, which is to return for a second season on Sept. 25. Almost every cast member is in an ad, some for more than one marketer, in a rush reminiscent of the ardor to use the actors from other popular shows like *Friends* and *Sex and the City*.

Eva Longoria, who portrays the sultry Gabrielle Solis on *Desperate Housewives*, is a voiceover announcer in commercials for Sirius Satellite Radio and the star of a campaign for the Vive line of hair care products sold by the L'Oréal Paris brand division of L'Oréal USA.

"The fact she's in more than 20 million households each week is not a bad thing to have," Carol Hamilton, president for the L'Oréal Paris division in New York, said, laughing.

Teri Hatcher, who plays the clumsy Susan Mayer, appears in ads for the trade publication *Variety*, owned by Reed Elsevier. She wears the magazine, a startled look—and nothing else. Nicollette Sheridan, who portrays the vixenish Edie Britt, is featured in magazine ads for Di Modolo, a brand of luxury jewelry.

The newest arrival to the ranks of ad fans of *Desperate Housewives* is the Cadbury Schweppes Americas Beverages division of Cadbury Schweppes, which has signed Ms. Sheridan and Marcia Cross, who plays the tightly wound Bree Van De

Kamp, to appear in commercials for the 7Up Plus line of flavored soft drinks. The humorous spots, created by the San Francisco office of Young & Rubicam, part of the WPP Group, are to start running Monday.

"We went through a litany of potential candidates," said Randy Gier, chief marketing officer for Cadbury Schweppes Americas Beverages in Plano, Tex. "Obviously, it doesn't hurt that they're on the No. 1 show on television." Hiring celebrities to endorse brands is one of the most time-honored tactics in consumer marketing. The silent-film star Pearl White appeared on calendars for Coca-Cola, for instance, and, after she was first lady, Eleanor Roosevelt, even appeared in a commercial for Good Luck margarine (her fee was donated to charity). Today, when increasing clutter makes the ability of a famous face to stand out more valuable, they are being used heavily.

"When you use celebrities, their personalities make that instant connection with the consumer," said Mr. Gier, who has also used two cast members from *Sex and the City*, Kristin Davis and Cynthia Nixon, in the 7Up Plus campaign along with Regis Philbin and Kelly Ripa from "Live With Regis and Kelly."

"If you spend the 30 seconds explaining the personality," he added, "then you can't spend the time talking about the product."

In this instance, Mr. Gier said, Ms. Cross's and Ms. Sheridan's playing "strong women" on *Desperate Housewives* was a reason to cast them for the new commercials, which promote the inclusion of calcium in 7Up Plus.

The fervor among marketers to bask in the reflected glow of the program has become so intense, even some of the actors who play the desperate househusbands and boyfriends are getting their 15 minutes in the advertising spotlight.

A print campaign to support the National Denim Day fundraiser for the Susan B. Komen Breast Cancer Foundation, sponsored by the Lee jeans brand sold by the VF Corporation, features Ricardo Antonio Chavira, who portrays Gabrielle's roguish husband, Carlos, and James Denton, who plays Susan's mysterious beau, Mike Delfino.

"When you've got a man next to a pink ribbon, it has stopping power," said Kathy Collins, a spokeswoman for Lee in Shawnee Mission, Kan.

Mr. Chavira and Mr. Denton made a "powerful pair" for the pro bono campaign, because both their mothers died of breast cancer. "Neither one knew about the other until we contacted them" for the ads, Ms. Collins said. The campaign was created by Design Ranch, an agency in Kansas City, Mo.

The use of the cast members in public service campaigns as well as product pitches is a sign their appeal is deemed broad enough, and potentially longlasting enough, to help draw support for causes.

"They're at the top of everyone's list," said Lisa Paulsen, president and chief executive of the Entertainment Industry Foundation in Los Angeles. Ms. Cross and Felicity Huffman, who portrays the put-upon Lynette Scavo, are the featured faces for the foundation's 2005 fundraiser, a "Shoes on Sale" show on the QVC shopping network scheduled for Oct. 26.

"The more noise we can create, the more money we raise," Ms. Paulsen said during the program, which is supported by the Fashion Footwear Association of New York. The proceeds are to be donated to benefit breast cancer research and education programs, she added, and the goal is to sell 100,000 pairs of shoes for more than $3 million.

One big risk of using the cast members of a hit series in ads is that the show's appeal will fade, rendering the campaign as hot as what the lyricist Dorothy Fields called yesterday's mashed potatoes.

Ms. Hamilton of L'Oréal agreed that marketers want to avoid "falling into the trap of the 'flavor of the month' club," adding that her company's ideal was to affiliate with stars like Ms. Longoria who have "such broad awareness and presence" that their appeal continues into "very long-term relationships." For example, Heather Locklear, the star of the once-popular series *Melrose Place*, has been a spokeswoman for L'Oréal Paris for eight years, Ms. Hamilton said.

There are also those seeking to ride the *Desperate Housewives* bandwagon without paying the fare. "Delighted housewives use Bosch appliances," declared an ad on the TV listings page of *USA Today*. An ad from MGM Home Entertainment to promote the DVD release of the film *The Graduate* said that Mrs. Robinson was "the original desperate housewife." *HX*, a magazine for gay men published in New York, ran a cover article about "Desperate Houseboys." And a campaign to promote reruns of a British series, *Footballers' Wives*, on the BBC America cable network carried this theme: "If you're desperate this summer, here is a whole new set of housewives."

The Walt Disney Company, which owns ABC, is certainly not going to let everyone else get into the act without some peddling of its own.

There is *Desperate Housewives* licensed merchandise like a calendar, T-shirts, a board game and a book, and the first season's episodes are to be released on DVD on September 20 by the Buena Vista Home Entertainment division of Disney. "Hungry for more *Desperate Housewives*?" a headline asks on DVD ads featuring a game, "Which desperate housewife are you?", that can be played online (video.com/desperatehousewives).

"We're hoping the awareness" generated by the cast's ad appearances "will always drive people back to the series," said Bruce Gersh, senior vice president for business development at ABC Entertainment in Los Angeles. "We look to *Desperate Housewives* as a franchise, and look for longevity."

During fall 2005 Ford announced that the company's Mercury division was introducing its first mid-sized car in ten years, the Milan sedan. The objective was to win over style- and fashion-minded urban professionals in their late twenties to mid-thirties. The marketing effort was less traditional and more grassroots (using down-to-earth ways to spread the news about a product or service, streetwise methods) and lifestyle-oriented. It specifically targeted style, rather than a generalized approach. Companies have become increasingly interested, aware, and proactive about reaching fashion-minded buyers.

Approaching the Marketplace

Graham, a first-time business owner, needed advice on promoting his business. He called his friend Lakisha, who worked as a marketing specialist for a furniture manufacturer, and asked her for help. When they met the next day, Lakisha had Graham describe his target market and asked him how he'd segmented the marketplace. Confused by the question, Graham asked Lakisha to explain.

"You have to have a strategy," she said. A **strategy** is a plan that addresses how competitors respond to consumers in the marketplace. "Think about that saying, 'Plan your work and work your plan,'" she told him. In *The Concept of Corporate Strategy*, Professor Kenneth Andrews of Harvard Business School (and also a former editor at *Harvard Business Review*) defines "business strategy" as the basis of competition for a given business. Michael Porter, another business author, says strategy is about competitive positioning and separating your company from others by

FIGURE 2.7. Fashion-Minded Buyers

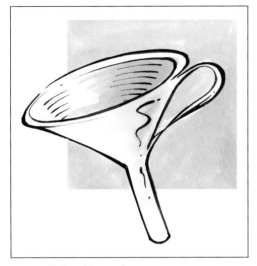

FIGURE 2.8. Funnel Approach

doing things differently than your competitors to modify the customer's perception.[8]

Lakisha said to Graham, "First, figure out who your customers are, where they are, what they like and don't like." But that's not always an easy thing to do. Then she told him about the **S T P** formula, a way to help organize marketing activities for greater effectiveness.

Step 1: S = *Segment potential buyers into similar groups (parts).*

Market segmentation divides markets into clusters of possible customers who reflect similar characteristics, wants, and needs.

Why segment? To identify the best market prospects. For example, customers at Ann Taylor or Talbots are likely to be somewhat more conservative than the youth-oriented customers of Abercrombie & Fitch. A businessperson segments his or her market by first identifying specific demographic or psychographic factors that describe the ideal customer, and then using a "funnel" approach to narrow each segment even further for greater efficiency in terms of reaching that particular segment while saving time and money.

How is segmenting done? Let's say we're selling shoes. Who might buy these shoes? Men? Women? On a separate sheet of paper, draw a pie graph (which is nothing more than a circle). The first step in segmenting potential buyers, as shown in Segmentation 1, is to designate a portion (in this case, 25 percent) to men and a portion (in this case, 75 percent) to women buyers. This shows you how the total marketplace is divided. Of course, the data needed to create this pie graph must come from reliable research (discussed in Chapter 10).

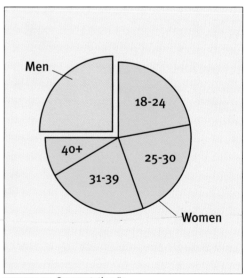

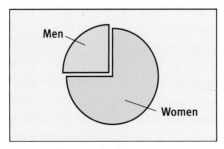

FIGURE 2.9. Segmentation #1

FIGURE 2.10. Segmentation #2

Table 2.1. Marketplace Segmentation Categories

Type	Example
Demographic	Age, Sex, Marital Status, Income, Education, Occupation
Dominant Benefit	Convenience, Value, Social Rank, Political
Geographic	Domestic: state, city, region; International: country, zone
Hybrid	Combination of any group
Psychographic	Lifestyle
Sociocultural	Culture, Religion, Ethnicity, Class, Family
Usage	Quantifying and Qualifying Criteria: rate/loyalty/activity/location

Segmentation 2 subdivides only one of the groups (from Segmentation 1) into smaller segments with similar characteristics. Segmenting group members by demographics divides them into subgroups according to some objective factors, such as age, marital status, income, education, and occupation. Segmentation 2 could include different age groups, such as 18–30 years, 31–41 years, and so forth, or financial brackets, such as $35,000 annual income, $65,000 annual income, and so on. If a businessperson segments the marketplace well, it makes the next step in the S *T* P process much more effective.

How else can groups be subdivided? Some general marketplace segmentation categories are listed in Table 2.1. (See Chapter 9 for a complete discussion of demographics and psychographics.)

Step 2: T = *Target (identify) a particular segment(s) to pursue.*

A target is a reference point to shoot at; it can also be defined as a goal to be achieved. Decide which subgroup or groups are important (this consists of people who are likely to buy your product or service). Effectively marketing to your target, a defined segment of the market that is the strategic focus of a business or a marketing plan, should save time and money. Why? Because with **target marketing**, you're promoting your product or service only to your specific segment(s), not the entire marketplace.

The following questions may help clarify whether selecting a desired target market is a good business decision:

- *Specify.* Can you actually designate and/or quantify specific segmentation parts, or are you using a series of guesses?
- *Enough.* Can you generate enough revenue (or interest) within the target market to satisfy all stakeholders? (A **stakeholder** is any person or organization with an interest in the company.)

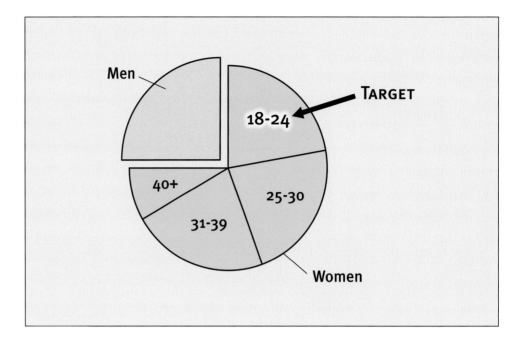

FIGURE 2.11. Target

- *Growth.* How much will the target market grow or change during business cycles?
- *Cost.* How cost-effective is it to reach that specific market segment?

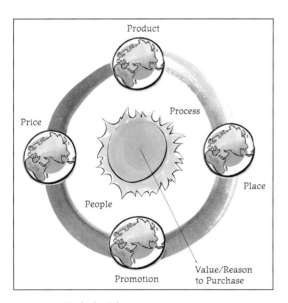

FIGURE 2.12. Marketing Mix

On the same sheet of paper you used for Step 1 (Segment), draw an arrow that points to one or more of the segments that identify your target customer(s). (See figure 2.11.)

Completing the first two steps of S T P, segmenting and targeting, helps to identify the specific market that is of interest. How can you make your product or service stand out from those of competitors? Chapter 1 defined positioning as creating a certain perception or image about the product or service in the minds of consumers; this is an idea we need to look at more closely.

Step 3: P = *Position the product or service and company.*

To **position** means to align or put in place. In the book *Positioning: The Battle for Your Mind,* authors Al Ries and Jack Trout describe how to create a leading "position" in

Table 2.2. Examples of Participants in a Supply Chain

Company Provides	Item	Some of the People Involved in the Supply Chain
Service	Restaurant	Raw materials supplier, farmer, truck driver, wholesaler, chef, server, hostess, and others until the customer actually eats
Product	Purse	Raw materials supplier, manufacturer, truck driver, wholesaler, boutique manager, salesperson, and others until the customer actually buys the purse

prospective customers' minds; that is, how to get the company's name and message into the "collective subconscious" of the target market and keep it there. It gives customers concrete reasons to select one competitor over another.[9]

In order to position a product or service or company, you need to implement six tools (described below). By doing so, the consumer will presumably come to believe that you provide the service or deliver the product in a better way than your competitor. Figure out how to best serve your customers based upon some objective factors (for example, more physical distribution locations or self-serve computer checkout counters). Understanding what the customer really wants and why he or she wants it, then combining that understanding with your study of how your competitors serve that same market segment, will help you succeed. (See Chapter 1 for additional information on positioning.)

These six marketing tools (variables in the marketing mix) are the consideration of *product, place, promotion, and price* plus two ancillary tools: *people (employees) and procedures (factors of efficiency and comfort for both internal and external customers, employees, and consumers, respectively).* These ideas were further developed and put forth in the 1970s by E. Jerome McCarthy, a professor and marketing consultant who identified the marketing mix—that is, the four areas of concentration for marketers: product, place, promotion, and price—commonly referred to as "The 4 P's."[10]

Successful companies pay attention to details, and these details (tools) add value to various levels of the **supply chain**, the organizations and related activities associated with the manufacture and delivery of a product or service. The supply chain represents the workflow from supplier to manufacturer to wholesaler to retailer to the end user, the consumer. (See examples in Table 2.2.) The final result of the S T P process is the perception by the customer that the product or service has value and is worth purchasing. Perception, the process of interpreting our surroundings through our senses, implies awareness and comprehension and can vary tremendously from segment to segment.

Customizing each of the variables of the marketing mix itemized below more effectively than the competition—so the benefits exceed customer expectations—should result in a competitive advantage for the company. Keeping current with research and adding value (for example, through new products or improved services) to the customer's experience should sustain a company's growth and revenue generation.

The Marketing Mix

Product. Is it the best it can be? Get feedback about it; improve it; use research to anticipate evolving needs and wants.

Place. How can customers get the product or service more easily, quickly, conveniently? Improve access and the distribution channels (the ways that customers get the products and services).

Promotion. What promotions, media, and technology will interest and encourage customers to buy?

Price. What pricing strategies make sense, add value, and stimulate purchases?

Ancillary Tools

People. How do you hire, train, motivate, develop, and retain employees to provide excellent service to customers?

Process/procedure. What will make the delivery of the product or service more efficient and cost-effective?

As technology and the marketplace continue to evolve, so too will successful marketing tools. (See Special Focus 2.3.)

❯ ❯ ❯ SPECIAL FOCUS 2.3: PUTTING SCANNERS IN SHOPPERS HANDS ❮ ❮ ❮

Word of the future rarely arrives in the form of ordinary junk mail. But sometimes established (read: old) technologies are the best way to introduce new ones. In this case, a simple postcard brought news of a digital—yes, that dreaded, wonderful word again—innovation that could remake the retail experience.

Container Store

The mailing came from the Container Store, a chain as remarkable for the simplicity of its concept (it sells stuff in which you store stuff) as Starbucks. It's a tad smaller at 35 U.S. stores and $440 million in sales, but equally renowned for its focus on customer service and employee training.

Rather than pitching the latest storage solution, the Container Store mailing touted a new customer service with a clunky label, GoShop Scan & Deliver, but a potentially transformative premise.

As of this month, shoppers at the Container Store in Manhattan can register a credit card number at the counter and get a wireless hand-held scanner. As they walk the aisles, they scan in barcodes on desired items then pay for the purchases, which are delivered to their homes the same day.

Such customer self-service devices have been talked about and tested for years, and various retailers such as sporting-goods chain Modell's have armed store clerks with wireless devices to assist customers and track inventory.

Scanners for Shoppers

But few stores have actually put scanners in customers' hands, so it's far from an everyday shopping experience. Where scanners have been used, it's mostly been in places that are already self-serve environments, like gas stations or grocery stores. Even then, customers have to place groceries in a cart, scan them with a handheld or checkout device, bag them and carry them away.

But the Container Store is going the next step, eliminating the need to carry around items, wheel around carts or lug purchases home. That also eliminates physical and psychological limits on how much is purchased in a single trip.

The average purchase of a delivery customer in Container Store's New York outlet is 10 times that of a shopper who carries away her goods, said John Thrailkill, vice president, stores for the chain. "So you can see how the wheels started to turn." While supermarkets and the like see such devices primarily as a way to improve the bottom line by cutting labor costs, the Container Store insists it views them as a way to grow the top line by creating a better shopping experience—particularly in Manhattan, which is unique from even other major markets in its reliance on home delivery since few people here have cars and those who do refuse to give up their parking spaces. Shoppers in Manhattan can already order groceries and even books over the Internet for same-day delivery.

Radio Frequency ID

This isn't just a New York thing, though, nor is it merely a Container Store gimmick. As the use of Radio Frequency ID technology grows and mobile devices improve, shoppers will walk into retail outlets of all stripes and use cell phones and PDAs to order and pay for goods while stores track their purchases and offer customized sales pitches. That will change everything from inventory management to marketing to the size of stores and number of employees in them.

Like everything else in the digital age, the common thread is consumer empowerment. "We're seeing more and more people demanding the ability to dictate the shopping experience," Thrailkill said. "If you ignore that, you're setting yourself up for lost sales. We're trying to stay in front of it.

>>> Source: Scott Donaton, "Check It Out: Hand-held Scanners Will Change the Way You Shop," AdAge Online, August 29, 2005. Retrieved on August 31, 2007, from http://adage.com.

FIGURE 2.13. Satisfying customers: The marketplace at work

Let's Talk
Have you ever used the self-service checkout lane at the grocery store? When you want to know the price of a store item, isn't it convenient to physically scan it yourself? This is an example of the process/procedure element.

Satisfying Customers

The **marketing concept** focuses on knowing your customers or clients (the buyer), satisfying their needs, and doing so more effectively than the competitors. This makes the buyer the center of all business initiatives. Simply put, marketers must find out what customers want, and then give it to them at a profit, for the profit enables the company to stay in business. The more an organization understands and addresses the real wants and needs of its customers, the more likely it is to have satisfied buyers who become not only repeat purchasers, but also influence their friends' decisions about where to shop and/or which brands to buy. A successful, effective marketing program also includes feedback mechanisms; companies should listen to both customers and suppliers, be alert to changes in the marketplace, and continuously track the business activities of competitors. It is then on the path to creating a win-win situation, satisfying both its customers and its own strategic goals.

In the early 1960s, marketers started to use this knowledge to sell more products more efficiently. They began to test the waters through **market research** (also discussed in Chapter 1), the collecting of information about the marketplace that results in planned marketing activities and generates revenues. This research helped marketers to identify consumer needs and wants.

In 1954 Peter Drucker, the father of modern business management, noted that "What the customer thinks he/she is buying, what he/she considers 'value' is decisive—it determines what a business is, what it produces, and whether it will prosper."[11] However, many companies continued to practice the **selling concept,** which focused on trying to sell what the company had already made, not what the customer wanted. Today we know better.

Why do today's companies follow the marketing concept and not the selling concept? According to the American Marketing Association, the marketing concept is preferable for several reasons: [12]

• Surveys demonstrate that it costs as much as five times more to acquire a new customer than it does to service an existing one.
• Customers tell twice as many people about a bad experience as about a good one.

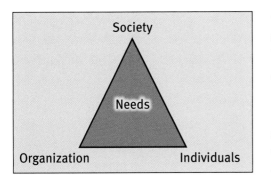

FIGURE 2.14. Societal Marketing Concept

- The association claims that an average company gets 65 percent of its business from its present and satisfied customers.

In a nutshell, organizations that address the needs and wants of customers stand a better chance of sustaining a competitive advantage in the marketplace. Additionally, a new way of thinking has gained traction in the marketplace in recent decades; one that brings another perspective—the customer's—to the activities as previously described in this chapter.

> *"It is what we do when we don't have to that determines what we will be when we can no longer help it."—Anonymous*

> *"Hold yourself responsible for a higher standard than anybody else expects of you."—Henry Ward Beecher (mid-nineteenth-century clergyman and abolitionist)*

> *"Ethics are . . . the reverence for and the maintaining, promoting, and enhancing of life . . ."—Albert Schweitzer (1952 Nobel Prize recipient)*

The above quotes are intended to help illustrate that there are times when merely satisfying customers' needs better than the competition is just *not* enough. What if these solutions (as products and services are sometimes referred to) are harmful to people, the environment, or future generations? These days, businesses carefully balance the needs of individuals, the organization, *and* society, because ethics and responsibility are key components for the success of today's companies—not merely food for thought.

The **societal marketing concept** considers the interests of stakeholders—any people (from administrators to vendors, from stockholders to members of the cleaning crew, as well as clients and customers) who have an interest in an organization. The four key ideas that must be balanced for this concept to work are as follows:

1. Customer wants
2. Competitors' actions
3. Society's interests
4. Company profits

This concept both embraces and reflects the idea that companies *should balance customer interests and wants, competitive intelligence, and long-term consumer and societal well-being.* In 2005, for example, Dove began to use women with average body builds, rather than very thin women, in its advertisements; the company suggested that this might help improve self-image issues among females (in addition to increasing sales).

Some fast-food restaurants incorporate menu choices that contain less fat, and "smart" homebuilders provide convenient safety and energy management options for disabled individuals. StarKist Seafood Company is committed to protecting dolphins and will not purchase any tuna caught by means that endanger these creatures. The American Marketing Association specifically addresses the social obligations companies have to all stakeholders in the responsibility and citizenship sections of its code of ethics.[13] (Ethics and responsibility are discussed in greater detail in Chapter 15.)

Taking this issue further is the concept of **cause-related marketing,** the public association of a for-profit company with a nonprofit organization. The for-profit company pairs with the nonprofit's social cause. One of the front-runners in this effort was American Express. In 1983 it participated in the restoration of the Statue of Liberty, pledging a minimum of $3 million through its various fund-raising efforts. Companies that employ this concept increase corporate sales and customer loyalty while demonstrating social concern and involvement. Today companies and individuals want to do good things; philanthropy (helping others through charitable contributions) has become very fashionable. (See Chapter 13 for more details.)

Developing fashionable solutions, from the company's perspective, means understanding what is currently valued and wanted by its customers. But what about the consumer's perspective? What is it that helps create that perspective—at a very basic level? How do consumers interpret and learn? The next chapter provides some answers.

Summary

Buying and selling come together in the exchange process when the buyer perceives value, tangible or intangible attributes that improve the desirability of a product or service. After the marketer identifies that perceived value in specific market segments, products or services that address those client needs and wants are sometimes customized to increase their appeal to the consumer.

A company that creates a strategic marketing plan (a road map that connects and positions product and service solutions to buyers) and adapts, as needed, to evolving fashion expectations, will thrive in today's marketplace. The emerging expectation is that organizations will provide products and services that add value in a socially responsible manner—not just generate revenue for the company.

Key Terms

Buyer's market	Secondary data
Cause-related marketing	Seller's market
Customization	Selling concept
Market research	Societal marketing concept
Market segmentation	Stakeholder
Marketing concept	Strategic marketing plan
Perceived cost	Strategy
Position	Supply chain
Primary data	Target marketing
Quantifying	Value

Questions for Review

1. Describe the differences between buyers' and sellers' markets and give a specific example of each.
2. Explain the equation P (Price) ÷ V (Value) = C (Cost), and provide a numerical example showing what happens to C when the denominator increases. How do actual and perceived costs differ?
3. What is meant by "quantifying" and why is it an important business tool? Support your answer with two examples.
4. What is the S T P process, why is it important to a marketer, and what steps are involved?
5. Discuss the differences between the selling, marketing, and societal marketing concepts.

Activities

1. Price, value, and cost (P/V = C): You are a buyer, not the seller. Assume that you have the extra dollars to make the purchase. Select three items in the same product or service category that have low, medium, and high price points (for example, Jeans: $35/$75/$195).
   A. Explain this equation in terms of the product or service at the lowest and highest price levels.
   B. Identify specific value factors.
   C. List other value-added factors that might motivate you to spend more on the product or service.
2. Customization: Select a company that's both *product* and *service* oriented. Discuss the following:

    A. Ways the company customizes its offerings

    B. Your perception of this customization

    C. How you would improve it

3. Quantifying (measuring and expressing a result as a number equivalent): Think of a particular company that provides a service, and identify three areas in which quantifying results is important. Then:

    A. List and explain one specific method of measurement for each area.

    B. Recommend one improvement to maximize efficiency in each area.

4. Buyer's and seller's market: Select two designed products or services and explain how they moved from a buyer's market to a seller's market (for example, blue jeans).

5. Societal marketing concept: Find the mission statements of three not-for-profit organizations. Then pair each one with an existing company, explaining why you feel each is a good match (for example, Kenneth Cole and the Save the Children Foundation).

Mini-Project

S T P Process (Segment–Target–Position)

    Assume the role of a business owner. Dream for a moment: What kind of business interests you? What product(s) do you sell or what service(s) do you provide? Then identify a new line or a service add-on you think would be good for your bottom line. Remember, you don't want to add a new product or service blindly. Illustrate and explain the S T P process at work by segmenting your market, and targeting and positioning your product or service.

References

1. Adam Smith, *A Wealth of Nations*, www.bibliomania.com/2/1/65/112/frameset .html.
2. Susan Chandler. "What Do Shoppers Want," *Chicago Tribune*, September 25, 2005.
3. Peter Drucker, www.peter-drucker.com.
4. Catherine Getches, "Brand Boggled," *New York Times*, September 1, 2005.
5. Henry Mintzberg and Joseph Lampel, "Customizing Customization," *MIT Sloan Review* 38 Topic: Corporate Strategy Reprint 3812, no. 1 (Fall 1996): 21–30.
6. www.photostamps.com.
7. James B. Arndorfer, "Grappling with Marketing's 'Tsunami,'" AdAge.com online edition, October 7, 2005, http://adage.com/news.cms?newsId=46320#.
8. Michael Porter, *The Concept of Corporate Strategy*, 2nd ed. (Homewood, IL: Dow Jones-Irwin, 1980).

9. Al Ries and Jack Trout, *Positioning: The Battle for Your Mind* (New York: McGraw-Hill, 2001).

10. J. McCarthy, *Basic Marketing: A Managerial Approach*, 13th ed. (Homewood, IL: Irwin, 2001).

11. Peter Drucker, *The Practice of Management,* 1954.

12. Peter D. Bennett, ed., *Dictionary of Marketing Terms,* 2nd ed. (Chicago: American Marketing Association, 1995).

13. "American Marketing Association Code of Ethics," www.ama.org; www .marketingpower.com/content435.php

Additional Resources

American Express. "American Express Launches National Campaign to Help Reopen the Statue of Liberty; Pledges A Minimum Of $3 Million with Cardmember Support." November 25, 2003. http://home3.americanexpress.com/corp/pc/2003/statue_liberty.asp

Borden, N. "The Concept of the Marketing Mix." *Journal of Advertising Research* 4 (June, 1964): 2–7.

Brandweek. November 4, 2005. www.brandweek.com/bw/news/autos/article_display .jsp?vnu_content_id=1001434575.

Hughlett, Mike. "A Field's, Frango Frenzy." *Chicago Tribune*, December 23, 2005.

Davis, Wynn. *The Best of Success: A Treasury of Success Ideas.* (Great Quotations, Inc., Lombard, Illinois: 1988).

Elliott, Stuart. "Housewives Is a Big Hit on Madison Ave." August 24, 2005. www .nytimes.com and www.infosyncworld.com/news/n/5249.html.

England, Lizabeth. "Marketing with a Conscience: Sales and Ethics." Chapter 10 in *Business Ethics* volume of *Language and Civil Society* journal. Published online at http://exchanges.state.gov/forum/journal/bus10background.htm.

Investor Words.com. www.investorwords.com.

Investor's Glossary. Contra the Heard Web site. www.contratheheard.com/cth/glossary.

MarketingProfs Web site. www.marketingprofs.com/5/kaden1.asp.

Martin, James. "Color Trends for Custom Homes." *Residential Design & Build*. April 2007.

"Motorola Pininfarina i833 Announced." MobileTracker Web site. August 18, 2004. www.mobiletracker.net/archives/2004/08/18/motorola_pininf.php.

Mplans.com Web site. www.mplans.com.

Nobelprize.org Web site. Biography of Albert Schweitzer. http://nobelprize.org/nobel _prizes/peace/laureates/1952/schweitzer-bio.html.

Porter, Michael. *Competitive Strategy.* (Cambridge, MA: Harvard Business School Press, 1986).

Schweitzer, Albert. *Civilization and Ethics.* (New York: Macmillan, 1949.)

Scott, David L. *Wall Street Words: An A to Z Guide to Investment Terms for Today's Investor.* (Boston: Houghton Mifflin Company.)

SmartHomeUSA Web site. www.smarthomeusa.com.

Vielkind, Jimmy and Nancy Dillon. "Swoosh! Big Women Taking Ads by Storm." New York Daily News. August 16, 2005.

Voorn, R. *The Marketing Plan Made Simple.* 3rd ed. Costa Mesa, CA: James Publishing, 1997.

Webster's New World Dictionary. 3rd ed. New York: Simon & Schuster.

"What Is Strategy?" *Harvard Business Review,* November–December, 1996.

Wikipedia. "Consumption" entry. http://en.wikipedia.org/wiki/Consumption.

www.trexfiles.com/2007/02/why_fashion_has_turned_to_cause_marketing.php

"What is cause-related marketing?" From the Foundation Center's Web site. http://foundationcenter.org/getstarted/faqs/html/cause_marketing.html

PART II

Internal Factors Influence Fashion Consumers

Numerous psychological and behavioral elements influence individual consumers in their actions and attitudes toward fashion—some of these elements are explored in Part II.

Chapter 3 describes how people perceive, learn, and remember. The various human needs and wants that motivate purchases, especially those that reflect self-image, are examined in Chapter 4. The consumer's attitudes and values, and how those traits influence behavior, are the topic of Chapter 5. Part II concludes with the Chapter 6 discussion of how personality and self-concept relate to the consumption of fashion.

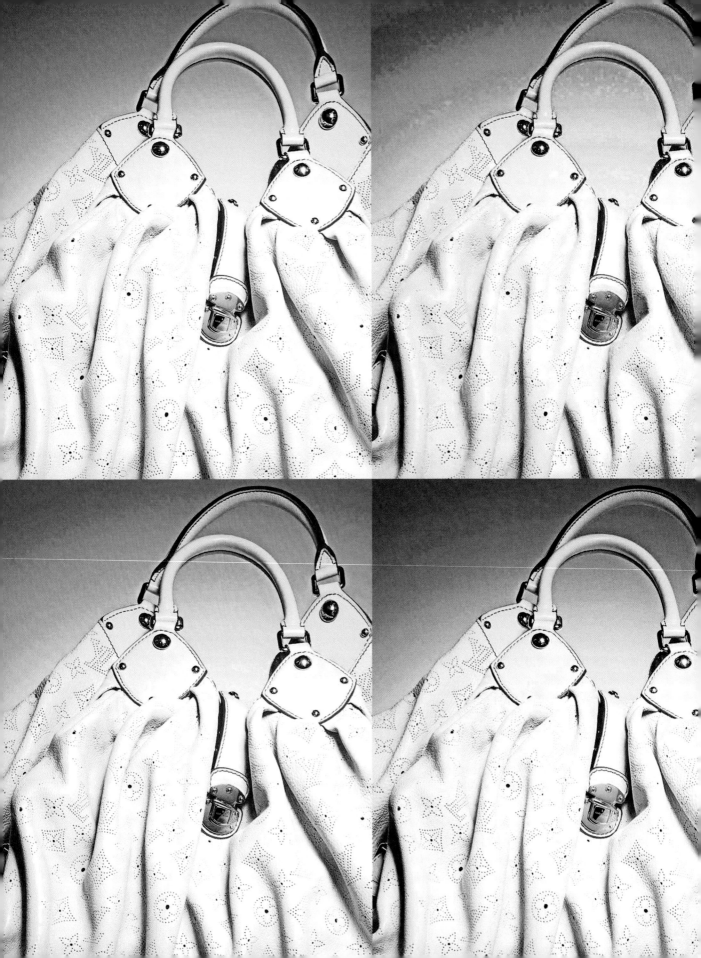

merc
time:
cult,
prof:
"lool
chase
Acce:
and c
roon

How
As n
and t

Visic
In fa
desig
show
walk
silho
has :
and
good
befo
Cole
colo
lates
furr
prin
war
selv
whi
Tar
ma

Tou
Ess
vet,
phy

CHAPTER 3

How Fashion Consumers Perceive, Learn, and Remember

Before people can react—form an opinion or reach a decision—they must be exposed to a physical sensation such as the colors in a display of bright T-shirts; **exposure** then happens when we encounter a stimulus through our senses: seeing, hearing, smelling, touching, or tasting. Stimuli such as jazz on the radio, the aroma of coffee, or strong light bombard us constantly, and we cannot possibly register everything we encounter. Instead, we choose the exposure we want. For example, to discover fashion trends, women may flip through hundreds of ads in *Elle* or *InStyle*, noting only those looks that appeal to them. Fashion marketers work to maximize the possibility of exposure for their products, creating eye-catching ads and commercials and placing these products prominently in stores.

To better understand this concept, let's look at an example. Stacy has been working as a cashier at a Ralph Lauren Polo store on weekends for several months to help pay for college (with a major in fashion). The job fits her schedule, but the store's merchandise certainly is not the edgy look her friends at school are wearing.

help her own customers choose what's right for them. The sincerity and enthusiasm of the salesperson, along with the tone and sound of her voice, give Stacy a feeling of confidence about the merchandise. Marketers reach customers many ways through sound.

Taste

One day, Stacy decides to have a Dove bar. She had seen an ad showing a silky curtain in chocolate brown emphasizing the smoothness of that candy compared with less expensive brands.[7] Not a designer chocolate, but quite fashionable in its appearance and taste, just the same. Stacy realizes that there are fashions in food, just as there are fashions in apparel and home furnishings. Her friends were eating fewer hamburgers and more vegetables and fruit, and were experimenting with the flavors and cuisines of places as far away as Argentina, Ethiopia, and Thailand. Obviously, taste can introduce new experiences. Most humans recognize four flavors: sweet, sour, salty, and bitter; the Japanese claim a fifth flavor called "umami," with a taste similar to MSG.

The way we respond to these sensory stimuli makes up a part of the emotional aspect of our relationship to purchasing products and is known as **hedonic consumption**. For example, with the scent of roses a young woman recalls her grandmother's garden and the summer parties there. By purchasing rose-scented hand cream, she remembers the pleasant memories of those gatherings each time she uses it.

> *Let's Talk*
> *What fashion goods have you noticed recently whose appeal to consumers is based on hedonic consumption, the emotional/relationship aspect of the purchase?*

How We Perceive

Because as humans we can only process some of the stimuli that bombard us, we call the process of interpreting our surroundings through our senses **perception**. Since perception is about our individual interpretations, marketers continually study how perception motivates us as members of specific consumer groups. In addition to exposure to sensory stimuli (discussed in the previous section), the perception process includes attention and interpretation.

❯❯❯ SPECIAL FOCUS 3.1: VIRTUAL SEEING, HEARING, TASTING BY AIMING ULTRASOUND AT THE BRAIN ❮❮❮

The film series *The Matrix* showed some of the characters hooked up to a huge computer that was able to influence their vision, hearing, tasting, and other senses, but only in their imagination. While these "sensory experiences"—sounds, smells, tastes, and moving images—were fictitious in the movie, the entertainment corporation Sony has taken out patents to create the actual technique. The project's goal is to use ultrasound to stimulate the brain to create sensory experiences. The idea has long been a tool of science fiction writers, but what's the real use?

There are several. First, according to Sony, developer of popular electronic entertainment including the Walkman and PlayStation and coinventor of CDs and DVDs, a film or game offering a "personal sensory environment" would be an enhancement, taking its entertainment systems to the next level by letting participants believe they were really taking part in the situation—seeing, hearing, and smelling what was going on.

In the field of health, such sensory technology might well enable deaf and blind people to hear and see. In law enforcement, this technology could replace the rather unreliable lie detector by using "thermal facial imaging," which shows the flow of blood changing in the blood vessels when someone is not telling the truth.

For example, bright circles show up around a person's eyes when faced with a question that he or she feels must be answered with a lie. Obviously, businesses could use thermal facial imaging in screening potential employees to eliminate potential problems from dishonest applicants and substance abusers.

>>> Source: Adapted from "To Tell the Truth," Trends Magazine Online, August 22, 2005.

Absolute Threshold

Now that we have seen several examples of exposure through our five senses, we need to take this information one step further. The lowest level at which our senses can recognize a stimulus is called the **absolute threshold**. The music in a store, in order not to detract people from shopping, is set at a scarcely discernible volume, an absolute threshold for many shoppers. When our senses can barely distinguish between two stimuli such as popular music and jazz, this represents the "**just noticeable difference**" (**j.n.d.**). The just noticeable difference is important to designers and marketers who want to make sure that customers can distinguish, for example, the difference between two sweaters priced $20 apart or two chairs priced $50 apart. Certain features of the more expensive item, perhaps the fiber content or the trimmings, must make it worth the higher price in the mind of the consumer. Or, if shirts are on sale, the reduced price must have a j.n.d. in price from the original price. In the mind of the customer, there is no j.n.d. in a sweater or a chair reduced from $80 to $78. In this instance, the j.n.d. becomes another way consumers are encouraged to buy.

Let's Talk
What recent examples can you think of that illustrate j.n.d.?

Weber's Law

A nineteenth-century German experimental psychologist, Ernest Weber, gave us the basis for explaining j.n.d. when he developed the theory bearing his name. **Weber's Law** states that the more intense the first stimulus is, the stronger the next stimulus must be in order for people to see it as different.[8] For fashion marketers, Weber's Law has applications in design, color, pricing, and other areas. This season's fashion looks must stand out from last season's, or they will not excite fashion editors, professional buyers, and, eventually, customers. This season's color palette must appear different from last season's so that customers will be enticed to want the latest looks. In the area of price, Weber's Law is most important. Near the end of the summer, a set of wicker garden furniture marked down from $600 to $589 will hardly warrant a customer's glance, but a reduction to $449 could well attract interested buyers. In other words, there must be a lot more than a j.n.d. for Weber's Law to have an effect.

Subliminal Perception

An area exists below the absolute threshold where we perceive but are not capable of overtly recognizing stimuli. Suppose you were exposed to a fashion commercial on TV that flashed the words "plaids are in" at a speed you could not consciously see. The purpose of this message, repeated several times, would be to encourage viewers to buy plaid garments and home furnishings. The perception of stimuli by our senses below the level of conscious awareness (absolute threshold) is known as **subliminal perception**. The word "subliminal" comes from "limen," which is another term for "threshold." Subliminal perception was once a hotly debated topic. In 1957, a market researcher named James Vicary conducted an experiment at a movie theater in Fort Lee, New Jersey. He had the words "Drink Coca-Cola" and "Eat Popcorn" flashed subliminally on the movie screen (3/1,000 of a second, once every five seconds), and snack bar sales soared during the next several weeks. When the experiment couldn't be replicated with similar results and subsequent tests failed, interest waned in the use of subliminal advertising for marketing purposes. Nevertheless, many people see messages embedded in films, commercials, and print ads. The federal government believes that while subliminal advertising is an attempt to manipulate consumers and therefore is against public well-being, without proof that it actually works, legislation seems unnecessary.[9] Next, we will investigate how we continue to perceive and process stimuli.

FIGURE 3.3A and B. The work of designers like Eunyoung Song and Shuji Wada reflect changing looks that draw the attention of fashion editors and customers from season to season.

How We Pay Attention

Just because we are exposed to a variety of sights, sounds, and smells doesn't mean we really notice all of them. Only when we apply our minds to a stimulus does it have our attention. **Attention**, then, is focusing our thoughts on a certain stimulus. Children and pets have a way of grabbing our attention (as you can tell from the soulful stare of the puppy in Figure 3.4).

Or, returning to Stacy, she is thumbing through the latest issue of *Martha Stewart Living*, idly turning the pages until she sees a new home-decorating idea. The room design is the focus of her attention. Marketers work to accomplish this very goal: getting our attention is the first step in convincing us to buy. Notice some characteristics of attention, however. It does not last. Soon Stacy turns the pages in search of even more appealing décor. Nor does the magazine have her full attention; she is listening to her iPod as she flips the pages.

How do we choose which stimuli will merit our full attention? That depends on the kind of stimulus, what experience has told us to expect, and our current needs and desires. Let's first consider the stimulus itself, and then look at our personal characteristics.

FIGURE 3.4. The winsome look of a pet draws attention to an ad.

Stimulus Characteristics

Certainly the type of item we focus attention on is essential and highly individual. An ad for a fishing rod may appeal to your grandfather, whereas an ad for a leather jacket is what really grabs your attention. Several factors are involved here; two of them are size and contrast. Large billboards along the highway draw our attention to nearby stores or restaurants, while small, exclusive jewelry store display windows might show a single diamond ring or clip. Using color is another way to draw attention. Consider the silver GAP package designs, more sleek than the company's previous use of navy blue with white lettering; the bright red envelope of an Internet marketer; or the Nike "swoosh" on a red or white cap, shirt, or shoes. The position of an ad in a magazine, or of a product logo on a package (such as Bloomingdale's "Brown Bag"), is also designed to attract attention.

Let's Talk

Of the stimulus characteristics mentioned above, which would be the strongest draw for you in an ad promoting a product such as an automobile, furniture for your living room, or a new pair of dress shoes?

Personal Characteristics

Since we cannot possibly process all of the stimuli we encounter, we pay attention to stimuli that touch on our needs and wants and (we hope) will meet our expectations. We practice **selective perception**: We choose to pay attention to the stimuli that connect to our needs. (To relate stimulus characteristics and personal characteristics, see Table 3.1.) When Stacy wants to add a new skirt to her wardrobe, she skims the fashion magazines, surfs the Internet, and searches through the skirt racks in several stores. She looks just at those skirts that interest her and disregards the rest. In reality, because we can deal with only a limited number of stimuli, we screen out others; we are practicing selective exposure and selective attention as well as selective perception. But we make sure to be continually on the lookout over time for the things we need. For example, when Stacy is at the beauty salon, she notices that a friend is wearing a skirt similar to the one she wants and learns that it is from a J. Jill catalog.

❯❯❯ SPECIAL FOCUS 3.2: SUPERMARKET SHOPPING BUDDY: CONSUMER PROBLEM-SOLVING MADE EASY ❮❮❮

People like to pick out their own groceries, but writing a shopping list is hard to do and then remembering everything we need may well be impossible. Never fear, Shopping Buddy is here—or at least being tested in Massachusetts supermarkets. A computer resting on the handles of a grocery cart helps us get the job done. Developed by Accenture Technology Laboratories, a division of the business consulting group Accenture, this device is able to communicate with customers as they go through the supermarket.

Shopping Buddy works like this: Consumers log in with the store's frequent shopping card. On the Buddy screen, a shopping list appears, and not just any list but one based on individual past purchases. While rolling through the store, consumers pick items off of the shelves and scan them, yielding an instant tally of what's in the basket. Since shopping lists are personalized, when consumers come across a brand they normally buy, such as Ben & Jerry's ice cream, there may be a promotion with coupons or a sale price that they are awarded automatically. Because the Buddy list is detailed, it serves as a reminder of items consumers may have neglected to write down.

Once finished, Shopping Buddy scans and tallies up purchases so customers don't wait in line to check out. Decision making is easier and without taxing long-term memories!

❯❯❯ Source: Adapted from Shia Kapos, "High-Tech Shopping Lists Guide Grocery Shoppers," *Chicago Tribune*, June 20, 2005, Sec. 4, pp. 1 and 4.

Table 3.1 Chart of Stimulus and Personal Characteristics

Stimulus Characteristics	Personal Characteristics
Type of item	What we expect
Size and contrast	What we select to
Color	Perceive
Position, placement	Reject

How We Process

How do we as consumers decide what to buy? Our first step is to organize the stimuli we have perceived into some meaningful form. The process of organization is explained by **gestalt psychology,** meaning that people reach a conclusion after seeing a total picture. The German word "Gestalt" means "pattern" or "configuration." Gestalt psychology is sometimes compared to a lightbulb turning on. Maybe you've seen a comic strip where the main character "gets the point," and to illustrate that, there is a lightbulb glowing over his or her head. That's the gestalt or "aha!" experience.[10]

Three elements of perceptual organization are similarity, figure-and-ground, and closure. *Similarity* tells us that we like to group together similar ideas and objects. Retailers use the concept of similarity to group similar merchandise so that customers can see related items together. Think, for example, of the display windows of Williams-Sonoma where you could see a group of red, yellow, or green kitchen appliances such as mixers, bread makers, waffle irons, and bowls displayed with coordinated print kitchen aprons and dish towels.

Another organizing concept, *figure-and-ground,* tells us that we organize stimuli so that part of the stimulus (the *figure*) is more prominent than the rest (the *ground*). Marketers use this principle in planning advertisements and merchandise displays so that the main objects, perhaps garments or jewelry, are distinct from the background. Interior designers place a solid-red sofa on a black-and-white floor so that the sofa stands out as the focal point.

Humans have a need for a complete picture. When what we see is incomplete, we tend to see it as complete anyway; this is known as the closure principle. A while ago, the Kellogg Company ran a billboard for its cereals, substituting a pair of bananas for the two letters "l" in the company name, and viewers automatically used closure to make the name complete. Marketers use the closure principle in ads to gain attention and to urge us to perceive and remember their messages. Interior designers group a collection of pictures on a living room wall, sometimes using the closure principle to create a complete look. As consumers, we develop an *organized* set of beliefs about a topic or product that is known as a schema. A client develops a schema when she or he learns that the grouping of pictures adds to the total effect of the interior.

FIGURE 3.5. The "aha" of the Gestalt experience.

How We Learn

When we're thinking about buying something new, we often want to find out as much as we can about that particular product or service. Stacy noticed that customers frequently read the labels on the apparel and home furnishings in the outlet store where she works. They were learning about fabric content and care. **Learning** is a process that changes behavior through experience. For example, two customers looking at a Ralph Lauren sheet set wanted to be certain of 100 percent cotton fabrication because only natural fibers would suit them.

People learn in several ways. Two major learning theories are **behavioral learning** and cognitive learning. Behavioral learning occurs when we respond to certain stimuli. Cognitive learning is a problem-solving process.

Behavioral Learning

The behavioral learning concept theorizes that learning takes place after exposure to external stimuli; two major types of behavioral learning are *classical conditioning* and *instrumental conditioning*. If you wonder sometimes why you see or hear advertising messages over and over again, behavioral learning theory could possibly be an element of that particular ad campaign. Classical conditioning and instrumental conditioning are both based on training that elicits a response to a stimulus. **Classical conditioning** pairs an artificial stimulus with a natural one and eventually gains a response from the artificial stimulus alone. This theory was developed in Russia when physiologist Ivan Pavlov experimented with the way dogs anticipate food. Pavlov fed the dogs while ringing a bell. The dogs salivated naturally when given the food, but after much repetition, they began salivating when they just heard the bell. This is an example of a conditioned response.[11] The repeated experiment is the basis for the reason we may sometimes see the same furniture store commercial several times during a TV show, or notice the same Estée Lauder ad in four different fashion magazines. (See Figure 3.7.) This idea of conditioned response could be the reason why the private label on a regional drugstore's brand of shampoo almost mirrors that of the best-selling national brand and why so many food products in addition to soup bear the family brand name of Campbell's.

When we have choices and begin to prefer a choice that produces a "reward" over one accompanied by "punishment," we encounter learning through **instrumental conditioning**. Suppose

FIGURE 3.6. Here the handbag attracts attention because it stands out clearly from the background.

Table 3.2.   Learning Theories

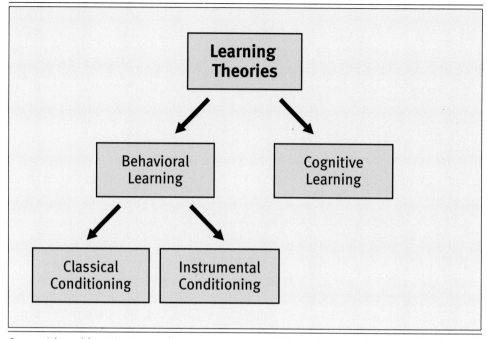

Source: Adapted from Henry Asseal. *Consumer Behavior: A Strategic Approach*. Boston: Houghton Mifflin, 2004. p. 59.

Stacy's class project is to create a plan for remodeling her bedroom. She knows she should complete her assignment in order to succeed and earn a good grade. But her friends invite her out to the movies. If she opts for the night out, her project will be slapdash, and her grade will reflect it; however, if she spends time on her assignment, chances are that she will present it well in class. As consumers, we learn to behave in ways that bring rewards—and avoid punishment.

American psychologist B. F. Skinner refined the theory of instrumental conditioning through his work with rats that were rewarded with food by pushing one lever as opposed to another. Classical conditioning and instrumental conditioning obviously differ; in instrumental conditioning, a choice exists and the experiment's subject has the power to choose. If the right choice is made, there is a reward. If the wrong choice is made, there is nothing—or worse, a negative stimulus such as a shock. The right choice with repeated rewards reinforces the behavior, whereas no reward or receiving actual punishment for a choice discourages a subject from continuing with that choice.[12] As consumers, we continue to buy the same brands of apparel or appliances when we are satisfied with them; conversely, we avoid those products that we find may shrink in the wash or break too easily. Marketers use advertising, coupons, and rebates as rewards to attract and maintain loyal customers. When these promotions are no longer rewarding, we sometimes discontinue purchasing a given product.

❯ ❯ ❯ POINT OF VIEW 3.2: HOW MARKETERS USE THE LEARNING PROCESS IN SELLING HOMES ❮ ❮ ❮

With more people owning not one but two or more homes and demanding custom touches such as professionally designed adjacent golf courses designed by pros, home builders are eager to see that the decision-making process is as appealing and convenient as possible. In addition, manufacturers of brand-name products such as General Electric, Kohler, and even John Deere are seeking out new markets through home developers' building projects.

When a prospective new home buyer can choose General Electric kitchen appliances, Kohler bathroom fixtures, Andersen windows, or a John Deere tractor-mower to mow the lawn, or can play golf on an Arnold Palmer course, these brand names are already stored in memory. Because they are familiar, they can reduce the home buyer's stress in decision making, at least for these products. And often there is a carry-over: If the customer has faith in the appliance brand names, that goodwill can spread to the builder.

For the marketer, the learning process is effective when customers have stored the brand names and product characteristics and recall them positively.

❯❯❯ Source: Adapted from Sharon Stangeness, "House Only Part of the Package," *Chicago Tribune*, June 18, 2005, Sec. 2, pp. 1 and 8.

FIGURE 3.7. Repeating the manufacturer's logo in an appealing ad helps consumers identify the image and learn product benefits.

Cognitive Learning

While behavioral learning occurs in reaction to a stimulus, **cognitive**

learning is a problem-solving process where, as consumers, we actively seek out information in order to make an informed decision. Cognitive problem solving can be active (as when Stacy tries several new paint colors on her bedroom walls until she finds the one she likes best), or it can occur through observation (as when she looks through a home-decorating magazine and selects the most appropriate window treatments for her room).

When do we rely on behavioral learning and when on cognitive learning? As consumers, we tend to be influenced through behavioral stimuli (for example, repeated ads for a brand of cereal or toothpaste) when the products we are considering are not high-involvement, that is, they don't represent expressions of our individuality and don't take a lot of energy to purchase. These low-involvement products are often staples such as dairy products or health and beauty aids. But we use cognitive learning strategies when considering goods that represent our personalities (such as a new outfit), or when making a substantial purchase (for example, a home or apartment, a new automobile, or a vacation destination). We are more highly involved with these purchases—not just because they may be costly but because they make up part of our persona. Notice the BlackBerry product information presented in Figure 3.8.

Let's Talk
What examples can you think of where fashion advertisers appeal to consumer learning behavior? Which type(s) of behavior?

How We Remember

Obviously, we need to be able to call on what we have learned when we need it. The process of storing and retrieving knowledge is called **memory**. There are three types of memory, each with a different purpose: sensory memory, short-term memory, and long-term memory.[13]

Our Three Memories

We receive sensory stimuli automatically in our *sensory memory*, which holds them briefly. When Stacy sees a family who is about to enter the store where she works (a visual stimulus), this image goes into her sensory memory for a few seconds and then disappears—unless she consciously records it, as she would if recognizing neighbors, for example.

If we do consciously record a stimulus, it enters our *short-term memory*, which allows us to remember something for a limited time. Stacy would remember the neighbors entering the store. If a customer were purchasing some Polo shirts, a decorative pillow, and a throw, Stacy would remember these items as she rings up the sale,

FIGURE 3.8. Information on new products and improved technology help consumers reach meaningful buying decisions.

but chances are that at the end of the day she wouldn't be able to recall every item in each sales transaction. Short-term memory is where most mental processing takes place in order to retain what we want to store.

To hold on to information readily, we encode it; in this sense, **encoding** means the way we select visual images or words in short-term memory to stand for what we want to store in our long-term memory. Visual images are often easier for us to store, and marketers devise brand symbols and corporate logos that are easy to remember. Marketers create symbols, or icons, such as the Ralph Lauren polo player, the Westinghouse W with a crown, and the Ford galloping Mustang horse that help us easily put those brands in long-term memory should those products be of interest to us.

The purpose of **long-term memory** is to store information we want to keep for permanent use and recall at will, almost like a computer's hard drive. Sometimes long-term memory retains items for years—even decades. For example, you can probably recall the name of your first really close friend, even though you may not have seen that person for 15 years or more. Marketers hope that by giving us symbols that are easy to encode, we will store them in long-term memory and retrieve them when considering purchases. We may store these symbols into knowledge structures made up of nodes, information that is linked to similar data in a kind of web. Humans can amass large amounts of encoded information on a topic, a process known as **chunking**. One example of chunking is when we add on to what we already know about appropriate fabrics for interior design as opposed to those for wearing apparel.

Often, we are bombarded with more information than we can process or store, a condition called **information overload**. When we learn that certain brands of cell phones not only send, receive, record messages, and have photo and e-mail capability, and still others print movie tickets, turn on lights, and open garage doors, we have too much information and run the risk of making a poor buying decision as a result. Chunking helps consumers who have researched a given product or idea store much more information about it than those who have not.

Storing and Retrieving Information

People can store information by its sensory interpretation, such as the brilliant yellow of a dandelion; semantically by its meaning in language, such as "surfers have great bods"; or autobiographically, as memories of events as they occurred to us, such as our high school graduation. Our semantic memories are interconnected through networks, sets of ideas, and schema (a set of beliefs and associations that trigger each other).

The process we go through to use information stored in memory is called **retrieval**. The strength of the associations in the memory network has an influence on the effectiveness of retrieval. If a student has a firm belief that the designs of Karl Lagerfeld influence both apparel and theatrical costuming trends, that person will be able to recall evidence to support this view. The speed at which information can be retrieved from the memory network is known as **activation**. Through spreading activation—that is, the linking of our memory nodes—we can recall a product through its brand name, a particular ad we saw, or some of its characteristics. For example, if we hear a radio commercial for a favorite restaurant, activation lets us recall the restaurant's location, the type of food it serves, and how the hosts treated us. The prominence of a product message also helps us retrieve information about it. A striking ad in *Vogue* or *Metropolitan Home* can cause us to remember other information about the work of the designer featured.

But we are not able to retrieve everything stored in memory. Perhaps we can't recall a friend's telephone number or the birthday of an uncle. If we haven't used the information for a while, it could just disappear. When we learn new information, it may replace the old, which is then lost. At times, we unintentionally forget. Research indicates that older people and children have more difficulty remembering than people who are between those age groups; older people perhaps because they have had many experiences to remember and youngsters because they have had relatively few to build on.

In the next chapter, we will explore the topic of motivation, a key factor in buying decisions.

Summary

We are connected to the world through our perceptions. The way we perceive is through our five senses: vision, hearing, smell, taste, and touch. We are constantly exposed to these sensations and are only able to register some of them, so we focus on the stimuli that gain our attention and then select what we want to use. Through the continuing process of learning, we are capable of changing behavior. Major learning theories include classical and behavioral conditioning and cognitive learning. Classical conditioning demonstrates that a new stimulus used repeatedly with an original stimulus eventually produces the same reaction alone. Behavioral conditioning offers a choice, with the correct response bringing a reward. Marketers employ incentives based on conditioning learning theories when they offer product samples, coupons, and discounts that encourage consumers to purchase their products. Cognitive learning views learning as a problem-solving process: People go through a series of steps to determine the correct course of action. As consumers, we tend to use cognitive learning when considering high-involvement products, those that are more costly and closely related to our personalities, such as a new vehicle or apartment.

When storing information for future use, we rely on memory. We have different forms of memory based on the length of storage time. Sensory memory stores perceived stimuli for a few seconds, short-term memory enables us to remember for a few minutes, and long-term memory for months or years. We encode information and store it, retrieving it through networks, finding most easily what is familiar and important to us.

Key Terms

Absolute threshold	Encoding
Activation	Exposure
Attention	Gestalt psychology
Behavioral learning	Hedonic consumption
Chunking	Information overload
Classical conditioning	Instrumental conditioning
Cognitive learning	Just noticeable difference (j.n.d.)

Learning	Retrieval
Long-term memory	Selective perception
Memory	Subliminal perception
Perception	Weber's Law

Questions for Review

1. Using examples from your experience in design or fashion, describe each of the five kinds of sensory stimuli humans perceive.

2. Explain the importance of the concepts of absolute threshold, just noticeable difference, and Weber's Law both to consumers and to marketers.

3. As consumers, when do we tend to learn through classical or instrumental conditioning techniques and when through cognitive learning methods?

4. Identify the three levels of memory humans possess, and state which of these we use in recalling the brand names and characteristics of products we are considering purchasing. How do marketers hope to make this recall easier?

6. Why are perception, learning, and memory important to us both as consumers and marketers?

Activities

1. Select three magazine ads, each of which appeals to a different sense. Identify which sense each ad appeals to and state what makes it appealing. Then explain how each ad attracts attention.

2. Visit the Web sites of two retailers, one with brick-and-mortar stores (such as www.Nordstrom.com) and one that is strictly point-and-click (such as www.Amazon.com). Describe the visual appeal of each site, indicating how each one promotes that retailer's image.

3. In small teams, visit a large supermarket to identify how customers use various learning theories. Look for examples of consumer behavior representing classical conditioning, instrumental conditioning, cognitive learning, and observational learning. Report your findings to the class.

4. Think of a brand of jeans or laptop computer that is marketed to your age group. Create a list of that product's characteristics that distinguish it from the competition. Select the features that would most appeal to your target market, and create the copy for a print ad or television commercial that would be based on cognitive learning theory. Share your results with the class.

5. Working in teams, recall as many product slogans and jingles as you can. Then create your own slogan or jingle. Ask other members of the class if they can

remember the brand names that match your slogans. Recite your own slogan first, then the others. After classmates have identified the products on your list, ask them for the first slogan you gave them. Then ask them to determine whether these slogans are stored in sensory, short-term, or long-term memory.

Mini-Project

As a group, develop the interior design for one room of a home. Create a household of three people and a clothing outfit for each. Explain how each group member (classmate) used perception and learning to select apparel for the residents and how together the group members applied cognitive learning theory in creating the design and selecting the furniture for the interior of the house. Present your project to the class.

References

1. Elaine Stone, *The Dynamics of Fashion* (New York: Fairchild Publications, Inc., 2004), p. 315.
2. www.colorbox.com.
3. Color Association of the United States Web site, www.colorassociation.com.
4. Michael Gross, *Genuine Authentic, the Real Life of Ralph Lauren* (New York: HarperCollins, 2003), p. 98.
5. Amir Vokshoor, "Anatomy of Olfactory Systems," *eMedicine*, March 22, 2006, www .eMedicine.com/ent/topic564.htm.
6. Ken Druse, "She Smells Me Not," *New York Times*, June 9, 2005, Sec. D.
7. Stuart Elliott, "Advertising," *New York Times*, April 4, 2005, Sec. C.
8. *Encyclopedia Britannica*, "Weber's Law" entry, www.britannica.com/eb/article -9076393/Webers-law#39123.hook; Lewis O. Harvey, Jr., *Psychology of Perception*, Psychology 4165-100 (Fall 2004), http://psych.colorado.edu/~lharvey/P4165/ P4165_2004_Fall/2004_Fall_pdf/P4165_Lab1.pdf.
9. Federal Register 39 Federal Register 3714, January 29, 1974. See also http://tribes .tribe.net/e388baea-51eb-417f-9390-06fe37f92e41/thread/99d62700-d8c2-4905 -b7dd-9426066cc759; http://www.psych.wright.edu/gordon/psy110/Psy110Mod 11a-outline.pdf
10. Answers.com, "Gestalt psychology" entry, www.answers.com/topic/gestalt -psychology
11. Ivan Pavlov biography, www.ivanpavlov.com
12. B. F. Skinner biography, www.bfskinner.org/bio.asp
13. April Holliday, "How Does Human Memory Work?," *USA Today*, March 12, 2007.

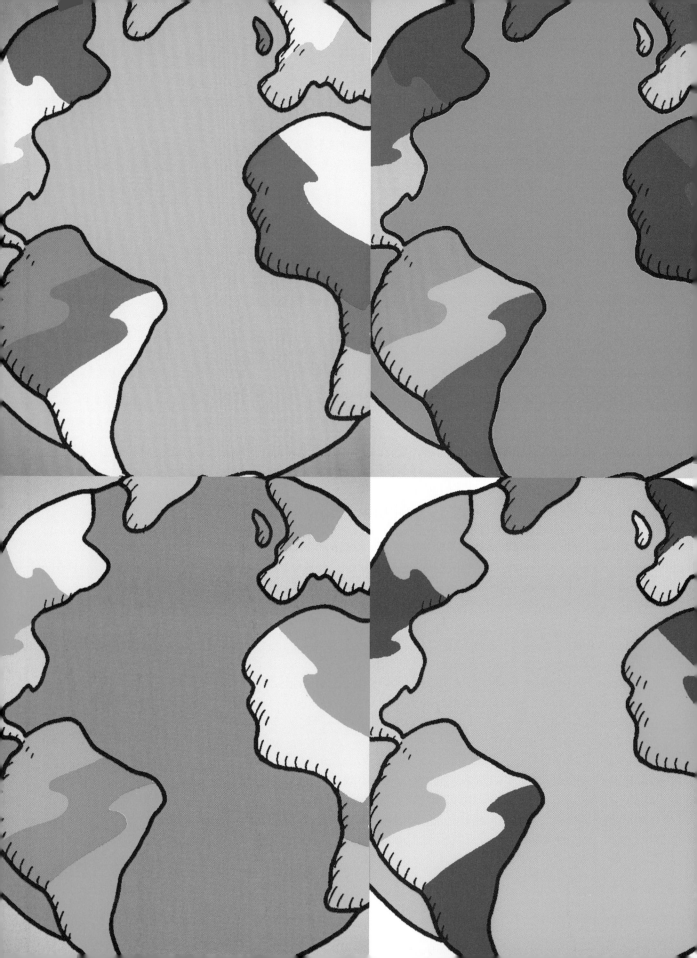

CHAPTER 4

Motivation and the Fashion Consumer

If you are among the growing number of consumers who are concerned about the environment and using eco-friendly products as a result, you probably look for clothing made with natural fibers, grown without the use of pesticides or man-made ingredients of any kind.

Other people may prefer the look and feel of real leather. Today, a variety of leather looks are achieved by applying various techniques, oils, and chemicals to the animal skins. From patent, metallic, and distressed to perforated, sueded, and pearlized finishes, leather clothing, accessories, and furniture are very popular.

Perhaps you have recently heard about the benefits of "functional foods," noninvasive, edible products that contain additives said to make users healthier and more beautiful. For example, the makers of collagen marshmallows (in blueberry, cherry, or grapefruit flavors) claim they keep lips plump, while aloe vera added to certain yogurts keeps skin moist and youthful. A friend of yours has scheduled a cosmetic procedure, but you want to try a functional foods diet before committing to surgery.

If you're about to purchase an engagement ring, you might be considering a diamond. Although diamonds are usually white, they also come in other colors. Premium colors, which are rare, and often more expensive, include canary yellow, pink, and blue, but shades such as champagne, cognac, and black might be less expensive. For some consumers, owning a diamond in an unusual color is an exciting prospect.

With so many choices, how do people decide what they really want? Why does one person choose bran flakes, another one oatmeal, and yet another scrambled eggs? What is at the core of each buying decision we make? How can marketers determine what customers want and present it to them in ways that please them?

These are the kinds of questions to which all marketers seek answers, and once they answer these questions, they should be able to predict *what* consumers are likely to want, or to understand *why* they want it. Are people interested in buying just to experience the act of consumption and ownership, because they consciously need something, or because of unrecognized, unconscious desires?

⟩ ⟩ ⟩ SPECIAL FOCUS 4.1: HOLIDAY SHOPPERS AS HUNTER-GATHERERS ⟨ ⟨ ⟨

"When you're at the mall, your natural instinct . . ."

Is to buy, yes. We are foragers. We see a sale sign, it's like a buffet in the forest. Besides, we're already here, right? Surely we need *some*thing. ("Need" in that flexible sense of the word, the way a couch needs a decorative pillow.)

Somewhere along the way, we got to be a nation that consumes instead of creates, that spends instead of saves. Ben Franklin wrote, "Rather go to Bed Supperless than rise in Debt," but now our mottos are "Born to shop" and "I shop, therefore I am." Now our money is plastic and our debt is real.

This didn't happen overnight. The last 150 years saw change after change that democratized consumption. We got sewing machines and readymade clothes, so even the less-well-off could dress well. We got department stores with fixed prices displaying the finest wares to everyone, instead of reserving them exclusively for the wealthy. We got inexpensive plate glass for window shopping, so the poor could see what they were missing out on.

We got the notion of buying cars on installment plans and of having things before we could pay for them. We got chains and self-service stores and the notion of packaging products no longer just for storage and transport—but in containers seductively decorated so as to sell themselves.

By the late 20th century, historian Daniel Boorstin wrote, Europeans still "went to market to buy what they wanted, while Americans went increasingly to see what they wanted."

Thus, the rise of impulse purchases, and to pay for them, a growing middle class. And something called the credit card.

There's heavy stuff going on when we shop. In the relatively new field of neuro-economics, which looks at how people spend money and manage risk, scientists have found that dopamine levels appear to rise when people come across unex-pected rewards. In shopping terms, that could be a well-priced designer handbag at Filene's Basement or a rare Elvis eight-track.

"Dopamine is one of the systems we use to learn how good or bad something is," says Paul Glimcher, a professor of neural science and psychology at New York University. "Shopping is fundamentally the same kind of foraging animals do every day. You move through a complex environment trying to find good stuff."

So, consider the mall our lab and let's study these creatures. Watch the way peo-ple enter a store. They slow down, trying to orient themselves and take everything in. Researchers will say they're looking for what's new and unusual. They stroke sweaters and lean in to smell tubs of sugar body scrub. They pick up plates, feel their heft, turn them over. They're thinking, *Does this say mom?* Or, *does this say me?*

Everyone is waiting for that shopper's eureka, the surge in the heart, the yes-yes-yes. Flash to a housewares store called Z Gallerie: Hear that? "Haaah," a sharp intake of breath and longing. "Haaah, *Mom*, look at the little room divider!"

That's the sound marketers are going for. They've studied us. They know why we're here. We buy for the rush, for beauty, maybe even for the sacrificial twinge when we surrender the plastic. We buy because these boots are the last in our size, or because a saleswoman looks so cool in this blouse, and we're hoping to be that cool.

>>> Source: Excerpted from Libby Copeland, "If Not Sublime, Then Silly: Holiday Shoppers Are the Hunter-Gatherers of the American Economy," *Washington Post*, December 19, 2005.

We need to understand human motivation in order to better explore what it is that creates in us the desire to buy in the first place. Is it a feeling that overwhelms people and can't be ignored? It might seem that way sometimes, and if that *is* what it is, where do these feelings come from?

Understanding Human Behavior

In order to successfully interpret consumer research data, some basic knowledge about the fundamentals of **psychology**, the study of individual behavior, and **sociol-ogy**, the study of group behavior, is needed. Once we agree that human behavior can be understood, and that we can access and interpret these dynamics using the appropriate methods, we begin to recognize that there are certain patterns in consumer buying behavior, and these patterns can be influenced by applying relevant marketing strategies. In other words, marketers are able to create motives or **motivate** customers—they can impel, incite, or move a person into action, and, in this case, the action is buying. Both "motive" and "motivate" come from the Latin word "motivus," which means "to move or be caused to move." Thus, **motivation** results from forces acting either on or within a person to initiate or activate certain behavior. These forces can be physiological (for example, hunger activates the desire for food), psychological (for example, sadness evokes tears), or environmental (for example, storms move people to seek shelter). And the behavior that marketers want to activate or initiate is the purchase of a particular product.

FIGURE 4.1.

How Motivation Works

Let's take a look at the following example to better understand motivation. Larry walks into a store that's well known for its state-of-the-art exercise equipment. What has brought him here? He could have been driven by several reasons. He wants to improve his stamina. He wants to increase his muscle mass. He's dieting and wants to tone as he loses weight. He let his health club membership lapse and has decided to work out at home. The store is currently offering some great discounts. His buddies mentioned that he looks like he's getting a little soft. Any or all of these reasons might serve as the motivating force behind his desire to purchase fitness equipment, and they all have one thing in common: They are causing Larry to experience some discomfort. That discomfort is referred to as a **stimulus**, an energizing force that causes a state of tension or arousal. (See Chapter 3 for a discussion of *stimulus characteristics*.) This tension has created in Larry a **need**, an internal state of discomfort that calls for a solution. Larry is trying to find a solution that will alleviate this feeling and provide some relief; he's trying to satisfy this need so that he can experience pleasure instead. By focusing on a **goal**, a particular outcome or end (which in this case is getting in shape), Larry is attempting to get rid of his discomfort. He hopes this will be achieved by the purchase of fitness equipment, resulting in **need satisfaction**, the experiencing of pleasure.

Needs versus Wants

"Listen, pal," his brother says when Larry tells him the plan, "you don't need to spend money on fancy equipment. Just do some running, and I'll lend you my weights. Then you can train without all that stuff around. It takes up a lot of room, and your apartment isn't that big." His brother is offering some good advice, but Larry is intent. He *wants* the equipment; he believes it will enable him to reach his goal more quickly. Both needs and wants are strong motivators, and both feelings emerge as the result of certain stimuli. But there is a difference between the two.

Studies have suggested that needs come from **instinct**, innate drives that we are born with, which are largely physiological, while **wants** are not necessities; although they can enhance the quality of our lives, they are not required for survival and, therefore, not driven by instinct, but rather by **desire**, a yearning or longing for something. Hence, what people *want* is largely the result of psychological and social forces in our environment.

❯❯❯ SPECIAL FOCUS 4.2: IDENTIFYING CUSTOMER WANTS ❮❮❮

Most of us have an occasional need for a good cup of coffee, and any restaurant or fast-food establishment can easily recognize and fulfill that need. But how many knew, years ago, that consumers also had a need for a café latté, café mocha, espresso, café au lait, cappuccino, and probably ten other teas or coffee drinks? Better yet, how many consumers knew they would willingly part with $3 or more for a cup of coffee?

Imagine you were a potential investor and Howard Schultz, the founder of Starbucks, explained in terms of needs, not wants, why you should invest in his company. I think your proposal would sound something like this: "Look, I've got this great idea. I mean a really great idea. I want to sell coffee and coffee concoctions nobody has ever heard of for $3 a cup. I want to open up stores nationally. In fact, I'd really like to open a couple thousand of them and maybe even more. So what do you think? Any chance of getting some money here?"

I think we all know what the answer would be—if, in fact, an answer was ever given before the guy was shown the door or nearest psychiatric hospital. So why is Starbucks so wildly successful? The answer is simple as well as profound: The company identified consumer wants that existed but no other business was perceptive enough to see or understand. What were those wants? People wanted a neighborhood place with attractive surroundings where they could go to talk. They wanted a place where they didn't feel pressured to eat and leave. Starbucks knew, too, that the general population was becoming better educated and well-traveled, believing itself to be more sophisticated and, therefore, willing and anxious to try a $3 café latté.

>>> Source: Roy Katz, Identifying Customer Wants, www.insideselfstorage.com/articles/2a1results.html.3. Retrieved on February 3, 2006.

Why can't consumers just explain to marketers why they buy what they buy? What are the reasons behind their purchases? The problem is that most people don't know what their motives are, and if they did, they probably wouldn't want anyone else to know. Motives can be **conscious**, in which case the individual is aware of what she wants and why, or **unconscious**, largely unknown to the individual because these motives are either repressed, dormant, or unrecognized.[1] To be sure, motives aren't always pretty (think of anger, fear, jealousy); that's why people often keep them secret—even from themselves.

Need Theories

It's for these reasons that marketers turn to psychologists like Abraham Maslow, who, in 1943, was one of the first to formulate a practical theory about human needs. Many well-respected scientists, including David McClelland and Henry A. Murray, have developed other theories, some based on as few as three essential human needs (power,

Table 4.1.   Maslow's Hierarchy of Needs

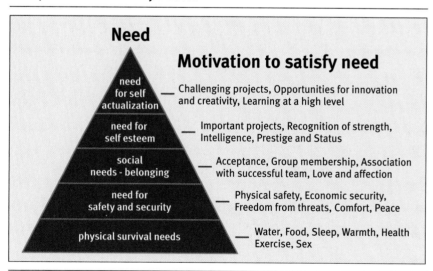

Source: www.pateo.com/images/maslowmaster4ts.gif. February 6, 2006.

affiliation, and achievement are the basic needs identified by McClelland), and others that number as many as 20 (see Table 4.2), but Maslow's theory has been used most frequently as the basis for understanding much of the modern consumer's behavior.

By looking at Table 4.1, you can see that humans' **basic** or **primary needs** are few: food, clothing, shelter, sleep, and so forth. Once these physiological needs are met, other needs can be addressed, such as the need to feel safe and secure, the need to feel connected to and valued by others, the need for praise and appreciation, and so on. Maslow has put these needs in a hierarchy, demonstrating that people put their efforts toward fulfilling their primary or "low" needs (also referred to as *biogenic* needs) before they attempt to fulfill "high" needs (also referred to as *psychogenic* needs). His theory contends that humans can't sufficiently progress, or even live normal lives, if basic physiological needs aren't met first. Only then can people attend to the other needs on his hierarchy, **acquired** or **secondary needs**, which are learned in accordance

Table 4.2. **Conflicting Needs**

Need	Definition
Abasement	To surrender and submit to others, accept blame and punishment. To enjoy pain and misfortune.
Achievement	To accomplish difficult tasks, overcoming obstacles and becoming expert.
Affiliation	To be close and loyal to another person, pleasing them and winning their friendship and attention.
Aggression	To forcefully overcome an opponent, controlling, taking revenge or punishing them.
Autonomy	To break free from constraints, resisting coercion and dominating authority. To be irresponsible and independent.
Counteraction	To make up for failure by trying again, seeking pridefully to overcome obstacles.
Defendance	To defend oneself against attack or blame, hiding any failure of the self.
Deference	To admire a superior person, praising them and yielding to them and following their rules.
Dominance	To control one's environment, controlling other people through command or subtle persuasion.
Exhibition	To impress others through one's actions and words, even if these are shocking.
Harm avoidance	To escape or avoid pain, injury, and death.
Inavoidance	To avoid being humiliated or embarrassed.
Nurturance	To help the helpless, feeding them and keeping them from danger.
Order	To make things clean, neat and tidy.
Play	To have fun, laugh, and relax, enjoying oneself.
Rejection	To separate oneself from a negatively viewed object or person, excluding or abandoning it.
Sentience	To seek out and enjoy sensual experiences.
Sex	To form relationship that leads to sexual intercourse.
Succourance	To have one's needs satisfied by someone or something. Includes being loved, nursed, helped, forgiven, and consoled.
Understanding	To be curious, ask questions and find answers.

Source: http://changingminds.org/explanations/needs/murrays_needs.htm

with the values of the specific culture a person is raised in. For example, people in the United States have developed acquired needs for money, education, freedom—things without which most Americans believe they could not survive. Could they?

Let's Talk

Read Table 4.2, adapted from Explorations in Personality (1938) by Henry A. Murray. Which of these needs are primary and which are secondary? Are there any needs on Murray's list that can't be satisfied by the purchase of a product or service?

Motivation Is Complex

Motives can be driven by both **internal/nonsocial factors** and **external/social factors**. A couple may purchase a house because they really love it, the result of *internal* motivation (which comes from within), or because living on that particular street will afford them the status they desire, a result of *external* motivation (which derives from desires that are independent of the actual behavior).

We can also be motivated by either **positive** or **negative motivation.** A 19-year-old who's worked in the stock room of a department store since high school may decide she wants more out of life, so she joins the army in order to travel and get a free college education (*positive*). But another employee of the same age, who's worked in the shipping department since she quit school at 16, feels that she'll never make enough money to move out of her parents' place, so she joins the army, figuring that at least she'll have somewhere to go and will no longer have to worry about where she'll be living (*negative*).

Additionally, people are often motivated by the need to experience both **stability** and **variety**, or constancy and changeability. For example, we don't want to paint the bedroom a new color every single day (we need *stability*), nor do we want to repaint it the same color when we're ready for something different (we need *variety*).

To complicate matters, people are frequently motivated by multiple desires that are experienced simultaneously and thus create **conflict**. A conflict occurs when we view the outcome of our behavior as potentially positive and potentially negative. That is, we may want to both do something and not do it at the same time; or we find

FIGURE 4.2. Many choices are available to meet the vast and diverse needs of consumers.

off the mark.com   by Mark Parisi

we must choose between two desirable outcomes; or we might even discover that we must choose between two undesirable outcomes. Essentially, there are three common types of motivational conflicts: **approach–avoidance**, **approach–approach**, and **avoidance–avoidance**.

Approach–avoidance. A simultaneous desire to engage in a certain behavior *and* to avoid it

Approach–approach. A choice must be made between two desirable options.

Avoidance–avoidance. A choice must be made between two undesirable options.

In the first instance, *approach–avoidance*, a man may find himself experiencing a strong desire to buy an extravagant engagement ring for his fiancée (consistent with the needs for affection and prestige). However, he may also feel that if he purchases that ring, he'll be putting himself in debt, and he knows that that's no way to begin a marriage (inconsistent with the need for security).

In the second type of conflict, *approach–approach*, a newly graduated art student has just been given a generous check by her grandparents and is deciding how to spend the money. Should she purchase a painting she really likes by a famous artist whom all her friends will recognize and admire (consistent with the needs for recognition and self-esteem)? Or should she enroll in a six-month educational program that will allow her to study art abroad (consistent with the needs for enrichment and self-fulfillment)?

The third kind, *avoidance–avoidance*, is experienced by a single mom on a limited income who doesn't want to buy an expensive outfit for her class reunion, especially if she feels she won't wear it again (inconsistent with the need for financial security). But she certainly doesn't want to look frumpy or out-of-touch in front of her successful former classmates (inconsistent with needs for acceptance and recognition).

Marketers Use Conflict to Motivate Consumers

By understanding the nature of conflict, marketing experts can create appealing ways to assist customers in the decision-making process, by either helping them resolve their conflicts or by tapping into those conflicts in ways that will encourage them to purchase. For example, marketers working in the professional selling field have developed programs that ease the minds of customers who may be conflicted about the amount of money they can comfortably spend, by allowing them to spread payments over extended periods. Or, if a customer has enough money for the required down payment, but needs time to raise the rest, sellers offer plans that let buyers delay paying their balances for as much as a year, thus resolving any conflict that might stand in the way of completing the sale.

FIGURE 4.3. This advertisement for suntan lotion attempts to resolve the consumer's conflict: tanning to look healthy but risking skin damage from the sun's harmful rays.

Marketers who specialize in product development also seek to create alternatives for customers who might be experiencing conflict. Many people are conflicted about buying fur because they've read or heard that extensive or unnecessary cruelty toward animals might be used in the process of creating fur garments and accessories. Thus, fake fur was developed, allowing those who want the warmth and look of fur to buy and wear those products without worrying about animal endangerment.

Marketers in the advertising field often make use of their knowledge regarding conflict when devising ad campaigns. A customer might be conflicted by the desire to look tan and the fact that sunbathing is unhealthy. An attractive ad for a product that promises that a person can actually look sun kissed while enjoying substantial protection from harmful rays will provide that customer with a resolution.

Rational versus Emotional Motives

Consider what happened when Veronica had an argument with her significant other. She was feeling extremely sad and very lonely, so when her friend called and invited her to go shopping, she said yes, rather than sit home by herself. Soon after arriving at the mall, she found herself trying on a great-looking coat. Veronica knew she didn't *need* it—she'd bought one the previous month, in fact, which she really liked and had barely worn. But she *wanted* the coat she was trying on, even though she couldn't come up with a single logical reason to buy it—it was quite expensive, and it even resembled the new one at home in her closet! But she bought it anyway, and for an hour or two she felt a certain amount of satisfaction and excitement. However, later that evening, she began to question her purchase.

Let's Talk
What might have motivated Veronica's impulsive purchase? Why did she feel such a strong desire to buy?

Early in this chapter, *motivation* was defined as the result of forces acting either *on* or *within* a person to initiate or activate certain behavior. Remember also that these forces can come from physical, psychological, or environmental stimuli. Thus, if Veronica had realized that she *actually* needed a coat to keep warm, she most likely would have followed the **consumer decision-making process,** the steps buyers take when deciding whether or not to make purchases:

- Need recognition
- Information search
- Evaluation of alternatives
- Purchase
- Post-purchase evaluation

Veronica would have been acting on the basis of **rational needs**, whereby the purchasing decision is the result of a process that uses reasoning and logic—she *needed* protection from the cold, so actual physical and environmental realities motivated her to buy a coat. But sometimes we act because of certain **emotional needs**; these can cause a buying decision that's made in a nonrational manner, without the benefit of an information search, a comparison of alternatives, and so on. In Veronica's case, the real motive was a desire to ease the distress and unhappiness caused by a recent breakup.

When this happens, a person's post-purchase evaluation could include **post-purchase dissonance** (also known as "cognitive dissonance") or "buyer's remorse," which is when doubt about making a purchase decision follows the actual purchase and creates tension, or a state of dissonance. This can occur for any number of reasons. (In this particular case, doubt was brought on by allowing emotions to overrule rationality.)

So, although it might seem that consumer choices are quite random, each decision has some meaning behind it, even if the choice doesn't always appear to be rational. Purchasing decisions are motivated by any number of factors, including emotions, social situations, goals, and values. Obviously, all purchases resulting from motives that are emotional in origin do not necessarily end in dissatisfaction; in fact, many times the customer's decision leaves him or her feeling quite satisfied.

Marketers Use Emotion to Motivate Consumers

Using their understanding of basic psychology, marketers are able to motivate consumers by devising creative strategies that evoke emotional responses. We've all experienced various forms of emotional motivation, some as a result of our own envy, love, sorrow, fear, surprise, and so on, and some as a result of having our emotions stirred by marketers.

When presented with merchandising methods that evoke feelings of nostalgia, such as a display that resembles a flea market, a window that incorporates antique toys, or a sound system that plays "golden oldies" while customers shop, those who value the "good ol' days" are being motivated to purchase because of the positive emotions they are experiencing. This technique is particularly effective in encouraging the purchase of **unsought goods**, products or services that consumers do not actually seek or plan to buy, such as items that are purchased impulsively, without advance need recognition.

Advertisers frequently use emotion to stimulate buying behavior. Think about the ads you see on a daily basis; many employ emotional appeals purposely designed to trigger positive emotional responses. Puppies, babies, beautiful scenery, grandparents playing with grandchildren, surprise visits from family members—the objective is that these kinds of images will become associated with the products that marketers are trying to sell. Marketers use beauty, humor, sex, camaraderie, and so on to encourage customers to buy, since chief among the benefits we seek from our purchases is simply to feel good. But they can also try to evoke negative emotions and imply that their products will eliminate our bad feelings.

Similarly, unpleasant images can be just as effective. A car skidding in a storm or a burglar breaking into a home—these images can arouse fear, an emotion that can be effective in motivating customers to purchase, for example, a new set of tires or a home security system.

The Power of Motivation

The science of evaluating and influencing consumer behavior is foremost in determining which marketing efforts will be used and when. Marketers spend a great deal of time and money discovering what compels consumers to make purchases.[2] There are two principal ways to evaluate the motivation behind consumer purchases: direction and intensity. **Direction** refers to what the customer wants from a product in terms of facts, features, or benefits. For example, if a customer is selecting a watch, she may like the fact that one watch is less expensive than another, but what she really wants is a timepiece that will last and keep accurate time, and she'll probably pay more if she thinks the more expensive brand will do those things more effectively. Marketers need to understand the principal motivation that leads to the purchase of each type of product in order to accurately target potential customers.

The other way to evaluate consumer behavior, **intensity**, refers to whether a customer's interest in a product is compelling enough that she will actually make the purchase. In other words, how badly does the customer want the particular item? Good marketing can create that kind of intensity. Positioning a particular handbag as not only chic, but also as a special limited edition signed by the designer, might create a sense of urgency that motivates the customer to buy that purse, and do so quickly.

Thus, understanding consumer motivation is the best way to increase buyer **incentive** (a reason to buy), that is, to move the consumer from an actual state to a desired state. Most importantly, the customer's attention must somehow be focused on the specific goods the marketer wants to sell—and not on anyone else's products, and the drive has to be powerful enough for the customer to be willing to pay the price in terms of time, effort, and money to obtain the goods.[3]

Motivation and the Desire to Acquire

"People like having stuff, and stuff is good for people," says Thomas O'Guinn, a professor of advertising at the University of Illinois and author of textbooks on marketing and consumption. "One thing modernity brought with it was all kinds of identities, the ability for [you] to choose who you want to be, how you want to decorate yourself, what kind of lifestyle you want. And what you consume cannot be separated from that."[4]

Marketers have had to adjust their strategies to accommodate ever-changing shopping habits. They also know that today's shoppers aren't as predictable as they once were. Perhaps that's why every day seems to bring something new to the marketplace, another enticement, a different method for arousing the desire to consume. One example of this is a retailing concept that's become popular recently: the temporary, or "pop-up," store, designed to open and close within a short time. Similar to carts and kiosks that pop up in shopping malls during the holidays, TILS (temporary in-line stores) look more permanent, but the owners typically sign leases of a year or less. This is seen as a great way to test new concepts and gauge customer response.[5] Even Target recently popped up on one of America's most famous shopping streets, Melrose Place, to launch a hip new line of clothing, Paul & Joe, by French designer Sophie Albou. Open for only about a month, the store generated lots of buzz—and lots of sales.

❯ ❯ ❯ POINT OF VIEW 4.1: JCPENNEY ROLLS OUT THE RED CARPET FOR NEW PRIVATE BRAND ❮ ❮ ❮

JCPenney rolled out its newest private brand—a.n.a., which stands for A New Approach—to all its stores in early 2006. The launch truly represented a new approach for the retailer, which traditionally has introduced new labels several hundred stores at a time during the course of a couple seasons. The nationwide rollout coincided with the largest marketing campaign in company history—which included an official a.n.a. debut during Academy Award commercial breaks—and a pop-up store in New York's Times Square, where JCPenney showcased its private brands for shoppers to purchase via Internet kiosks.

The a.n.a. line comprises casual but trend-right apparel (e.g., gauchos, tunics, skinny jeans) as well as handbags and shoes. According to the company, a.n.a. is geared toward 30- to 50-year-olds and is positioned as the casual counterpart to its Worthington brand.

>>> Source: Industry Outlook: Department Stores, July 2006, *www.retailforward .com.*

"Experiential retailers" want to make their stores into destinations for customers, using the idea of retailing as theater. Imitation of Christ, the offbeat clothing line, recently combined pop-up and theatrics, opening a moveable store encased in Plexiglas that appeared in a different place every day during New York Fashion Week.[6] American Girl is another destination retail site, where parents and kids can spend the day at the store participating in a variety of activities designed to encourage customers to buy. Borders, Virgin Megastores, and Apple all attempt to stimulate sales by creating experiences that engage consumers.

Other ways to motivate buying behavior include personalized products and customized goods. Timberland's Build Your Own Boot Program lets consumers choose the colors and monograms they want, while Fossil encourages consumers to design their own watches. A fragrance can now be created just for one person; jeans can also be customized to specifications. (See Chapter 2 for additional information about customization.) These are all ways to promote customer engagement.

FIGURE 4.4. Customers examine merchandise at the JCPenney pop-up store in New York.

Marketers can also connect with customers through convenience, an important issue for many of today's time-starved shoppers. Technology can play a key role in this regard. Some consumers are particularly interested in goods that can be easily purchased, especially when they're made available via automated phone ordering. In Japan, for example, young women buy everything from subway passes to mascara with a swipe of their cell phones.[7]

> > > SPECIAL FOCUS 4.3 < < <

I. Boutique in Hand

While more Americans expand their wardrobes with the click of a mouse, the Japanese are a step ahead, buying clothes on their cell phones. It's almost exactly the same as shopping on a computer, just smaller and more mobile.

In tech-savvy Japan, cell-phone commerce is an $83 billion industry. The leader is *Xavel*, which launched *girlswalker.com*, the first free-of-charge cell phone consumer portal. Six years later, it's the country's most popular shopping site, garnering 100 million hits a day. Its partner, *girlsauction.com*, boasts 1.5 million members and $43 million in monthly cell phone transactions. "If I was going to do business, I was going to do it with women in their 20s and 30s," says CEO Fumitaro Ohama. "I wondered why nobody thought of it, considering they are such a huge market."

Another thing nobody thought of was a buy-it-as-you-see-it fashion show. In August (2005), Ohama, 34, threw Japan's largest fashion event to date, the *Tokyo Girls Collection*. The 12,600 attendees—and 15 million people watching the live cell phone broadcast—could purchase items on their phones as soon as they appeared on the catwalk. Shin Akamatsu launched his *Joias* line at the festival and received more orders than the established labels did. "We struck gold right from the beginning," says the creative director, who saw $4.2 million in sales in five months. Other brands plan to present new lines at the next event.

Also catching is Japan's eBay, *Rakuten*. Cell-phone sales account for 34% of its transactions. "Cell phone companies realized the potential, so we too started taking cell-phone commerce seriously," says spokeswoman Kuniko Narita. "Our turnover increased drastically."

The Japanese aren't just shopping on cell phones but also with them. A new "wallet cell phone" functions as a credit, debit or ID card, among other things. The handset has a computer chip similar to that found in electronic key cards. Japanese girls are buying mascara, mints and magazines at convenience stores simply by swiping their phones past a scanner near the cash register.

So, what's next? "People have started buying big things," says Narita. "You can even buy a helicopter or a $3.2 million tanzanite gem on a cell phone."

>>> Source: Michiko Toyama, "Boutique in Hand," *Time*. Style and Design issue. Spring 2006.

II. A Fragrance for You, and Only You

For Parisiennes looking for bijoux that are even more precious and personal than a Trinity ring or a solitaire diamond, Cartier has the answer. To celebrate its new six-story flagship store on Rue de la Paix, the French jeweler has introduced a customized fragrance called *Bespoke*.

Cartier's resident "nose," Mathilde Laurent, will meet with clients at least four times in the store's *Salon des Parfums*. Over the course of two or three hours, Laurent will grill clients about why they like to wear perfume, what their favorite childhood fragrances were and which ingredients they use when cooking. In subsequent appointments, clients are given three prototypes from which to choose, and then Laurent adds the final touches to the fragrance. The process can take anywhere from six months to three years, depending on the client, and costs $72,600.The finished product arrives in a Baccarat crystal bottle, stamped with Cartier's 13 Rue de la Paix insignia.

Ironically, Laurent, who has worked as a perfumer for 11 years, does not wear any fragrance. "I want to stay clean," she says. "If you want to work well with fragrances, you have to have a fresh nose."

>>> Source: Nia E. Shepherd, "A Fragrance for You, and Only You." *Time:* Style and Design. *Spring 2006.*

Marketers Create Consumer Needs and Stimulate Demand

Studying the origins of motivation has enabled marketers to actually invent "needs" that people didn't know they had until marketers pointed them out. A recent TV commercial addressed the problem of "body soil," the invisible residue supposedly left in clothes after they've been washed, which can presumably irritate the skin, damage fabric, and so on. The solution? A specific bleaching product that claims to eliminate this problem. In this case, marketers actually *created a need*; people concerned with getting clothes as clean as possible were motivated to purchase by savvy marketers who aroused in them a need they hadn't previously recognized.

Some observers would say this is a good example of how marketers create or stimulate **demand**, the price that people are willing to pay to obtain a particular product. It is the job of marketers to create an atmosphere around a product or service that encourages consumers to take notice, experience a need/want, and ultimately purchase. However, some people question the ethics of creating artificial demand or **false need**, the desire for something to which we attribute more value than it is actually worth. In Herbert Marcuse's *An Essay on Liberation*, he argues that a capitalist system gives people what it wants them to want, and that it generates needs supportive of mass consumption rather than stimulating creative human development. Modern capitalist economies, he feels, are based upon a degree of production that can only be maintained through conspicuous consumption and a terrific degree of waste. It must, therefore, train its citizens to "need" the things it produces, whether they're good for us not. For example, adolescents often regard drinking alcohol as a cool thing to do, a sign of maturity, rather than a behavior that could lead to addiction, illness, and even death. However, the images they see in liquor ads are of glamorous models, often with glamorous friends in glamorous settings, and they seek to emulate that behavior. Because a teenager sees only the positive side of drinking, he overestimates the true worth of liquor and often uses a sizable portion of his allowance (and even phony identification) to buy it.[8]

❯❯❯ SPECIAL FOCUS 4.4: CONSUMER ANGST ❮❮❮

The Role of Surplus

The key change that separates modern from traditional societies is the concept of surplus, a condition in which there is more than enough of everything to sustain the lives of all the members of a society. As it happens, people are not designed to cope with surplus. We have many, many strategies to deal with perpetual deficit, some learned, some congenital, but surplus bewilders us.

This condition—a world of surplus, occupied by people programmed for deficit—is a perfect setting for modern consumerism. Modern consumerism is based on the triple premise that

- Luxuries are actually needs
- What you already have is not satisfactory
- No product is so basic that advertising is superfluous

The Little Lies

Here are some examples of the minor lies that are included in advertising:

- "New!" How can something be simultaneously new and absolutely essential to survival? Or, given the thesis that new is better, the advertiser should honestly list the ways that the old new product failed us, thus setting the stage for inevitable disenchantment with the new *new* product.
- "An exclusive offer!" This nationally televised, prime-time advertisement excludes only the dead, and those too penniless from responding to previous exclusive offers.
- "It costs more, but it is worth it." By implication, things that cost more are worth more, and by negation, things that have no price also have no value.
- "You deserve the best." A questionable premise, one intended to cloud your mind and distract you from the more practical question of whether you can afford the best, or whether the product is in fact the best.

CHAPTER 5

Attitude and the Fashion Consumer

In his Interior Design class, Juan's assignment was to design and furnish a small apartment for a young couple employed by a global nonprofit organization. Since the couple expected to travel overseas in the next decade and to live for two or three years each in several locations, they hoped to collect only a few easily stored or transported pieces of furniture. Also, since the employee earnings from nonprofit organizations are not high, this couple was on a strict budget. Finally, they had already done some traveling and wanted to show their interest in world cultures through the décor of their apartment.

After planning the space, Juan went first to the IKEA Web site to look for furniture. He was in luck. Among the items he found were a sofa bed with a washable cover, dining chairs and a table that could double as a desk, and a wall storage system that accommodated books and clothing. Next, he scouted the Costco Web site for a television and found a 20-inch Toshiba set with built-in DVD and VCR, plus remote and a front-panel connection for video games or a camcorder. Finally, he went to the nearby Target store, where he found sheets, towels, and blankets, plus cookware and dinnerware, as well as a few imported decorative items such as a brass planter and Buddha statue to complete the international look his clients wanted. Juan felt pleased as he put the finishing touches on his project; he knew he had been able to create what was required and to stay within budget.

What Is "Attitude"?

Juan obviously had a very positive attitude toward this project, but what does the term "attitude" really mean? An **attitude** is our settled opinion—either positive or negative—about people, places, ideas, or objects. By "settled opinion," we mean that attitudes are formed after some thought, they are learned, and they occur within given circumstances. For example, when he chose where he would shop for his project, Juan's positive attitude about each of the three retailers stemmed from what he had previously learned about the modern furniture at IKEA; the many bargains in electronics and other products at Costco; and Target's home furnishings, emphasizing style and design at discount prices. These retailers would meet the requirements of his project "clients."

Notice that we hold attitudes about people, ourselves included; objects, such as products, brands, manufacturers, places, and retailers, as we've just described; and ideas, such as those we see in print advertisements or on TV and the Internet. For example, in thumbing through a magazine, we may see ads about new digital cameras, certain kinds of tanning lotions, the latest foreign car, an exotic vacation spot, and our favorite discount store, all within a few pages, and as we look, we may form attitudes. In consumer research, those things that we form attitudes about are called **attitude objects**. When seeking out the right products for his project, Juan made use of his previously developed positive attitudes toward the attitude objects he selected (that is, retailers IKEA, Costco, and Target).

> *Let's Talk*
> *What is your attitude toward a well-known fashion attitude object such as a pair of shoes by Jimmy Choo or the latest iPod?*

Although we tend to maintain the same opinions over time, attitudes may change, and marketers continually strive to bring about attitude change, encouraging us to favor their offerings over others. For example, Target has carved out a niche in discount retailing by emphasizing its fashion connections and crafting agreements with designers such as Isaac Mizrahi, Mossimo, and Thomas O'Brien to create stylish goods at budget prices. Many consumers recognize and support this effort.[1]

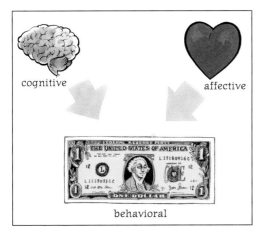

FIGURE 5.1. Affective, behavioral, and cognitive elements are the primary influencers of attitude.

What Goes into Our Attitudes?

Three elements contribute to the way we create attitudes: (1) *cognitive*—what we perceive and believe about an attitude object, as Juan believes that IKEA furniture can be easily stored or moved; (2) *affective*—how we feel about it, our positive or negative emotions, as Juan really admires the home furnishing designs he finds at Target; and (3) *behavioral*—what we do about it, as Juan would have recommended the products he found had this assignment involved actual clients.

But we do not develop attitudes in a vacuum. Our emotions play a part. If we are happy, sad, angry, or distressed, our attitude tends not only to reflect our feelings but also how we think and act. Attitudes are also affected by other influences such as our individual personalities, past experiences, family and friends, media, and marketing efforts.

The Cognitive Element

The **cognitive element** of our attitudes—that is, what we know—comes from what we have seen, read, or experienced concerning an attitude object; it forms the basis of our beliefs about that object. Juan had read about and seen the flexibility of Swedish modern furniture before formulating his beliefs about the benefits of IKEA's product line. A fashion student learning about the features of Spandex in apparel fabrics believes that garments with some stretch in them look neater and more fashionable than those made solely of traditional fabrics.

Marketers appeal to our cognitive element by providing information about the product they are offering. For example, advertisements for cell phone wireless headsets fully describe the many features of Bluetooth technology, such as its clear sound, unobtrusiveness, and hands-free ease of use, all of which appeal to our cognitive, or reasoning, capabilities.[2] In learning, when reaching a complex or expensive (high-involvement) purchasing decision, such as deciding on our career education or a place to live, we use problem-solving skills that rely heavily on our cognitive attitudes.[3]

Marketers appeal to our cognitive abilities by using credible sources, from a reputable computer manufacturer providing information about new product features to an appeal to stop smoking, as shown in Figure 5.2.[4]

FIGURE 5.2. Significant information about a product's benefits can appeal to the cognitive element of attitude

The Affective Element

The **affective element** of attitude is made up of our emotions toward an attitude object. Juan was delighted to see the style and color that went into the products of Michael Graves and other designers at Target. He felt that these looks were right with the times and could fit easily into the lives of his clients. Many fashion-sensitive people who see the eveningwear of Vera Wang or Badgely Mischka are drawn to these glamorous looks. Countless movie fans crowd into the theater to see the latest film of Scarlett Johansson, Samuel L. Jackson, or Matt Damon because they admire the work of these performers. Marketers appeal to the affective element by touching our emotions. For example, an interior designer tells a client how a certain demi-lune table enhances an entryway. Appealing subjects, such as photogenic models and celebrities, children and pets, and persuasive messages using humor or sex, reach out emotionally to a variety of consumers. Also, advertisers may also use emotional appeals to our affective side to counteract the fact that we might not be paying much attention to the purchase we're making, as when we buy staple goods like laundry soap or pet biscuits.[5]

Of course, how we feel internally when we encounter an affective appeal is also a contributing factor. For example, if we are happy when thumbing through a store catalog, we could have a positive reaction to an emotional appeal for an item, pick up the phone, and order it. But if we felt sad or distressed, our reaction could be negative to the very same ad, and the persuasive effort would escape us.

There are also times when we may select a product off the shelf almost automatically, with a minimum of thought or effort. Knowing that, some advertisers try to make an impression through repetition, using basic methods such as behavioral learning techniques (described in Chapter 3). This is the reason that duplicate advertisements for certain cosmetics appear in four fashion magazines during the same month, or why television ads for a particular product or store are sprinkled throughout a series of programs.

The Behavioral Element

The third part of attitude, the **behavioral element**, is how we intend to act toward the attitude object. We can act negatively (for example, avoiding a certain fast-food drive-in because a friend became ill there). Or, we can do nothing. Because Juan was working on a college project, he did not actually purchase the products he researched; however,

FIGURE 5.3. Emotional messages, such as those featuring celebrities or pets, can stimulate desire for a product.

many times we buy a particular product because all three attitude elements point in this direction. Thus, our intentions to act positively become our decision to buy. Marketers, of course, aim their efforts at dispensing information and techniques of persuasion toward this goal by making it as easy as possible to purchase goods and services. Advertisements appealing to our cognitive and affective elements, multichannel marketing (that is, selling through stores, catalogs, and/or Web sites), personable and knowledgeable salespeople, and pleasant shopping environments along with accessible credit all contribute to the behavior that both customers and marketers desire. Influencing consumer behavior is a major goal for many organizations, including both profit-making companies like Target, and nonprofits, such as Americans for the Arts. (In Figure 5.4, notice how the latter is seeking immediate response through persuasive techniques based on cognitive and emotional appeals.)

The Hierarchy of Effects

The term **hierarchy of effects** refers to the series of steps—beliefs, feelings, actions—that we go through in forming our attitudes. The order of these steps depends on how involved we are with the attitude object and is designated: (1) high-involvement hierarchy, (2) low-involvement hierarchy, and (3) experiential hierarchy.

High-Involvement Hierarchy

In the **high-involvement hierarchy**, customers use a problem-solving process to reach buying decisions about a product, usually when contemplating an important purchase, such as the TV that Juan found. We actively study product features and benefits; and what we learn—our cognitions—become beliefs about a product. These beliefs then lead to our forming affective (positive) feelings about the product. Juan liked the VCR/DVD feature plus the front-panel connection for video games and a camcorder.

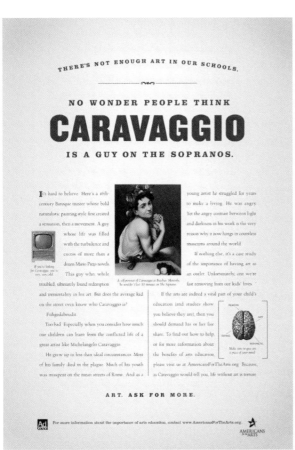

THERE'S NOT ENOUGH ART IN OUR SCHOOLS.

NO WONDER PEOPLE THINK

CARAVAGGIO

IS A GUY ON THE SOPRANOS.

ART. ASK FOR MORE.

After reviewing the features of competing television sets in that price range, he decided that the Toshiba would best suit his clients' needs. When, as consumers, we participate in the high-involvement hierarchy, we are serious about our planned purchase; we seek out information, evaluate the alternatives, and after a great deal of thought, decide. Marketers key into consumer problem-solving skills using advertising that is heavy on copy, containing complete explanations of product features and benefits, or communicating knowledge and values the consumer already understands.

Low-Involvement Hierarchy

With **low-involvement hierarchy** situations, the purchase is usually insignificant and we do not prefer one brand over another; here, we act before forming firm attitudes, and our attitudes emerge after we have used and evaluated a product. We may select a product out of habit or availability, such as paper towels. We do not identify with

FIGURE 5.4. By including a Web site, the advertiser encourages action after appealing to our emotions and thought processes.

Table 5.1.   Three Hierarchies of Effects

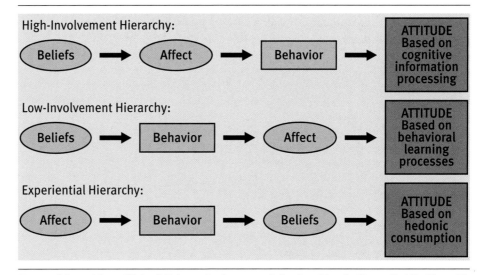

Source: Adapted from Michael Solomon's *Consumer Behavior,* 6th ed., Upper Saddle River, NJ: Pearson/Prentice Hall, 2004, p. 238.

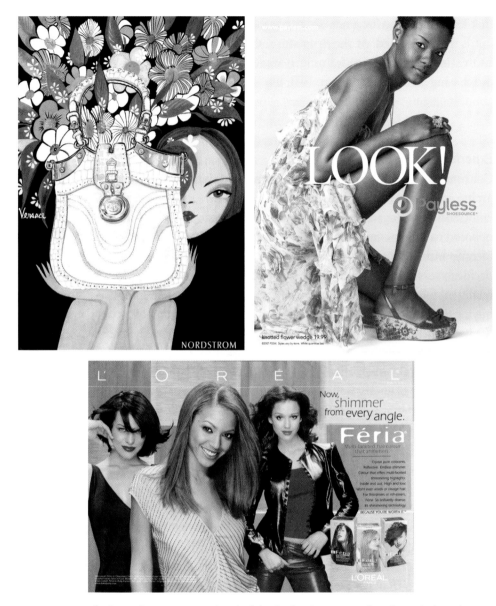

FIGURE 5.5A, B, and C. Depending on a consumer's attitude level, advertisers use a variety of appeals; here, the reputations of the designer and the retailer appeal to the high and low involvement hierarchy knowledge and beliefs, while experiential levels are influenced by affective appeals.

those items, nor do we care much about them. Therefore, our selection of a certain brand is passive, based on beliefs, and requiring minimum energy. Our positive or negative attitudes develop from our experience with the product after we purchase it. Here, while no single brand seems to be a favorite, emotional appeals in the form of television commercials, print advertising, and particularly point-of-purchase materials influence our beliefs and, hence, our decisions to buy. For example, say

emotional appeals and symbols are prominent, whereas in the high-involvement hierarchy, specific product features and customer benefits predominate. Many marketers understand this difference when framing their messages to consumers. Automobile manufacturers that emphasize a vehicle's ease of handling, interior comfort, and convenient accessories are reaching out to the experiential hierarchy, while those that promote low gas consumption, low maintenance, and economy are appealing to the high-involvement hierarchy.

Let's Talk
For each of the last three fashion purchases you made, which of the three elements of the hierarchy of attitude was the greatest influence? Explain.

How Do Attitudes Serve Us?

Attitudes help give us a sense of balance in life. Psychologist Daniel Katz developed a theory on the **functions of attitudes**, which tells us that attitudes serve us in the following four classifications:

- Utilitarian
- Value-expressive
- Ego-defensive
- Knowledge [6]

The *utilitarian function* of attitude helps us reach our goals by focusing on product benefits. For example, if we want to prevent slipping on winter ice, we will shop for boots with nonskid soles and avoid those with smooth leather soles. Marketers work to change our attitudes about utilitarian function by indicating the problem-solving capabilities of their products. In the case of the boots, for instance, L. L.Bean advertises its "chain grip rubber outsole."

In applying the *value-expressive function* of attitude, we are expressing our personality and self-image through the goods we buy. For instance, the saying "Dress for the job you want, not for the one you have" means that if you want a promotion, give the appearance that you already have it (that is, you are moving toward your ideal self-image). Marketers make great use of the value-expressive function of attitude by promising a more successful or happier life when you possess their products, whether paintings, cosmetics, or Zen meditation classes.

We also form attitudes to protect us from anxieties; this is the *ego-defensive function*. We are concerned about acceptance in business, so we pay attention to our grooming and use products that eliminate body odors. We know we should pay attention to our health; marketers promoting smoking-cessation methods are appealing to our ego-defensive functions by offering ways to combat the addiction.

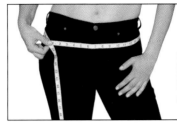

Every day, we are inundated with more stimuli than we can ever absorb. The *knowledge function* of attitude helps us to order the information we encounter. Marketing information proclaiming new product features and new products themselves reaches us through all kinds of media, including billboards, magazines, the Internet, and television. An editorial feature in this month's *Vogue* shows the latest fashions from Milan and Paris, describing new fashion trends—information we store and use when considering our next apparel purchases. A print ad in *Metropolitan Home* tells us about the features and advantages of indoor–outdoor carpeting for balconies and patios; if the information is relevant, we may store it for later use. Humans are naturally inquisitive and collect information on many topics.

Because we differ in our values—what is important to us— the way we use our attitude functions varies. Marketers are aware of these differences and reach out to us in a number of ways: through the utilitarian function of attitude, as when Colgate toothpaste promotes its cavity-fighting capabilities; or through the value-expressive function of attitude, making claims about Colgate's teeth-whitening capabilities.

FIGURE 5.6. (A) How does this ad appeal to the utilitarian function of attitude? (B) To which values does this Cotton council ad appeal?

What Influences Our Attitude Formation?

Many influences contribute to how we form attitudes, including: (1) our own personality, (2) the experience and information we encounter, (3) our family, and (4) our friends and peer groups.

Personality

Human **personality** consists of the individual psychological characteristics that routinely influence the way people react to their surroundings. Those characteristics that make us unique from other people, characteristics such as whether we are

FIGURE 5.7. (A) In what ways does this L. E. I. jeans ad appeal to the ego-defensive function of attitude? (B) How does this Yaz ad target the knowledge function of attitude?

more extroverts or introverts, passive or active, leaders or followers, are part of our personality. (For additional information on personality, see Chapter 6.) For example, when considering adopting a new fashion look, someone who is more of a follower than a leader will wait until she sees others wearing that style before she will adopt it. Each person's own individual sets of characteristics influence the attitudes he or she forms, as well as that person's decisions and resulting behavior.

〉 〉 〉 SPECIAL FOCUS 5.1: SEAN JEAN CHANGES PUFF DADDY ATTITUDE 〈 〈 〈

Starting out in Harlem with next to nothing except a family fashion tradition and his own musical and entrepreneurial skills, by delivering newspapers at age 13, Sean Jean Combs was earning $300 a week. In college, he decided to pursue a music career, and the rap music he produced as Puff Daddy or P. Diddy became a hit among urban teens. As a rapper he won Grammies, enabling him to begin his first business, Bad Boy World Entertainment.

His love for apparel became evident when he created urban styles for teens including jailhouse stripes, low-crotch pants, and baggy logo-embossed T-shirts and hoodies. His company, Sean Jean, accounts for some $400 million in urban goods.

Realizing the baggy urban look had peaked, Sean Jean set out to change his fashion emphasis and his customers' attitudes toward his brand. His main project is creating casual men's wear with an edgy yet mainstream look. He also is producing a line of women's apparel with Zak Posen, known for his fashion-forward ideas. Most of these garments will be produced in the United States, for Combs advocates keeping U.S. citizens in jobs. His lines are carried by stores such as Saks, Bloomingdale's, and Macy's. In addition, Sean Jean has a fragrance agreement with Estée Lauder; the total merchandise package creates an image distant from that of the urban rapper. So far, his offerings are right in tune with the changing attitudes of his customers.

>>> Source: Adapted from Tracie Rozhon, "The Rap on Puffy's Empire," *New York Times*, July 24, 2005, Sec. 3, pp. 1 and 6.

Experience and Information

Our personal experience with a product, plus what we have learned about it, influence the kinds of attitudes we form. For instance, if we have experienced success with a certain brand of suntan lotion, we do not hesitate to buy the same brand again. Or, we may have purchased a North Face jacket and found it sturdy, dependable, and fashionable enough over several years. Having formed a positive attitude about that brand, we look for the brand again when it's time to replace that jacket. Or, when purchasing a laptop computer, after studying information about each model, we know we can make a buying decision that is most appropriate for us. To help us gain experience, we gather information. Often we don't even have to look for it, because the media bombard us with marketing messages that may or may not be targeted to us and, if so, may or may not be useful, depending on our attitude and buying intentions.

Consumers develop attitudes not only toward products but also toward the advertisements for those products. For example, if we are interested in a new cell phone and see an ad for one, we might study the copy seriously to learn more about its capabilities and form beliefs (cognitions) about the product. Another time, an exciting TV commercial for a new film could send us straight to the theater. Both beliefs and affections defined through advertising can lead us to form positive attitudes toward the advertisement as well as the product.

Family

Our families can play important roles in the formation of our attitudes, particularly when we are young because they are the dominant factor in our lives as children. Also, they influence us heavily during that time because we simply have not yet lived long enough to be exposed to other influences for a sustained period. Say, for example, the adults in a family believe that a certain brand of cereal like Special K is more nutritious than other brands. Their children would tend feel the same way about that cereal, whether or not they enjoyed eating it. As we mature, we become more independent and develop our own attitudes that, in many instances, may be similar to those of our parents but in others may be quite different. Today, children tend to express their own attitudes at earlier ages than in the past. When it comes to choosing their own apparel or decorating their own rooms, many children are influencing their parents' buying decisions at a younger age. (For more information on the influence of family, see Chapter 7.)

Friends and Peers

Friends and peers can also influence our attitude formation from childhood on. For example, teens hanging out together often have similar attitudes toward a number of things, including fashions in apparel, food, hobbies, and entertainment. Teens' influences on each other's buying behavior are heavy and contagious. In the world of work, other employees contribute to our forming attitudes toward the culture of the workplace, proper dress, and business etiquette. Acquaintances at college or clubs, as well as our very good friends, contribute to our attitude formation; a tennis partner may praise the performance of his new racquet; a good friend may suggest shopping at a certain Web site. (For more information on the influence of friends and peers, see Chapter 8.)

> *Let's Talk*
> *Consider a recent significant purchase made by your family—a car, home, or vacation. What roles did personality, experience and information, family members, and friends play in the purchasing decision?*

How Do Marketers Use Attitudes?

Marketers study our attitudes in order to learn the effectiveness of their strategies and to plan for the future. To more fully understand and better connect with consumers, marketers divide the total market (all of the possible customers) for their goods or services into smaller, more homogeneous units in order to most effectively reach the most likely customers, a process known as market segmentation. They may do this in any number of ways, depending on what they want to find out. For instance, to learn about consumer attitudes toward products, researchers may segment markets according to consumer benefits. (For a more detailed discussion of market segments, see Chapter 1.)

Through a graphics technique known as **perceptual mapping**, shown frequently in two dimensions, marketers can visualize consumers' attitudes toward their existing products and see where their goods stand in relation to their competitors. Map dimensions are created by selecting relevant attributes to be measured such as quality, timeliness, or customer service. For example, items appearing close together on a perceptual map are often seen by customers as "me too" products, while gaps indicate that no products exist and perhaps there is opportunity to satisfy an unmet consumer need. Marketers can then position their products to meet those needs. Thus, perceptual mapping also helps marketers focus on planning distinctive advertising and promotional activities.

Table 5.2.   Perceptual Map of Martin + Osa

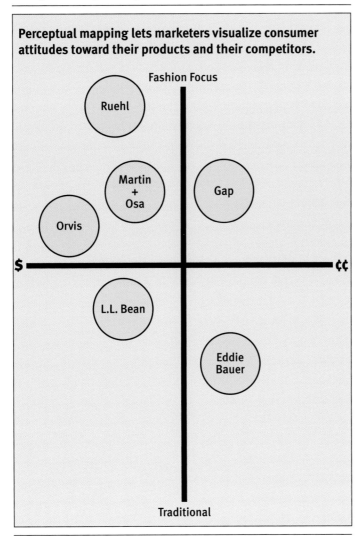

FIGURE 5.8. American Eagle Outfitters established Martin + Osa to keep its customers as they matured.

Table 5.2 presents a perceptual map for American Eagle Outfitters' division for 25 to 40 year olds, called Martin + Osa.[7] The company wanted to retain its original younger customers as they matured, and its executives believed that this older market was underserved, so they developed the Martin + Osa concept. Martin and Osa Johnson were twentieth-century explorers from Chanute, Kansas, who trekked through much of Africa and Southeast Asia before exploring became popular. The stores emphasize outdoor wear, with classic looks featuring denim. In this perceptual map, similar retailers are positioned according to fashion focus and price. Competitors include Eddie Bauer, L.L.Bean, Gap, and Orvis. Notice that Ruehl is more fashion-focused and higher in price than either Gap or Martin + Osa. Orvis is high in price but not as fashion-forward as Ruehl or Martin + Osa. Eddie Bauer and L.L.Bean, on the other hand, both feature a more traditional look, and Bauer is lower in price. You can see why American Eagle executives believed that the over-25 customer seeking daytime denim and sportswear could use more options.

What Is the Effect of Attitudes on Our Buying Behavior?

Marketers know that sales volume for their products depends not only on positive consumer attitudes about their offerings, but also on consumers' acting on these attitudes by purchasing their goods. Therefore, marketers are vitally interested in the ways our buying behaviors are influenced by the cognitive and affective elements of our attitudes, since our purchasing behavior reflects the effectiveness of marketers' promotional strategies. Advertising that leads consumers to develop positive attitudes about a product may well encourage them to buy that product, and successful experience with the product could well mean repeat purchases.

The Relationship between Beliefs and Attitudes

While there are several theories explaining the relationship of beliefs and attitudes in the marketplace, most point out that consumers want to maintain harmony in their buying activities. Among the theories, two of the most relevant are balance theory and multi-attribute theory (the basis for the Theory of Reasoned Action).

Balance Theory

Balance theory states that people want to maintain harmony or balance in their attitudes—that is, their beliefs and feelings, whether positive or negative. An example of balance theory happened when Sears tried to enhance its apparel fashion image by promoting "the softer side of Sears." One part of its strategy was to purchase the nautical sporting goods and apparel firm Lands' End. At the time, Lands' End had many loyal customers, while fewer people purchased apparel from Sears. When Sears started offering Lands' End apparel, the negative object (Sears) connected to a positive one (Lands' End), creating a negative imbalance, and customers saw them both as negative. Lands' End apparel, when made by Sears, took on a negative appeal and consumers began buying less of it. Sears apparel sales also fell below expectations, resulting in a total negative balance. The huge retailer put Lands' End up for sale, then had second thoughts and created Lands' End boutiques in Sears stores, hoping to achieve balance in apparel sales. To date, these departments appear to be successful for Sears, but the long-term outcome is unknown.

As previously mentioned, the main concept of balance theory is that people are more comfortable when their attitudes are in balance. Moreover, as consumers, we like to associate ourselves with positive attitude objects.[8] Serious fashion apparel consumers are drawn to the quality and style of names such as Prada, Burberry, and Chanel; many interior design practitioners have high regard for names such as Baker, Miele, and Kohler.

Balance theory also helps explain the use of celebrity product endorsements. The

Table 5.3. Illustration of Balance Theory

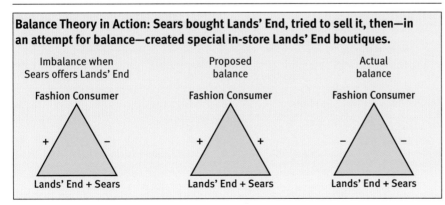

Source: Adapted from Henry Assael. *Consumer Behavior*. Fig. 8.3. p. 224.

balance is created because consumers like to identify with positive attitude objects, here represented by a well-known person. Marketers hope to transfer our positive feelings toward the celebrity to the product the celebrity endorses, thus creating a favorable balance in our minds toward the product. Celebrities such as Donald Trump and Sarah Jessica Parker, among others, endorse new fragrances in hopes that we as consumers will buy them because we have transferred our positive attitudes toward these celebrities to the products. Popular athletes such as Tiger Woods endorse golf wear and accessories. Celebrity Jennifer Lopez has introduced her own in-store boutiques, The World of J.Lo, in places such as Moscow, Chicago, and Las Vegas, featuring her Sweetface Fashions, which include sportswear, accessories, and fragrances, believing her star image will transfer positively to the merchandise.[9] A celebrity's negative image also can influence consumers' attitudes, as when model Kate Moss's drug use was publicized. This caused the cancellation of a number of her commercial contracts, such as one with the Swedish apparel retailer H&M. At this time, however, she has managed to overcome the negatives and is modeling again.

Multi-Attribute Models

The idea that consumers purchase products based on the latter's characteristics or attributes became the basis for the development of Fishbein's **multi-attribute model**, which states that a combination of consumers' beliefs, derived from their knowledge about the attributes of a product, reveals the consumer's overall attitude toward the product.[10] For example, when searching for furniture for his project, Juan had developed beliefs about IKEA's attributes and how they filled his clients' needs.

The multi-attribute chart in Table 5.4 compares three furniture retailers: IKEA, Crate & Barrel, and Pier 1. The furniture attributes Juan sought are listed in the first

Table 5.4.   Multi-Attribute Theory

Attributes	Importance	Ikea	Crate & Barrel	Pier 1
Modern-looking	3	8	9	6
Sturdy	5	6	10	5
Flexible construction	4	9	3	6
Accommodating design	6	8	9	4
Easy-to-move	2	9	3	5
Inexpensive	1	10	3	8
Total		50	37	34

Source: Adapted from Michael Solomon's *Consumer Behavior,* 6th ed., Upper Saddle River, NJ: Pearson/Prentice Hall, 2004, Table 7.1, p. 252.

column. In the second column are Juan's rankings, on a scale of 1 to 10, of the importance of each attribute in this situation, with low cost being the most important attribute. Then each retailer is accorded points based on Juan's evaluation of that company's attributes. Adding up the attributes, we see that for Juan's purposes, his beliefs about IKEA's furniture are that it would best fulfill the goals of his assignment. For his clients, price and transportability are the most important factors. Neither Crate & Barrel (with a score of 37) nor Pier 1 (with a score of 34) fulfills each of the attributes as well as IKEA (with a score of 50).

> *Let's Talk*
> *What are three or four of the attributes of your college that influenced your decision to attend? How would you prioritize them?*

Theory of Reasoned Action (TORA)

While we as consumers may hold favorable attitudes about products, those attitudes may not lead to our purchasing them. For example, we might think highly of a BMW convertible or a Pierre Deux chaise lounge in a Provençal print, but something, perhaps money, keeps us from signing a purchase order. Realizing that positive attitudes do not necessarily mean increased sales led to the creation of a more precise theory dealing with consumers' intent to purchase. The **Theory of Reasoned Action** (**TORA**) includes the affective, cognitive, and behavioral components of attitude in addition to other influences on our decision making. These influences, known as **subjective norms**, include our **normative beliefs**, that is, the opinions about the purchase held by other people who matter to us (such as friends and family), plus the extent to which we're motivated to go along with others' opinions.

For example, Pam, a college design student, hears about a school trip to Paris and wants very much to go. Analyzing Pam's attitude using TORA, we can determine the likelihood of her intention to take the trip. Her attitude toward the excursion is that it will be

FIGURE 5.9. What seems to be a major attribute in this student's college selection?

"My first choice college should have lots of closet space."

Table 5.5.   TORA

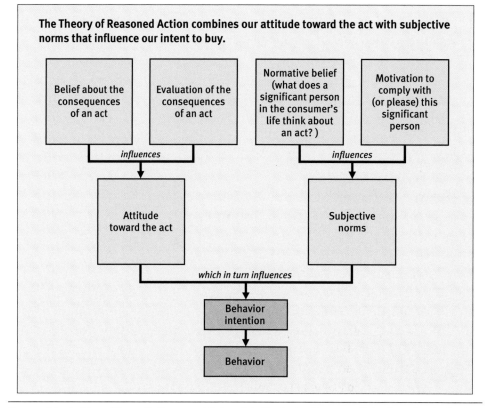

Source: Adapted from Wayne D. Hoyer and Deborah J. MacInnis, *Consumer Behavior*, 4th ed., Boston: Houghton Mifflin Company, 2007, Exhibit 6.4, p. 135.

educational, somewhat costly, fun, but foreign and perhaps unsettling. Her beliefs about the educational value and the fun outweigh her concerns about both the cost and the fact that she has never been to a foreign country before. Evaluating the consequences of the trip, she will need to borrow money to pay for it, plus she will miss the income from her job while she is away. But her attitude toward the trip remains positive. She asks her parents for their opinion, and they are enthusiastic, even offering to underwrite some of her expenses. She then turns to her boyfriend; he is totally against her going away at all. While she is quite fond of him, she believes that if their relationship is to last, whether or not she takes the trip will not be the deciding factor. She is motivated to take the trip and intends to sign up for it. TORA is a more precise gauge of consumer behavior because it strives to measure consumers' attitudes toward *intending* to buy rather than their attitudes toward the object being considered for purchase.

One application of TORA can be seen in a recent survey by *Women's Wear Daily* on how people perceive fashion brands, namely that style and color outrank marketing efforts such as celebrity promotion. Consider the information in Point of View 5.2 on how consumer attitudes can be changed.

❯ ❯ ❯ POINT OF VIEW 5.2: ARE FASHION MARKETERS DOING ENOUGH TO SWAY CONSUMERS' ATTITUDES? ❮ ❮ ❮

Apparently not. At least not in great numbers. According to a study conducted by the marketing consulting firm Brand Keys, too few fashion brands sway consumer attitudes favorably enough in their direction. In a recent survey, 500 men and women, ages 18 to 59, ranked 50 fashion brands in terms of attributes they value such as style, color, and comfort, along a continuum ranging at the low end from price-driven commodities to the high end designated human brands.

Of the brands rated, only five (10 percent of the brands surveyed) made it to the highest or human level: Chanel, Donald Trump, Isaac Mizrahi, Ralph Lauren, and Victoria's Secret. Consumers' attitudes toward these brand attributes were most positive. Surprisingly, only two brands relied on celebrity mojo: Chanel, through its successful promotions enhanced by Nicole Kidman, and Donald Trump, (marketing his fragrance and menswear), through his real estate and reality television image of over-the-top living that appeals to some wannabe affluents.

The second level, twenty-first-century brands, contains 34 brands (17 percent) positive in consumers' attitudes but not high enough to rank as human brands. These include Abercrombie & Fitch, Christian Dior, Louis Vuitton, Nike, Skechers, among others. (See Table 5.6 for the complete list.) At the third level, designated label, containing 12 brands (24 percent), consumers' positive attitudes toward the brand attributes were weakening. Some of these brands include Anne Klein, Dockers, Gucci, and Tommy Hilfiger. The commodity group, primarily driven by price, contains 16 brands (32 percent), among them: Champion, Gap, Guess, JCPenney, Old Navy, and Wrangler.

The survey produced some astounding results for fashion marketers. First, of the 50 fashion brands included, only a small number of five reached the very highest level. Second, of the many brands with strong attributes in the next category (over a third of all brands surveyed), not enough of them were seen to have influenced consumer attitudes sufficiently enough to rate as human brands. Additional research pointed out that celebrity promotions of fashion goods influence the purchasing of 9 percent of clothing bought by men and women, whereas style, color, and comfort are far stronger influences on buying behavior (62 percent for the first two; 44 percent for the third. The percentages amount to

Table 5.6. How People Perceive Brands

Commodity	Label	21st-Century Brand	Human Brand
Adidas	Anne Klein	Abercrombie & Fitch	Chanel
Champion	Bill Blass	Giorgio Armani	Donald Trump
Ellesse	Calvin Klein	Brooks Bros.	Isaac Mizrahi
Fila	Dockers	Burberry	Ralph Lauren
Gap	Donna Karan	Christian Dior	Victoria's Secret
Guess	Eddie Bauer	Ferragamo	
INC	Fendi	J. Crew	
J.C. Penney	Gucci	Louis Vuitton	
Lands' End	Hugo Boss	Lucky	
Lee	Lacoste	New Balance	
Levi's	Kate Spade	Nike	
London Fog	Tommy Hilfiger	The North Face	
Old Navy		Prada	
Reebok		Polo	
Sears		Sean John	
Wrangler		Skechers	
		Versace	
Totals: 16 (32%)	12 (24%)	17 (34%)	5 (10%)

Source: Brand Keys Commodity-to-Brand Continuum, third quarter, 2005.

more than 100 percent because consumers have multiple reasons for purchasing). Clearly, fashion marketers have more to do in their efforts to influence consumer attitudes!

>>> Source: Adapted from Valerie Seckler, "There's No Banking on Star Power," *Women's Wear Daily,* November 16, 2005, p. 8.

Theory of Cognitive Dissonance

After buying a product, we want to assure ourselves that we have made the right decision, an effort that helps us maintain balance. According to the **theory of cognitive dissonance**—sometimes called buyer's remorse—we are uncomfortable when we have conflicting attitudes or behaviors concerning an attitude object and work to resolve them. For consumers, cognitive dissonance tends to appear after making a large purchase. For example, perhaps you spent a lot of money on a new outfit. When you get it home and try it on, you ask yourself, "Should I have bought the gray one that had a more stylish jacket?" or "Was the striped one more flattering?" You think about your answers and decide that you were right in the first place, or you take steps to return the outfit and find something more suitable, thus restoring balance. Marketers are quite aware of the power of cognitive dissonance, one of the reasons why salespeople at stores such as Nordstrom send customers notes of appreciation after a significant purchase, and why, for customers buying a new car, automobile dealers like Cadillac include a CD that lauds the features of the vehicle (to be played as the new owner drives away from the showroom).[11] Marketers work to reinforce doubts about the features of the brands we rejected by emphasizing the attributes of the one we actually purchased.

Common Methods Marketers Use to Change Fashion Consumers' Attitudes

Marketers use numerous ways to change our attitudes; one is repetition, which stems from Pavlov's system of classical conditioning (described in Chapter 3). We see over and over again the latest fashions promoted by manufacturers and marketers in a multitude of newspaper and magazine ads and articles, through the Internet, in catalogs, and on television.

Attitude Change through Repetition and Emotion

The act of repetition (repeated exposure through advertising and promotion) can make a product or service seem familiar to us, so, if it meets our needs and we develop a favorable attitude toward it, then we buy it—and the marketing goal has been achieved.

When the message itself is appealing to us, with attractive visuals (children, pets, or celebrities), when the sound of a commercial features pleasant music, when there is humor, or even better, sex—perhaps the most powerful of all attitude changers and a gargantuan selling tool in the world of fashion—marketers are hoping to change our beliefs and feelings toward a new fashion look, or for just about any product, service, or company.

FIGURE 5.10. Fashion promotion of all kinds frequently contains sexual overtones.

Changing the Multi-Attribute Model

Changing beliefs, attitudes, and intentions to purchase by altering aspects of the multi-attribute model is another approach marketers use to increase sales. One popular method is to change beliefs about product attributes. What customers believe about a fashion look affects its popularity. For example, if fashion leaders are wearing knee-length gaucho trousers, then fashion followers who had been wearing ankle-length pants begin to believe that knee-length is the latest look, and to be in fashion they must adopt the new length. Another way that fashion marketers work to change consumers' beliefs is by adding a product attribute. With fashion goods, adding an attribute may be as simple as putting lace on the neckline and cuffs of this season's "hot" silk blouse, or altering the look of a room by placing colorful cushions on the sofa. Changing beliefs about a competitor is another way fashion marketers work to change attitudes. In the budget fashion market, Wal-Mart—not generally perceived as a fashion leader—introduced Metro 7, a trendy line of women's wear, hoping to lure young urban consumers away from the pull of Mossimo and Isaac Mizrahi at Target. Unfortunately, the fashion change was too swift for Wal-Mart's mainstream customers, so the company decided to introduce fashion elements more slowly in its misses' ready-to-wear product line.[12]

Also, by making buying easier, fashion marketers can sway customer attitudes about owning an attitude object (product). Carpeting, furniture, and appliance retailers, for instance, promise introductory discounts or low interest rates and "no payment until next year" to customers who are considering doing some interior decorating. Or, some promotions may be based on changing our normative beliefs, that is, others' opinions of certain fashion decisions. The group People for the Ethical Treatment of Animals (PETA), renowned for its disapproval of the commercial treatment of fur-bearing animals, actively campaigns against the use of fur in fashion apparel and home furnishings in hopes of convincing all consumers that the many possible substitutes available today make fur unnecessary.

How do our attitudes relate to our individual personalities? We'll find out more about that topic in Chapter 6, "Personality and the Fashion Consumer."

Summary

We all hold attitudes; these are our settled opinions (either positive or negative) about people, ideas, places, or objects. Our attitudes consist of three parts: cognitive, our beliefs; affective, our feelings; and behavioral, our actions. In forming attitudes, we go through the hierarchy of effects, a series of steps, the order depending on our level of involvement with the attitude object. In a high-involvement situation, we use a problem-solving process, first gaining knowledge, then developing positive feelings, and finally taking action. In a low-involvement situation, we act on our beliefs—in this case, buying the product—and then develop positive or negative feelings about it as we use it. In an experiential situation, based on consumption for pleasure, we are caught up by the emotional appeal of the product, and by using it, we develop beliefs about it.

Our attitudes give us balance by meeting our needs through their functions: utilitarian, being useful in problem solving; value-expressive, representing our personalities and self-image; ego-defensive, protecting us from anxiety; and knowledge, ordering our information-processing. Influences on our attitudes include our personalities; our experience and information; as well as our family, friends, and peers.

Through perceptual mapping, fashion marketers use their knowledge of consumer attitudes toward their products both to assess their current strategies and to reveal new marketing opportunities.

By studying the relationship between beliefs and attitudes, marketers have learned that customers like to maintain balance (balance theory) and do so by association with positive attitude objects such as celebrities. Consumers develop attitudes about products by citing product attributes and weighing their importance. To go beyond attitudes and learn consumers' intent to purchase, marketers use the Theory of Reasoned Action (TORA), which factors in attitudes plus the importance of others' influence in the purchasing decision.

Some of the most popular ways of influencing attitudes in fashion marketing include the use of repetition and attractive messages featuring celebrities, pleasant visuals, sound, sex, and humor. Changing our perceptions of a product's attributes and making the purchase of fashion goods easy are also marketing efforts designed to encourage us to buy.

Key Terms

Affective element

Attitude

Attitude object

Balance theory

Behavioral element

Cognitive element

Experiential hierarchy

Functions of attitudes

Hierarchy of effects

High-involvement hierarchy

Low-involvement hierarchy

Multi-attribute model

Normative beliefs

Perceptual mapping

Personality

Subjective norms

Theory of cognitive dissonance

Theory of reasoned action (TORA)

Questions for Review

1. Explain the relationship of an "attitude" to an "attitude object," and describe each of the elements that compose an attitude.

2. Name the three classifications of the hierarchy of effects, and explain why appealing to each is useful to fashion marketers.

3. Cite the four classifications of the functions of attitude, and supply an example of how a fashion goods marketer could appeal to each.

4. Describe four influences on attitude formation, with examples of each.

5. Explain what is meant by "perceptual mapping" and how fashion marketers would use it.

6. Give examples of how fashion marketers could apply the following: balance theory, multi-attribute model, and TORA.

Activities

1. Select one designer about whose work you have developed strong feelings—either positive or negative—and state whether your attitude stems mainly from cognitive or affective elements, or a combination. Cite the contribution of each element to your attitude formation, and state their combined effect on your purchase behavior.

2. Think of a fashion item you have purchased, and explain how your feelings, beliefs, and behavior developed, and in which order. Create a diagram of the hierarchy of effect that depicts your choice, and describe it to the class.

3. From recent fashion magazines, select a series of advertisements that appeal to the four functions of attitude. Try to find at least one ad that appeals to each function. Share your findings with the class. Ads appealing to which attitude function were easiest to find? Why?

4. Working with one or two partners, select a fashion goods manufacturer retailer, and create a perceptual map positioning that business in relation to its competition. Based on your findings, what are your suggestions for advertising campaigns for this company? Are there gaps that the company might fill with new divisions or products?

5. List four or five attributes of your college. Then applying TORA, indicate how you arrived at the decision to attend this school as opposed to others you could have selected.

Mini-Project

Working alone or with a team, think of three stores (or fashion goods designers or manufacturers) you have a positive or negative attitude about. Create a multi-attribute model for your chosen subjects consisting of the attributes you have selected, their importance, and the ranking of your beliefs about each one. Add up each attitude score, and report your findings to the class.

References

1. Alex Kuczynski, Critical Shopper column, "Consumer Philosophy by Tar-zhay," *New York Times,* July 2, 2005, Sec. E.

2. Shawn Young and Li Yuan, "You Talkin' to Me?" *Wall Street Journal,* September 16, 2005, Sec. B.

3. Martin E. Goldberg et al., eds., *Social Marketing* (Mahwah, NJ: Lawrence Erlbaum Associates Publishers, 1997).

4. Robert J. Marzano, *Designing a New Taxonomy of Educational Objectives* (Thousand Oaks, CA: Corwin Press, 2001).

5. Brian Mullen, *The Psychology of Human Behavior* (Mahwah, NJ: Lawrence Erlbaum Associates, 1990).

6. Daniel Katz, "The Functional Approach to the Study of Attitudes," *Public Opinion Quarterly* 24 (Summer 1960): 163–204.

7. Michelle Dalton Tyree, "American Eagle Evolves: Retailer Unveils Concept for the Post-College Crowd," *Women's Wear Daily*, (October 20, 2005): 2, 8.

8. John C. Mowen, *Consumer Behavior* (New York: Prentice Hall, 1997).

9. Beth Wilson, "Field's Kicks Off World of JLo," *Women's Wear Daily* (September 26, 2005): 18.

10. Kenneth Miller, "A Situational Multi-Attribute Model," *Advances in Consumer Research* (Association for Consumer Research) 2 (1975): 455–464.

11. Robert A. Wicklund and Jack W. Brehm. *Perspectives on Cognitive Dissonance.* (Hillsdale, NJ: Lawrence Erlbaum Associates, 1976).

12. Michael Barbaro, "Wal-Mart Goes Urban with Clothing Line," *New York Times,* October 7, 2005, Sec. C.

CHAPTER **6**

Personality and the Fashion Consumer

"Honestly, Mother. I don't see why you insist on putting plastic covers on the furni-ture. It looks *so* tacky!" cried Kim Alexander as she stopped by for a visit and surveyed her mother's living room.

"Those covers may look tacky to you, dear, but now your 11-year-old brother Matthew and his pals can eat their pizzas here while playing their video games, and I don't have to worry about redecorating tomorrow. And the dog can sit wherever he wants and no harm done," Mrs. Alexander responded.

"But what will visitors say, people like Matthew's teacher and Reverend Baxter? When they see these shiny things, they'll think our family is tacky plastic too."

"No. They're smart enough to see below the surface. Besides, for occasions like those, I can whip off the covers and have immaculate furniture for guests to sit on," replied Mrs. Alexander.

"Why didn't you get upholstery that doesn't show spots in the first place?" Kim asked. "That would save you time and energy."

"I just don't have that kind of personality," responded her mother, firmly ending the discussion.

What Is Personality?

As you can tell from Mrs. Alexander's conversation with her daughter, while our perceptions and attitudes play an important part in how we choose fashion goods, our personalities also influence our actual purchasing behavior. As we defined in the previous chapter, personality is made up of those individual psychological characteristics that routinely influence the way people react to their surroundings. In addition, while personalities are lasting, they can change, through maturing, or after an accident, illness, or other very significant event. One example of this could be a mean-spirited relative who "mellowed out" after either marrying or divorcing his or her spouse.

Effect of Personality on the Fashion Consumer

Although marketers often segment consumers by obvious means such as gender, income, or occupation, by using personality-based dimensions, they also probe to discern more about customers' deep-seated purchasing behavior. For example, fashion experts know that when shopping for apparel and home furnishings, assertive and outgoing customers tend to choose bright colors and patterns harmonizing with their personalities, while more timid people, in order to blend in, tend to stick to basic neutrals and pastels.

Major Personality Theories

In order to look more deeply into the core aspects of consumers' buying behavior, marketers examine some of the major theories of personality, including: (1) psychoanalytic theory, (2) social cultural theory, (3) self-concept theory, and (4) trait theory.[1]

Psychoanalytic Theory

During the early twentieth century, Austrian psychiatrist Sigmund Freud studied many aspects of human behavior, developing theories that revolutionized the study of personality and making major contributions to the advancement of psychoanalysis. According to Freud's **psychoanalytic theory**, many of our behaviors and our dreams come from our unconscious, where thoughts we are largely unaware of are stored. The personality develops as a reaction to the ways one deals with childhood conflicts and is influenced by the three components of personality: the id, the ego, and the superego. The **id**, or libido, while unconscious, is the component that controls our biological drives of hunger, sex, and self-preservation; it is with us from birth and its impulses require immediate gratification. The purpose of the id is to seek pleasure and avoid pain. If unchecked, it is wild and acts freely, and can be a source of destruction—and of creativity.[2] The id plays a significant role in the lives of many people in the fields of design and fashion.

The second component, the **ego**, is the conscious part of our personality, our sense of ourselves; it reacts to reality in a socially acceptable way, serving as a mediator between the desires of the id and the restraint of the superego.[3] Operating under the ego's influence, a consumer purchasing an outfit for work would select something that both blends into that environment and accurately reflects how she feels about herself. The designer Gianni Versace, interpreting the ego in his own way, at one time remarked, "I like to dress egos. If you haven't got an ego today, you can forget it."[4]

The third component, the **superego**—manifesting the traditional values of society customarily transmitted by parents—acts as a conscience, promoting acceptable standards of behavior and restraining the impulsive id by creating feelings of guilt to punish misconduct, real or imagined. A graduate student who would like very much to own an expensive watch, but also not wanting to see his debts mount, opts for a Timex instead. His superego puts a brake on his id's demand for immediate gratification, and the ego tells him the watch he chose is practical, durable, and completely acceptable for now. In this situation, the ego has acted to balance the desires of the id and the superego in a way that maintains the personality's equilibrium; this is known as the *reality principle* and takes place in the unconscious, so that the consumer often may not know the real basis for some buying behavior.

Let's Talk
Can you think of an example of a recent fashion item that you, or someone you know, chose where id, ego, or superego could have played a part leading up to the purchase decision?

FIGURE 6.1. What messages are this ad conveying to the ego, superego, and id?

Through the work of Freud, marketers are able to envision the relationship between our biological urges (represented by the id) and our human consciousness (shown by the ego) to the customs and traditions of society (represented by the superego). These three influences are the basis for understanding the needs and motivations of consumers and their behavior. Marketers can use psychoanalytic theory to create and advertise new products that appeal to the id, ego, and superego.[5]

The field of **motivational research**, developed when researchers applied some of Freud's theories to marketing, studies the effect of the unconscious id and the superego on motives in purchasing behavior. *Depth interviews*, prodding for unconscious motives through a series of questions, and *focus groups*, guided discussions on marketing behavior, both grew out of the psychoanalytic approach. (For a more detailed discussion of motivation, see Chapter 4.)

Social-Cultural Theories

Two students of Sigmund Freud, Carl Jung and Alfred Adler, carried the psychoanalytic view a step further. They believed that the social and cultural influences on personality were far stronger than the biological drives cited by Freud. They also felt that knowledge about personality would best reveal itself through studying people behaving normally in their environments, as opposed to Freud's methodology of working primarily with abnormal patients. Jung developed the concept that shared memories of the past were the basis for the present culture; he called these memories **archetypes**. Some of these archetypes relating cultural memories included wizards, enchanted beings, and the "earth mother." To convey the shared meanings, advertisers sometimes incorporate archetypes into their campaigns. For example, the French government has used actress Catherine Deneuve and other stars to depict Marianne, France's national symbol of courage and freedom ("earth mother"). The characters from *The Chronicles of Narnia* or *Harry Potter* are archetypes that enthrall us today. In the *Pirates of the Caribbean* series, Johnny Depp's Captain Jack Sparrow represents the swashbuckling adventurer coping with the eternal powers of the sea.

> *Let's Talk*
> *What archetypes can you think of that play a role in today's marketing of fashion goods and services?*

Alfred Adler, an early twentieth-century Austrian physician and psychologist, worked with Sigmund Freud in Vienna for a while, but then broke away to develop the school of individual psychology. Adler's emphasis centered on the individual's relationship to his or her environment and on maturing by overcoming feelings of inferiority. Contemporary marketers incorporate Alder's theories by showing how consumers sometimes gain feelings of superiority through association with the products of luxury brands such as Rolls-Royce, Rolex, and Ritz-Carlton, and even with other goods and services that are more moderately priced.

FIGURE 6.2. Recalling archetypes such as the characters in *Harry Potter* relates shared memories to today's culture.

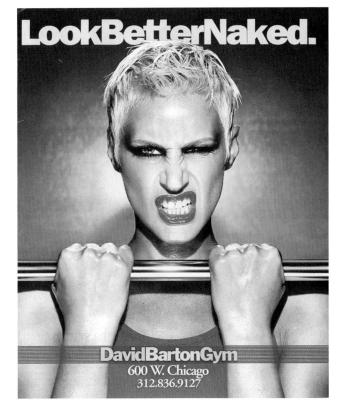

FIGURE 6.3. Which personality characteristics are the focus of this advertisement?

Karen Horney was another twentieth-century social theorist. A physician by training, she worked at the Chicago Institute for Psychoanalysis, founded the Association for the Advancement of Psychoanalysis, and later taught at the New York School of Medicine. Her theories were based on the idea that personality develops as an individual learns to cope with anxieties originating in childhood relationships with parents. She developed three hypotheses that describe ways people deal with this anxiety: compliance, an effort to move toward people, to be accepted and loved by others; aggressiveness, to move against people, to compete and gain power; and detachment, to move away from people, to be independent and self-sufficient. She believed that the reality-based ego was more influential than aggressive or sexually driven motivations in guiding human behavior and sought to strengthen her patients' feelings of competency and self-worth.[6]

Joel Cohen built on Horney's theories by creating the CAD scale, a device that measured degrees of compliance, aggressiveness, and detachment. He discovered that compliant people used more mouthwash than others and postulated that this was part of their ongoing efforts to be accepted; aggressives, he learned, bought more aftershave—possibly as a means to dominating a group; and detached people drank more tea,

entertaining with great music and food at her parties. In her ideal social self-image, Kim wants to be known for entertaining gatherings of designers, musicians, and other celebrities in her own elegantly furnished home.

Self-concept theory includes the ideas of consistency and of working to improve one's self-esteem, or opinion of oneself (described in greater detail in the following paragraph). It grows out of psychoanalytic theory in that the actual self is close to the ego, our internal mediator, while the ideal self is similar to the superego, both concerned with their version of the way things *should* be. Marketers of fashion goods of all kinds such as jewelry, clothing, automobiles, homes and interiors, as well as travel (also a consumer item) frequently appeal to our ideal self-images with advertisements that portray an ideal. One outstanding example of this is Ralph Lauren, with his tailored British looks for men and clubby upper-class British furniture, fabrics, and wall paint. The company's promotions as much as declare, "Buy these goods and live the life!"

Let's Talk
When considering buying fashion goods, which manufacturers and stores do you feel most comfortable patronizing? Why?

Self-Esteem

The concept of the ideal self focuses on **self-esteem**, that is, our positive and negative opinions of ourselves and our estimate of our self-worth. The closer the resemblance between the actual and the ideal self, the higher one's self-esteem. Having an ideal and working toward it can obviously influence buying behavior—and self-esteem. Unfortunately, much advertising that appeals to the ideal self tends to accentuate the differences between the real and the ideal, frequently contributing to a viewer's diminished

FIGURE 6.6. What does this cartoon say about the self?

self-esteem. The advertisements themselves are unreal, creating their own ideal by using models whose bodies are often surgically enhanced and graphics technology such as airbrushing to alter reality. Consider any fashion model in an advertisement. What real people do you know with such proportions, such smooth complexions, and such perfectly arranged hairstyles? Striving for such unattainable ideals can be disappointing and stressful, and can result in compulsive and unfulfilling buying behavior, at the extreme.

❯ ❯ ❯ SPECIAL FOCUS 6.1: CELEBRATING DIVERSITY LETS AUTHENTIC PERSONALITIES SHINE THROUGH ❮ ❮ ❮

Defying the fashion trend to pinch, pad, and puff, many consumers today, men as well as women, are opting for a more natural look. According to Faith Popcorn, head of Brain Reserve, a New York research organization, the interest in a more realistic look began when, as a society, we started celebrating the black and Hispanic cultures where having a visible derrière and even a mustache are totally acceptable and often "cool."

In marketing, the natural look may have started when Jamie Lee Curtis appeared in an ad wearing sports gear but no makeup and without photo retouching. The advertising industry was quick to act on consumers' desires to see advertisements with more realistic models. To promote its Intensive Firming Lotion and other products, the health and beauty aids brand Dove created billboards and ads featuring six women of various sizes, who were not professional models, dressed in their underwear. Their appearance caused a stir in the media and society in general and included a segment on the *Today* show and a *New York Times* editorial. This moderately priced beauty aids manufacturer was reaching real women. Nike was quick to follow, showing people with outsized shoulders, thighs, and backsides in its ads for exercise outfits.

Dove's emphasis on promoting the natural look grew from more than a whim to counter consumer dissatisfaction. As part of the British conglomerate Unilever, and in order to learn consumers' views on beauty, Dove surveyed girls and women in the United Kingdom, Canada, and the United States. Some of the results were disturbing; for example, in Britain, more that half of those surveyed said their bodies "disgusted" them. Six out of ten girls believed they would be happier if they were thinner, but actually fewer than two out of ten were in fact overweight. Apparently, fashion's images of artificially curvaceous models and celebrities had wreaked not a little havoc on young self-concepts. From their findings, Dove created a self-esteem fund to help girls and women build confidence. In Britain and Canada, the fund devotes itself to combating eating disorders, 90 percent of which are found in young girls. In the United States the fund works with the Girls Scouts to build self-image through the *uniquely ME!* program to build self-esteem. Activities include exercises in recognizing one's strengths, identifying core values, and handling stress, among others. The message conveyed: An attractive, natural appearance grows from a healthy outlook on life.

>>> Sources: Stuart Elliott, "For Everyday Products, Ads Using Everyday Woman," *New York Times*, August 17, 2005, pp. C1 and C2; Rich Thomaselli, "News Steers Advertising toward Reality Anatomy," AdAge.com, online edition, August 15, 2005; Rob Walker, "Social Lubricant," *New York Times* Magazine, September 4, 2005, p. 23; Dove Support: the Dove self-esteem fund, www .campaignforrealbeauty.com.

The Extended Self

The relationship between ourselves and our possessions is known as the **extended self**; in other words, "We are what we own." In the film *Pulp Fiction,* one of the main characters, Butch (Bruce Willis), although running for his life, must drive back to his apartment and a potentially lethal situation to pick up the watch he inherited from his father and grandfather. That watch was part of Butch's extended self. Per-

FIGURE 6.7. A piece of heirloom jewelry such as this pearl necklace by Stefani B, can become part of a consumer's extended self.

haps you have been given a gift that you enjoy and treasure highly; owning it adds to your self-esteem. Or, if you lost or gave up that item, you feel diminished in self-esteem. Consider Eleanor, who is in a public restroom. After removing an heirloom sapphire ring to wash her hands, she inadvertently leaves it on the edge of the sink. Realizing her forgetfulness just a few minutes later, she rushes back to retrieve the ring, but finds it is gone. Eleanor is devastated, ashamed of her carelessness; her self-esteem tumbles. Possessions as forms of our extended selves can have numerous meanings. According to research, they can actually enhance or extend our personalities in these ways: (1) *actually*, as in learning a new skill by using new scuba diving equipment; (2) *symbolically*, as winning a contest prize for creating a garment; (3) *conferring status*, as being the first among friends to own a wide-screen plasma TV; (4) *bestowing symbols of immortality*, as preserving a wedding gown for future family brides; and (5) by *containing magical powers*, as did Dorothy's red slippers in *The Wizard of Oz*.[8, 9]

Let's Talk
Think of a fashion item you would like to own. In what ways might it enhance your self-esteem? Then consider one of your possessions that you believe represents your extended self. In which of the five ways described above do you see this item as part of your extended self?

Trait Theories

Another way of studying personality is by looking at our traits or personal behavioral tendencies. We each have **traits**—distinct characteristics that differentiate us from others and contribute to our behavior. Many psychologists have identified and studied traits such as friendliness, innovativeness, and the desire for power. It was Carl Jung, however, who identified people according to whether they were **introverts**, choosing to turn inward, or **extroverts**, sociable and outgoing, concerned with external matters.[10] As consumers in the decision-making process, introverts do not ask others for product information but prefer to rely on themselves, whereas extroverts get product advice from various sources and tend to buy products that are accepted by others.

To better understand consumer behavior, many researchers have undertaken studies of personality traits. Because its results apply to almost all cultures, one of the most important theories is the five-trait model. These traits are (1) extroversion, (2) neuroticism, (3) openness to experience, (4) agreeableness, and (5) conscientiousness.

Researchers have also noted various personality traits that designers and marketers are interested in understanding better. These are discussed below.

Extroversion and Introversion

Extroverted people are active and outgoing as opposed to introverts, who are more centered inwardly. According to research, extrovert consumers tend to react more positively than negatively to certain upbeat TV commercials.[11] Therefore, marketers aim cheerful and optimistic messages, such as travel agencies depicting fun-filled vacation resorts, or design firms emphasizing the glamour and efficiency of a new kitchen. Viral or "buzz" marketing (word-of-mouth promotion, discussed in Chapter 1) is a popular way of enabling extroverts to become part of a promotion, as when teens talk, talk, and talk about the latest look in denim—and then all want to own it.

Negativism

A person's level of negativism is shown by the tendency to express negative rather than positive emotions, as opposed to having a more realistic or balanced outlook.

Negativism can be a manifestation of a **neurosis**, a mental disorder with emotionally painful symptoms that can surface as anxiety, compulsion, and depression. A marketing appeal to neurotic tendencies would cue in on negative feelings of insecurity and inadequacy. A fashion magazine touting the season's newest looks has a not-so-hidden agenda of making readers feel dissatisfied with their present outfits. A more realistically oriented personality would identify the information that could be useful in wardrobe planning and put aside feelings of discontent about not being able to acquire an entire closet full of the latest fashions.

One extreme form of neurosis—compulsion—is seen in the fashion world when consumers purchase goods indiscriminately, which is known as **compulsive buying behavior.** Consider Imelda Marcos, wife of a former president of the Philippines; at one time she owned over 2,000 pairs of shoes! Extreme compulsive shopping is an illness, a form of addiction, similar to other addictions to activities such as gambling and drug use.

Desire for Knowledge

Some consumers have a strong urge to learn everything they can about a product before purchasing it; others do not need to know all the details. The desire for knowledge is

FIGURE 6.8A. In this Apple ad aimed at verbalizers, the copy clinches the message.

called the **need for cognition** (NC). Studies have shown that consumers with a high NC react positively to advertisements explaining product features and customer benefits in great detail, while consumers with low NC seem to prefer attractive illustrations featuring celebrities.[12]

While some people prefer to learn through reading, others are more open and respond better to images. Cognitive research has developed two classifications for consumers: *visualizers*, consumers who prefer to learn through viewing pictures in movies or DVDs, and *verbalizers*, those who prefer to learn by reading texts or ads or listening to lectures.[13] Advertisers of fashion goods, aiming at visualizers, stress the assets of their products in appealing illustrations, while marketers of technical products such as electronics, aiming at verbalizers, provide extensive written information about these items. (See Figure 6.8A.)

Innovation and Opinion Leadership

Some people are the first to buy new designs for themselves and their surroundings. The people who buy the earliest and are the first visual communicators of the season's styles are known as **fashion innovators**.[14] In the rarified atmosphere of haute couture,

FIGURE 6.9. The popularity of Mary-Kate and Ashley Olsen contributes to their influence on fashion trends.

they are often among those 1,500 or so individual clients of the famous couturiers. They are also the ones who can recognize and afford the newest in design. Fashion innovators want to stand out from the crowd, to be the first to own a new product; they are often said to have a *need for differentiation or uniqueness*. To be an acknowledged fashion innovator takes a lot of originality and a big checkbook, although a few very creative fashion devotees are able to originate looks putting imagination to work with items they already own, or can devise.

People who recognize and endorse what innovators are wearing and doing are known as **fashion influentials** or the visible elite; they are usually members of an aggressive, fast-moving group of opinion leaders. They include royals, the wealthy, and celebrities worldwide.

They are not necessarily fashion innovators but rather set the standards for apparel worn for a given event or the surroundings created for a certain lifestyle.[15] Current fashion opinion leaders include David Linley (grandson of Britain's Queen Elizabeth) and his wife Serena, whose house in Provence is the subject of articles in high-end shelter magazines such as *Architectural Digest*; socialites, such as Anne Hearst and Mercedes T. Bass; the wealthy, such as Donald Trump (whose hairstyle and face seem to be everywhere in the media); and others in the public eye, such as Beyoncé Knowles, Ashley and Mary-Kate Olsen, Brad Pitt, Tiger Woods, Martha Stewart, Matt Damon, Nancy Pelosi, and Oprah Winfrey. In accepting and approving new fashion looks, fashion innovators and influencers are frequently tolerant of and open to new ideas, as opposed to people who are rigid and dogmatic or closed-minded and do not readily accept innovation.[16] For this reason, fashion marketers direct their promotions to the affluent, socially mobile, and fashion-centered, those who tend to accept new looks readily and who consciously seek out the latest styles among friends and in the media.

Need for Stimulation

Some people have a greater need than others to explore their surroundings and seek stimulation; they may also be more open to new ways of thinking than other people are. For example, Mark might feel invigorated, alert, and ready to party after completing a brisk walk or run, while a lively discussion of the season's latest hues might energize Chris to devise new color combinations for his interior designs.

According to the theory of **optimal stimulation level (OSL)**, people have different needs for stimulation, most preferring moderate stimulation over high stimulation. People with a high need for stimulation seek out strenuous physical activities such as mountain climbing, paragliding, or bungee jumping.[17] As consumers, those with a high need for stimulation react differently than do people with a low need. For example, according to research, consumers with high OSL traits tend to seek out information about products and are often innovators looking for uniqueness who are willing to make riskier decisions (such as buying a controversial work of contemporary art) than consumers with low OSL. When encountering advertising, those with high OSLs search for more information but become bored with repetitive ads.[18] To reach high OSL consumers, marketers try to provide a variety of promotional approaches with the

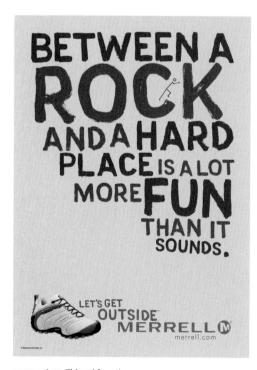

FIGURE 6.10. This ad for athletic shoes reaches out to men seeking OSL.

advertising containing more product information than usual and not repeated in the same way. For example, two Pepsi commercials presented during a recent Super Bowl employed the same story line—actors as agents "representing" the product—but with different actors for each airing; this was based on the idea that many Super Bowl viewers have a high need for stimulation.

Need for Affiliation, Achievement, and Power

Some people are quite independent, preferring to be by themselves or with just one or two friends or family members. Others place strong emphasis on gaining friends, maintaining close relationships, and belonging to groups; these people have a strong **need for affiliation**. They often buy products to reinforce their affiliations. For example, affiliation to one's employment is obvious: The uniforms worn by members of the military, postal employees, train conductors, airline employees, and others overtly indicate a work affiliation. Scout pins and wedding rings are signs of other affiliations. College posters, pennants, sweatshirts, and dorm room furnishings instantly signify students' school affiliations. Marketers of these products stress achieving a sense of belonging through buying and using these goods. Many consumers striving to maintain a particular standing in society patronize certain restaurants, theaters, museums, resorts, and charities, all to validate their affiliation with a social class. To encourage these patrons, marketers promote the sense of uniqueness and quality in their offerings in order to appeal to consumer needs for affiliation.

Some people want to stand out from the crowd, to do better than others; this trait is the **need for achievement**. An example of this can be seen in the behavior of competitive people who want to excel; they would have a tendency to look for features in products that would add to their expertise. A marketing manager might find the latest BlackBerry most efficient in handling work outside his or her office. An interior designer realizes her work would be more accurate and professional with the most recent room-planning software. A boutique owner consulting with an advertising

FIGURE 6.11. The desire to affiliate (to belong to a group) comes through in this Eileen Fisher ad for women's apparel.

YOUR LEFT HAND SAYS "WE," YOUR RIGHT HAND SAYS "ME." YOUR LEFT HAND LOVES CANDLELIGHT. YOUR RIGHT HAND LOVES THE SPOTLIGHT. YOUR LEFT HAND ROCKS THE CRADLE. YOUR RIGHT HAND RULES THE WORLD. WOMEN OF THE WORLD, RAISE YOUR RIGHT HAND.

FIGURE 6.12. The ad for diamonds encourages women to achieve on their own.

agency learns that a multimedia promotional campaign with mailers and magazine ads is likely to produce a higher sales volume for her next designer trunk show. Marketers appealing to the need for achievement stress the superiority of their products and services in fulfilling their customers' goals to succeed.

While some people have traits stressing a need to belong and others to achieve, still others want to be powerful. People who want to influence or control others are said to have a **need for power**. When people are taking charge, displaying their authority, and seeking attention, they may well be showing their need for power. Certainly, infamous tyrants Genghis Khan, Adolph Hitler, and Pol Pot displayed this trait in excess; thankfully, few people in history have possessed it to that degree! Tests measuring the need for power, however, do reveal that business executives, psychologists, and teachers (among other professionals) can score high on the power trait.[19] People with a strong power trait often want to focus attention on themselves. In the 1980s when businesswomen as a group were beginning to rise to executive levels, they made the broad-shouldered "power suit" the fashion trend, perhaps in part to show that their shoulders could bear the heavier job responsibility. Obviously, the "power look" is found not strictly among women. Male and female lawyers, stockbrokers, and bankers have a certain look to their apparel aimed at conveying power, control, and authority. In addition to apparel, consumers purchase many other items to boost their sense of power, including the latest electronics, expensive cars and homes, club memberships, and even trips to outer space. These goods and services draw admiration and indicate that the consumer has some degree of control over his or her surroundings. Marketers appealing to the power trait emphasize how consumers using their products become the center of attention and are in charge of the situation. (For additional information on human needs, see Chapter 4.)

Let's Talk
Which trait or traits described above do you recognize as influencing your fashion purchase behavior, or that of someone you know? Describe the trait and the fashion item.

While personality traits can strongly influence individual purchases at times, and while marketers can appeal to a given trait—for example, as a Hummer H2 advertisement appeals to some consumers with a desire for power—researchers have also found that traits alone are not always an accurate predictor of consumer behavior.

FIGURE 6.13. This Hummer H2 advertisement, appealing to the power trait, shows the vehicle taking charge of the road.

By combining trait information with statistics such as age or income, marketers can obtain more reliable indicators of buyers' behavior, such as customers' willingness to try healthier food items.[20] What marketers can do to appeal to personality traits is to endow their products and brands with personalities that key into consumer needs.

Products and Their Personalities

As we saw in the earlier discussion of self-concept, people tend to shop in stores and choose goods and services that make them feel comfortable. Plus, as consumers, we want the goods we buy (such as apparel, home furnishings, and automobiles) to say something about us, to reflect our personas. We tend to look at products as symbols of certain qualities; the study of symbols and their meanings is called **semiotics**. Consider the attorney who wears a gray pinstripe suit, white shirt, and regimental tie. In semiotic terms, these product symbols say he is smart, conservative, and well organized. The real estate agent in her designer dress and matching coat, accessorized with Ferragamo pumps and Prada handbag, conveys an image of style, knowledge, and success. Semiotics is important to marketers because consumers often express their personality characteristics through the symbolic meanings of the brands they purchase.

>>> POINT OF VIEW 6.2: FASHION AND SEMIOTICS: THE HIDDEN MEANINGS OF A STYLE <<<

When we look at a startling fashion, or any new product for that matter, we try to make sense of it. We do this in the context of our own experience and our own culture. Cultures around the world differ in their interpretations, and this dissimilarity creates a challenge for global marketers.

Take a recent Paris fall showing of the designers Viktor Horsing and Rolf Snoeren. Their collection, rooted in the fifties, with polished trench coats and silvery frocks, underline Viktor Horsing's statement, "Fashion is the biggest thing in our lives. We want to heirloom it, make it timeless." Yet, for the runway, each of the models was outfitted with a grid mask, giving the effect, as noted in *Women's Wear Daily*, of a cross between a fencer and Hannibal Lector.

Interpreting symbols and their meanings, in this case, the masks, hoods, and other drapings obvious in a number of collections that season, is the work of semioticians. In marketing, semiotics reveals the meanings that consumers assign to products, permitting advertisers to create symbols targeted to fulfill consumer desires and enhance their personalities. In semiotic terms, each marketing message has three parts: (1) the *object* (a product such as the mask), (2) the *symbol associated with the product* (obscuring the model's face), and (3) the *interpretant* (the meaning of the symbol). In this case, depending on the consumer's viewpoint and origin, there could be a number of meanings to the use of masks in a fashion showing. Since more than a few designers shrouded models' faces, one interpretation could be misogyny, the hatred of women on the part of some designers; another could be a kind of cultural malaise, reflecting anxiety about political conditions today; a third could be a form of homage to Muslim culture; and another might be the view that the mask is an "in" trend of fashion this season. The work of searching out the symbolic meanings of products in order to reach consumers is complex and not always clear. Semioticians can help marketers lift the fog of uncertainty.

>>> Sources: "Ladies and Gentlemen," *Women's Wear Daily*. February 28, 2006, pp. 6 and 7; Stephanie Rosenbloom, "The Obscure and Uncertain Semiotics of Fashion," *New York Times*," March 5, 2006, Section 4, p. 16.

Recent studies by Alan Hirsch, published in his book, *What Flavor Is Your Personality?*, show the relationship between consumers' personality characteristics and their ice cream preferences. Participants were given a battery of standard personality tests and then asked to select their favorite among six flavors of ice cream. Six personality types appeared. You would think that respondents choosing vanilla would be mild with bland personalities. Not so! According to the findings, they are risk takers, even overcommitted. The results are summarized in Table 6.1.[21]

Brand Personality

Because our personalities are reflected in the products we choose, marketers seek to create personalities for their brands that match what we want. For example, at a recent Paris auto show, Daimler-Chrysler promoted its new Mercedes-Benz as being innovative, created with passion, and possessing high quality.[22] Advertisers give certain brands human characteristics that relate to personality characteristics, like those of friends whom consumers would like to associate with; this is called **brand personification**. Consider the following list of characteristics and sample brands that have been promoted to reflect those characteristics:

- *Sincere, down-to-earth, family-oriented.* These terms could be used to describe Kodak, Hallmark, or Coca-Cola, products that are respected like a well-regarded friend.
- *Young, modern, outgoing.* In the soft drink category, this describes Pepsi, a friend to hang out with during free time.
- *Competent, influential, accomplished.* Hewlett-Packard and the *Wall Street Journal* are representative of these characteristics, like a business leader or teacher you respect for his or her achievements.

Table 6.1. Selected Ice Cream Flavors and Personality Characteristics

Ice Cream Flavor	Personality Characteristics
Vanilla	Colorful, gregarious risk takers, possibly overcommitted, impulsive, set high goals, enjoy close relationships
Double Chocolate Chunk	Charming, lively, want attention, extroverts, romantic, trustworthy, followers rather than leaders
Strawberries and Cream	Shy, but emotionally strong, have high standards, can seem cranky and irritable, pessimistic
Banana Cream Pie	Easy-going, well-adjusted, good listeners, good marital partner
Chocolate Chip	Competitors, go-getters, can't stand losing, charming, generous
Butter Pecan	Set high standards, ethical, fair, tend to be rigid, aggressive in athletics

Source: Alan Hirsch, *What Flavor Is Your Personality?* Naperville, IL: Sourcebooks, 2001, pp. 69–71.

- *Sophisticated, wealthy, condescending.* These terms might describe brands such as Chanel or Baccarat, as opposed to Tommy Hilfiger or Mikasa. It has been suggested that a consumer's relationship with the first two brands might resemble one with a rich relative.[23]

Table 6.2 describes five components of brand personality: sincerity, excitement, competence, sophistication, and ruggedness. Below each component are contributing aspects.[24] You can gather, for example, that the ruggedness of the Orvis line of apparel for men is emphasized in its newspaper ads and catalogs with its information about fishing gear and fly-casting seminars.

In his book *Why Customers Do What They Do,* Marshal Cohen, chief industry analyst for the research organization The NPD Group, declares, "Branding is what makes the consumer associate himself or herself with the product. Branding gives the product personality and image, and, even more important, gives the consumer something to share with others."[25]

How Marketers Create Brand Personality

Marketers create personalities for companies as well as for products. Consider Macy's, for example; many people think of this retailer in terms of wide assortments, up-to-

Table 6.2.   Brand Personality

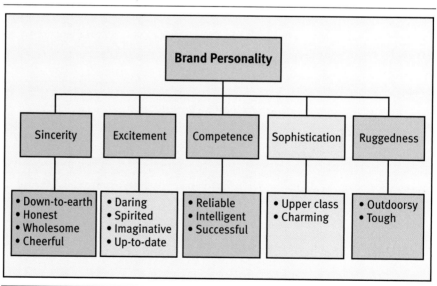

Source: Adapted from Schiffman and Kanuk, Fig. 5-7. p. 139. *Original source*: Jennifer L. Aaker, "Dimensions of Brand Personality," *Journal of Marketing Research* 35, August 1997, p. 352. Permission American Marketing Association.

date fashions, and fair prices. The goal of a successful effort to create an effective brand personality is to build brand equity, that is, to gain a loyal customer for the long term. In developing a brand personality for a product or a company, one way is to build a personality that closely resembles that of the consumer. Below are the steps for developing a brand personality:

1. Define the target market.
2. Determine what those customers want, need, and like.
3. Create a consumer personality profile.
4. Build a product personality to coincide.[26]

Companies such as Levi-Strauss research their target markets thoroughly and find that building brand personalities is very useful. The company discovered the following characteristics for its master brand personality: original, masculine, sexy, youthful, and rebellious. For its signature button-fly 501 jeans, Levi's created the following brand personality that the company could market worldwide: romantic, sexually attractive, rebellious, strong, resourceful, and independent.[27]

Color and Brand Personality

According to research done by NPD Group, the main external influence on customer purchases is style (which includes color), followed by price, comfort, and fit; this is true not only for apparel but also for household appliances and electronics.[28] In describing how Apple changed the look of the office, home, and classroom by introducing computers in colorful housings (which strongly contrasted to the drab off-white and gray electronics then in use), graphic designer and consultant Beatrice Santiccioli said, "Giving things color is a way of inventing personalities."[29]

Think of the image that color conveys for fashion organizations: The cosmetics firm Elizabeth Arden and the online gift purveyor Red Envelope are nearly as recognizable as Coca-Cola for their use of that color; Alexander Julian, creator of apparel and home furnishings, is known for his signature "Colours by Julian"; Clinique and Tiffany have their own shades of green and blue; Chanel and Nike make great use of black and white; Dior's gray is known worldwide. Even Kermit the Frog, who used to sing, "It's not easy being green," changed his tune when he saw a recent Ford Escape Hybrid! Some colors have certain personality characteristics, as indicated in Table 6.3.

Table 6.3.   Personality-Like Associations of Selected Colors

Color	Personality link	Marketing insights
Blue	Commands respect, authority	• America's favored color • IBM holds the title to blue • Associated with club soda • Men seek products packaged in blue • Houses painted blue are avoided • Low-calorie, skim milk • Coffee in a blue can perceived as "mild"
Yellow	Caution, novelty, temporary, warmth	• Eyes register it fastest • Coffee in a yellow can tasted "weak" • Stops traffic • Sells a house
Green	Secure, natural, relaxed or easygoing, living things	• Good work environment • Associated with vegetables and chewing gum • Canada Dry ginger ale sales increased when it changed sugar-free package from red to green and white
Red	Human, exciting, hot, passionate, strong	• Makes food "smell" better • Coffee in a red can perceived as "rich" • Women have a preference for bluish red • Men have a preference for yellowish red • Coca-Cola "owns" red
Orange	Powerful, affordable, informal	• Draws attention quickly
Brown	Informal and relaxed, masculine, nature	• Coffee in a dark-brown can was "too strong" • Men seek products packaged in brown
White	Goodness, purity, chastity, cleanliness, delicacy, refinement, formality	• Suggests reduced calories • Pure and wholesome food • Clean, bath products, feminine
Black	Sophistication, power, authority, mystery	• Powerful clothing • High-tech electronics
Silver, Gold, Platinum	Regal, wealthy, stately	• Suggests premium price

Source: Schiffman and Kanuk, Table 5-9, p. 141. *Original source*: Bernice Kanner, "Color Schemes," *New York* magazine, April 3, 1989, pp. 22–23.

Let's Talk

What additional fashion businesses or individuals can you think of that are associated with certain colors? What personality characteristics do these colors convey?

To encourage consumers to want the newest in fashions, and to move along the product life cycle, the apparel and home furnishings industries introduce new color combinations each season. Coordinating this effort, color-forecasting organizations provide advance trend information to manufacturers, retailers, and the media, enabling them to synchronize production and promotion. These organizations include companies such as Color Box and the Color Marketing Group, and associations such as the Color Association of the United States (CAUS) and the International Color Authority (ICA).

In addition to the internal influences on consumer behavior, such as learning, motivation, attitude, and personality, that we have seen in Part II of this text, in Part III we will look at external factors such as family and society that constitute other revealing components of the why of the buy.

Summary

Our personalities are made up of those individual psychological characteristics that routinely influence the way we react to our surroundings. Four significant areas of personality theory are (1) Freud's psychoanalytic theory, (2) social-cultural theories, (3) self-concept theories, and (4) trait theories.

According to psychoanalytic theory, the unconscious, pleasure-seeking id often conflicts with the superego, or conscience; the realistic ego mediates these conflicts to create harmony. Since this activity occurs at the unconscious level and we may not be aware of the reasoning behind some purchase decisions, marketers use motivational research and focus groups in part to understand unconscious buying motives. Shared memories of the past, archetypes, can also influence our purchasing habits, as can the sense of superiority that some products strive to convey.

Social-cultural theories tell us that the conscious mind plays a big role in our decision making, and that our decision making may be compliant, aggressive, or detached. Each of these responses calls for a unique marketing approach, appealing to that specific characteristic.

Self-concept and self-image theories identify the many roles that humans play—that is, our multiple selves, such as student, employee, son, or daughter. Also, privately, our actual selves represent the way we are, and our ideal selves, the way we would like to be. Our social self-image is the way we appear to others; our ideal social self-image is the way we would like to appear to the world. Our self-esteem is made up of our positive and negative opinions of ourselves and our concept of self-worth. The term "extended selves" is used to describe the relationship between ourselves and our possessions.

Trait theories seek to examine and describe the distinct characteristics that distinguish us from others. Research in personality traits useful to fashion marketers includes (1) extroversion and introversion, (2) negativism, (3) desire for knowledge, (4) innovation and opinion leadership, (5) need for stimulation, and (6) need for affection, achievement, and power. For example, when offering new color combinations or fabric innovations, fashion marketers can key into consumer traits such as the desire for knowledge and the desire to innovate.

Products, and often the symbols representing them, also have personalities. Semiotics is the study of symbols and their meanings. Consumers express their personalities through the brand symbols they purchase. Advertisers often give brands human characteristics, called brand personification, in hopes that consumers will respond by purchasing those brands that relate to their personalities.

In creating product or brand personalities, marketers go through steps that include defining the target market and building a product personality to match. Color adds personality to products, and certain colors contain specific personality traits (for example, red represents excitement in some Western cultures). Each season the fashion industry offers a new color palette providing fresh product choices to consumers, keying in to consumer and brand personalities.

Key Terms

Actual self	Need for achievement
Archetypes	Need for affiliation
Brand personification	Need for cognition (NC)
Compulsive buying behavior	Need for power
Ego	Neurosis
Extended self	Optimal stimulation level (OSL)
Extroverts	Psychoanalytic theory
Fashion influentials	Self-concept
Fashion innovators	Self-concept theory
Id	Self-esteem
Ideal self	Semiotics
Ideal social self-image	Social self-image
Introverts	Superego
Motivational research	Traits
Multiple selves	

Questions for Review

1. Name and describe the three components of personality according to psychoanalytic theory.
2. What were Karen Horney's and Joel Cohen's respective contributions to the social-cultural theory of personality?
3. Explain the various "selves" in the self-concept theory. What is the relationship between self-concept and buying behavior?
4. Cite the six personality traits presented in the text, and for each identify a marketing strategy that fashion businesses might use to target that trait.

5. Why are many fashion goods marketers concerned with creating brand personalities for their products?

Activities

1. Select two apparel, home furnishings, or other fashion goods advertisements with origins in psychoanalytic theory, and two ads that stem from social-cultural theories. What is the main point of each ad?

2. With a classmate or by yourself, visit a fashion retail store where you are comfortable shopping and that appeals to your self-concept. Note the store layout and displays, the merchandise, and the salespeople. Determine how each of these elements enhances your self-concept. Then visit a store where you are not necessarily comfortable and that does not harmonize with your self-concept. Describe the displays, merchandise, and sales force, and contrast your findings from the second store with those of the first. Which store element has the greatest influence, positive or negative, on your self-concept? Why?

3. Develop a profile of a college student based on the selected traits described in this chapter. How might fashion businesses use this information?

4. Describe your color preferences for apparel and home furnishings. According to Table 6.3, how do these relate to your personality? Select five advertisements for apparel and/or home furnishings that appeal to you because of color, and state how the promotion matches your color preferences and personality. For more information on your color preferences, take an Internet color quiz such as the one given at www.colorquiz.com.

5. Describe two fashion brands that portray definite personalities. Explain the target market for each of these brands according to their brand personalities. State the relationship between the personality of the product and that of the targeted customer.

Mini-Project

Create a customer profile and corresponding brand personality with at least four components for each of two fashion brands within the same product classification, for example, jeans, men's suits, dining or living room sets.

References

1. Henry Asseal, *Consumer Behavior: A Strategic Approach* (Boston: Houghton Mifflin Company, 2004), p. 295.
2. Sigmund Freud—Life and Work: www.freudfile.org/

3. Eric Arnold et al., *Consumers*, Chapter 11 (New York: McGraw-Hill Higher Education, 2002).

4. Gianni Versace obituary, *The Guardian*, July 16, 1997.

5. Asseal.

6. Karen Horney, *Neurosis and Human Growth* (New York: Norton, 1950).

7. Joel B. Cohen, "An Interpersonal Orientation to the Study of Consumer Behavior," *Journal of Marketing Research* 4 (August 1967): 270–278; P. K. Tyagi, "Validation of the CAD Instrument: A Replication," in *Advances in Consumer Research* (Association for Consumer Research, Ann Arbor, Michigan) 10, (1983): 112–114.

8. Russell Belk, "Possessions and the Extended Self," *Journal of Consumer Research* 15 (September 1988): 139–168.

9. Amy J. Morgan, "The Evolving Self in Consumer Research," *Advances in Consumer Research* (Association for Consumer Research, Provo, Utah) 20 (1992): 429–432.

10. Carl G. Jung, *Man and His Symbols* (Garden City, NJ: Doubleday, 1964).

11. Todd A. Mooradian, "Personality and Ad-Evoked Feelings: The Case for Extraversion and Neuroticism," *Journal of the Academy of Marketing Science* 24 (Spring 1996): 99–109.

12. Susan Powell Mantel and Frank R. Kardes, "The Role of Direction of Comparison, Attribute-Based Processing, and Attitude-Based Processing in Consumer Preference," *Journal of Consumer Research* 25 (March 1999): 335–352.

13. Leon J. Schiffman and Leslie L. Kanuk, *Consumer Behavior,* 8th ed. (Upper Saddle River, NJ: Pearson Prentice Hall, 2004), p. 131.

14. Evelyn J. Brannon, *Fashion Forecasting,* 2nd ed. (New York: Fairchild Publications, Inc., 2005), p. 92.

15. Elaine Stone, *The Dynamics of Fashion,* 2nd ed. (New York: Fairchild Publications, Inc., 2004), pp. 59–61.

16. P. S. Rajou, "Optimum Stimulation Levels in Relationship to Personality, Demographics and Exploratory Behavior," *Journal of Consumer Research* 7 (December 1980): 273.

17. Marvin Zuckerman, *Sensation Seeking: Beyond the Optimal Level of Arousal* (Hillsdale, NJ: Lawrence Erlbaum, 1979).

18. Jan-Benedict, E. M. Steenkamp, and Hans Baumgartner, "The Role of Optimum Stimulation Level in Exploratory Consumer Behavior," *Journal of Consumer Research* 19 (December 1992): 434–448.

19. D. G. Winter and A. J. Stewart, "The Power Motive," in H. London and J. Exner (eds.) *Dimensions of Personality* (New York: Wiley, 1978).

20. Gordon R. Foxall and Ronald E. Goldsmith, "Personality and Consumer Research: Another Look," *Journal of Marketing Research Society* 30, no. 2 (April 1988): 111–125.

21. Alan R. Hirsch, *What Flavor Is Your Personality?* (Naperville, IL: Sourcebooks, Inc., 2001).

22. www.idsa.org/idea 2005/b.1082.htm.

23. David A. Aaker, *Building Strong Brands* (Riverside, NJ: Free Press, 1995).

24. Jennifer L. Aaker, "Dimensions of Brand Personality," *Journal of Marketing Research* 35 (August 1997): 352.

25. Marshal Cohen, *Why Customers Do What They Do* (New York: McGraw-Hill Companies, 2006).

26. www.indiaco.com/resource-center/building-brands-personality.html.

27. Ibid.

28. Cohen, p. 33.

29. www.aedo-to.com/eng/library/aedo-02/art06.html.

PART III

External Factors Influence Fashion Consumers

Obviously, consumers do not make buying decisions in a vacuum. In addition to internal motivations, outside influences have a profound effect on fashion consumers—the focus of Part III.

Chapter 7 discusses the roles that family, friends, and other groups and events play in influencing consumers' purchasing behavior. The social and cultural elements of the media, technology, and fashion are examined in Chapter 8, and Chapter 9 describes how marketers create profiles of consumers, using demographics, psychographics, and value-driven behaviors to target an ideal customer audience for their products.

MARRIEDS
Preteens
HUSBAN

MARRIEDS
Preteens
HUSBA

MARRIEDS
Preteens
HUSBAN

MARRIEDS
Preteens
HUSBA

CHAPTER 7

Age, Family, and Life Cycle Influences

The makeup of the American population is changing. Americans vary greatly in their attitudes, opinions, and lifestyles, and appear to be splintering into more and more diverse groups with more and more distinct behaviors and purchasing practices. What does this mean for marketers? Will a time come when marketers will have to anticipate and accommodate the desires of an even greater variety of consumers, with needs, attitudes, values, and expectations so vast that eventually there will be product and service options too numerous to count, and target markets so disparate that consumer researchers will continuously be identifying new groups and looking for new and better ways to satisfy them? What a nightmare!

The Changing Face of the American Consumer

Guess what? That time is already here! In addition to the fact that shopping habits vary among people of different ethnicities, occupations, geographical regions, ages, cultures,

FIGURE 7.1.

and educational backgrounds (see Chapter 9 for detailed profiles of various market segments), through the media we also learn about consumers categorized in groups such as Gen Xers, yuppies, metrosexuals, boomers, tweens, and so on. It seems that every few months a new group of buyers with unique preferences emerges, often identified by age and/or family life cycle.

❯ ❯ ❯ SPECIAL FOCUS 7.1: AMERICAN CONSUMERS: THE WORLD'S BIGGEST SPENDERS ❮ ❮ ❮

Americans are the biggest spenders on the planet. Collectively, U.S. consumers spend more each week than the annual gross domestic product of Finland.

Will U.S. consumers continue to consume as they have in the past decade? Or will they—horrors!—get real and start living within their means?

Ascent of the Mass Affluent

During the past decade, the number of U.S. homes valued at more than half a million dollars tripled to more than 6 million units. And now more than 5 million American homeowners—about 5% of households—own two or more homes. During that same period, the median value of stock portfolios at least tripled for about 22 million U.S. households.

The number of U.S. households that spend more than $100,000 a year on everything—with lots of money for expensive second homes and worldwide travel—is growing by more than 7% a year compared with an overall household growth rate of around 1%. These households, when combined with the really big spenders, are what we call the mass affluent.

They're growing rapidly and account for a disproportionate share of consumer spending. The U.S. Bureau of Labor Statistics reports that only 13% of households it surveyed had an annual income of $100,000 or more, but those households accounted for almost half of all consumer spending on jewelry, other lodging and related travel expenses.

The influence of the mass affluent on our consumer economy extends well beyond their personal household spending. Transitioning from a manufacturing-based economy to a more knowledge-based one has meant greater reliance on intellectual capital instead of factory equipment capital.

If our nation's intellectual-capital assets can spread fast enough, then the mass-affluent segment of consumers will continue to grow at least as rapidly as it has in the recent past and sustain our consumer economy for years to come.

Aging Baby Boomers

Baby boomers have created more wealth than any preceding generation in part because of their cohort size (78 million Americans born 1946–64; 26% of the population), but in large part because so many them went to college. The best-educated men in America are 55- to 59-year-old baby boomers. But the oldest boomers are turning 60, and some people are starting to worry about them.

There have been more than a few articles about looming economic collapse because baby boomers are on the verge of retiring. The story line is that they will sell their stocks and their big homes, and stop spending as they wait for the end. Anyone who's paid attention to boomer behavior over the past several decades knows that nothing of the sort is likely to happen.

Baby boomers have delayed or transformed every life-stage transition they've ever been involved with, and they're likely to do the same for retirement. They will almost certainly delay retiring.

The average income for households headed by 50- to 59-year-olds is $75,000 a year. In many cases, they're making more than that and enjoying their work. For millions of older baby boomers, the pressure to retire won't be as great as the desire to maintain their present income and present lifestyle.

The long-term trend toward early retirement has reversed. Today about 65% of men and 50% of women aged 60–64 are in the work force. But at ages 65–69, that percentage drops to 37% of men and 29% of women.

During the next 10 years, baby boomers will fill that sixty-something space. That will mean another 9 million workers aged 60-69 who will add at least $400 billion a year to consumer spending.

>>> Source: Peter Francese, "American Consumers: The World's Biggest Spenders." www.AdAge.com, January 10, 2006.

Age Influences Purchasing Behavior

There is one variable that appears to govern both the customer preferences and the marketing strategies discussed in each of the scenarios in Point of View 7.1. That variable is age. Age is one of the biggest determinants of what people want; with changes in age come changes in the products and services a person seeks. Think of a boy you know. At age 3 he only wanted toy cars, at 4 he wanted to be Superman, at age 5 it was Spider-man, and at 6 the Power Rangers ruled. Each age brings different priorities and desires.

⟩ ⟩ ⟩ POINT OF VIEW 7.1: PURCHASING PATTERNS AND MARKETING PRACTICES IN DIFFERENT SEGMENTS OF THE POPULATION ⟨ ⟨ ⟨

The Kaiser Family Foundation recently completed a study on *advergames*, product promotions in the form of Internet games that food manufacturers are putting on their Web sites to sell cereals and fast food products to children. The findings showed that three quarters of the 77 product Web sites and 4,000 Web pages visited encourage kids to play endlessly in an interactive name brand world. Nearly 40 percent of the sites offered incentives for children to purchase food to collect points, which they can exchange for access to other games or gifts. A quarter of the Web sites enabled kids to sign up for new products, special offers, and upcoming commercials. Only half required parental permission, and almost two-thirds of the sites encouraged users to e-mail friends about the products.

> ⟩⟩⟩ Source: Goldstein, David. "Food Makers' Web Sites Market Products to Pint-Sized Customers, McClatchy Newspapers, July 19, 2006.

Women 35 and older accounted for about half of the $101.6 billion total spent on women's clothing from March 2005 to February 2006, according to The NPD Group, a consumer and retail information company.

> ⟩⟩⟩ Source: Amie Streater. "Stylish after 35," *Columbus Dispatch*, June 26, 2006.

Once, pregnancy was viewed primarily as an awkward condition to be endured with grace and modesty. Today women flaunt their pregnancies, showing them off with low-slung jeans, baby doll dresses, and belly-baring tops. Total maternity wear sales are said to have jumped 28 percent from 2000 to 2005; this is largely attributed to the fact that expectant mothers over 30 are now a sizable portion of the 5.5 million women a year who buy or receive maternity clothing.

> ⟩⟩⟩ Source: Ruth La Ferla, "Showing? It's Time to Show Off," *New York Times*, June 8, 2006.

Some 10,000 baby boomers turn 50 every day, and they are entering their later years with lots of money and adventurous spirits. That's why more and more companies are developing products just for them. Home Depot offers free home improvement clinics for people over 50, which include ideas for turning rooms vacated by children into great new spaces. Procter & Gamble's Olay division promotes anti-wrinkle treatments to them, and P&G's drug division has more than 30 products aimed at the 50-plus crowd. And AARP (American Association of Retired People), originally a not-for-profit organization, is now developing its own products for the 50-plus crowd, which include an investment fund for people over 50, senior friendly cell phones, and easy to open luggage.

>>> Source: Claudia Deutsch, "AARP Wants You (to Buy Its Line of Products)," *New York Times*. October 28, 2005.

Disney officials kicked off the CTIA Wireless 2006 cell phone convention by touting its *Disney Mobile Phone Service*, which includes tools that allow parents to monitor and control calls by family members, and a Global Positioning System locator that can provide real-time maps and addresses of family members. [Note: In 2006 approximately 45 percent of 13-year-olds owned a cell phone.]

>>> Source: Ryan Kim. "Disney to Market Phones: New Devices Will Let Parents Restrict Use, Keep Tabs on Kids," *San Francisco Chronicle*, www.SFGate.com. April 6, 2006.

Not that long ago, the "birth to 12" age group was quite satisfied with a variety of colorful toys, including dump trucks, bicycles, dolls, and the like. However, current research indicates that marketers should no longer approach this age group as a whole, but should treat it as four distinct segments: newborns to 3-year-olds, 3- to 5-year-olds, 5- to 8-year-olds, and 8- to 12-year-olds. Why? Because members of each of these age groups demonstrate very different preferences. Today's children differ from their parents in that they are much more technologically savvy; they've grown up in a world with ready access to gaming gadgetry and Internet connections. When marketing to members of these age groups, it is important to focus on the new media available, as well as the products themselves. Of course, products and marketing campaigns still should be fun; after all, no matter how techno-savvy they are, 3- to 12-year-olds are still children.

〉〉〉 POINT OF VIEW 7.2: STUDIES OF TEENS HINT WRISTWATCH MAY BE GOING WAY OF THE SUNDIAL 〈〈〈

Is time running out for the wristwatch?

Surveys and sales numbers show that young shoppers are shunning watches for snazzier time-telling gadgets, such as cellphones and iPods.

For many in the cellphone generation, watches now seem about as relevant as grandfather clocks. Bare wrists were plentiful last week at The Lab, a Costa Mesa, Calif., shopping center that caters to teens and young adults. Shoppers dived into purses or pockets to retrieve cellphones when a reporter casually asked the time.

Kamlyn Snyder said she hasn't worn a watch since she plucked one from a cereal box many years ago.

"The inconvenience of strapping it on in the morning," said the 21-year-old student. "My grandma does; that's how she tells time. She's not that old. She's, like, 60, but still . . ."

Many older people, too, would make the cellphone their primary timepiece if it didn't mean digging around for their reading glasses, said Marshal Cohen, chief industry analyst for market research firm The NPD Group, which tracks consumer trends.

"Once the cellphone manufacturers recognize that not everybody has X-ray vision, they'll begin to make the cellphone clock a little bit bigger and it will very quickly replace the fashion watch as the No. 1 timepiece," he said.

>>> Source: Leslie Earnest, "Wristwatches Get the Back of the Hand," April 16, 2006, *Los Angeles Times*, p. A1.

Generally speaking, today's 13- to 17-year-olds have developed a view of consumption that differs from their parents. Teenagers are now much more accustomed to being the target of sales pitches, and tend to be more aware and sometimes skeptical of sales techniques as a result. And because today's teens are accustomed to multitasking and are besieged by competing advertising and other promotional devices, marketers need to position products in ways that really stand out; otherwise, they'll just become part of the clutter that teens have learned to ignore. Knowing what's important to teenagers (customization, green products, online networking) enables marketers to develop tactics and strategies that help them connect with this age group. Businesses have a greater chance of getting teens' attention when they use methods highlighting teens' interests and habits.

> > > SPECIAL FOCUS 7.2: MARKETERS GET THEIR MASCOTS IN ON ACTION AT MYSPACE < < <

Who knew being square was cool?

On MySpace.com, Wendy's cartoon marketing mascot Smart has more than 81,000 "friends" who've linked to his page and posted notes such as, "i luv u."

In his profile, the Wendy's burger-patty-shaped icon lists metal music, Angelina

Jolie, and TV show 24 as interests. Favorite nosh: Wendy's bacon mushroom melt. Hero: Wendy's founder Dave Thomas, of course.

Smart is an example of how marketers are riding the online community craze: seeding social-networking sites with faux profiles to connect with consumers.

Among others with profiles for ad characters:

- Wendy's rival Burger King has a MySpace page for its "king."
- Columbia Pictures posted a profile for Ricky Bobby, the fictional NASCAR racer played by Will Ferrell in the studio's *Talladega Nights.*
- News Corp. sibling FX, the cable channel, even has a MySpace profile for The Carver, a serial killer from its *Nip/Tuck* TV show. Joan Crawford and George Steinbrenner are among The Carver's heroes.

Many of the faux profiles, including the FX listing, are paid deals with Fox Interactive Media, the News Corp. unit that sells advertising on MySpace. Buyers get fancy features for the page, and the profile is promoted on the site to other users with banner ads and text links. The cost ranges from $100,000 to more than $1 million, depending on the page's technical complexity and the level of MySpace promotion, says Michael Barrett, chief revenue officer at Fox Interactive.

Paid profiles aren't the only corporate fiction on MySpace, however. Other companies post profiles for free, the way any other user can. Volkswagen put up a profile for Helga, the sexy engineer from its commercials. Among her likes: "the smell of gasoline."

MySpace says it monitors unpaid commercial profiles and has taken down some down. A firm no-no: directly selling products from the page. (Also banned sitewide are offensive content, profanity and nudity.)

There Are Risks

Limiting the number of commercial messages is "critical" for social-networking sites, says Max Kale Hoff, vice president of marketing at Nielsen BuzzMetrics, which tracks consumer-generated content on the Web.

Advertisers also take a risk: The goal of most marketing profiles is to draw in those coveted "friends" and build buzz, but marketers have to accept that not all the buzz will be positive.

"There's a fine line for most marketers when they venture into the social media space," Barrett says. "You're going to hear all sorts of feedback . . . Sometimes it's not going to be all that flattering, but that's what makes it even more genuine."

MySpace offers more-intense monitoring for ad clients and removes negative postings on request.

"We monitor it, but we don't control it," says Ian Rowden, Wendy's chief mar-

FIGURE 7.2. There are many buyers in all phases of the family life cycle whose needs and wants are studied by consumer researchers.

keting officer. "It's a social dialogue. If we took the posts down, it would send a message that's not consistent with the character."

Ads OK If You Make Them Fun

Eliza Madison, a 20-year-old student at Fordham University in New York, hasn't connected her MySpace profile to any corporate sites yet but says she doesn't mind that marketers mix business with pleasure.

"It's a good way of using the network if they make (the profiles) funny and people enjoy it," she says. "But they have to do it in a way that it doesn't make you feel like you're being attacked by the company to go out and buy their stuff."

>>> Source: Laura Petrecca, "Marketers Get Their Mascots in on Action at MySpace." *USA Today* August 30, 2006. Retrieved on August 31, 2007, from www.usatoday.com/money/advertising/2006-08-30-myspace-usat_x.htm.

The 18 to 34 market segment includes those who were raised on MTV and are old enough to remember the 9/11 tragedy, as well as the challenges brought about by increases in gas prices, the Iraq war, and other unrest in the Middle East, all of which have left them with feelings of insecurity. Members of this market segment tend to look for value in the products they buy, and seek items that are environmentally safe, connected to a cause, and community friendly. For example, shopping at the local farmers' market allows them to feel socially responsible. Of course, like any other sizable segment, this group has diverse members, but for marketers' purposes, 18 to 34-year-olds share a common attraction to well-designed, well-performing products that imply luxury, but are of good value.

The 35 to 54 generation is characterized by both spending a lot and spending carefully. Most have the money for purchases, so price is not necessarily the deciding factor, even though many are still raising children. Members of this market segment are also quite capable of using technology, and their purchasing habits reflect that. Other priorities for people in this age group include fitness, health, and adventure. Marketing efforts directed at this group should appeal to their desired state of well-being and their focus on "getting out there and doing things," such as taking exotic trips and participating in extreme sports. Members of this group also buy second homes.

The 55-plus generation is generally thinking about retirement, and seeking fulfillment or self-actualization (see Chapter 4 for a discussion of Maslow's Hierarchy of Human Needs). Many are energetic and prosperous, and want to hold off old age as long as they can. Thus, they are giving marketers opportunities in the areas of

Table 7.1. "Buy Words"—Marketing Approaches That Appeal to Different Age Groups

Phase	Phrase
Teens	This is what you *need* in order to *belong*.
Twenties	This is what your *friends expect of you*.
Thirties	This is for a *good, solid person like you*.
Forties	This is what the *pros and experts* buy.
Fifties	This is something to *judge for yourself.*
Sixties+	This is very *effective and economical.*

Source: www.wcupa.edu/_Academics/sch_cas.psy/CareerPaths/Consumer/

finance, hospitality, and wellness. Products and services that promise to keep them youthful are in high demand. Many people in this group have enjoyed the benefits of higher education, real estate investments, and so on, but they are still concerned about the future. After all, living longer could increase their need for extended care. Today's marketers are hurrying to accommodate seniors who inevitably will become less mobile as they reach their eighties.[1] Product enhancements for the home, such as easily accessible bathtubs, special lighting, safer kitchen equipment, and elder-friendly technology are all intended to meet the needs of older consumers.

Data on population trends, age-related preferences, and all of the other valuable information supplied to marketers by consumer researchers enables companies to develop new products and services in a timely manner, advertise in media most likely to be accessed and trusted by their target markets, devise persuasive and effective promotions (including making prices appear more appealing), and ultimately move goods and services into the hands of consumers more efficiently. Marketers also have to learn the special language cues that can evoke responses from members of different age groups. At each stage of life, there are certain words that hold greater meaning than they did in the past or might in the future; using those words effectively can be an important marketing tool. This idea of "a phrase for a phase" is illustrated in Table 7.1.

Family Influences on Consumer Behavior

There are a multitude of powerful forces that help determine purchasing behavior, most of which derive from observing the actions of various **reference groups**, any person or group serving as a point of comparison or frame of reference for an individual when that individual is forming his own beliefs and behaviors. (See Chapter 8 for an in-depth discussion of reference groups.) The first and primary reference group a child uses to gauge his behavior is the family. No matter what your age, you can probably remember a time when you were a child, shopping with your parents or grandparents, and how you were expected to behave. Perhaps you had to dress up a little to go to a fancy store. Maybe you were told in advance that you would not be getting a toy during that visit—and that there would be no whining or else you'd be taken straight home. Or you might have been asked what you thought about a certain item and then treated to ice cream for being "good." Consumer researchers have discovered that the behaviors and values parents teach their children and continuously reinforce as they grow are the ones that will guide them through their teens and into adulthood. Although children have numerous experiences each day outside the home, the family remains the strongest influence.

FIGURE 7.3. Families today take on many forms and are more aptly termed "households" by consumer researchers.

> > > SPECIAL FOCUS 7.3: PARENTS BUY CASHMERE FOR INFANTS AND TODDLERS < < <

As couples wait longer to have children and raise smaller families on higher salaries, they are spending more on their kids. A lot more.

The market for expensive baby fashions and accessories is booming, according to Michael Silverstein, vice president of Boston Consulting Group. He estimates the high-end baby market at $45 billion, growing at a 10 percent annual rate over the last decade.

Over the past 30 years, the average family size has dropped to about 3.2 people, from 3.6 people, while inflation-adjusted family incomes have risen 50 percent, according to Boston Consulting's analysis of U.S. census data. And the number of first-time mothers age 40 and older has tripled in the decade that ended in 1997, according to the National Center for Health Statistics.

All these dynamics are helping offset a financial crunch caused by rising interest rates and fears about job security as well as the higher energy prices.

"We see a growing population and that bodes well for infant apparel," said Matt Nitowski, a director for global franchise management at Disney's consumer products unit. He added that he saw no direct risks to the luxury segment's growth.

Disney, known for its movies and theme parks, has contracted with premium infant clothing maker Icky Baby to make $90 cashmere rompers that are being pitched to high-end department stores like Saks Inc.

"People are spending more and they want their kids to look good," said Kate Somerset, president of Icky Products. "We play into that trend."

But what happens when an 18-month-old spits up on his or her cashmere sweater?

>>> Source: Chelsea Emery, "Parents Grab Up High-End Duds for the Playpen Set," *Washington Post,* August 15, 2006, p. C2.

Today's Family

Traditionally, a **family** is defined as a group of individuals who live together and are related either by blood, adoption, or marriage. Some of these groups are **nuclear:** the father, mother, and children live together; some are **extended:** grandparents, aunts, uncles, and other relatives may also live with the nuclear family. Curiously, although many people in the United States view the nuclear family as "typical," it is by no means the norm. In fact, that traditional view of the American family does not represent many of the groups of people who live together today. Rather, today's "family" is more often thought of as a **household**, a term that refers to any single person or a group of persons who live together in a residential setting, regardless of whether they are related. Many researchers agree that the American family began to change soon after World War II, when married women began working outside the home and sought increased earnings. This reduced the demand for children and encouraged a substitution for motherhood.[2] Additional reasons for changes in family structure include increased acceptance of both cohabitation without marriage and nonmarital births. For example, children born to unmarried women accounted for 3.8 percent of recorded births in 1940, while in 2003 it was 35.7 percent.[3]

Many different kinds of households exist, including the traditional nuclear family, single-parent families, step-families, heterosexual and homosexual couples, single people who are roommates, married couples without children or whose children are not living at home, elderly parents who live with their grown children. Needless to say, the family of today takes many forms.

Marketers obviously need to keep track of the ongoing evolution of the modern household. As the composition of the family changes, the needs and wants of each household change—hence, the rise of furniture stores that cater to singles, resorts that target families, communities exclusively for retirees, and do-it-yourself classes for women who take care of their own cars and build their own sundecks.

< < < **POINT OF VIEW 7.3: TOOLS DESIGNED**
JUST FOR WOMEN > > >

Barbara Kavovit, a single mother, is successfully marketing herself as a home-repair expert with a sleek set of tool kits for women who want to be their own "handy men."

Her tools are designed to better fit a woman's size and strength, such as lighter hammers with female friendly curves and screwdrivers with thumb rests that are easy to handle.

Prior to her divorce and as owner of a Manhattan construction company, her income was over $1 million several years. But after September 11, 2001, the company crashed, leaving her millions of dollars in debt, scared, and feeling inade-quate, especially when her son would ask her to do certain things, like put up a basketball net.

She was fortunate to have a background in construction, but she realized other women needed help too. She also knew that a growing number of women were buying homes without men and needed some manly skills for small tasks. So she went to work designing tools. Soon, she had a display window at a Fifth Avenue department store and contracts with Home Depot Inc., Bed Bath & Beyond Inc. and Target Corp. She says she is determined to continue to make women's lives easier.

>>> Source: Larry Neumeister, *Columbus Dispatch*, August 7, 2006.

Regardless of composition, the spending patterns of household members primarily depend on age, income, the members' relationships to one another, and the presence or absence of children. These factors are all part of the con-sumer decision-making process, which involves multiple influences and steps. (See Chapter 11 for an in-depth discussion of decision making.) For now, however, we will focus our attention on the family, since it is the primary influencer and the unit that teaches each member the skills eventually needed to make buying decisions.

The Primary Functions of a Family

The family, no matter its size and composition, has two main functions:

1. To create security (emotional and economic)
2. To educate and socialize the children

Both functions include preparing children for the future. Encouragement of positive qualities, self-respect, confidence, and the satisfaction of basic needs (as discussed in Chapter 4) all contribute to feelings of security, a sense of safety. Families educate and socialize children through **socialization,** the process of teaching the skills, attitudes, and general knowledge necessary for a person to effectively integrate into society. From a consumer behavior standpoint, socialization also includes conveying to children the specific skills and knowledge needed to function as consumers in the marketplace. The socialization process continues throughout adulthood. The task is ongoing and changes as the family or household evolves; it appears to be changing as our society evolves, as well.

Let's Talk

Are there specific skills we all have to learn in order to become productive members of society? What knowledge must we possess in order to successfully interact with others in settings such as classrooms, stores, sporting events, and so on?

The Family Life Cycle, Defined and Redefined

The **traditional family life cycle** comprises the time-honored stages through which people predictably progress as they age (see Table 7.2); it has been used by marketers for decades as a guideline for the development of new products and the creative strategies used to sell those products. However, more and more people belong to **nontraditional families,** like blended step-families or same-sex parents raising children; therefore, for this textbook, we have reworked and expanded these stages to create a representation of the twenty-first-century family life cycle (see Table 7.3) in hopes of making the stages more relevant for today's marketing professionals.

Table 7.2. The Traditional Family Life Cycle

Stage	Description
I	**Bachelorhood**—Single, no longer living with parents
II	**Honeymooner**—Newly married
III	**Full Nester**—Parenthood, raising children of varying ages (infants to teenagers)
IV	**Empty Nester**—Post-parenthood, children have left home (parents are still working or newly retired)
V	**Dissolution**—One spouse dies, the widow(er) survives and lives alone

Table 7.3. The Twenty-First-Century Family Life Cycle

Stage	Description
I	**Child/Teen**—Living with parent(s), dependent
II	**Single/Independent**—Usually young, dating, lives in residence separate from parents for first time, beginning career or job, answers only to self
III	**New Couple/Partnership**—Living together, adjusting to life together, two incomes usually allow for a comfortable lifestyle
IV	**Mid-Adulthood**
	A. Parenthood—Three scenarios:
	P-1—Raising young children, under age 6
	P-2—Raising children, ages 6–12
	P-3—Raising teenagers
	At any point in Stage IV, the following variations can be introduced:
	V-1—*Separation*: Creates single-parent household
	V-2—*Re-coupling*: Single parent remarries, introducing step-parent to household
	V-3—*Blending*: Step-siblings introduced to household
	B. Partners without children—Partners do not become parents
	C. Single household—Individual remains independent, does not partner
V	**Empty Nest** (Two phases)
	Phase 1—*Send-off*: Children have left home, adult(s) still working, looking forward to new experiences
	Phase 2—*Retirement*: Adult(s) no longer working, slower pace is adopted
VI	**Dissolution**—One partner dies; remaining partner lives alone or with adult children and possibly grandchildren (infants to teenagers)

Note: This discussion of households and life cycles refers primarily to those in the United States. In other countries, the family relationships and the obligations of the members can be very different (see Chapter 14 for more information).

Source: © Stefani Bay, 2006.

Different Stages, Different Needs and Products

Regardless of whether marketers are targeting members of a traditional or a nontraditional family, two ideas are clear:

1. The various stages of the life cycle create different needs, resulting in different allotments of available money, and different buying behaviors and patterns, all of which lead to the purchase of very different kinds of products and services.

2. For each life cycle stage, marketers must not only develop new products, but also new marketing strategies, since what attracts a person in the midst of one stage might not interest him or her during another.

> > > POINT OF VIEW 7.4: TWO VIEWS OF THE TRADITIONAL FAMILY LIFE CYCLE < < <

I. Family Life Cycle—A Psycho-Social Approach

The emotional and intellectual stages one passes through, from childhood to the retirement years, as a member of a family. In each stage, one faces challenges in his/her family life that result in the development of new skills.

Not everyone passes through these stages smoothly. Mastering the skills and milestones of each state allows people to successfully move from one stage of development to the next. If one doesn't master the skills, he/she may still move into the next phase, but is more likely to have difficulty with relationships and future transitions. Fortunately, if skills are not gained in one stage, they can still be learned in later stages.

>>> *Source:* www.everettclinic.com/kbase/topic/special/ty617/sec1.htm.

II. Family Life Cycle—A Consumer Behavior Approach

A sociological concept that describes changes in families across time. Emphasis is placed on the effects of marriage, divorce, births, and deaths on families and the changes in income and consumption through various family stages.

Families account for a very large percentage of all consumer expenditures. Much of this spending is systematic and stems from natural needs that change as a family unit goes through its natural stages of life. These range from the *young single* and the *newly married* stages to the *full nest* as the children are born and grow, to the *empty nest* and the final *solitary survivor* stage. Each transition prompts changes in values and behavior.”

>>> *Source:* American Marketing Association, family life cycle” entry in *Dictionary of Marketing Terms*, www.marketingpower.com/mg-dictionary-view3937.php.

Needs and wants are fluid during each life cycle stage; what might be viewed as superfluous during one stage could be seen as a necessity during the other, and vice versa. Consider the following list of products and services. Which do you think a person in the initial stage of parenthood would consider a top priority? Which product or service would be a top priority for someone in the empty-nest stage, or a person in the single household stage?

- Car
- Digital camera
- Bed linens
- Personal trainer
- Patio furniture
- Handbag
- Investment opportunity
- Stain remover stick
- Health care plan
- Subscription to GQ

And with so many types of different household scenarios now common throughout American society, how can marketers determine which household members are actually making the final purchasing decisions?

Let's Talk

Do you live with another person, or more than one? How do you make purchasing decisions? Who ultimately decides what to buy when it comes to shared items?

Household Roles in the Family Decision-Making and Purchasing Process

In your family, who decides what to buy? Is it your mother or your father? Your younger sibling? Is it the person who's the most aware of what's new and exciting? Or is it the one who speaks with the loudest voice?

Suppose your family was thinking about buying another car. Who would have the last word on make, model, style, color, special features: the person who was paying for the car, or the one who would be driving it? Or would you decide by family vote? Suppose your mother knew very little about flat-screen TVs, but you really wanted her to buy one. How would you approach her? Would you try to explain the benefits of owning one, or maybe have your persuasive sibling talk to her instead? Or would you just have to be satisfied with the flat screen you watch on weekends at your dad's house?

Each household does things differently, of course, but as a unit, all members must participate in some way, so together they can function as a whole. Developing positive interdependence is the key. In other words, members learn to operate as a team. In most households each member has a certain role to play in the decision-making process, whether conscious or unconscious. A **role** can be defined as the behavior expected of a person in a given setting. Roles are often performed automatically, but sometimes they change. The kinds of issues a person in a dominant role in a household might decide typically involve a child's bedtime and how chores are delegated (for example, who will wash the dishes, walk the dog, mow the lawn and so on.).

Additionally, each household member usually plays a certain role regarding buying decisions, although these roles may shift slightly, depending on the product sought. Five primary roles exist in regard to consumption in a given household; each role is described in Table 7.4. A single member might assume several roles, depending on the size of the household, the particular shopping context (supermarket, hardware store, boutique), or even the prevailing cultural attitudes (for example, a male should have a more dominant role than a female).

Consumer researchers have found that the household decision-making process can sometimes cause tension and conflict resulting from numerous issues, including disagreements about how limited funds should be spent. In large families, two or more members might share a role, and in smaller households, one person might act in more than one capacity. Additionally, the person who uses the product isn't necessarily the one who actually buys the product. When conflicts arise, the role of the ultimate decision maker can be difficult because that person has the responsibility and power to determine what, where, when, which product, whether to buy, and how much to spend.

Let's Talk

Why should marketers be concerned about which members play which roles in household purchasing decisions (for example, husband vs. wife or teen vs. grandparent)? How could marketers apply information about household decision-making roles to create more effective marketing strategies?

Household Decision Making Today

When it comes to purchasing practices in the modern household, consumer researchers have detected several new patterns. Most important are the changes in decision-making styles and **consumption roles,** the expected/prescribed behaviors of consumers within a household. In the past, fathers traditionally served multiple roles as **information gatherers** (also called influencers), providers of information and guidance to other family members about products, services, newness, and availability; **gatekeepers,** those who screen and control access to product information and can veto purchases; and **decision makers,** who ultimately determine, with or without input of other members, which items will be considered, purchased, and how they will be used and discarded. Mothers might have participated with fathers as **purchasers,** those who actually make product purchases, and, along with children, shared usage with fathers (those who actually consume the products or services are called **users**).

Today, however, household members often collaborate when it comes to purchases and prefer a certain amount of interaction during the decision-making process. Preteens and teenagers are increasingly becoming information gatherers, influencers, purchasers, and users.

There are several reasons for this shift in consumer behavior. Primary is the change in the makeup of the U.S. household. As previously mentioned, the traditional family is no longer the norm. Often both parents/partners work, and children are more likely—and more able—to discover new products and/or product advancements simply because they have more unregulated free time.

Second is the daily barrage and evolution of media. We now live in the Information Age; not only is more information available, but there are many more ways to access that information than ever before. Some older household members might be uncomfortable with technology, electronics, and the latest gadgets, so they depend more on younger members for new information. For example, your grandmother probably isn't interested in accessing her e-mail through her cell phone, but she wants an e-mail address so she can get photos from family members who live in another state.

Much of today's marketing and advertising is targeted directly at children. Of course, marketing to kids is not new; since the early 1900s, characters from the world of entertainment (such as Shirley Temple, Superman, and Davy Crockett) have endorsed products for children in print, movies, and on TV. However, the Internet has become a more powerful advertising medium than any of those vehicles. (See Point of View 7.1.) Through "advergames," a product-placement strategy that uses digital game-like entertainment organized around images and references to specific products, marketers like Kellogg's, Hershey's, and Burger King can reach kids with Web features that appear to be entertainment but are actually marketing communications.[4]

Whether or not this is good for society, or even ethical, is debated extensively by consumer groups, who feel that these efforts are destructive and

FIGURE 7.4. The role of the ultimate decision maker can be difficult.

Table 7.4.   The Five Primary Consumption Roles of Household Decision Makers

Household Role	Accompanying Behaviors
Information gatherer/influencer	Provides information/guidance to other members about products/services, newness, and availability
Gatekeeper	Screens/controls household members' access to product information; can veto purchases
Decision maker	Ultimately decides, with or without input of other members, which items will be considered, purchased, and how they will be used and disposed of
Purchaser	Secures/buys product(s)
User	Consumes (uses) product(s)

should be stopped because young children do not have the ability to discriminate between games and marketing devices that offer inducements to buy.

A third factor that has contributed to changing consumer behavior in the market-place is the growing influence of young people, many of whom have definite ideas about how to express gender, political ideals, affiliations, creativity, and independence through their belongings—especially their clothing and accessories. Certainly young people have long differentiated themselves from the rest of society by wearing certain types of products (think raccoon coats of the 1920s and black eyeliner of the 1960s), but today those under the age of 18 generally have much more input into purchases and can substantially affect how household members spend their free time (for example, where they will go for vacation, which movies or TV shows they will watch, at what restaurants they will have dinner). They also can influence where household members buy products, such as toys and electronics, and can also help decide which actual products will be purchased. Furthermore, many preteens and teenagers today have more ready access to money than in the past (courtesy of debit and ATM cards) and are willing to spend it to convey their uniqueness and personal style.

⟩ ⟩ ⟩ SPECIAL FOCUS 7.4: STUDY SAYS RETAILERS UNHIP TO YOUNG SHOPPERS ⟨ ⟨ ⟨

If retail marketers are going to capture the loyalty of the next generation of spenders, they're going to have to get hip to the new Web, according to a report from Forrester Research.

Always Online

Young shoppers break into two distinct age groups, under 18 and 18 to 21 years old. While the over 18 crowd has more money to spend—

US$193 a month, compared to $76—both market segments have one thing in common.

"They're always online," Forrester reported. "The majority of both groups have broadband at home and go online daily. The online behavior of older teens illustrates that this is a generation that has hardly known life without the Web."

Selling to young shoppers is challenging marketers because the buying segment leans so much on the wired word.

"Just as teens bring along friends to the mall, they find ways to incorporate their friends into online research," the report said. "They use tools like 'e-mail a friend' links on retail sites, wish lists, and IM when shopping to get purchasing help from friends."

"The majority of all teens also seek out social content and shopping tools like consumer ratings on Shopzilla and Shopping.com and reviews and peer-to-peer sales channels like eBay and Craigslist," the report added.

They also are great users of search engines, according to Vikram Sehgal, research director for Jupiter Research in New York City. "Across the different age groups, they're the most likely to use search engines," he told *E-Commerce Times*. "So search engine marketing would be a very effective tool in reaching this age group."

Promotions that work with teens, [the Forrester report] said, include advergames, instant-win games, online coupons, streaming video ads and cell phone promotions.

Loyal . . . to a Point

Forrester's analysts also disparaged the notion that most young shoppers are fickle.

"Although they admit to shopping around before making a purchase, more than half of both younger and older teens agree that when they find a brand they like, they stick with it," the report said. That's true, but only up to a point, according to Patton. "You can develop their loyalty, if you get in quickly enough, for long-term things — household products and stuff like that," she opined. "But in the trendy stuff, they're not that loyal."

>>> Source: John P. Mello Jr., "Study Says Retailers Unhip to Young Shoppers", *E-Commerce Times*, www.etcnews.com, May 16, 2006.

Families, households, and the roles of their members are definitely changing, as is the marketplace and the incredible array of new products and possibilities. Now that we understand how important it is that marketers consider, among other factors, age and household composition to determine customer needs and desires, in Chapter 8 we will explore additional variables that influence consumers every day.

2. Using Table 7.4, create a 3- to 5-minute skit with a few classmates that illustrates the various roles played by household members in the decision-making process, and how they might function as a unit in the purchase of a fashion or design-related product or service. Present your skit in class.

References

1. Erika Rence, "What Drives Consumer Behavior? Preferences of Age Groups," Article summary, *Let's Talk Business* (Issue 116), April 2006, www.uwex.edu/ces/cced/publicat/documents/LTB0406.pdf.
2. Gary Stanley Becker, *A Treatise on the American Family*. (Boston: Harvard University Press, 1991), p. 135.
3. Ron J. Lesthaeghe and Lisa Neidert, "The Second Demographic Transition in the US: Exception or Textbook Example?" http://sdt.psc.isr.umich.edu/pubs/online/US_SDT_text.pdf. July 3, 2007.
4. http://adage.com/point/article?article_id=110592<br. Retrieved on August 20, 2006.

Additional Resources

American Marketing Association. *Dictionary of Marketing Terms*. "Family life cycle" entry. www.marketingpower.com/mg-dictionary-view3937.php. Retrieved on August 6, 2006.

Assael, Henry. *Consumer Behavior: A Strategic Approach*. Boston: Houghton Mifflin Company, 2004.

Boone, Louis E., and Kurtz, David L. *Contemporary Business*, 11th ed. Mason, OH: Thomson South-Western, 2005.

Carter, B., and M. McGoldrick, eds. *The Expanded Family Life Cycle*, 3rd ed. Boston: Allyn and Bacon, 2005.

Deutsch, Claudia. "AARP Wants You (to Buy Its Line of Products)." *New York Times*, October 28, 2005. Retrieved on August 20, 2007 from www.nytimes.com.

Earnest, Leslie. "Studies of Teens Hint Wristwatch May be Going Way of the Sundial." April 6, 2006. *Los Angeles Times*. April 6, 2006. p. A–1.

Emery, Chelsea. "Parents Buy Cashmere for Infants and Toddlers." *Washington Post*. August 13, 2006. www.washingtonpost.com.

Henry J. Kaiser Foundation. Menlo Park, CA, 2006.

Falcone, Lauren Beckham. "Pricy Preteens: When It Comes to Beauty, Adolescents Go High-End." *Boston Herald*. August 28, 2005. www.BostonHerald.com.

Francese, Peter. "American Consumers: The World's Biggest Spenders." An American Demographics Report. January 10, 2006. www.AdAge.com.

Goldstein David. "Food Makers' Web Sites Market Products to Pint-Sized Customers." July 19, 2006. McClatchy Newspapers. Retrieved on August 20, 2006 from www.mcclatchydc.com.

Kim, Ryan. "Disney to Market Phones: New Devices Will Let Parents Restrict Use, Keep Tabs on Kids." April 6, 2006. www.SFGate.com.

La Ferula, Ruth. "Showing? It's Time to Show Off." *New York Times.* June 8, 2006.

Mello, John A. Jr. "Studies Show Retailers Unhip to Young Shoppers." May 16, 2006. www.etcnews.com.

Michigan State University Extension. *"Communicating with Your Family: The Family Decision-Making Process."* www.fcs.msue.msu.edu/ff/pdffiles/familystress2.pdf August 9, 2006.

Neumeister, Larry. "Do-it-Herself: Home-Repair Guru Barbara Kavovit Finds Niche Designing Tools for Women." August 7, 2006. www.dispatch.com/business-story.

Perner, Lars. "Consumer Behavior and Marketing Strategy." www.consumer psychologist.com. Retrieved on July 28, 2006.

Petrecca, Laura. "Marketers Get Their Mascots in on Action at MySpace." August 30, 2006. www.usatoday.com/money/advertising/2006-08-30-myspace-usat_x.htm.

Streater, Amie. "Stylish after 35." June 26, 2006. www.dispatch.com/business-story. www.consumerpsychologist.com/ July 28, 2006.

www.marketingpower.com/mg-dictionary-view3937.php. Retrieved on August 6, 2006.

www-rohan.sdsu.edu/~renglish/370/notes/chapt05. August 10, 2006.

CHAPTER 8

Social Influences on Fashion Consumers

Question: What do strangers, our environment, friends, family, celebrities, and assorted messages from the media all have in common?

Answer: They provide us with information, they influence us, and they often exert a kind of social pressure on us, to which we respond by modifying our behavior, both as individuals and as consumers.

Forces That Influence Behavior

Each day we take part in activities, buy products or services, or share our points of view with other people. Think of a typical day—haven't many of your activities been influenced by someone or something? Previous chapters have addressed the impact of varied individual and family forces on the buying and selling of products and services; our discussion will now focus on social forces that change and drive our decisions.

FIGURE 8.1. Seeing the big picture: Understanding the social influences affecting consumers clarifies the task of marketers, helping them to see a bigger picture.

In her book, *Fashion Forecasting*, Ellen Brannon writes about the balancing a person must do when trying to live in the moment, which often involves efforts to conform (perhaps by imitating others) and, at the same time, the desire to demonstrate uniqueness.[1] We all engage in these divergent, apparently contradictory behaviors—the simultaneous effort to both fit in and stand out. A multitude of social forces tip the scales to one side or the other, and it is the job of marketers to identify, categorize, and make use of those forces for the benefit of both the organizations they represent and the consumers they seek to attract.

Different Types of Influence

In a marketing context, **social influence** refers to the information or pressure that an individual, group, or type of media presents or exerts on consumers. Variables and related pressures (friends, marketers, politicians, TV, radio, and so forth) come into play between the moment of stimulation and the resulting action (see Chapter 3 for information about stimuli and how we respond). For example, if a marketer were interested in accelerating the buying process that people use when purchasing new cars, she would want to know who (individuals or groups) wields the influence, what

FIGURE 8.2. Who said that?

types of influence they exert, and how those influences affect the ultimate purchase. In their book *Consumer Behavior and Marketing Strategy,* marketing professors J. Paul Peter and Jerry C. Olson discuss how both direct (for example, firsthand communication) and indirect (for example, observation) social interactions influence consumers' behaviors.[2]

More than 50 years ago, psychology professor Solomon Asch researched three responses to social influence; his discoveries are still valid today. He classified the responses in the following way: **conformity**, which occurs when a person is behaving like others in order to be accepted or feel like "one of the group"; **compliance**, when someone chooses to do something because he's been asked to do it; and **obedience**, when a person strictly obeys an order from an authoritative person or group.[3] These behaviors are illustrated in the following scenario. Assume you're alone in your aunt's apartment, and her 40-inch plasma flat-screen TV (with the deluxe home studio sound system) is blasting.

- A neighbor asks you to turn the volume down and, unhappily, you *comply.*
- A police officer rings the doorbell; he tells you to turn down the volume, and you *obey.*
- After a while, you realize that the right thing to do is to turn the volume down; you know it's what your aunt would expect, so you *conform.*

Of course, numerous other influences exist (many of which are discussed in this book), but marketers are most interested in the ones that mold buying behaviors, particularly when it comes to the purchase of designed goods.

Influences on Fashion and Design

As previously mentioned, influence affects us in myriad ways, such as in what consumers buy and wear, what designers create, and what media marketers use; there are many sources of influence. Some of these sources we don't often consider, but they nonetheless have lasting effects on our choices and behavior. Three examples of such forces include social class, culture, and subculture. These forces in particular often determine the roles that are assigned or ascribed to us—that is, the roles we didn't choose, such as firstborn, only child, aunt—as well as the ones we strive for and achieve, such as designer, buyer, manager.

Social class refers to groups of individuals belonging to different levels of society; social classes are hierarchical and, for the most part, depend on levels of prosperity and opportunity. Culture includes the learned customs, values, and beliefs of a group of people who usually live close to each other, although proximity is not a requirement. Younger members of a culture are taught by older members to behave in expected and accepted ways, which were learned from the members of the previous generation. According to the authors of the book *Consumer Behavior in Fashion,* culture is society's personality and the lens through which we screen products and services.[4] **Subcultures** are smaller groups or "mini-cultures" that function within larger cultures; examples of subcultures include flappers, hippies, punks, Goths, and cowboys.

Influences outside our immediate sphere are all part of the unending array of external influences we encounter on a daily basis. These include salespeople, advertisers, our favorite entertainers, athletes, politicians, teachers, role models, mentors, as well as TV shows and movies, Web sites, blogs, and so on. Review some of the Web sites that appear when you search for "fashion/design/culture/political. . . . blog" on the Internet. You'll see comments posted from both large and small organizations as well as from individuals that provide insight, education, updates, and points of view that might influence our fashion and design behaviors. Web-based communication is no longer a trend; it's a fact of life for many people. A July 2007 issue of the *Wall Street Journal* discussed microblogs (short text messages where recipients get updates but don't really need to respond). Interestingly, the article also mentioned the phrase "information pollution."[5] These and other sources, known and currently unknown, can certainly influence our consumption activities.

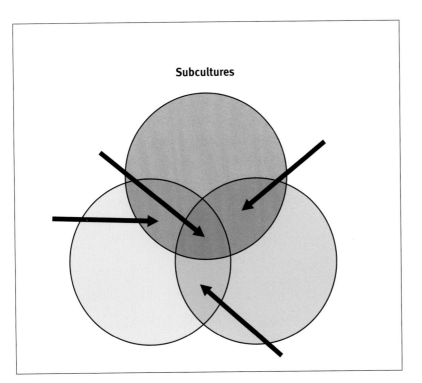

Subcultures

FIGURE 8.3. This visualization identifies several subgroups within larger groups.

Social Influences and Fashion Diffusion

Obviously, members of "society" influence the fashion behaviors of others. How and where did this social influence begin? In the late 1800s, Thorstein Veblen, the Norwegian-American sociologist and economist, described a group of people whom he termed "the leisure class," wealthy members of society who spent their time and money acquiring extravagant clothing, homes, and art objects. Since they didn't have to work, their main pastime was buying for themselves; Veblen referred to these people as participating in a lifestyle that revolved around "conspicuous consumption." They purchased in order to entertain themselves and to show off. Since they were at the top of the social ladder, they were celebrities, of a sort, and those who rubbed shoulders with them wanted to imitate their style and attempted to do so (within their more limited means).[6] Thus, the first theory of **fashion diffusion**, the spread of a fashion throughout different societal groups, became known as the **downward flow theory** (trickle-down theory), whereby people look to those they consider to be above them (the upper classes) for fashion guidance, and the styles they've adopted continue to trickle down the social ladder. Of course, by the time members of the lower classes are wearing their version of that fashion or style, members of the upper class have moved on to something new.

Let's Talk

In 1929, "puttin' on the Ritz" was slang expression for dressing fashionably and the title of Irving Berlin's song about "different types who wear a day coat, pants with stripes and cut away coat, perfect fits." What song lyrics have recently given you new insights into fashion? How have these same songs touched your friends?

Variations of this theory have emerged over the years, including the **upward flow theory** (trickle-up), the concept that a great new fashion idea can also start among the lower echelons of society and work its way up. One example of this is urban wear, which originated in the 1990s with people who lived and worked in cities; the style was eventually embraced by the most esteemed social groups. Phat Farm is a clothing company that combines fashion elements of both urban and preppy culture; this business was launched by Russell Simmons in 1992. The clothing was adapted and became so influential in the look of the urban subculture of rap and hip-hop that Russell is often referred to as the founder of the hip-hop movement.[7]

The trickle-up concept can also be used to explain how an idea can "take hold" in other fields. For example, many companies use customer data that "trickles up" from routine client e-mails and letters to help the organization "become much more responsive, flexible, and efficient," according to writer Marc Haskelson.[8] This shows that consumer researchers can actually use a fashion theory to enhance their business practices.

The **horizontal flow theory** (trickle across) is the third theory of fashion movement (how fashion ideas move across the population) and contends that influences among members of peer groups with similar demographic or psychographic profiles are what determine the adoption of fashions. (Psychographics is defined as the study of attitudes, values, lifestyles, and opinions.[9] See Chapter 9 for a detailed discussion of this topic.) For example, your college roommate got an iPod in a hot new color, or an Internet-ready video cell phone, so you find yourself wanting one. Or perhaps a fashion leader in a particular group of suburban moms knowingly or unknowingly influences others in that same group to do something, wear something, dine somewhere, or purchase a specific product or service.

These three fashion-diffusion theories have themselves each been in fashion at various times. Juliet B. Schor, a professor of sociology at Boston College, noted that in the new millennium, "horizontal desire" (trickle-across theory), or the coveting of a neighbor's goods, seems to have been replaced by "vertical desire" (trickle-down theory), or coveting the goods of the rich and powerful, who are seen on television and in the movies.[10] Her research showed that "increased exposure to TV (the modern babysitter) increases individuals' annual spending because of lifestyle interests for the upper middle class and wealthy."[11]

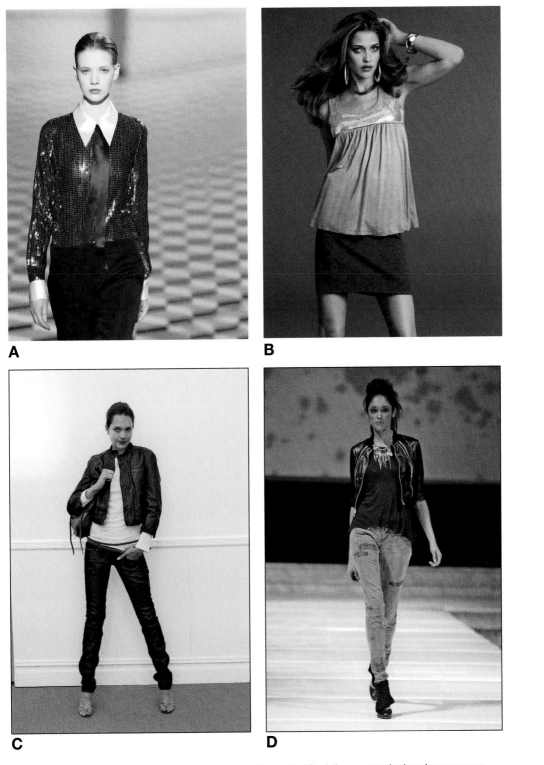

FIGURE 8.4A AND B. Once seen as a runway extravagance and impractical for daily wear, sequins have become a common accent for women's sportswear. FIGURES 8.4C AND D. The "rocker chic" look, featuring skinny jeans and cropped leather jackets, has made the step up from the streets to the runway platform in fashionable form.

Let's Talk
Which fashion-diffusion theory do you think is most applicable in America right now? Which influences are the most powerful?

Types of Social Influence

To further increase our understanding of how influences impact us, we can divide them into two main categories. As mentioned earlier, sometimes people do things simply because that's "the way things are done." If we follow this pattern of not questioning our behavior, we know we will generally be rewarded with acceptance and approval. So, we identify and follow certain societal guidelines or rules of behavior that serve the common good (doing the right thing/serving humanity). This is referred to as **normative social influence**, a type of pressure that requires a person to conform to the expectations of others. We might conform to avoid rejection or to gain acceptance. Society sets standards of behavior, evaluates subsequent performance, and uses rewards or punishments in response to the performance.[12, 13]

Examples of normative social influence are easy to see. People frequently wear clothes they believe will grant them greater acceptance. (For example, a young entrepreneur might believe that his well-tailored suit helps him to be seen as a both a mature adult and serious, successful businessperson at a chamber of commerce event.) Friends socializing in a club may order the same type of drinks. Or a shopper might select a specific gift because of an expectation that the recipient has expressed, either directly or indirectly. In a sense, our society has "programmed" us (via our parents and relatives, friends, employers, and members of institutions such as churches and schools) to believe that when we meet the expectations of others, good things happen. Maslow's Hierarchy of Needs, one of the models discussed in Chapter 4, can help us relate conformity to the belonging and esteem needs we seek to meet through the approval and friendship of others. Conformity can be a very powerful change agent (something or someone that motivates change), as we often modify our attitudes, actions, beliefs, and values so they are more in line with those of our key social groups and respected elders or authority figures.[14] On the other hand,

FIGURE 8.5. "Obviously the applicant has not read the best seller, *A Guide to Normative Social Influence*."

I guess he's not that interested in the position.

sometimes we prefer not to conform for a variety of reasons, such as wanting to differentiate ourselves from these same groups. Avant-garde (leaders in new or unconventional movements) designers exemplify a nonconforming group.[15]

Other times people seek specific guidance and direction in order to make the right choice. **Informational social influences** affect us when we copy the behavior of others because they directly or indirectly offer information to assist in our decision making. "Social proofing" is another term that describes this type of influence; we often think that others really know how to handle certain situations better than we do. For example, a college student might read *Vanity Fair* because her

FIGURE 8.6. Informational social influence.

instructor does, and she believes her instructor to be very much "in the know." Perhaps a college graduate accepts a job in a specific city because, although he doesn't want to move, a respected family friend in the same field succeeded there. Or a newly married couple decides to accessorize their kitchen with black appliances instead of stainless steel because their developer told them black was the "in" color. Another example of informational social influence can be seen in Figures 8.6.

In Figure 8.6, Alisha did no research before making her decision; she was satisfied to rely on her friend. Of course, fashion marketers would prefer that Alisha not depend on Megan (except for those working for Ralph Lauren, of course!), but rather on the messages about their brands they disseminate via TV, radio, the Internet, magazines, and so on. In this situation, marketers for Ralph Lauren competitors, such as Calvin Klein and Donna Karan, want potential customers to look at their offerings before deciding to buy. Marketers encourage consumers to spend time learning about product or service alternatives instead of buying just because of informational influencers' opinions. Naturally, marketers want to be the ones to provide the influences that people respond to, and they use those influences effectively to encourage the "right" buying behavior.

What kinds of information do people consider most important when deciding to buy?

1. The ease of use of the product or service; how much work is required to use the components of the goods as compared to the competitor's offerings.

2. The types of risks involved in the purchase.
3. The levels of expertise of both themselves (the consumers), as well as the seller and the influencer.
4. The degree of comfort, security, and convenience that comes with the goods.

How does this information, and the idea of relying on the opinions of others, relate to the Internet? Research indicates that potential Internet shoppers wait to learn how others like a specific Web site before making it part of their routine.[16] This suggests that many people do not want to be the first ones to do a specific activity; they don't want to experiment and prefer instead to seek the feedback of others before trying new things. Designers and marketers adapt these same ideas and "help" potential customers see others using similar products first.

Let's Talk

What are some of your own shopping and buying habits—do you "rely on a friend"? Do you want other people to "test the waters" first with a particular product before you buy a similar item? Do you feel more secure about a product when you know that others are already buying and using it?

Researchers have also determined that a physical presence of some kind can also lead people to make decisions more quickly than if no one was around. The 2005 study published in the *Journal of Consumer Research*, "The Influence of a Mere Social Presence in a Retail Context" (see Special Focus 8.1), noted that "the mere presence of another person or group of people is sufficient to elicit emotional and behavioral responses on the part of the consumer." So, a retail manager who maintains an amount of "social presence" (for example, sales associates, consultants, etc., who move around the store) could influence customers to make buying decisions more quickly.

››› SPECIAL FOCUS 8.1: THE INFLUENCE OF A MERE SOCIAL PRESENCE IN A RETAIL CONTEXT ‹‹‹

Overview of the Research

Fellow shoppers in a grocery aisle, audience members at the theatre, and consumers lined up at the check-out are all examples of a mere social presence. This mere social presence is one which is physically present, but is not involved nor attempts to engage an individual in any way. Given that a mere social presence is often found in a variety of consumption situations, it raises the question—does the mere physical presence of another consumer influence how you feel and what you do (e.g., what brand you select) when you are shopping? Further, do characteristics of the mere social presence, such as its size (i.e., number of people) and its proximity to you, determine the extent of the influence? The present research sought to address these questions using two field studies where participants made a small consumer purchase in a retail setting.

Using Social Impact Theory (SIT) as a basis for our predictions, we expected that as the size of a social presence increased and moved physically closer in proximity to a consumer, he or she would experience an increase (decrease) in negative (positive) emotions. Further, a consumer was also expected to be more willing to buy the most expensive brand name alternative under these conditions as there would be heightened impression management concerns. However, when the social presence was located further away, its impact on a consumer's feelings and behavior was expected to decrease regardless of the number of people present.

The findings of this research provided some support for SIT and the predictions forwarded. When the size of the social presence increased, two distinct patterns arose. Consistent with SIT, when the consumer was alone in the shopping aisle (i.e., a social presence did not exist), he or she spent the least amount of money by buying the cheapest, generic brand alternative. In contrast, when a social presence, comprised of either one or three people, was standing next to the consumer in the aisle, he or she was most likely to spend more by purchasing a more expensive brand. In fact, when the social presence consisted of three people, the consumer never once purchased the generic alternative.

In terms of emotions, counter to expectations, consumers felt the least annoyed and frustrated and the most pleased and happy when there was another shopper next to them in the aisle as compared to when they were by themselves (i.e., no social presence existed); however, when the number of people in the aisle increased beyond one, consumers began to feel more annoyance/frustration and less pleasure/happiness. Finally, when the mere social presence was at the far end of the shopping aisle, its influence on the consumer's emotions and brand choice were reduced regardless of how many people were present.

Significance of the Research

Although previous research in marketing has shown that social influences can play an important role in the consumption process, the majority of the work in this area has focused on the impact of an interactive social influence (e.g., salespeople greeting or persuading consumers, groups of consumers debating over a product choice). However, social influence situations in consumption are not limited only to interactive situations but also include those that occur without an interaction (i.e., a mere social presence). The results of two studies provide evidence that the mere presence of a social influence standing next to a consumer while he or she is selecting a product can have an impact on how he or she feels and which brand he or she will buy. Our research contributes to the existing literature by refining Social Impact Theory through the identification of a situation under which the theory does not hold. At a more general level, we validate the importance of a non-interactive social influence in the consumption context and point to important opportunities for future research.

Implications of the Research

Given the finding that simply the mere presence of another person or group of people is sufficient to elicit emotional and behavioral responses on the part of the consumer, it is important for managers to understand the influence and importance of social presence in a retail context. The findings of this research demonstrate that the ideal situation for managers is to create a situation in which there is some level of social presence within the retail environment as consumers feel the most pleasure/happiness and spend the most money in this situation. However, management should also be careful to avoid situations of overcrowding in shopping aisles and throughout the store, as consumers were shown to respond negatively to a heightened level of social presence. Thus, it is critical for management to recognize a balance in creating a comfortable social environment for the consumer.

FIGURE 8.7. The importance of others.

>>> Source: Jennifer J. Argo, Darren W. Dahl, and Rajesh V. Manchanda, "The Influence of a Mere Social Presence in a Retail Context," *Journal of Consumer Research*, 32 (2005): 207–212.

How Many Influencers Are Too Many?

Are people more likely to be influenced in a given situation when there are fewer people or more people involved? The **social impact theory** suggests that the probability of influence increases depending on the number of people involved and the importance and proximity of the influencers. However, when the number of influencers increases, the influence of any one person is reduced. So, if one person goes shopping with ten other people, that shopper is more likely to disregard the opinions of the ten influencers. But if only three people were shopping together, each person's opinion would weigh more heavily (would have stronger influence).

The Impact of Groups

Sometimes situations involve multiple influencers that are grouped together and exert collective pressure on the person(s) making a decision. Consider the following example. One day Inez, 18, came home from school and said to her parents, "Everyone is going on the trip to Disney World. It only costs $750. All the other parents are letting their kids go, so can I go?" Her parents discussed it for a few minutes and said, "Well, if everyone is going, and it's sanctioned by the school, you can go." In this case, the impact of the group's behavior on the parents (in this case, the decision makers) was powerful. A **group** is two or more people who share similar values and beliefs and communicate interdependently, sharing and relying upon another's opinion. Her parents agreed to let Inez go on a trip because they regarded her school group positively. In this example, the school group is a reference group, a specific type of group composed of individuals we respect, admire, and value; we use these groups as a guide when developing our own beliefs and behaviors.

Reference group members don't necessarily tell a person what to do; rather, the person is influenced by the group members' actions and the opinions they have. An example of this kind of influence is role modeling, but at the group level. When problem solving, the person might ask, "How would my uncles handle this situation?"

FIGURES 8.8A,B, and C. What do these groups have in common? They each influence their respective group members.

Just how strong is the influence of groups in our lives? Groups with which you have the most contact, such as family or close friends, serve as **direct** or **primary influencers**; their opinions are very powerful. **Indirect** or **secondary influencers** do not have as much power; they may include mere acquaintances or members of political/sports/entertainment groups you admire, but they are not included in your circle of closeness. Either group may exert pressure on you when it comes to prioritizing values, attitudes, and behaviors and in buying or not buying specific items or brands. For example, if a close friend (rather than someone you just know casually) suggests that you'd like a specific vacation destination, restaurant, or MP3 player, that comment could have an influence on you.

How the Reference Group Influences

Different types of reference groups serve different influential purposes. The American Marketing Association notes the three following purposes informational, utilitarian, and value-expressive.

Informational influences come in the form of facts, figures, data, and so on to those seeking opinions from professionals who are familiar with a specific subject or brand. This can save consumers time and reduce the perceived risk involved with many purchases. Marketers can dispense information in the form of educational and/or awareness campaigns, positioning their products as the ones experts prefer. For example, an ad for a tooth-whitening product could feature the American Dental Association's endorsement of that particular whitening system.

Utilitarian influences are in effect when an individual yields to another person's or group's influence to gain recognition and reward or avoid punishment.[17] For example, if your boyfriend tells you he prefers the smell of gardenias over lilies, you may very well give up one fragrance and purchase another. You might do this to please your boyfriend, that is, to maintain favor with him. If a product helps you achieve a desired goal, your resulting attitude toward it will be positive.[18]

Table 8.1. Examples of Reference Groups

Acquaintances
Authority figures
Close friends
Cultures: One's own/others
Family
Famous people: Entertainers/people in the news/politicians/
sports heroes . . .
Gangs
Internet chat groups
Social class: One's own/others
Subcultures

Value-expressive influences are those that address core values (for example, working hard is good for you; the customer is always right; be good to the environment), or the values a person believes one should possess to enhance his or her image in the eyes of others. One example of this is buying clothing that bears the "Made in the USA" tag, reflecting the value of national loyalty. Again, the marketer's goal is to identify these potential influences and respond in a manner that benefits all parties.

Reference groups impact our decision making in both obvious and subtle ways. Once marketers understand the shared beliefs of specific reference groups, they can use the group's influence to help promote their product or service, either directly or indirectly.

Membership Influences

We can also be influenced through membership relationships. Consumers consciously align themselves with potential influencers through individual and organizational memberships. The groups we do not actually belong to, but wish we did, are called **aspirational groups**. For example, we might want to belong to an admired downhill ski group or dream of joining an award-winning hip-hop dance troupe.

Associative groups are those we already belong to. For example, we might be members of the neighborhood volleyball team or a professional association. On the other hand, **disassociative groups** are those that do not interest us; in fact, we might

FIGURE 8.9 A AND B. Social influences: Direct (8.9A) and Indirect (8.9B)

disapprove of them. For example, we might decide to avoid someone who belongs to a certain political party.[19]

As was the case with the concept of "relying on a friend" (discussed earlier in the chapter), research indicates that when consumers either don't know about a product or service or are just not sure about it, they may look to others—in this instance, specific membership groups—as credible sources.[20] Consumer researchers use this type of information to help create strategies targeting appropriate market segments, using individuals who are perceived as reference group members and positive influencers for that segment. For example, if a woman's appearance-related aspirational group includes Angelina Jolie, then companies that sell lip enhancers might hire the actress as their spokesperson or hire a model who resembles her to appear in ads or at special events.

Control

In addition to all the influences we've discussed in this chapter, there's yet another group of influencers: the ones we don't know. What is their impact on consumer purchasing behavior?

Figure 8.10 shows examples of how gatekeepers, knowledgeable individuals who control access and information flow to their respective followers, influence people to act or not act in specific ways. In the fields of fashion, design, and art, we are constantly bombarded by information from critics, seasoned professionals, high-profile influencers, and others who impact our decisions with their words or actions. We don't know them, yet they influence our choices. Additionally, as a result of advances in technology and the Information Age, a new group of influences exists in cyberspace: "e-gatekeepers," direct and indirect electronic data providers who try to influence users to do or not do something.

But are e-gatekeepers really powerful; do they actually have genuine influence in the real (nonvirtual) world? In his article "The New Gatekeepers," writer Tristan Louis discussed the blogosphere (social online community) and asked what might happen if a false rumor were perpetuated by an online gatekeeper. Would "top-ranked online bloggers" begin impacting the "non-blog world"? According to the writer, some gatekeepers use a combination of traditional and new technologies to guide their followers. For example, using a phone or fax to spread a rumor would be considered traditional in contrast to spreading a rumor via e-mail, blog, YouTube posting, or audio e-clip. This illustrates another concern about the potential power of gatekeepers in society and the role of technology. In 1999, for example, both Liz Claiborne and Tommy Hilfiger were the targets of rumors accusing them of being racist by anonymous Internet sources that seemed intent on harming their businesses.

FIGURES 8.10 A,B, and C.   Gatekeepers influencing the actions of their followers. Clockwise from top right: Helen Mirren and David Beckham; Victoria Beckham; Serena Williams.

❯❯❯ SPECIAL FOCUS 8.2: SOMEBODY'S AFTER TOMMY HILFIGER. SOMEBODY'S GOT IT IN FOR LIZ CLAIBORNE, TOO ❮❮❮

Both clothing designers are targets of gossip that seems aimed at hurting their businesses. Both are accused of making racist remarks about minority groups wearing their clothes.

It's all over the Internet. Haven't you heard?

Lie No. 1—Hilfiger went on Oprah Winfrey's television show and said if he'd known blacks, Asians and Hispanics were going to buy his clothes, he wouldn't have made them so nice. He intends them for upper-class white people. Oprah had to order him off the show.

And . . .

Lie No. 2—Claiborne was on *Oprah* and a member of the audience asked why her skirts were cut so small. And she said it was because she didn't like the way black women looked in her clothing. Oprah was wearing a Claiborne outfit at the time and she went right to commercial, and she came back and finished the show in a bathrobe.

These stories have everything going for them except the truth.

Hilfiger says he's never been on *Oprah* and never said any such thing, anytime, anywhere. Executives at Claiborne's offices say that she was never on the show, that the company opposes practices that generate prejudice or racial division and "these unfounded stories are completely false." On Jan. 11, Winfrey opened her show by denouncing the gossip, saying: "It just never happened. Tommy Hilfiger has never appeared on this show . . . I've never even met Tommy Hilfiger."

But that doesn't end it. The talk goes on, unstoppable, difficult to trace to the source. The dark side!

Hilfiger and Claiborne both appear to be victims of the dark side of the Internet—a rumor mill where charges are anonymous and nasty. It's sort of the modern-day version of the old urban legend. Who started it? Competitors? Disgruntled buyers? Nobody can say. But who's passing it on now? Ordinary people. Folklorists say every ethnic group tells its own myths, and sometimes the accounts are so gripping they break through racial barriers.

A generation ago the talk—almost entirely within white groups—was that the moon and the stars on Procter & Gamble's logo proved the company was controlled by Satanists. Then came a spell when almost everyone, black or white, was hearing the story of the Kentucky Fried Rat.

As chronicled by Patricia A. Turner, who teaches African-American studies at University of California, Davis, in her book *I Heard It through the Grapevine*, it goes like this: "A friend or relative of the narrator stops by a branch of the fast-food franchise at night and orders a bucket of chicken to go. Taking a bite in the dark, the individual is disturbed to taste hair. When the lights are turned on in the car, a deep-fried rat is revealed."

A Tool for Myth, Smears

Folklorists are intrigued and somewhat stumped by these tales. Jan Harold Brunvand, author of numerous books on modern myths, including *The Vanishing Hitchhiker* and *The Choking Doberman*, notes that folk tales once were thought of as obsolete and unsophisticated traditions passed on by cackling crones in the backwoods. But he says urban legends have become a subclass in which humans of modern times replace the ancient demigods.

"One of the great mysteries of folklore research is where oral traditions originate and who invents them," writes Brunvand. "One might expect that at least in modern folklore we could come up with answers to such questions, but this is seldom, if ever, the case." Once the originator might have been the town meanie passing gossip over a back fence. Today, it's a button pressed on a keyboard, shooting countless copies at an instant across cyberspace. The Internet is the best tool for myth and smears since the development of vocal chords.

"Foaf"

In trying to trace urban legends, the narrator so often attributes it to a "friend of a friend" that Brunvand has coined a word for this source: "Foaf." That's who saw it, or heard it, or to whom it allegedly happened. No matter how far back folklorists track the tale, it remains "friend of a friend" and "friend of a friend of a friend"— forever. It's "Foafoaf."

In slurs such as those about Hilfiger and Claiborne, could it be somehow a jealous competitor trying to wreck their profits? Turner, whose research has focused on legends about corporations in black communities, says she doesn't think so. "It would be stupid. If a competitor tried to start something, they'd be damning themselves. It's too dangerous. Eventually you'll be painted by the same brush."

For example, she says, the old myth about Reebok supporting apartheid is sometimes told with the villain being Converse or Pumas or Nike. She's collected versions of the Claiborne slur when it's attributed to Gloria Vanderbilt. Sometimes a legend is told about a mouse tail found in a can of Coke, and sometimes it's in a Pepsi. "That's one of the clues to me," she says. "What people are responding to is not necessarily a particular company but something about the product." As she explains it, Claiborne was one of the first haute designers to reach out to working women. Claiborne wanted to make blazers that working women could afford. So instead of pricing them at $2,000, they were sold for

$200. "Now, that's a lot cheaper. But for lots of women it's still pricey for a blazer."

It's the same problem for Snapple (falsely said to be owned by the Ku Klux Klan). Turner notes that Snapple appeared with designer ice teas selling for $1.25 when soft drinks were usually sold for 60 cents.

"Those tend to be the consumer products around which urban legends develop," says Turner. "It's consumer ambivalence toward some kinds of products they simultaneously want and yet can't justify the expense of. Urban legends provide an out: I don't have to yield to peer pressure to buy this Tommy Hilfiger shirt, because this person is supporting things I don't believe in."

Believing What's Not True

And so, says Turner, people will firmly believe what is not true. She says she knows that Claiborne never said on Oprah's show anything derogatory about black women. Nevertheless, "There are people who tell me they can find the tape."

Hilfiger's company has tried to fight the legend, releasing statements that practically plead: "Tommy Hilfiger did not make the alleged inappropriate racial comments . . . Tommy Hilfiger wants his clothing to be enjoyed by people of all backgrounds . . . Tommy Hilfiger features models of all ethnic backgrounds in his fashion shows and advertisements."

Still, spokeswoman Peggy Chong says, "It's so frustrating and terrible. It's a domino effect. Fifty years ago, maybe you could find the source in the barber shop. Now we can't track it down. People assume it's true because it's on the Internet."

>>> Source: John Lang, "Somebody's after Tommy Hilfiger. Somebody's Got It in for Liz Claiborne, Too," March 23, 1999, *San Diego Union-Tribune*.

Let's Talk
What information about celebrities have you found on the Internet that turned out to be simply rumors? What mainstream media ran the same story?

Whom do you go to for advice or guidance on subjects you don't really understand? You'd probably seek out an "expert" on that particular topic. An **opinion leader** is someone who is highly regarded by his peers and serves as a credible source or a liaison, who transmits and translates information from mass media to those seeking advice.

These advisors do not necessarily have to be famous (although they can be); they just need to have specific expertise in the area of concern to you. Opinion leaders might include the following:

- A friend who is a certified mechanic with eight years' experience working on Ferrari engines
- The hair colorist or stylist who works with well-known celebrities
- A highly trained and well-respected plastic surgeon
- Stella McCartney
- Donald Trump

Let's Talk
What opinion leaders have influenced your selections of music, movies, dress, friends, social events, or career paths?

Consumer Socialization Process

Also mentioned in Chapter 7, consumer socialization is a process by which children acquire the skills, knowledge, attitudes, and experiences necessary to function as consumers.[21] Obviously, children learn from their parents, siblings, other relatives, friends, classmates, teachers, the media—and marketers. Marketers educate and motivate children to want goods by using TV programs, movies, and product placements in multimedia targeted to that specific market segment. Fast-food companies such as McDonald's or Burger King create marketing campaigns that entice young people to buy toys and other nonfood items at these restaurants. Another example is Webkinz, the "Web site partner" that children are encouraged by marketers to use after purchasing a stuffed pet toy. The site teaches children how to care for stuffed toys and provides 2000 KinzCash that children use to pay for the redecorating of a virtual computer pet room, furniture, clothing, and food.[22] Marketers can use creativity as a way to teach children how to function as consumers.

When we shop, watch TV or a DVD, listen to our iPod, thumb through our favorite magazines, or read poster ads on public transportation vehicles, we are seeing marketers' efforts to educate and motivate us to try, buy, or switch products and services—to have some influence on both our thoughts and actions. Marketers also seek to develop a better understanding of the social forces affecting consumers, and then use that information about influencers to generate more product interest and sales. But marketers also need other statistics and "hard data" to accurately identify market segments and determine which potential customers to target; this type of research is discussed in Chapter 9, "Demographics, Psychographics, and the Fashion Consumer."

Summary

Marketers study the effect of influence on consumers in order to both predict and guide consumer behavior, as well as to understand the degree of impact that the influences have on buying behavior. Reference and other groups' (for example, positive and negative memberships) influences guide people to consider, reject, or accept products and services, among other things. These combined variables and the efforts of traditional and nontraditional marketing gatekeepers and new technologies make our buying decisions even more complicated. Purchasing choices are most certainly impacted by the influence of other people and/or forces. Because of this, marketers know that the ongoing process of consumer socialization is ever-changing, and they must adapt if marketing messages are to reach and impact consumers effectively before, during, and after a purchase. Marketers are therefore better able to create more successful campaigns when they understand the processes by which consumers allow people, places, events, culture, and so on, to affect their buying habits.

Key Terms

Aspirational groups	Informational influencers
Associative groups	Informational social influences
Compliance	Normative social influence
Conformity	Obedience
Direct primary influencers	Opinion leader
Dissociative groups	Social class
Downward flow theory	Social impact theory
(Trickle-down theory)	Social influence
Fashion diffusion	Subculture
Group	Upward flow (Trickle-up theory)
Horizontal flow theory	Utilitarian influences
(Trickle-across theory)	Value-expressive influences
Indirect secondary influencers	

Questions for Review

1. Define and discuss normative and informational social influence. Provide examples of each from your own life.
2. Explain what the term "social class" means. How are the concepts of culture and subculture related? Illustrate their influences on consumers in relation to choosing designed goods.

3. How do the three "trickle" theories differ and why are they important to consumer researchers and marketers?
4. What is meant by the term "consumer socialization"?

Activities

1. Select an element of home décor such as kitchen appliances or cabinetry, a piece of furniture, bathroom fixtures, or paint colors. Apply one of the diffusion theories (trickle up/trickle down/trickle across) by researching the origin and history of your selection and demonstrating how designed goods of all kinds spread through a population.
2. Select two items or services that cost more than $100 that you bought while shopping with a group of three or more people. Explain whether they were direct or indirect influencers and how their comments (pressure) persuaded you to buy (or, if appropriate, *not* buy) the product or service.
3. Select two items you've considered purchasing that exemplify how either informational influencers, utilitarian influencers, or value-expressive influencers affected your buying decision.
4. Review your typical week at work, school, and in social situations. List two potential gatekeepers from each of these categories. Explain why you consider them gatekeepers and tell how and why you responded to their input.

Mini-Projects

1. Identify two opinion leaders, one found on the Web and one from another source. Compare and contrast the influence of each, taking into account traditional media, the reach of the Internet, and blogosphere opportunities.
2. Cite two memberships for each category (aspirational, associative, and disassociative) that you would personally consider joining or not joining, and explain the motivation behind your choices.

References

1. Evelyn L. Brannon, *Fashion Forecasting* (New York: Fairchild Publications, 2005).
2. J. Paul Peter and Jerry C. Olson, *Consumer Behavior and Marketing Strategy* (New York: McGraw-Hill Irwin, 2008).
3. Solomon E. Asch, "Effects of Group Pressure upon the Modification and Distortion of Judgement." In *Groups, Leadership and Men*, ed. H. Guetzkow. (Pittsburgh: Carnegie Press, 1951).

4. Michael R. Solomon and Nancy Rabolt, *Consumer Behavior in Fashion* (Upper Saddle River, NJ: Prentice Hall, 2004).

5. *Wall Street Journal,* Marketplace Section, July 11, 2007.

6. Michael R. Solomon, *Consumer Behavior: Buying, Selling, and Being,* 7th ed. (Upper Saddle River, NJ: Pearson Prentice Hall, 2006), pp. 385—388 and 474–475.

7. Phat Farm Web site, www.phatfarm.com/about.

8. Marc Haskelson, *The Trickle Up Theory,* April 2005, www.findarticles.com/p/articles/mi_qa3947/is_200504/ai_n13602220.

9. *The American Heritage Dictionary of the English Language,* 4th ed. (Boston: Houghton Mifflin Company, 2007).

10. Jennifer Steinhauer, "When the Joneses Wear Jeans," *New York Times,* May 29, 2005,.www.NYTimes.com.

11. Juliet Schor, "The Overspent American," Interview on Time.com, May 20, 1998, www.time.com/time/community/transcripts/chattr052098.html.

12. M. Deutsch and H. B. Gerard, "A Study of Normative and Information Social Influences upon Individual Judgement," *Journal of Abnormal and Social Psychology* 51 (1955): 629–636.

13. H. C. Kelman, "Compliance, Identification, and Internalization: Three Processes of Attitude Change," *Journal of Conflict Resolution* 2 (1958): 51–60.

14. ChangingMinds Web site, www.ChangingMinds.org

15. *Webster's New World Dictionary,* 3rd ed. (New York: Simon & Schuster, 1988).

16. Matthew K. O. Lee, , Christy M. K.Cheung, , Choon Ling Sia, , and Kai H. Lim, "How Positive Informational Social Influence Affects Consumers' Decision of Internet Shopping," HICSS, Proceedings of the 39th Annual Hawaii International Conference on System Sciences, Koloa, Kauai, Hawai'i (HICSS'06) Track 6, p. 115A, 2006.

17. Tudor and Carley, "Informational social influence" definition, 1998, http://ciadvertising.org/sa/spring_03/382J/jamie/term.html.

18. Nessim Hanna and Richard Wozniak, *Consumer Behavior: An Applied Approach* (Upper Saddle River, NJ: Prentice Hall, 2001) p. 177.

19. Katherine White and Darren W. Dahl, "To Be or *Not* Be? The Influence of Dissociative Reference Groups on Consumer Preferences," *Journal of Consumer Psychology* 16, no. 4 (October 1, 2006): 404–414.

20. Solomon.

21. Leon Schiffman and Leslie Kanuk, *Consumer Behavior,* 8th *ed.* (Upper Saddle River, NJ: Prentice Hall, 2004), p. 349.

22. Webkinz Website, www.webkinz.com.

Additional Resources

Argo, Jennifer J., Darren W..Dahl, and Rajesh V. Manchanda. "The Influence of a Mere Social Presence in a Retail Context." *Journal of Consumer Research* 32 (2005): 207–212.

Asch, S. E. Studies of Independence and Conformity: A Minority of One against a Unanimous Majority. *Psychological Monographs* 70 (Whole no. 416), 1956.

————. "Opinions and Social Pressure." In A. P. Hare, E. F. Borgatta, and R. F. Bales, eds., *Small Groups: Studies in Social Interaction* (New York: Alfred A. Knopf, 1966), pp. 318–324.

————. "Forming Impressions of Personality." *Journal of Abnormal and Social Psychology* 41 (1946): 258–290.

ChangingMinds.org. "Informational Social Influence." http://changingminds.org/explanations/theories/informational_social_influence.htm.

Cialdini, R. *Influence: Science and Practice.* 3rd ed. New York: HarperCollins. 1993.

Latané, B. "The Psychology of Social Impact." *American Psychologist* 36 (1981): 343–356.

Latané, B., and S. Wolf. "The Social Impact of Majorities and Minorities." *Psychological Review* 88 (1981): 438–453.

Tanford, S., and S. Penrod, "Social Influence Model: A Formal Integration of Research on Majority and Minority Influence Processes." *Psychological Bulletin* 95 (1984): 189–225.

Tristan, Louis. "The New Gatekeepers." www.tnl.net/blog/entry/The_New_Gatekeepers. Retrieved on February 9, 2006.

CHAPTER 9

Demographics, Psychographics, and the Fashion Consumer

Ashley and her twin sister, Leslie, had been working all summer at a lake resort. Both were college fashion students—Ashley in merchandising and Leslie in interior design— and the girls had taken the jobs to earn money to help pay for their last year in college and to buy a few special things. Ashley worked in the resort's dining room and Leslie at the snack bar by the pool. "I'm going to get a knock-out dress to go Salsa dancing," Ashley said to her sister. "What are you going to do with your extra earnings, Leslie?" "There's a new computer program that helps create more realistic interior design layouts; I think I'll have enough saved to get one," Leslie answered.

When consumers consider how to spend the incomes they have earned, their decisions are based on what is important to them and are reflected in their buying behavior, two of the topics of this chapter. Let's start by looking at some of the measurable statistics and personal characteristics that marketers consider important in analyzing and interpreting consumer behavior. First of all, what makes up a consumer market?

Markets consist of people, specifically those people with an interest and ability to buy goods and services. Of the some 6 billion people on the planet, just a small but growing number have much spending power, particularly discretionary spending power, a major concern for fashion marketers.

According to information presented in Table 9.1, the countries with the highest population are China and India, each with over a billion inhabitants, and each with a rapidly developing a middle class (due to massive industrialization) whose spending power is increasing. No wonder Wal-Mart is leading other retailers in expanding its presence in China, and site planners are designing in double digits shopping malls ten times larger than the Mall of America!

Although many people in highly industrialized nations such as the United States, Japan, Germany, and France enjoy a higher standard of living in comparison with citizens in developing countries, the former simply do not have the burgeoning societies and economies of China and India, and others such as Indonesia and Brazil.[1]

Considering the world's population from a different perspective, if there were only a hundred people on earth, and the existing human ratios remained the same, there would be an equal number of men and women; 61 would live in Asia; 85 would be nonwhite and 15 would be white; 60 percent of the world's wealth would be in the

Table 9.1.   The World's 50 Most Populated Countries

Rank	Country	Population	Rank	Country	Population
1.	China	1,313,973,713	26.	Ukraine	46,710,816
2.	India	1,095,351,995	27.	South Africa	44,187,637
3.	United States	298,444,215	28.	Colombia	43,593,035
4.	Indonesia	245,452,739	29.	Sudan	41,236,378
5.	Brazil	188,078,227	30.	Spain	40,397,842
6.	Pakistan	165,803,560	31.	Argentina	39,921,833
7.	Bangladesh	147,365,352	32.	Poland	38,536,869
8.	Russia	142,893,540	33.	Tanzania	37,445,392
9.	Nigeria	131,859,731	34.	Kenya	34,707,817
10.	Japan	127,463,611	35.	Morocco	33,241,254
11.	Mexico	107,449,525	36.	Canada	33,098,932
12.	Philippines	89,468,677	37.	Algeria	32,930,082
13.	Vietnam	84,402,966	38.	Afghanistan	31,056,581
14.	Germany	82,422,299	39.	Peru	28,302,000
15.	Egypt	78,887,007	40.	Nepal	28,287,147
16.	Ethiopia	74,777,981	41.	Uganda	28,185,254
17.	Turkey	70,413,958	42.	Uzbekistan	27,907,134
18.	Iran	68,688,433	43.	Saudi Arabia	27,019,731
19.	Thailand	64,631,595	44.	Iraq	26,763,381
20.	Congo, Dem. Rep.	62,660,551	45.	Venezuela	25,730,435
21.	France	60,876,136	46.	Malaysia	24,385,858
22.	United Kingdom	60,609,153	47.	Korea, North	23,113,015
23.	Italy	58,133,509	48.	Taiwan	23,035,081
24.	Korea, South	48,846,823	49.	Ghana	22,409,522
25.	Myanmar (Burma)	47,382,633	50.	Romania	22,903,552

Source: U.S. Census Bureau. International Database.

hands of only six people—predominantly U.S. citizens; 46 would live in urban areas; 47 would be living on $2 a day or less and 25 (one-fourth of the world's population) would be living on $1 a day or less. Only 14 would be able to read, and just 2 would be college-educated.[2]

What Are Demographics?

What do these figures mean to marketers of corporations such as Home Depot, Gap, and Nike? Clearly, only a small fraction of the world's population are potential customers for goods offered by these global retailers; marketers, therefore, have to determine whom they can best serve in order to earn a profit. To locate their best customers, then, businesses segment markets (discussed in greater detail in Chapter 1). Among the oldest and most efficient methods of market segmentation is according to **demographics**, the measurable statistics concerning a population, particularly its size, composition, and distribution. We will also discuss income, gender, education, and occupation. Other demographic measurements of interest to marketers are age and life cycle stage, family composition (both discussed in Chapter 7), ethnicity and religion, and social class (discussed in Chapter 8).

Marketers use demographic information to learn more about their markets—for example, where their customers live, what they do, how they spend their time, and the kinds of goods and services they need. They also use the information to identify trends, such as when products like the BlackBerry become popular, causing a greater demand in the personal electronics industry. And demographic information is used by marketers to increase sales, to learn, for example, when American Girl's successful store in Chicago would be ready for replication in New York and other regions of the country.

Examples of Typical Demographics

One of the most important demographic dimensions is population. As we saw earlier in this chapter, while the United States, plus the world's other industrialized countries such as France, Germany, and Japan, may not have the largest populations, the citizens do possess substantial disposable income (a topic discussed later in this chapter). First, let us consider the approximately 300 million consumers in the United States.

Whose information goes into demographic measurements? To gain an idea, let's take a look at the "average American." According to Sam Roberts, author of *Who We Are Now: The Changing Face of America in the Twenty-First Century*, the following is a portrait of the American population based on the 2000 census:

The average American is still a woman, aged thirty-five (if not a little older), living in a metropolitan area of the West or the South, more likely than not in a suburb.

She owns her own home and probably lives with only one or two other people. More than a quarter of all Americans live alone. About 1 in 10 adults are divorced. More that 80 percent are high school graduates, and more than 3 in 5 women are in the work force. About 1 in 4 Americans are Black, Hispanic, or Asian.[3]

As you can tell, a significant amount of demographic information is provided in the preceding paragraph: gender, age, location, home ownership, household composition, education, employment, and ethnicity/race. This type of information helps marketers better connect with consumers.

Population Growth and Distribution

And where are the average and not-so-average Americans living today? Many tend to prefer the two coasts and warmer states of California, Texas, Nevada, and Georgia, or scenic ones such as Colorado. Cities such as New York, Los Angeles, and Chicago also thrive; four out of five Americans live in metropolitan areas.[4] Home ownership is at a record high, with two-thirds of all households choosing to own rather than rent. Furthermore, most households also possess at least one automobile. According to the U.S. Census conducted every ten years, over the decades the population center has moved steadily westward and more recently also southward, from Chestertown, Maryland, in 1790, to Edgar Springs, Missouri, in 2000.[5] In the Southwest, two rapidly expanding metropolitan sites in terms of population are Las Vegas, Nevada, and Phoenix, Arizona. Also, many people choose to leave the states where they were born; it is estimated that one out of every five people in the United States moves each year.

Moving to a new location frequently means repairing and even remodeling. In a recent year, 11 percent of homeowners spent up to $1,500 for improvements, while around a third devoted more than $5,000 to priority projects such as buying furniture, painting a room, and landscaping.[6] When they move, many people want more space in the form of larger homes, leading some places such as Marin County, California, to require those planning to build homes larger than 4,000 square feet to obtain approval from authorities, and communities such as Delray Beach, Florida, in an effort to safeguard its historic district, to ban construction of homes larger than 2,000 square feet.[7] Nevertheless, the demand for home-building supplies and equipment and home furnishings provides opportunities for businesses ready to sell those types of products, such as Lowe's, Home Depot, and Menards, plus niche home furnishings retailers and design services. National chain supermarkets and pharmacies such as Supervalu, Safeway, and CVS quickly occupy the newest shopping centers in American communities, as do clothing retailers like JCPenney, Kohl's, and Bon-Ton. Apparel designers are quick to understand consumer needs for home-related products, also. Liz Claiborne attaches its brand name to home flooring products, and Vera Wang to mattresses.

FIGURE 9.1. Frequent moves call for new household goods.

Let's Talk

If you had your "druthers," where would you choose to live? Why? What kinds of retailers would you need to create the surroundings you prefer?

Tables 9.2 and 9.3.   Changes in Population and the Ten Largest Cities in the United States

Gains in Population

Change in population between 1990 and 2000.

Fastest-Growing Metropolitan Areas	POPULATION IN 2000	PERCENT CHANGE SINCE 1990
Las Vegas, Nev.	1,563,282	+83%
Naples, Fla.	251,377	+65
Yuma, Ariz.	160,026	+50
McAllen-Edinburg-Mission, Tex.	569,463	+49
Austin-San Marcos, Tex.	1,249,763	+48
Fayetteville-Springdale-Rogers, Ark.	311,121	+48
Boise City, Idaho	432,345	+46
Phoenix-Mesa, Ariz.	3,251,876	+45
Laredo, Tex.	193,117	+45
Provo-Orem, Utah	368,536	+40

Ten Largest Cities

New York, N.Y.	8,008,278	+9%
Los Angeles, Calif.	3,694,820	+6
Chicago, Ill.	2,896,016	+4
Houston, Tex.	1,953,631	+20
Philadelphia, Pa.	1,517,550	−4
Phoenix, Ariz.	1,321,045	+34
San Diego, Calif.	1,223,400	+10
Dallas, Tex.	1,188,580	+18
San Antonio, Tex.	1,144,646	+22
Detroit, Mich.	951,270	−8

Source: Sam Roberts, *Who We Are Now*, New York: Times Books, Henry Holt and Co., 2004, p. 190 and Appendix K.

Population Size Factors: Birthrate, Life Expectancy, and Immigration

The size of a country's population depends on the following factors: birthrate, life expectancy, and immigration. **Birthrate** means the number of babies born each year; there must be a sufficient number to replace the population if a nation is to maintain its economy, and more if it is to expand. **Life expectancy** means how long people will live, and, more important, how long they can be productive in the economy and in society. **Immigration** refers to the number of people who come into a country; it must be greater than the number leaving in order for the rate to remain constant.

Birthrate

Approximately 4 million babies are born in the United States each year, or 13.9 per 1,000 people.[8] American women today are having just enough babies (2.1 for the average woman) to keep the population size constant.[9] While the rate of teenage births is down, the birthrate for women from ages 35 to 44 is up.[10] This last fact has further implications for marketers.

Marketers take note of the current birthrate for several reasons. First, all women giving birth have certain needs for consumable goods for themselves and their families, needs for maternity wear, infants' wear, and nursery furnishings (among others).

FIGURE 9.2. Young families have many needs for goods and services.

Through their use of demographic statistics, marketers such as Sears, Target, The Baby's Room, and others are able to offer products for this market segment. But the needs of women who decide to defer having families until they are older sometimes differ from those of younger mothers-to-be. In all likelihood, older women have been in the work force for a decade or more, and have been increasingly significant consumers of fashion apparel, home furnishings, entertainment, automobiles, and travel. Second, as women mature, their fashion tastes have also had a chance to develop so that when they are ready to raise a family, their choices of maternity wear, infants' layettes, baby clothes, and nursery

FIGURE 9.3. Fashion marketers are paying attention to the older consumer's apparel needs.

furnishings are different and probably more sophisticated than they would have been earlier. Third, their need for services could increase—particularly for those mothers planning to return to work—to maximize family time, they might hire people to provide housecleaning, landscaping, pet grooming, grocery delivery, and meal preparation services instead of doing these things themselves. Table 9.4 indicates projected changes in U.S. population growth between the years 2000 and 2020. No wonder fashion marketers are paying close attention to the needs of older age groups for apparel (think Chico's and Coldwater Creek); cosmetics, health and beauty aids (think Lancôme "invisible night repair"); and travel and entertainment (think Elderhostel trips and home theaters).

Life Expectancy

People in the United States are living longer than ever; due to progress in fighting diseases, life expectancy for American men is around 76 years, and for women 81. The two leading causes of death, heart disease and cancer, are both in decline.[11] The fact that people are living longer, healthier lives presents all kinds of marketing opportunities to meet the consumer needs of seniors, for example, comfortable apparel; secure living conditions; home furnishings such as chairs, tables, and draperies that are easy to operate; as well as relaxed recreation, travel, learning, and entertainment opportunities.

FIGURE 9.4. Today many people live longer, with more opportunities to enjoy life.

Immigration

The United States has traditionally been a haven for people from other countries, and much of the nation's growth is due to immigrant talent and tenacity. After all, unless we can trace our ancestry to an indigenous American background, we all stem from immigrant stock. Due to the increases in birthrate and immigration, the growth of the U.S. population reached a peak in the decade from

Table 9.4. Projected Population of the United States, by Age and Sex: 2000 to 2050 (In thousands except as indicated. As of July 1. Resident population.)

Population or percent, sex, and age	2000	2010	2020	2030	2040	2050
POPULATION						
TOTAL						
TOTAL	282,125	308,936	335,805	363,584	391,946	419,854
0–4	19,218	21,426	22,932	24,272	26,299	28,080
5–19	61,331	61,810	65,955	70,832	75,326	81,067
20–44	104,075	104,444	108,632	114,747	121,659	130,897
45–64	62,440	81,012	83,653	82,280	88,611	93,104
65–84	30,794	34,120	47,363	61,850	64,640	65,844
85+	4,267	6,123	7,269	9,603	15,409	20,861
MALE						
TOTAL	138,411	151,815	165,093	178,563	192,405	206,477
0–4	9,831	10,947	11,716	12,399	13,437	14,348
5–19	31,454	31,622	33,704	36,199	38,496	41,435
20–44	52,294	52,732	54,966	58,000	61,450	66,152
45–64	30,381	39,502	40,966	40,622	43,961	46,214
65–84	13,212	15,069	21,337	28,003	29,488	30,579
85+	1,240	1,942	2,403	3,340	5,573	7,749
FEMALE						
TOTAL	143,713	157,121	170,711	185,022	199,540	213,377
0–4	9,387	10,479	11,216	11,873	12,863	13,732
5–19	29,877	30,187	32,251	34,633	36,831	39,632
20–44	51,781	51,711	53,666	56,747	60,209	64,745
45–64	32,059	41,510	42,687	41,658	44,650	46,891
65–84	17,582	19,051	26,026	33,848	35,152	35,265
85+	3,028	4,182	4,866	6,263	9,836	13,112
PERCENT OF TOTAL						
TOTAL						
TOTAL	100.0	100.0	100.0	100.0	100.0	100.0
0–4	6.8	6.9	6.8	6.7	6.7	6.7
5–19	21.7	20.0	19.6	19.5	19.2	19.3
20–44	36.9	33.8	32.3	31.6	31.0	31.2
45–64	22.1	26.2	24.9	22.6	22.6	22.2
65–84	10.9	11.0	14.1	17.0	16.5	15.7
85+	1.5	2.0	2.2	2.6	3.9	5.0
MALE						
TOTAL	100.0	100.0	100.0	100.0	100.0	100.0
0–4	7.1	7.2	7.1	6.9	7.0	6.9
5–19	22.7	20.8	20.4	20.3	20.0	20.1
20–44	37.8	34.7	33.3	32.5	31.9	32.0
45–64	21.9	26.0	24.8	22.7	22.8	22.4
65–84	9.5	9.9	12.9	15.7	15.3	14.8
85+	0.9	1.3	1.5	1.9	2.9	3.8
FEMALE						
TOTAL	100.0	100.0	100.0	100.0	100.0	100.0
0–4	6.5	6.7	6.6	6.4	6.4	6.4
5–19	20.8	19.2	18.9	18.7	18.5	18.6
20–44	36.0	32.9	31.4	30.7	30.2	30.3
45–64	22.3	26.4	25.0	22.5	22.4	22.0
65–84	12.2	12.1	15.2	18.3	17.6	16.5
85+	2.1	2.7	2.9	3.4	4.9	6.1

Source: U.S. Census Bureau, 2004, "U.S. Interim Projections by Age, Sex, Race, and Hispanic Origin," <http://www.census.gov/ipc/www/usinterimproj/>
Internet Release Date: March 18, 2004

Table 9.5. Comparing U.S. Population Growth by Decade 1960–2000

		Census Population		Change, 1990 to 2000	
Rank	Area Name	April 1, 2000	April 1, 1990	Number	Percent
1	New York–Northern New Jersey–Long Island, NY–NJ–CT–PA	21,199,865	19,549,649	1,650,216	8.4
2	Los Angeles–Riverside–Orange Country, CA	16,373,645	14,531,529	1,842,116	12.7
3	Chicago–Gary–Kenosha, IL–IN–WI	9,157,540	8,239,820	917,720	11.1
4	Washington-Baltimore, D.C.–MD–VA–WV	7,608,070	6,727,050	881,020	13.1
5	San Francisco-Oakland-San Jose, CA	7,039,362	6,253,311	786,051	12.6
6	Philadelphia-Wilmington-Atlantic City, PA-NJ-DE-MD	6,188,463	5,892,937	295,526	5.0
7	Boston-Worcester-Lawrence, MA-NH-ME-CT	5,819,100	5,455,403	363,697	6.7
8	Detroit-Ann Arbor-Flint, ML	5,456,428	5,187,171	269,257	5.2
9	Dallas-Fort Worth, TX	5,221,801	4,037,282	1,184,519	29.3
10	Houston-Galveston-Brazoria, TX	4,669,571	3,731,131	938,440	25.2
11	Atlanta, GA	4,112,198	2,959,950	1,152,248	38.9
12	Miami-Fort Lauderdale, FL	3,876,380	3,192,582	683,798	21.4
13	Seattle-Tacoma-Bremerton, WA	3,554,760	2,970,328	584,432	19.7
14	Phoenix-Mesa, AZ	3,251,876	2,238,480	1,013,396	45.3
15	Minneapolis-St. Paul, MN-WI	2,968,806	2,538,834	429,972	16.9
16	Cleveland-Akron, OH	2,945,831	2,859,644	861,87	3.0
17	San Diego, CA	2,813,833	2,498,016	315,817	12.6
18	St. Louis, MO-IL	2,603,607	2,492,525	111,082	4.5
19	Denver-Boulder-Greeley, CO	2,581,506	1,980,140	601,366	30.4
20	San Juan-Caguas-Arecibo, PR	2,450,292	2,270,808	179,484	7.9
21	Tampa-St. Petersburg-Clearwater, FL	2,395,997	2,067,959	328,038	15.9
22	Pittsburgh, PA	2,358,695	2,394,811	-36,116	-1.5
23	Portland-Salem, OR-WA	2,265,223	1,793,476	471,747	26.3
24	Cincinnati-Hamilton, OH-KY-IN	1,979,202	1,817,571	161,631	8.9
25	Sacramento-Yolo, CA	1,796,857	1,481,102	315,755	21.3
26	Kansas City-MO-KS	1,776,062	1,582,875	193,187	12.2
27	Milwaukee-Racine, WI	1,689,572	1,607,183	82,389	5.1
28	Orlando, FL	1,644,561	1,224,852	419,709	34.3
29	Indianapolis, IN	1,607,486	1,380,491	226,995	16.4
		1,592,383	1,324,749	267,634	20.2

Source: U.S. Bureau of the Census, http://numbersusa.com/overpopulation/decadegraph.html.

1990 to 2000, causing concerns about overcrowding and the resulting stresses on the infrastructure (highways, bridges, and communications systems) and the environment.[12]

The U.S. immigrant population is huge and its various groups have certain consumer needs that marketers are eager to fulfill. In addition to the basic human needs of food, shelter, clothing, and health care, many immigrants have families here and the children require education, recreation, and supplies. And many want to remember the traditions, customs, and food of their origins; thus, marketers also have an opportunity to meet immigrants' needs for ethnic foods, apparel, household goods, and entertainment tailored to their tastes. In Los Angeles, for example, the most popular radio station broadcasts in Spanish. Because of California's large Hispanic population, *supermercados* (supermarkets) featuring Mexican foods and spices dot the landscape, and Mexican holidays such as Cinco de Mayo provide occasions for festivals and celebrations. For other daily living requirements, fashion marketers create apparel and home furnishings in bright colors to cater to the tastes of the Hispanic market.

Income

Perhaps the greatest single demographic indicator of consumer spending is **income**, the money or other assets that people receive typically in a year from their work, property, and other investments. Supermarket chains and other marketers in general are interested in two types of income: **disposable income**, the amount of money after tax deductions that people have for necessities such as food, shelter, utilities, and transportation, and **discretionary income,** the amount consumers have after meeting all expenditures for necessities (of particular interest to fashion and luxury goods marketers). Consumers tend to spend more when their discretionary income is up and they feel positive about general economic conditions—that jobs are secure, that there are no imminent or foreseeable threats to their well-being, and that life in general is moving along fairly well. The level of **consumer confidence**, how consumers feel about the state of the economy, is another indicator that businesses monitor closely. If consumer confidence is high, people are willing to take greater economic risks (such as buying a more expensive home than originally planned), but if consumer confidence is low, people hold back, postponing major purchases in particular. Organizations such as The Conference Board periodically conduct surveys to determine the level of consumer confidence; fashion businesses can use this economic information to gauge planning for inventories and promotions.

FIGURE 9.5. In this promotion, Kmart is targeting the Hispanic customer.

Income Distribution

Obviously, the distribution of income throughout the population of a country is not even; recently it has become more polarized in the United States. In a recent year, the average income for the top 0.1 percent of the U.S. population (just under 200,000 people) was $3 million. In the lowest brackets, 28 million people reported incomes of $0 to $13,476. The top 20 percent of taxpayers earned from $80,000 to $67 million or more, whereas the bottom 80 percent earned under $80,000.[13] While some companies such as Neiman Marcus, Gucci, Henredon Furniture, and Tauck Tours target their promotions to the high-income top 20 percent of consumers, others such as Lowe's, Old Navy, Wal-Mart, and K-Mart pay significant attention to the 28 million-plus people in the lower income brackets; this is an example of market segmentation based on the demographic of income.

The amount that consumers can spend is based on personal income. In 2005, the **per capita personal income,** total income divided by total population, in the United States was $34,586, up 4.6 percent from the previous year. As can be imagined, income distribution was not equal among states. Residents of Connecticut produced the highest per-capita income at $47,819, while residents of Louisiana, a large percentage of whom were severely destabilized by Hurricane Katrina in late August of that year, had the nation's lowest per-capita income of $24,820 (28 percent below the national average). Income growth was also uneven: Wyoming's mining industries created the nation's greatest percentage increases in both population and income, while the Great Lakes region had the slowest growth.[14] The distribution of income (as well as population) has an effect on fashion marketers, who are concerned with supplying their various retail stores throughout the country with the kinds of goods consumers need just before they recognize that need. Retailers from Macy's and Dick's to Home Depot and Crate & Barrel identify the economic conditions in each geographic region they serve in order to successfully plan for the new season's merchandise distribution.

Spending Patterns

Obviously, the amount of money people spend varies according to income level, and age is also a significant factor (discussed in Chapter 8). Consider children as consumers. Of the approximately 36 million children in the United States who are between the ages of 3 and 11, their recent **purchasing power**—the amount of goods and services the dollar will buy—amounted to $18 billion. That figure is expected to reach $21 billion by 2010. Currently, families spend $115 billion on children's needs, which include food, clothing, personal care items, and entertainment, with total expenditures estimated by 2010 to be $143 billion. While half of this amount goes for food, substantial proportions are devoted—by both children as individuals and with their families—to apparel and accessories.[15]

The U.S. teenage population, expected to be approximately 35 million by 2010,

Table 9.6. Distribution of Wealth in the United States

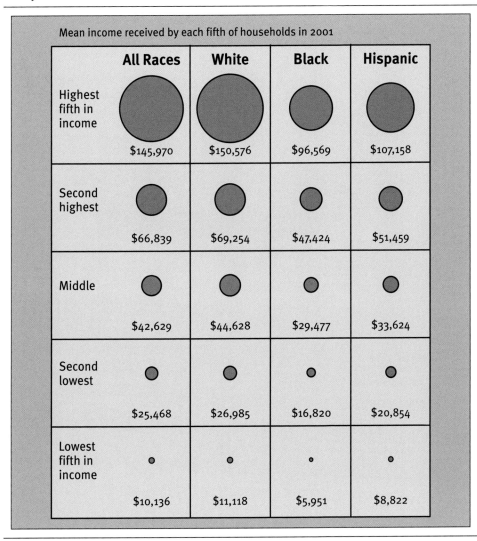

Mean income received by each fifth of households in 2001

	All Races	White	Black	Hispanic
Highest fifth in income	$145,970	$150,576	$96,569	$107,158
Second highest	$66,839	$69,254	$47,424	$51,459
Middle	$42,629	$44,628	$29,477	$33,624
Second lowest	$25,468	$26,985	$16,820	$20,854
Lowest fifth in income	$10,136	$11,118	$5,951	$8,822

Source: Sam Roberts, *Who We Are Now,* New York: Times Books, Henry Holt and Co., 2004, p. 172

shops both in its favorite stores and online, with eBay accounting for 5 million teen visitors in one recent month.[16] Teens spend more on apparel than their younger siblings—girls alone spent nearly $6 billion on apparel in a recent year—yet because teen tastes change so swiftly and unpredictably, they create a "moving target" for retailers such as Forever 21, American Eagle Outfitters, H&M, Urban Outfitters, Pacific Sunwear, and Abercrombie & Fitch.[17] Among the 18- to 30-year-old college crowd during a recent school year, spending on apparel, personal care, and beauty products amounted to approximately $9 billion. And furnishing freshman dorm

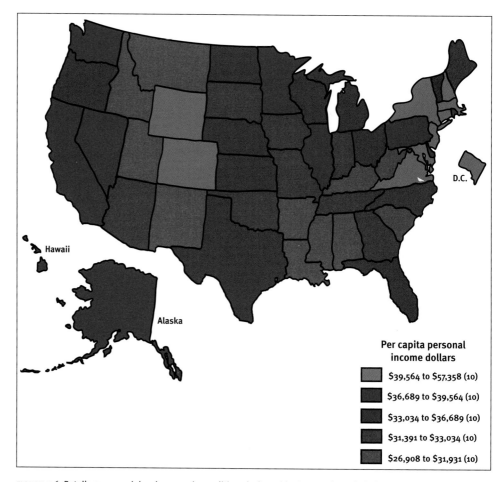

Per capita personal
income dollars

$39,564 to $57,358 (10)

$36,689 to $39,564 (10)

$33,034 to $36,689 (10)

$31,391 to $33,034 (10)

$26,908 to $31,931 (10)

FIGURE 9.6. Retailers research local economic conditions before shipping goods to their destinations.

rooms with bed linens, drapes, rugs, televisions, and other electronics can easily run $5,000 to $7,000.[18]

Affluent Generation Xers (born between 1965 and 1980) have spending patterns that reflect their interests, which are often centered on family and home—to be expected, as this generation is currently in its peak reproductive years. They seek out flat-screen TVs, brand-name baby strollers, Miele kitchen appliances, Marc Jacobs accessories, and Land Rovers.[19]

It is the baby boomers (born between 1946 and 1964 and accounting for nearly one-fourth of U.S. consumers) who are the nation's biggest customers, with an annual spending power of $1.1 trillion. Annual average spending per household amounts to nearly $46,000 for this generation. And for apparel, boomer expenditures are 13 percent higher than other age group. For boomer customers, fashion is part of their identity.[20] Fashion marketers are realizing this in a number of ways: Luxury stores such as Neiman Marcus, Nordstrom, and Saks Fifth Avenue are paying greater attention to consumers ranging in age from 35 to 60, and specialty stores such as Coldwater Creek and Chico's are catering to this consumer segment as well. Boomers are also traveling more, both for work and recreation, opening up the travel apparel market for retailers such as Travel Smith, L.L.Bean, and Magellan.

FIGURE 9.7. Back-to-school purchases by consumers make that season the retailers' busiest time of year, next to Christmas.

Boomers are also demanding customization, not just in their music and clothing selections but also in their home theater systems, closets, and kitchen cabinets. New home builders encourage their customers (many of them boomers) to visit builder design centers and select customized tile, colors, and moveable non-load-bearing walls.[21]

But not every member of this demographic is affluent; one study indicates that one-third of boomers, men and women, have assets of $10,000 or less.[22] Among working families in the United States, although the median income (or exact middle, with half above and half below) is $62,732, a third earn less than $37,000, and one of every four working families earns such low wages that they have to strain to make ends meet. Although nearly three out of four of these people were born in the United States, many lack sufficient education to be hired for the many technical—and higher-paying—jobs needing workers. They spend one-third of their income on housing, and often one of the parents has no health insurance.[23] In such instances, covering necessities with disposable income is rarely feasible, and the concept of discretionary income does not exist.

Due to the sharp increase in the U.S. birth rate after World War II and increased longevity, the most rapidly expanding group of consumers is people age 50 and older. This group comprises 40 percent of this nation's population, controls 75 percent of the financial assets, and does 55 percent of all consumer spending on a variety of consumer goods including travel, housing, and entertainment. Seniors are shopping on the Internet more frequently for goods such as apparel, accessories, gifts, and flowers. A recent Nielsen survey showed that while all adult online purchases declined slightly in a recent year (from 112 million to 107 million), senior online buying grew from

FIGURE 9.8. Many boomers have considerable discretionary income to spend on fashion goods.

26.5 million to 27 million people in just one 6-month period.[24] The second-fastest growing age group in the "senior" category is made up of 35 million people aged 65 and older.[25] This group possesses nearly half of the nation's discretionary income, an estimated $400 billion. As seniors live longer and healthier lives, their interests remain vital, and their purchasing power active.

Let's Talk

Think of a shopping center or downtown area you know, and name three or four popular stores there. Which income and age groups do these stores cater to?

Gender

It used to be that both marketers and consumers were quite certain about who bought what products, and advertisers knew whether to aim their promotions at men, women, or both. For example, men bought the family's car, while women bought its clothing—and marketers designed and directed their promotions accordingly. Automobile advertising stressed power and engine performance to men; department stores touted fashion and value to women. Today, however, marketers realize that women comprise a significant market segment for a much wider variety of products including automobiles, homes, electronics—even extreme vacations like sky diving. In automobile advertising, along with the attributes of power, engine performance, and fuel conservation, traditionally of interest to men, manufacturers also highlight safety, aesthetic, and comfort features, considered strong draws for women.

Likewise, manufacturers of cosmetics and beauty aids, traditionally marketed to women, are targeting an increasingly important group of male customers. In addition to using shaving cream and deodorants, many men are also applying moisturizers, masks, aftershave lotions, and fragrances, spending nearly $8 billion throughout the world on grooming products each year. Young men particularly find that these products not only make them feel better but can also enhance their appearance.

Table 9.7. Where Women Shop Most Often for Apparel

WHERE WOMEN SHOP MOST OFTEN FOR APPAREL

Type of Apparel Store	Share of Shoppers		Share of Shoppers by Age, 2006		
	2004	2006	18-34	35-54	55-70
Department stores	42%	32%	23%	32%	40%
Discount apparel	7%	19%	25%	17%	16%
Specialty apparel	21%	18%	27%	17%	11%
Supercenters with food	6%	10%	6%	11%	12%
Mass merchants	17%	7%	9%	7%	5%
Catalogues	2%	5%	2%	4%	10%
Online	1%	4%	6%	4%	1%
Dollar stores	0%	1%	1%	0%	0%
Warehouse clubs	0%	1%	1%	1%	0%
Other	4%	3%	0%	3%	4%

Source: Women's Wear Daily, April 26, 2006, p. 6.

❯❯❯ POINT OF VIEW 9.1: THE SOFTER SIDE OF MEN, THE NEW CLIENTS FOR SPAS AND MARKETERS OF BEAUTY AIDS ❮❮❮

How does a beauty salon or spa, traditionally the domain of women, begin to appeal to men? First of all, it doesn't look like a traditional beauty shop. The private club look of dark wood and leather often replace the feminine décor of a salon. Instead of leafing through a magazine while waiting for service, the male client can view a sports event on wide-screen television while sipping a drink.

Many of the spa services for men are similar to those for women: manicures, pedicures, facials, massages, and haircuts, but the names are often changed. A man's facial becomes a "men's cleanse," while a manicure is "handshake maintenance," and a pedicure is titled "foot repair."

When obtaining these services men prefer privacy, so one salon has set up acrylic dividers between the booths, guaranteeing that one client cannot not glimpse another, say, whose hair is being tinted. Another salon even provides a private room featuring a leather chair for pedicures. While undergoing spa transformations, male clients can continue their television viewing at each station and enjoy another beverage. Many men are realizing that the benefits of a spa need not be just for women.

While some men are enjoying spa services, others have entered the retail field of selling health and beauty aids to men as well as women. Avon, the direct-marketing cosmetics organization that calls itself "the company for women," now boasts some 12,000 men among its 500,000 sales representatives. Its products for men, under the brand ProExtreme, include, among other items, face moisturizer and eye cream. For many male Avon reps, the job is part-time, bringing in $10,000 or so annually. Recently, one part-time rep sold four times that amount and won a cruise to British Columbia. Clearly, many men are not only taking advantage of improving appearance, they are . . . also marketing the idea to their colleagues!

>>> Adapted from Nick Burns, "Putting the Manly in Manicure." *New York Times,* July 6, 2006, p. E3; and Kayleen Schaefer, "Knock, Knock. Who's There? Avon Man." *New York Times,* June 29, 2006, pp. E1 and E3.

Moving toward Gender Equality

The saying "He brings home the bacon and she cooks it" might well have been true for families in the twentieth century, particularly before World War II, but today it takes two incomes to just get some of the hog. In the majority of today's U.S. households, even those with children, both spouses work.[26] The rise of women in the work force has added to the growth of family income, and according to some experts, 100 percent of the growth of discretionary income. The earnings of women working full-time, on average, still have a way to go before catching up to those of men. For every $100 a man earned in the early twenty-first century, a woman brought home $77.50.[27] However, women are making progress, and in more than 25 percent of all dual-income families, the woman earns more than the man.[28]

Emerging Trends in Consuming

According to Michael Silverstein of the Boston Consulting Group and author of *Treasure Hunt: Inside the Mind of the New Consumer,* women's earnings are rising rapidly. Women outnumber men in colleges and graduate schools. Their knowledge obviously includes shopping savvy, which they combine with control over the discretionary dollar. In the family, she makes the decisions about remodeling the kitchen, going on vacation, and dining out. When shopping, she is looking for pleasure, emotional "highs," and she finds them at both ends of the price spectrum, in small luxuries at one end (think Godiva chocolates) and fantastic values at the other (think Thomas O'Brien linens at Target).[29] Fashion stores such as Nordstrom, Tiffany, or designer boutiques display tempting luxuries, while Sam's Club, Filene's Basement, Price Chopper, and other discounters hone in on offering great bargains. Some marketers are responding to the small luxury preference by combining the desire for luxury with that for value. For example, the budget-priced Swedish fashion retailer H&M is known for collaborating with designers such as Karl Lagerfeld, Stella McCartney, and Viktor Horsting and Rolf Snoeren (Viktor and Rolf); the company offers name apparel especially created for its approximately 1,200 stores worldwide, thus providing luxury brands created to sell at bargain prices.[30]

Marketing to Alternative Lifestyles

Although they make up a small percentage of all consumers, gay, lesbian, bisexual, and transgender (GLBT) people make up a vital part of the consumer market. Estimated at between 1 and 11 percent of the total population, GLBTs do not fit into a single market segment, but their spending patterns are significant. With incomes estimated at $56,000 and above, many GLBTs are in professional and creative occupations, well educated, with an interest in the arts, travel, social reform, apparel, and home furnishings. Advertisers traditionally used print media (newspapers and magazines) and some network television to reach these customers, but targeting segments of this market proved difficult. For example, advertisers trying to reach gays and lesbians in particular through television programs such as *Will and Grace* (a TV show featuring gay characters) discovered that the audience actually contained a large number of heterosexuals, making the cost per targeted viewer prohibitive.

Today, advertisers are using a variety of ways, such as the Internet and films, to reach GLBT customers. Sports events such as the Gay Games attract participants and fans from across the nation and abroad, providing numerous advertising, promotional, and sponsorship opportunities. Film festivals for gays and lesbians are also an increasingly important venue. The Pernod Ricard USA organization, owners of the Stolichnaya vodka brand, involved itself in film festivals by creating a 53-minute film for gay and lesbian audiences. Titled *Be Real*, the film carries Stoli's theme that the product is genuine Russian vodka and also emphasizes the company's commitment to the viewers.[31]

Cable television is another way that marketers successfully reach the GLBT audience. The Logo channel, sponsored by Viacom, can be seen in 23 million households. Logo also created a Web site (logoonline.com) for gays and lesbians and their friends. Many major companies advertise on Logo, among them Continental Airlines, Dell, Sears Holdings, and Subaru, with commercials geared to the audience. For example, in a Subaru ad featuring two people together, both are men or both are women. Bravo cable network, home of *Queer Eye for the Straight Guy*, has joined with Planet Out to

THE MOST
ILLEGALLY
DOWNLOADED
VODKA
OF 2033

THE FUTURE OF ADULT ENTERTAINMENT

SVEDKA

SVEDKA.COM

FIGURE 9.9. Svedka vodka is one of the products marketers gear toward a particular market.

introduce a Web site (outzonetv.com) for gays and lesbians; the site features blogs, video clips, television shows, and social networking.[32]

Education and Occupation

Marketers also glean demographic information about customers by segmenting markets according to education and/or occupation. Often researchers combine these elements with others such as income or age. For example, a marketer wants to reach middle-aged weekend motorcycle enthusiasts with careers in law, advertising, or dentistry. Research done by Harley-Davidson has shown that many affluent professionals seek adventure on the road and release from job stress, and for them, Harley has produced appealing motorcycles with power and style. In addition, the look is enhanced by accessories such as saddlebags and apparel, including leather jackets and pants, to complete the fashion picture. Finally the company creates a social life—Harley Owners' Group—built around Harley road trips and gatherings.

Typically, a college graduate tends to bring in a higher income than someone who completes only high school. And for many women today, education has become the key to more interesting, rewarding, and higher-paying careers. Marketers know that the more educated consumers become, the more goods and services they will want for themselves, and the more demanding they will be in their purchasing behavior—a result of their level of exposure to new ideas through travel, education, and life experience.

Remember how Leslie, the interior design twin at the chapter's opening, was planning to spend some of her summer job income on a program to help her create more realistic interiors? Once she graduates, she might design for wealthy clients, begin to buy period furniture and antiques for herself as well, and travel to exotic places to find just the right room accessories, and learn to distinguish an original piece of period furniture from a reproduction. As a result, she will become a more discriminating consumer; as a professional, she will be able to offer the benefit of her added expertise to her clients.

Marketers also use the demographic of occupation to reach target consumers. For example, people marketing New York theater productions and Las Vegas spectacles might target fashion professionals because the latter attend live performances for inspiration as well as entertainment; they have a professional/occupational interest. Mailers, flyers, and ads distributed at hotels and convention centers herald the shows most touted to market-week fashion buyers. Another example is the sport of golf. Among business executives, playing golf is considered a sign of job-related success. Many business deals have been made on the golf course over the decades. To reach this market, manufacturers of golfing equipment and accessories advertise in magazines that executives read (such as *Fortune* and *BusinessWeek*). Another example of marketers targeting a segment of consumers by occupation is the uniform industry. Many people wear uniforms on the job, including members of the military, emergency services personnel, airline and bank employees, health care workers, and chefs.

FIGURE 9.10. Education helps designers refine their tastes.

Fashion marketers are interested in the following demographics: population growth and location, income (particularly as related to age and life cycle stage), gender, and occupation. Marketers need to know the size of potential markets and their location. Designers, noticing the population shift to the "sunshine states" (for example, Arizona), can respond by creating casual apparel for outdoor wear and furniture to be used in gardens and by swimming pools. The accumulation of wealth among a small percentage of people lets high-end fashion marketers (from tiny boutiques to Barneys) serve this demographic by offering distinctive apparel and accessories from prestigious designers. The great majority of consumers with more modest incomes create a market for retailers from Macy's to Costco to satisfy consumer wants. Apparel and home furnishings are designed with gender in mind, also, and often with occupation as well. Brooks Brothers offers conservative looks for men and women in business and similar professional fields, while Bed Bath & Beyond provides linens and home accessories created to appeal to women, men, or both.

FIGURE 9.11. Uniforms serve to identify the members of an organization.

FIGURE 9.12. Income, gender, and occupation are often essential consumer demographics for fashion marketers.

Let's Talk
As a college student, what three or four kinds of goods or services do fashion marketers aim specifically at you?

Values Driving Consumption

Our **values**, what is important to us, have an effect on what we do—including what and how we consume. We hold certain values, both as a culture and as individuals. For example, Americans in general believe in values such as freedom and democracy; the right to choose what we want to do in life, including the work we want to do; the connections to family we want to create; the lifestyle we prefer; and the right as individuals to pursue our own goals. Other cultures (particularly in Asia) have different values, among them the supremacy of the family; respect for age; and decision making that benefits the group rather than an individual.

Humans have always consumed goods and services, but for centuries we were the sole producers of what we consumed. In early civilizations, people would forage for food, shelter, and the makings of clothing, and would gather only what they needed to survive. Their connection with goods was intimate—they made what they ate, slept on, and wore. In fact, collecting more than they needed could cause hardship, as they regularly packed up and moved all they had from place to place. Life was simple, and resources were used efficiently.

Everyone needs to consume to survive, but the *way* we consume today is vastly different from the past. Over time, through population migration and wars, some people and nations gained control over resources. With control came waste, and great differences arose between those who were in charge of the means of production (such as farmland, mines and later, factories) and those who were not. Even in the nineteenth and early twentieth centuries in the United States and Europe, consumption among most people was limited to necessities, and spending on luxuries was thought of as wasteful. Only the very wealthy were able to obtain the luxuries they desired (estates, jewels, works of art), a practice that had gone on for centuries in that class. According to writer Anup Shah in the article "Behind Consumption and Consumerism, Creating the Consumer," today almost everyone has access to luxuries, and many of these indeed have become "necessities," like hot and cold running water.[33]

〉 〉 〉 SPECIAL FOCUS 9.1: DESIGNS ON MARKETING: INVOLVING THE CUSTOMER IN MOVING THE PRODUCT! 〈 〈 〈

A particularly compelling way to encourage customers to buy a product is to have them take part in designing it! That's what shoe designer John Fluevog has been doing for the past several years, and the results have earned him high praise from fashion models and rock stars. His Web site invites consumers to vote for shoe fashion favorites from sketches submitted earlier by customers. A walking shoe titled Urban Angel Traffic, priced at $179, was designed by a woman in Moscow. Another, a retro pump called Fellowship Hi Merrilee, retailing for $189, was the brainchild of a customer in Provo, Utah.

Sometimes it's the package design as well as the product that attracts customers. The beverage company, Jones Soda of Seattle, reaches out to the teen and young adult market with off-the-wall flavors such as Fufu Berry, Lemon Drop, and Blue Bubblegum. The labels, changed periodically on the glass bottles—showing photos of scenery, animals, or friends submitted by customers—are then displayed on the company's Web site and voted on by viewers. A photo selected as a label bears the name and town of the person who sent it in.

A Chicago company, Threadless.com, sells T-shirts through its extensive online catalog, with all of the designs created by Threadless customers who send in their ideas. From the artwork it receives each week, Threadless management chooses five or so designs, prices the T-shirts at $15 each, and awards the winning designers a check for $1,500, plus $500 in merchandise. Involving the customer in creating the product takes market segmentation to another level!

〉〉〉 Source: Adapted from William C. Taylor, "To Charge Up Customers, Put Customers in Charge," *New York Times*, June 18, 2006, BU5.

The Rise of Consumerism

Somewhere along the way in Western society, the rise of individualism and the popularity of an individual's pursuit of his or her own needs became more important than concern for the needs of society in general. Moreover, being able to pursue individual goals meant having the capability to consume whatever one could obtain.[34] The concept that emerged from this point of view has become a central issue in most modern societies. Known as **consumerism**, it has three meanings: (1) the movement protecting consumers by requiring honest packaging and product guarantees, (2) the theory that the greater consumption of goods is economically beneficial, and (3) attachment to materialistic values and possessions. The consumerism movement (protecting consumers) is discussed in Chapter 16; the theory presented in the second point reflects the idea that consumerism is actually beneficial to society (for example, by creating more jobs and a higher standard of living). The following discussion addresses the third definition of consumerism: the attachment to materialistic values and possessions.

What is the price of this lifestyle? The way modern humankind practices consumption produces the inequalities that accompany it across the globe, inequalities that are damaging to the world's resources (one example is the contribution of air pollution to global warming), according to the United Nations. Consumption affects people and the environment all over the planet. Consider the following figures: Worldwide, 20 percent of the world's population lives in the highest-income countries such as the United States, Canada, Japan, and Western Europe. This group accounts for 86 percent of the world's private spending. The world's poorest 20 percent of people account for just over 1 percent of private spending. The richest 20 percent consume nearly two-thirds of the world's energy and own 87 percent of the world's automobiles, while the poorest 20 percent consume less than 4 percent of the world's energy and own less than 1 percent of its vehicles.

A dire need exists to erase poverty, hunger, and disease; to provide education and job opportunities; and to conserve and keep the environment free from degradation.[35]

Materialism Today

The importance that we attach to the things we own is called **materialism**. People in the world's richest nations tend to be materialistic; they have accumulated the means to purchase many goods and services, which are readily available. And the people most devoted to materialism reside in the United States. We are fortunate in having access to so many products, and many of us in having the wherewithal to own them. But contrary to popular belief, owning and consuming products does *not* make many people truly happy. A recent consumer survey of American attitudes on materialism and consumption, commissioned by Merck Family Fund, revealed four major points regarding Americans' feelings about consuming:

- Many Americans believe our priorities are out of kilter, that materialism, greed, and selfishness are overtaking our public and private lives, and crowding out our dedication to family and sense of responsibility to society.
- Americans are concerned about their future. "The American Dream" is now defined by what people own and "keeping up with the Joneses," rather than by an opportunity to create a better society. In general, children are very materialistic—too centered on consuming things.
- People feel ambivalent creating changes. They want to be financially independent and comfortable, but they also have nonmaterial goals for the future (for example,

raising healthy, well-rounded families). They know they buy more than they need, yet they cherish the idea of freedom to live as they choose.

• People connect materialistic concerns with the environment, realizing that the desire to consume more and more is not ecologically sustainable and, to maintain balance, priorities require serious changes—such as consuming far less oil and gas.[36]

> *Let's Talk*
> *Of the four concerns cited above, which, in your opinion, is the most important or urgent? Why?*

What's to Be Done?

According to anthropologist, professor, and writer Dr. Leslie Jermyn, consumers have lost touch with the human element in the goods they purchase. If you knew Aunt Jessie had knitted that sweater just for you, you'd tend to keep it as long as you possibly could. A similar item made by a stranger overseas, however, could easily be replaced by next season's latest look. Dr. Jermyn has developed some ideas for "successful consuming":

• *Value what we have.* Appreciate the time and other resources that went into creating the wardrobes, furniture, and electronics that we already own. When it's time to dispose of an item, we can find out how someone else might use it. Give it to a charity.

• *Repair and reuse.* If a garment needs mending, instead of discarding it, we can fix it. If it's not the latest look, alter it. If slipcovers and spreads look out-of-date, dye them. They'll last longer and you can use that money for other purposes.

• *Shop alternatively.* When we need something, let's think of the many places we could obtain it: discount stores, thrift shops, vintage clothing and antique stores. A Kansas City vintage clothing store on the second floor of a warehouse consists of several rooms, each of which is dedicated to a decade—the 1990s, 1980s, and so on to before World War II. Called Reruns, the store is visited by the general public as well as by costumers from Hollywood studios when they are doing period films, such as *Forrest Gump* and *Road to Perdition*. All of the apparel is sold at discount, and people come for miles to shop there. While other cities might not have stores exactly like this, towns of all sizes have thrift shops offering bargain assortments of vintage fashion goods.

• *Think before you buy.* Owning a certain product does not guarantee happiness. Owning a designer outfit does not make you a fashion plate. Using a certain soap or cosmetic will not change your basic appearance, so examine carefully what you need. By buying less often, you'll find you get more use out of what you do purchase, and you'll enjoy it longer.[37]

Let's Talk
From your experience, what are some examples where you or someone you know is practicing "successful consuming"?

What Are Psychographics?

We have examined how marketers can analyze customers and segment consumer markets according to demographics—measurable statistics of population growth and distribution, gender, income, and education—but numbers alone don't give the full picture. To further explain (and try to predict) consumer behavior, many marketers make an effort to learn what goes on inside the consumer's mind, which can't be measured in numbers. The field of **psychographics**, the study of consumer personality and lifestyle, provides another dimension for marketers to understand and influence consumer behavior. Our **lifestyles** include our values and the way we express them in what we consume. A young woman who reads *Marie Claire* may have the same demographic characteristics as one who reads the *New Yorker*, but their psychographics and resulting buying behavior might be very different.

Marketers use psychographics in a number of ways, including defining a target market, positioning a product, and creating a marketing strategy. In defining a target market, a fabric store might try to reach college-age design students; in positioning a product, Callaway golf equipment might focus on the equipment needs of middle-aged country club golfers; in creating a far-reaching marketing strategy, an apparel specialty chain might offer an online catalog in addition to its stores and mail order catalogs.

❯ ❯ ❯ SPECIAL FOCUS 9.2: FOCUSING ON THE PRODUCT, CONSUMERS REVEAL INNER FEELINGS ❮ ❮ ❮

Marketers are keen to learn what customers like and, perhaps more telling, *don't* like about their products. While demographics and psychographics help create sophisticated consumer profiles, the deeper questions about how customers feel about a marketer's product often remain unanswered. To find out why customers are buying some goods and not others, researchers have created focus groups, or guided consumer discussions about a product's features and benefits. For example, a fragrance company, before creating a new scent, may describe the lifestyle of the intended target customer to a focus group—that is, a small gathering of consumers meeting at research headquarters. The focus group, in turn, will fill in the target consumer's interests and activities, creating a profile that then becomes the foundation for the fragrance company's new scent.

Much of this research is done in the Midwest. The Chicago area is a center for market research including focus groups; 78 market research companies call the Chicago area home. Los Angeles is second, with 48 research organizations, and New York third, with 23.

Like many other innovations with business applications today, focus groups can be traced back to the military in the mid-twentieth century. The purpose then was to evaluate propaganda films with viewers offering opinions about a film's intended message. In addition to obtaining "quantitative research" statistics, such as those that are discovered through demographic segmentation, researchers now could put to use information from "qualitative research"—that is, how consumers feel about products.

A focus group, consisting of up to a dozen people selected to participate and paid for their time, meets with a leader at the research organization's offices to discuss a certain product whose manufacturer is interested in learning their opinions. These manufacturers, clients of the research firm, want to discover what a demographically targeted consumer will think of a new product, its marketing and advertising, and even its name. The discussion may be recorded on video for future reference, or sometimes a two-way mirror is used, as when observing the length of time children may play with a new toy. The discussion session lasts about an hour, when researchers analyze group comments and the tape, and then supply the client with the focus group results, which are often keys to determining the next step in the marketing process.

>>> Source: Adapted from Ruth Solomon, "Will You Buy It? Chicago, a Center for Study of What Will Sell, What Won't," *Pioneer Press*, June 22, 2006, pp. 149 and 150.

The Origin of Lifestyles

We frame our lives around what we consider important—that is, our values. Based on our values, our lifestyles consist of our activities, interests, and opinions (AIOs) and the goods and services we buy to confirm and support them. Psychographic analysis— done periodically through surveys (often online today)—reveals what people consider important and how they are consuming accordingly. For example, lifestyle research can indicate emerging trends in shopping preferences, such as going to the mall, buying from catalogs, shopping online, or ordering products from TV shopping channels. Table 9.8 shows popular AIO elements.[38]

Summary

Marketers seek to more thoroughly understand and influence consumer behavior through studying consumer demographics and psychographics. Demographics are measurable human statistics; the most significant for marketers are population growth and distribution (including birthrate, life expectancy, and immigration), income distribution and spending patterns, and gender. The population of the United States today is approximately 300 million; however, we and the other industrialized nations consume a far larger proportion of the world's resources than do the rest of the world's population (approximately 6.3 billion total). Fashion marketers adjust their product offerings according to the information they gather about population and income distribution.

As economic equality between the genders increases, more products such as automobiles, homes, and electronics are being bought by women. In addition, the development of gay, lesbian, bisexual, and transgender (GLBT) market segments has increased demand for media, sporting events, and vacations specifically designed and marketed to these groups. Also, marketers value information about occupation and education, and have found that people with more education are aware of a wider variety of goods and services, including fashions in apparel and interiors. For marketers of products like golf equipment and uniforms, targeting consumers by occupation can be a beneficial strategy.

Our consumption patterns are driven by what we consider to be important. In many societies, particularly American, we value the right of individuals to achieve the goals they set and, along the way, to buy and consume what they want. As a nation, Americans are materialistic—we attach great meaning to the objects we possess.

To further understand our lifestyles (the way we live), fashion marketers make use of psychographic systems such as VALS to determine whether we are motivated by ideals, achievements, or actions, and how our resources (including energy and commitment as well as income) influence our buying behavior. And through geodemographic segmentation such as PRIZM NE, marketers can identify consumers throughout the United States by their ZIP codes and lifestyle characteristics.

Key Terms

Birthrate

Consumer confidence

Consumerism

Demographics

Discretionary income

Disposable income

Geodemographics system

Immigration

Income

Life expectancy

Lifestyles

Materialism

Per capita personal income

PRIZM NE

Psychographics   Values
Purchasing power   VALS

Questions for Review

1. What are three or four of the most useful demographic market segment categories and why is the information obtainable through demographic segmentation valuable to fashion marketers?
2. What is a major trend in income distribution in the United States and why is that information important to fashion marketers?
3. Give three examples of the ways marketers have become more sensitive to segmenting by gender.
4. As fashion consumers, what are three or four ways we can benefit from materialism, or successful consuming, according to Dr. Leslie Jermyn?
5. Why are segmentation systems incorporating psychographics, such as VALS, and those utilizing lifestyles and demographics, such as PRIZM NE, useful to fashion marketers?

Activities

1. Organize a merchandise assortment for two small women's apparel stores, one geared to upper-middle income boomers in a suburb of Los Angeles, the other to lower-middle income seniors near Tampa, Florida. Include in your merchandise assortment items such as casual wear (pants and tops), rainwear and jackets, accessories, swimwear, and shoes. For each category of merchandise, describe the fashion look and fabrications you are seeking at each store.
2. Go to the Web site www.consumerworld.com and create a consumer profile of its target market in terms of the audience income range, gender, and education.
3. Survey three people your age, friends and classmates, concerning their views on each of the four points of the Merck Survey about materialism. Then ask three people from older age groups, such as boomers or seniors, about their views on these four items. In what ways do your respondents agree or disagree with the Merck Survey results? Do the two age groups you surveyed agree or disagree with each other on some issues? If so, which ones? What might be the reasons for these differences?
4. Select five or six fashion advertisements that you believe would appeal to a movie star, celebrity athlete, or someone you know, and state how each advertisement is geared to an aspect of that individual's demographics or psychographics. Write a paragraph for each ad, explaining the demographic or psychographic element, and why you selected it.

5. To further explore the VALS system of market segmentation, collect a series of a dozen ads for fashion apparel and accessories and home furnishings. Three of these ads should be directed toward consumers guided by ideals, three toward those driven by achievement, and three to those guided by self-expression. The last three are ads of your choosing for any of the categories. Arrange your ads according to the VALS categories and, for each group, write a description explaining your reasoning in selecting the ads. Also, for each group, add a statement about the kinds of resources that would assist in motivating the consumer to buy.

Mini-Project

Using the PRIZM NE system as a guide, go to www.MyBestSegments.com to find your own ZIP code. Using that ZIP code or another, create a print advertisement for a product or service that could be successfully aimed at one or more segments of that target market. Explain the reasons behind your choices.

References

1. Geography High Web site. www.geographyhigh.connectfree.co.uk
2. www.popconnect.org (March 2005), Blackwell, p. 237.
3. Sam Roberts, *Who We Are Now, The Changing Face of America in the Twenty-First Century* (New York: Henry Holt and Company/Times Books, 2004).
4. Ibid, pp. 11–12.
5. Ibid, pp. 60–71.
6. Earl. Swift, "Is It Time to Buy or Sell?" *Parade Magazine.* May 21, 2006, p. 5.
7. Ibid, p. 7.
8. www.usatoday.com/news/nation2003-06-birth-rate_x.htm
9. Pregnant Pause Web site. February 27, 2002, www.pregnantpause.org/overpop/usbirth.htm.
10. www.usatoday.com/news/nation2003-06-birth-rate_x.htm
11. http://hhs.gov/news/press/20011010.html
12. NumbersUSA Web site. "Comparisons of 20th Century U.S. Population Growth by Decade, http://numbersusa.com/overpopulation/decadegraph.html.
13. David Kay Johnston, "Richest Are Leaving Even the Rich Far Behind," *New York Times*, June 5, 2005, pp. 1, 17.
14. www.bea/gov/bea/newsel/SPINewsRelease.htm
15. WorldScreen.com Web site, "U.S. Kids' Buying Power Tops $18 Billion," May 9, 2006, http://www.worldscreen.com/newscurrent.php?filename=kids50906.htm.
16. Bob Tedeschi, "Teenagers are Among Online Retailers' Most Sought-After Customers," E-Commerce Report, *New York Times*, February 23, 2005, p. C3.

17. Meredith Derby, "Niche Specialty Stores Win Teen Dollars," *Women's Wear Daily* (November 4, 2004).

18. Valerie Seckler, "Why College Students Keep Spending More," *Women's Wear Daily*, (September 21, 2005): 10–11.

19. Nina Munk, "My Generation: Hope I Shop Before I Get Old," *New York Times,* August 14, 2005, p. BU5.

20. Meredith Derby, "The Indulgent Boomers: Generation to Propel Apparel Again in 2005," *Women's Wear Daily* (December 30, 2004): 1, 12, 13.

21. Douglas Brown, "Baby Boomers Demand a Custom-Tailored Lifestyle," *Chicago Tribune*, September 30, 2004, Sec. 5, p. 11.

22. Derby.

23. Brian Rose, "1 in 4 Working Families is Low Income, Study Finds," *Chicago Tribune*, October 12, 2004, p. 1.

24. Bob Tedeschi, "Older Consumers Flex Their Muscle (and Money) Online," *New York Times*, E-Commerce Report, June 12, 2006, p. C8.

25. Roberts, p. 58.

26. Ibid, p. 40.

27. Ibid, p. 171.

28. Susan Chandler, "Women Direct More Dollars," *Chicago Tribune.* May 7, 2006, Sec. 5, p. 3.

29. Michael Silverstein, *Treasure Hunt: Inside the Mind of the New Consumer,* New York: Portfolio, 2006.

30. Robert Murphy, "H & M's Growing Empire: Retailer Plans Launch of New Format in '07," *Women's Wear Daily* (June 22, 2006): 1, 15.

31. Stuart Elliott, "Hey, Gay Spender, Marketers Spending Time with You," *New York Times*, June 28, 2006, pp. C8, C31, C32.

32. Ibid.

33. Anup Shah, "Behind Consumption and Consumerism, Creating the Consumer," May 14, 2003. Retrieved June 10, 2006, from www.globalissues.org/TradeRelated/ConsumptionRise.asp.

34. Ibid.

35. Anup Shah, "Behind Consumption and Consumerism," June 10, 2006, www.globalissues.org/TradeRelated/Consumption.asp.

36. "American Attitudes about Materialism, Consumption, and the Environment," *Sustainable Consumption and Production Linkages Virtual Policy Dialog,* www.iisd.ca/consumer/mer_5.html.

37. Leslie Jermyn, "Great Temptations: The Trap of Materialism and How to Escape," www.globalaware.org/Articles_eng/greatexpectations.htm.

38. William D. Wells and Douglas J. Tigert, "Activities, Interests, and Opinions," *Journal of Advertising Research* (August 1971): 27–35.

39. vals@sricbi.com.

40. Claritas Web site, www.claritas.com.

Additional Resources

Barber, Benjamin. *Consumed*. New York: W. W. Norton & Company, 2007.

Frank, Robert. *Richistan, a Journey through the American Wealth Boom and the Lives of the New Rich*. New York: Crown Publishers, 2007.

Thomas, Susan Gregory. *Buy, Buy Baby*. Boston: Houghton Mifflin Company. 2007.

PART IV

How Fashion Marketers Communicate and Consumers Decide

News about fashion innovations spreads rapidly in today's world, influencing both consumer behavior toward fashion and the way fashion marketers communicate their messages to the consuming public—subjects that are explored in Part IV.

Researchers help to identify and interpret consumer views; Chapter 10 discusses some of the research methods by which fashion businesses obtain consumer data and explains how they use that information to formulate effective marketing strategies.

When making buying decisions, consumers take both conscious and unconscious steps during the process; these are described in Chapter 11. Chapter 12 examines the topic of how fashion consumers buy, and looks at issues such as the influence of fashion leaders and of the shopping environment. Chapter 13 addresses questions about how organizations buy and use fashion goods, while Chapter 14 tackles the topic of the consumption of fashion goods as a culturally driven global practice.

CHAPTER 10

How Marketers Obtain and Use Consumer Information

Julia was frazzled by the time she got home from running errands. The mall had been crowded, and she hadn't been able to find a pair of comfortable shoes that looked nice enough to wear to work. Then, on top of it all, a young man with a clipboard had stopped her on the way out to ask her questions about the number of stores she'd visited, how often she shopped at that mall, and so forth, and it had taken a little longer than the "only a minute" he had promised.

After relaxing for a bit, Julia felt reenergized and decided to go online and check out an Internet shoe store her friend had been raving about. First she checked her e-mail and found three messages from retailers alerting her to new products and special sales at their stores. She glanced at two and deleted them, but saved the one from Kohl's to look at later, since it showed some pretty sweaters at a good price, with an extra 15 percent off if she used her store credit card.

Finally, typing in the Web address of the shoe site, Julia was immediately impressed, not only by the variety of shoes but also by the number of ways to search for what she wanted—by brand, size, price, style, and more. There were even reviews from other customers about some of the styles. It was difficult to decide between two pairs that she really liked, especially without being able to try them on, but Julia also noticed that the e-tailer offered free shipping, and free return shipping if the shoes didn't suit. Figuring she had nothing to lose, she decided to order both pairs, and completed the transaction without a hitch. When a new window popped up asking if she'd be willing to take a quick survey about her shopping experience, she was so happy that she didn't hesitate to click "Yes." She typed in that she was delighted with the selection and how easy it was to find styles she liked in her size, and answered the final question, "How likely are you to recommend our site to others?," with a resounding "Extremely likely!"

Conducting Market and Marketing Research

Having studied the preceding chapters, you now understand how complex consumer behavior is—and why marketers work hard to decipher those complexities so that they can try to best meet the needs and wants of their target customers. But how do they do that? In large part, they do it by collecting information from and about consumers through research.

The field of market research was pioneered by Arthur C. Nielsen, Sr., who founded the ACNielsen company in 1923. (You probably know that name from the often-cited Nielsen Television Ratings, which monitor how many households are tuned in to a given TV show, among other statistics.) Nielsen developed many innovative research methods and techniques that are now standard industry practice, including the first objective and reliable methodology for measuring retail sales and competitive market share, and the impact of marketing and sales programs on revenues and profits.[1] Market research became even more important starting in the early 1960s when companies changed from using the selling concept to using the marketing concept (discussed in Chapter 2). Rather than trying to persuade consumers to buy products they'd already made, companies began making products they had confirmed, through research, that consumers wanted.

Today, research has reached new levels of sophistication and—although they are often used interchangeably—a distinction is being made between the terms "market research" and "marketing research." While market research involves gathering information about a specific market or industry's size and trends, including number of competitors, product pricing, government regulations, and so on, **marketing research** goes further by analyzing a given marketing opportunity or problem and finding solutions through understanding the behaviors and preferences of the market's consumers.

These two areas of research go hand in hand and are used either alone or together depending on the issues a marketer is facing. For example, if a watchmaker noticed that sales had dropped off for its less expensive styles typically bought by younger consumers, it might conduct market research to determine how many 18- to 25-year-old consumers were currently buying watches in the $30 to $100 price range. If results showed that those consumers were indeed purchasing fewer watches, the same company might use marketing research to discover why teens and young adults were not buying watches—for example, because they were using their cell phones to tell time (see Point of View 7.2)—and to determine what new watch styles or features might appeal to those consumers in order to reinvigorate that segment of the market. In general, market research is conducted periodically, such as when major changes occur in the market, or when a business is considering entering a new market or product category. Marketing research, on the other hand, should be an ongoing function within the sales and marketing department of a business as a way to stay in tune with its customer base.[2]

In this chapter, we'll look at different types of research and how each is conducted, and also explore how research helps marketers refine their message and better communicate it to their target consumers.

The Research Process

Market and marketing research can take many forms and can range from formal, statistically sound surveys to informal, personal observations. Political pollsters, for example, create objectively worded questions and use scientific methods to reach a

representative cross-section of voters when they track how candidates are faring before an election. By contrast, the owner of a high-end women's clothing boutique is conducting her own informal, yet equally valuable, research every time she scrutinizes the merchandise in her competitor's shop, or when she randomly observes customers in her own store or talks to them to learn what they like and don't like, and why. In all cases, however, research comes from one of two sources: secondary or primary.

FIGURE 10.1. Retailers conduct informal research just by watching customers browse and select merchandise.

Types of Research

Before undertaking any research, marketers must define the **objectives** of the study; they must identify specific information they want to learn. Once their objectives are established, they can determine what the best source of data will be. In some cases, the information might be available for them to cull and analyze from an existing source. Locating that existing data is called **secondary research**. If the information they want to gather is more specialized to their own business or otherwise unavailable from secondary sources, marketers conduct **primary research**, their own original study designed to address their specific objectives.

Secondary Research.   The advantage of secondary research is that it can save marketers the time and expense of conducting their own original research. Plus, depending on a marketer's needs, secondary data may be enough to answer the questions or solve the problem. A printed T-shirt company that was considering extending its line with graphics in Spanish, for instance, could turn to statistics from the U.S. Bureau of Economic Analysis and see that the Hispanic population was projected to increase by 14 percent over the next five years,[3] confirming that the new shirts would have a growing market of potential consumers. Or a retailer considering whether to expand its selection of private-label apparel could base its decision in part on an ACNielsen study that found 77 percent of respondents in the United States agreed that "private label brands are a good alternative to other brands."[4]

There are numerous sources available for secondary research, and in some cases, their data is free. The federal government and many of its agencies, for example, offer a wealth of free information. The Census Bureau provides details on the number, geographic distribution, and social and economic characteristics of Americans, among other data; figures on employment, consumer expenditures, prices and living conditions, and other subjects are available from the Bureau of Labor Statistics, to name just two. Links to statistics from more than 100 government agencies are organized by subject and compiled online at www.fedstats.gov.

Other sources of secondary data are newspapers and magazines, including trade magazines. In the fashion industry, trade publications such as *Women's Wear Daily* (*WWD*) and *Daily News Record* (*DNR*) not only report on the results of research conducted by other organizations, but often do their own market research. Marketers themselves can also be a source of secondary data through information found in annual reports or other corporate material, as well as when they publicize findings of research they have done. In fact, a company's marketing department can often delve into its own sales department's statistics on orders, returns, pricing analysis, and other information for a "built-in" source of secondary research.

Trade associations, market research firms, and advertising agencies, among others, can also provide secondary data. Full results of their studies are often available only to clients or members, or to others for a fee. But key findings are sometimes made public in a press release or other published report. For example, highlights from a study by the market research company Packaged Facts titled "The U.S. Men's Market: Examining the

Attitudes, Buying Habits, and Lifestyles of the Elusive Adult Male Consumer" were published by some media, although the full report would cost several thousand dollars to obtain. See Figure 10.2 for examples of the wide variety of sources for secondary research.

Primary Research.   When secondary research is not current or does not supply all the information a marketer needs, primary research can either provide all the necessary data, or, more often, supplement basic information from secondary sources. Depending on what information the company wants, it might do its research with existing customers, potential consumers, employees, vendors, or others, or possibly a combination of audiences.

Some companies may undertake the primary research themselves, but for most major studies, they will more likely hire a consultant or market research firm. In either case, the marketer's objectives will determine what research method should be used and how the study should be designed, whether by personal contact, written communication, or observation—techniques we'll discuss next.

Research Methodologies

In any marketing research, there are two types of methodologies: quantitative research and qualitative research. **Quantitative research** is objective, focusing on collecting numbers and facts that can be analyzed statistically. The surveyor who stopped Julia at the mall in the opening scene of this chapter was collecting quantitative data

---

A Few of the Many Sources of Secondary Data . . .

Federal Government
- Bureau of Economic Analysis
- Bureau of Labor Statistics
- Census Bureau
- Small Business Administration

Publications
- *Advertising Age/American Demographics*
- *Daily News Record*
- *Journal of Consumer Research*
- *Stores Magazine*
- *Women's Wear Daily*

Market Research Firms
- ACNielsen
- Claritas
- Forrester Research
- The NPD Group
- SRI Consulting Business Intelligence
- Yankelovich Partners

Trade Associations
- American Apparel and Footwear Association
- Cotton Incorporated
- Fashion Group International
- International Mass Retail Association
- National Retail Federation

FIGURE 10.2.

to create statistics on how often shoppers went to the mall, how many stores they visited per shopping trip, and so on. **Qualitative research**, on the other hand, is subjective, focusing on people's opinions and attitudes toward a product or service. When the online shoe store asked Julia to describe in her own words what she liked and didn't like about her shopping and buying experience, the retailer was conducting qualitative research, meant to help the company better understand how customers *felt* about shopping at its site.

Quantitative Research. Quantitative research is conducted in two main ways: through surveys and by observation.

Surveys are a flexible tool for quantitative research because they can be provided to respondents in written form by mail, e-mail, or through a Web site; they can also be administered by an interviewer in person (for example, at a store or mall, or over the phone).

Surveys are conducted with questionnaires; the questions reflect the research objectives and include demographic questions to help identify respondents by population segment. Questions are generally closed-ended, meaning they can be answered with a simple response such as a number or a "yes" or "no," or by selecting from a multiple-choice list. This allows researchers to compile exact statistics and develop percentages for specific questions or categories. For example, a recent study conducted by The NPD Group on back-to-school spending provided quantitative data about where consumers planned to shop and what they planned to buy. The report found that 81 percent of consumers intended to shop at mass merchants, vs. 38 percent at chain stores and 27 percent at department stores; and 71 percent planned to purchase apparel, as compared to 60 percent purchasing footwear, 13 percent cosmetics and other beauty supplies, and 45 percent school bags and knapsacks.[5]

In addition to simple-response questions, surveys can also include ways for consumers to express their feelings about a product or service. This is most frequently done with **attitude scales**, a device that lets respondents indicate their level of favorable or unfavorable opinion. The most popular attitude scale is the **Likert scale**, which presents a statement and asks consumers to select a degree of agreement or disagreement with the statement, with numbers usually representing the different levels. For example, a survey might include the statement, "I would be willing to spend twice as much money on a jacket if it had a designer label," and the respondent would choose a response ranging from 1 for "strongly disagree" to 5 for "strongly agree." (See Figure 10.3 for examples of the Likert attitude scales.)

Let's Talk

Have you been asked recently to complete a survey using an attitude scale? Why do you think marketers seem to be using this type of survey more frequently?

Typical Uses of the Likert Scale

Measure of Agreement

For each of the following statements, please check the response that best describes the extent to which you agree or disagree with each statement:

I enjoy shopping online.

☐ Strongly Agree   ☐ Somewhat Agree   ☐ Neither Agree nor Disagree   ☐ Somewhat Disagree   ☐ Strongly Disagree

I worry about identity theft when shopping online.

☐ Strongly Agree   ☐ Somewhat Agree   ☐ Neither Agree nor Disagree   ☐ Somewhat Disagree   ☐ Strongly Disagree

Measure of Satisfaction

How satisfied are you with the selection of jackets at retailer X? Please check one:

☐ Very Satisfied   ☐ Somewhat Satisfied   ☐ Neither Satisfied nor Dissatisfied   ☐ Somewhat Dissatisfied   ☐ Very Dissatisfied

Measure of Importance

For each of the following features relating to bed sheets, please check the response that best expresses how important or unimportant that feature is to you:

All natural fabric

☐ Extremely Important   ☐ Somewhat Important   ☐ Neither Important nor Unimportant   ☐ Somewhat Unimportant   ☐ Extremely Unimportant

Thread count

☐ Extremely Important   ☐ Somewhat Important   ☐ Neither Important nor Unimportant   ☐ Somewhat Unimportant   ☐ Extremely Unimportant

Price

☐ Extremely Important   ☐ Somewhat Important   ☐ Neither Important nor Unimportant   ☐ Somewhat Unimportant   ☐ Extremely Unimportant

FIGURE 10.3.

〉 〉 〉 SPECIAL FOCUS 10.1: FASHION ACCESSORIES ARE 'IN THE BAG' 〈 〈 〈

Handbags are replacing shoes as the signature accessory—and that's even with price tags reaching three and four digits. A report on the accessories market by The NPD Group, "Women's Fashion Accessories: It's All in the Bag," found that 44 percent of women ages 13 and over have bought at least one new bag in the past year. "That's a huge thing, because the number has been climbing in recent years. Five years ago, it was 26 percent," says Marshal Cohen, chief industry analyst for NPD.

The report also found that women with incomes of $35,000 and under say they are willing to pay $200 for a handbag.

Bags are expensive but "still a way to get designer merchandise that is more affordable than a lot of ready-to-wear," says Hope Greenberg, fashion director for Lucky magazine, whose twice-a-year handbag issues are among its most popular. Nearly 200 bags were featured in one spring issue, ranging from a low of $17 for a Payless bag to a high of $1,190 for a suede number by Gucci.

Table 1.   **Most-Often Carried Bag**

Rank	Style
1	Shoulder bag
2	Carry by hand
3	Backpack
4	Sling
5	Messenger bag
6	Tote bag
7	Mini-bag/ wristlet
8	Clutch

Source: NPD Group's Women's Fashion Accessories: It's All in the Bag.

〉〉〉 Source: Adapted from Maria Puente, "Hottest Trend? Handbags Are a Shoo-In," *USA Today*, May 3, 2005, http://usatoday.com/life/lifestyle/2005-05-03-handbags_x.htm.

Research that relies on observation has the advantage of not needing the active participation of the research subjects, and can even be conducted without their knowledge. The boutique owner mentioned earlier, for example, can learn which styles and colors her customers are gravitating toward by simply observing their browsing and noting which items they choose to try on. Fashion reporters observe celebrities and other people attending fashion shows, benefits, and similar events to discover the most popular cut of men's suits or whether skirt lengths are trending up or down. If more formalized results are necessary, researchers might conduct a **count**, where an observer or team of observers keeps a written tally of the category being studied.

Observational research can also be done mechanically or electronically. A department store, for instance, might use a counting device to track how many customers enter a department featuring a category of merchandise that is new to the store. Frequent-shopper cards or store credit cards, which are scanned at the cash register and record information every time a customer makes a purchase, provide a wealth of data about the customer's product preferences, buying frequency, and more. Similar information can be obtained when consumers shop online; in many cases, to facilitate that process, online merchants place invisible "cookies," or small text files that are saved to a computer user's hard drive when he or she visits a Web site. For the most part, cookies are harmless, and simply enable an e-tailer or other site to identify a returning customer and retrieve stored information about past purchases or present new information that is personalized to that customer's preferences. Sometimes, however, Web sites install tracking cookies that "follow" consumers as they browse other sites and report that information back to the original site. Many consumers and consumer advocates consider tracking cookies to be unethical and an invasion of privacy, and some Internet surfers routinely run anti-spyware programs to delete them. (See Chapter 15 for a detailed discussion of ethics.)

Qualitative Research. Qualitative research, with its purpose of gleaning respondents'
feelings and inner beliefs, has its roots in psychology, and requires a skilled researcher to conduct a study. In contrast to a quantitative study's closed-ended questions, qualitative research involves open-ended questions designed to encourage respondents to express their thoughts and opinions in detail. The two most common forms of qualitative research are focus groups and depth interviews.

A **focus group** is a gathering of a small group of perhaps 8 to 12 consumers and a moderator to discuss and offer opinions about a product, service, or other

FIGURE 10.4. Focus groups encourage free discussion of ideas and opinions about a product or service.

marketing-related topic. The moderator has a specific agenda and guides the discussion in order to accomplish the study's objectives, but participants are also encouraged to respond to each other's comments and elaborate on their thoughts and beliefs.

Focus groups usually take place in special conference rooms that are equipped with one-way mirrors; this allows researchers or representatives from the client company to observe without being intrusive or influencing the discussion. Video and/or audio recording equipment may also be hidden behind the glass so that participants will not be distracted or intimidated, and the tapes can be used for review of the session. Actual products or product prototypes may be used for participants to react to and evaluate, or the discussion may focus on intangible concepts to help marketers judge the viability of a new idea or direction.

Based on the objectives of the research, focus group researchers carefully select the participants for each study, screening potential respondents according to specific criteria defined by the marketer. A study about a new style of backpacks designed with pockets to hold an MP3 player and speakers to play music without earphones, for example, might be restricted to teenagers, the most likely consumers of that type of product. Research regarding a new anti-wrinkle cosmetic formula might require participants to be between the ages of 35 and 55, and already users of a particular brand of cosmetics. Because a focus group session takes an average of two hours to conduct, participants are usually paid for their time.

Let's Talk

Think of a new product that has recently reached the stores in your area. Do you think its manufacturer could have benefited from focus group research about the product? What types of consumers might have been involved? What specific features of the product might they have been asked about?

Depth interviews are similar to focus groups but involve just one participant offering thoughts and opinions to a researcher. The interview, which typically runs between a half hour and an hour, also takes place in a room with a one-way mirror and recording equipment. But since there is only a single respondent, the interviewer can delve more deeply into the person's feelings, or present several products or concepts about which the subject's responses can be compared.

For example, a depth interview might be used to test several different advertising approaches. Perhaps a retailer is ready to launch a new campaign and needs to know whether a fast-moving, flashy, hip-hop style of TV commercial will draw a better response than one with a whimsical, humorous tone. A skilled interviewer can show examples of commercials in each style and then draw out the respondent's conscious, and sometimes unconscious, reactions to each and reasons why the person liked one better than another.

Because quantitative and qualitative research provide different types of data, a research project will often combine both methods, providing marketers with more

How often do you shop for clothing for yourself, whether or not you actually intend to buy anything?				
	All Shoppers	Down Market	Middle Market	Up Market
At least once a week	7%	5%	7%	9%
Two to three times a month	19%	13%	21%	21%
Once a month	19%	16%	18%	22%
Once every 2–3 months	25%	23%	24%	27%
Once every 4–6 months	21%	24%	22%	17%
Once a year	5%	9%	4%	3%
Less often than once a year	4%	10%	3%	2%
Never	1%	1%	1%	0%
Source: Retail Forward Shopper Scape™				

FIGURE 10.5. The results of a research study are often presented in charts or tables.

FIGURE 10.6
wearing a p
a strong inf
emulate th
and othe
to the cl
 In to
even mo
even th
obvious
ated ne
but wh
most lil
tool to
lifestyle

comprehensive results. An example is a recent Nickelodeon/Youth Intelligence Tween Report, which investigated whether and to what extent the 9- to 14-year-old age group influences family purchasing decisions. The report combined results from a quantitative telephone survey and a separate series of focus groups, and found that while tweens rely on their parents to pay for "necessities" such as clothing, food, and room décor, nearly three out of four tweens have "a lot of say" when buying clothes for themselves.[6]

Analyzing and Reporting Research Data

Once the data for a research project has been collected, the information is organized, processed, and analyzed to determine the results. Responses to each quantitative research question are tabulated, usually through a computer program, and the numbers can be categorized according to the study's objectives. For qualitative research, the person or persons conducting the study generally review and analyze their own results.

Once the research has been analyzed, the researchers create a report, which often begins with a brief executive summary of the findings and then provides full details of the results, including charts, graphs, and other supporting information and illustrations. The report also describes the methodology that was used, along with a copy of any questionnaire used in the research. Perhaps most important, the research report may suggest a plan of action based on the findings. Suggestions to the marketer might consist of broad recommendations or specific marketing tactics that the research indicates might be successful.

Joe
fold
pro;

expanded to include "digital product integration," in which products are digitally inserted into scenes of TV episodes after they've been filmed.

Let's Talk
What is your opinion of product placement in TV shows and movies? Do you think this an acceptable way to get exposure for a product, or do you feel that marketers are trying to "trick" the audience?

In-store marketing is also constantly evolving, and new technologies are playing a role there as well. The use of interactive displays is still relatively limited, but units such as those in Niketown stores allow marketers to create two-way communication with consumers—in this case, letting shoppers order custom shoes that are delivered in two weeks by mail.[9] Other marketers, addressing an aspect of shopping they've learned their customers want, are redesigning their stores to create "environments," complete with cozy fireplaces (at Timberland) or afternoon tea (American Girl Store).[10] Even fashion shows are being updated for today's consumers. Target, for example, once created a "vertical" fashion show, with suspended models "walking" a runway down the side of a building at Rockefeller Center in New York City.[11] And New York's ready-to-wear fashion shows have been streamed live over the Internet—complete with cell phone videos and podcasts—in an initiative by organizer IMG Worldwide Inc.[12]

New Media

Even as marketers update their use of traditional media, they are also actively seeking ways to reach target consumers, particularly the younger generation, through newer channels. As a recent *New York Times* article stated, "The number of vehicles through which young people find entertainment and information (and one another) makes them a moving target for anyone hoping to capture their attention."[13] It is not only young people, either. Marketers are actively pursuing the attention (and dollars) of women via the Web vs. the more customary media used to reach them. Why? Because a recent survey found that the number of women online and the amount of time they spend online is outpacing men.[14]

Among the Internet-based communication tools marketers are using is e-mail, which can provide newsletters, notices about special sales or events, and even personalized messages based on information the marketer has about a regular customer. Some companies are also advertising in e-zines, such as DailyCandy, which are online magazines covering a range of topics that deliver daily e-mail updates on what's hot to consumers who register for the free service. Apparel retailer Scoop NYC, which operates stores in four states, has found that just being mentioned in an e-zine boosts sales at its Web site.[15]

Marketing rese...
Objectives (for...
Primary resear...
Qualitative rese...

Questions for...

1. Explain the...
   an exampl...
2. What are s...
   doing seco...
3. What is th...
   Name two...
4. What is ar...
   on one.
5. Why is ma...
   sumers?

Activities

1. Read thro...
   can find t...
   an examp...
   know.
2. Look onli...
   summary...
   involved (...
   were targe...
3. Pick a fasl...
   etc.), and...
   own obse...
   and share...
4. Imagine y...
   shoes and...
   tude scale...
   would hel...
5. List a vari...
   other stu...
   the same...
   groups di...

Marketers are also using richer content and interactive content on their own Web sites to communicate with consumers online, and a growing number are also jumping into the blogosphere. Blogs are appealing to many people and businesses because they feature two-way communication; marketers also appreciate this aspect because it lets them have a dialog with consumers. Among the fashion companies that have created or connected to blogs are Lands' End and Piperlime, Gap's online shoe store.

Other new media that marketers are using to reach consumers include cell phones, with some companies sending advertising that ranges from simple text messages to video clips. Even video games have become a channel for marketing communications. Knowing that video games are a $7 billion-plus market in the United States, activewear companies such as Nike, Adidas, Reebok, and Puma are entering agreements with game companies to feature their apparel on characters in the games. In one golf video game, for example, a digital Tiger Woods is wearing a cap with an instantly recognizable Nike swoosh.[16]

Other Communication Vehicles

There are many other methods that marketers use to communicate with consumers today. For example, some companies know they can reach their target audience through sporting events, and may advertise during televised games and matches, or they might even sponsor certain events. A growing number are also using buzz marketing (discussed in Chapter 1), the technique designed to generate excitement among a key group of consumers so that they will start a word-of-mouth campaign

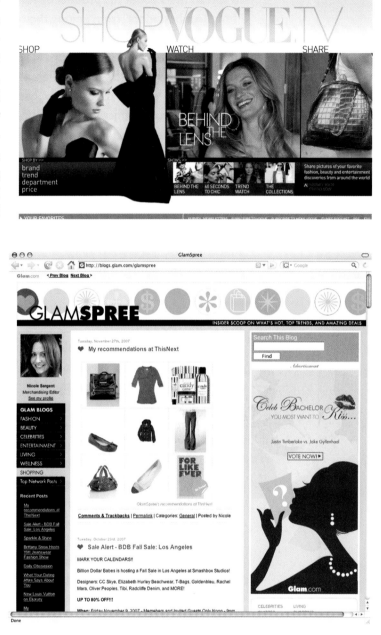

FIGURES 10.8A AND B. The fashion world is increasingly capitalizing on the number of consumers using the Internet and blogs to communicate to its target audiences.

Mini-Project

Working with one or two other students, choose a fashion product or category and create a mock research study about it. Define the objectives of the research, and determine whether it would be qualitative or quantitative (or both), what research methods you would use, and what types of consumers you would survey. Create a sample questionnaire that reflects your objectives and methods.

References

1. ACNielsen, "Our History," http://acnielsen.com/company/history.shtml.

2. Whipple, Sargent & Associates, "Market Research Guidelines," Corporate brochure, www.whipplesargent.com/mrguide.pdf.

3. Peter Francese, "American Consumers: The World's Biggest Spenders," *American Demographics*, January 10, 2006, www.adage.com/news.cms?newsId=47374.

4. ACNielsen. "Private Label Widely Seen as 'Good Alternative' to Other Brands, According to ACNielsen Global Survey," News release, August 11, 2005.

5. The NPD Group, "Retail Alert: Planned Back-to-School Spending Flat, as Shoppers Expect to Shop Later This Year," News release, July 24, 2006.

6. The Intelligence Group/Youth Intelligence, "Money Savvy Tweens Have a Big Say in Spending," News release, August 10, 2005.

7. Frappa Stout, "How To Be 'Juicy,' " *USA Weekend*, March 18–20, 2005.

8. Kortney Stringer, "Advertising: Pop-In Products," *Detroit Free Press*, February 16, 2006, www.marathondigital.com/news_ad_pop_up.html.

9. Betsy Spethmann, "Tuning In at the Shelf," *Promo Magazine*, April 1, 2005, http://promomagazine.com/mag/marketing_tuning_shelf/.

10. Wendy Mendes, "Showcasing Brands," GlobeSt.com, June 6, 2005, www.globest.com/retail/advisor/1_35/advisor/15173-1.html.

11. Emily Kaiser, "Retailers Shift Ad Strategies in Digital Age," Reuters, February 12, 2006, http://today.reuters.com/news/articlebusiness.aspx?type=media&storyID=nN10184324&imageid=&cap=&from=business.

12. Valli Herman, "Designers Refashion for Internet Age," *Los Angeles Times*, February 3, 2006, E1.

13. Tom Zeller Jr. "A Generation Serves Notice: It's a Moving Target," *New York Times*, January 22, 2006. Retrieved from www.nytimes.com/2006/01/22/business/yourmoney/22youth.html?ex=1295586000&en=d23bc480d739c911&ei=5088&partner=rssnyt&emc=rss.

14. Theresa Howard, "Marketers Go Fishing for Female Web Surfers," *USA Today*, March 19, 2006. Retrieved from www.usatoday.com/money/advertising/2006-03-19-webwomen_x.htm?CFID=507767&CFTOKEN=39368927.

15. Elizabeth Weinstein, "Retailers Tap E-Zines to Reach Niche Audiences," *Wall Street Journal*, April 28, 2005. Retrieved from http://online.wsj.com/article/ SB111411501158013598.html?apl=y.

16. Andrew LaVallee, "Sportswear Brands Now Playing in Video Games," *Women's Wear Daily* (May 18, 2005).

17. Kathleen Kiley, " 'Brand Ambassadors' Representing Consumer Products in Teen Nation," KPMG Consumer Markets Insider, July 28, 2005. Retrieved from www .kpmginsiders.com/display_analysis_print_nobuttons.asp?strType=&cs_id= 138056.

CHAPTER 11

Decision Making

It was time to fill up the car again, and Peter began to ask himself the same nagging questions. "Which fuel should I use? Should I buy gasoline, diesel, or clean-burning alternative fuels like ethanol or propane derivatives? Maybe I should try BioWillie, Willie Nelson's brand of biodiesel. I read that it's made from soybeans. After all, if a country music legend like Willie uses it, it must be great."[1] Peter goes through a number of steps before making a decision. He may consciously or unconsciously consider alternatives, and also evaluate those alternatives logically or emotionally.

This chapter addresses issues that surface before, during, and after a buying decision is made. We will discuss the components of the decision-making process, the effort involved in making different choices, and some considerations that may surface before, during, or after the selection.

❯❯❯ SPECIAL FOCUS 11.0: FILL 'ER UP: ALTERNATIVE FUEL STATION PROVIDES LOOK AT OPTIONS ❮❮❮

If the United States is going to end its addiction to oil, the fuel station of the future might look like Pearson Ford Fuel Depot. Along with gasoline and diesel, the one-of-a-kind station—part of a dealership near busy Interstate 15—offers a full range of clean-burning alternative fuels from ethanol to propane to BioWillie, a brand of biodiesel made from soybeans and promoted by country music legend Willie Nelson.

The station isn't profitable yet. But co-owner Mike Lewis said that could change if oil prices force consumers to seriously consider other fuels—especially in San Diego, which regularly pays among the nation's highest gas prices. "If you could make it profitable, you could do a whole lot more to preserve the environment than all the mandates in the world," Lewis said. At first glance, the facility looks like any other gas station—except there are pumps labeled "E85" and "compressed natural gas" along with recharging stations for people with electric cars.

The station is the only one in the country that sells such a wide range of fuels. And it's the only facility on the West Coast where private citizens can buy E85, a mix of 85 percent ethanol and 15 percent gasoline that can be used in a number of models that already roll from American assembly lines. Motorists who filled up recently had a number of reasons for using the alt-fuel oasis: helping the environment, keeping their money in the United States and just seeing how their vehicle ran on a different fuel.

Retiree Karl Evans wheeled in and spent $169.96 for 50 gallons of "BioWillie" to run a tractor he uses to clear his land. He hauled the fuel back home in a pickup truck rigged to run on propane. Evans said he doesn't like to buy gasoline. "You're sending the money out of the country, that's for sure," he said.

High gas prices coupled with President Bush's call for Americans to reduce their dependence on foreign oil are drawing more attention to alternative fuels that can be produced domestically, sold cheaper than oil and generate lower amounts of greenhouse gases. One of the most promising is E85, known for getting fewer miles to the gallon but higher octane, resulting in more horsepower. The fuel works in more than 30 models, including the Yukon sport utility vehicle from General Motors Corp., Silverado trucks and Impala cars from Chevrolet, and the Ford Taurus. Those flex-fuel cars can run on gas, E85, or combinations of the two.

Sales of alternative fuels at Pearson usually hinge on the cost of gasoline and diesel. When those prices are climbing, alt-fuels can account for as much as 30 percent of overall sales, Lewis said. On June 5, regular unleaded gas was selling for $3.29 a gallon, compared to $3.24 for diesel, $3.09 for E85, $3.29 for biodiesel, and $2.39 for natural gas. Lewis said high gas and diesel prices don't boost the station's bottom line, so it's adding a mini-market to increase income.

To attract the customers of the future, the EcoCenter for Alternative Fuel Education, also located at the dealership, offers tours explaining the benefits of alt-fuels over gasoline. Busloads of children—11,500 since the center opened in 2004—arrive daily for tours where guides discourage use of gasoline. At one exhibit, Eco-Center executive director Judy Bishop explains that drivers of electric-gas hybrids such as a Toyota Prius on display spend one-third as much on fuel as drivers of regular cars.

The anti-oil message is surprising at a center built with $1.4 million from Ford Motor Co. and $200,000 from the dealership owned by John McCallan. Lewis, chairman of the nonprofit center's board of directors, said Ford has no say in that message. Bishop, an environmentalist, designed the lesson plans. Lewis has been disappointed that automakers and oil companies haven't contributed to the operation of the center.

BP spokeswoman Cindy Wymore said the oil giant is impressed with the facility but declined to get involved because its goals are similar to BP's "A+ for Energy" program in which teachers receive grants to teach kids about alternative fuels. The company has said it's devoting $8 billion over the next decade to development of alternative energy. By then, Bishop hopes her young guests may be buying their first alternative-fuel or hybrid cars.

"Let's get the younger ones who are still receptive to new ideas," she said. "We're capturing them at an early age." Mike Pryor, a volunteer chaperoning his son's class, also paid attention to the tour. "It's actually better for me, I think, than for the kids," said Pryor, adding that he may eventually replace his van with a hybrid

>>> Source: Tim Molloy, Alternative Fuel Station Offers Look at the Future of Energy. Associated Press. June 11, 2006. Retrieved on August 31, 2007, from www.washingtonpost.com/wp-dyn/content/article/2006/06/11/ AR2006061100504.html.

Making the Right Choice

We make decisions because we don't have what we'd like to have. Decisions are required because we have options. If we didn't have options (that might result in favorable results), we'd probably live very simplified lives. In marketing jargon, a consumer who's making a decision is actually trying to "solve a problem." According to psychologist Lars Perner, Ph.D., a problem is "a discrepancy between a desired state and an ideal state, which is sufficient to arouse and activate a decision process."[2] So, when there are choices, people frequently think about and evaluate alternatives, move forward with a selection, then review the benefits to see if the final decision was a good one.

FIGURE 11.1. The Decision-Making Staircase identifies these steps in ascending order.

Five Basic Steps

While they may not realize it, most people go through five basic steps when making decisions, say authors Dr. Nessim Hanna and Richard Wozniak, who both teach marketing at Northern Illinois University. [3]

1. Recognize/Identify the Problem or Lack of Something

Problem awareness occurs when someone perceives an imbalance between his or her current situation ("as is") and an ideal ("should be") situation. If this gap (the distance between these two opposites) is large and important to the person, and alternative solutions are available, the person becomes aware that there must be a change. If, on the other hand, this gap is not large enough to cause some level of discomfort, the person is not likely to make a change (see Figure 11.2). We become aware of a "problem" because of a stimulus, something that attracts or directs our attention and opens our eyes to a possible lack of something, causing a state of discomfort brought about by a unsatisfied want or need. (Stimulus is discussed in greater detail in Chapters 3 and 4.) In turn, this stimulus motivates a response, some kind of reaction to the stimulus.

For example, if Rachel looks at herself in the mirror when she puts on her new pair of jeans and thinks she looks OK or pretty good, she probably will not be very con-

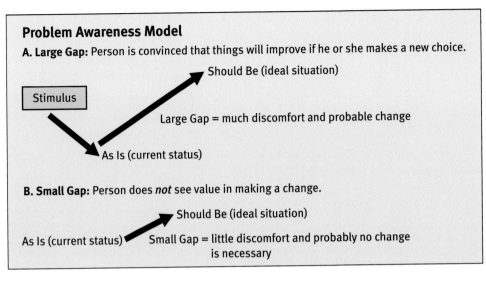

Problem Awareness Model

A. Large Gap: Person is convinced that things will improve if he or she makes a new choice.

Should Be (ideal situation)

Stimulus

Large Gap = much discomfort and probable change

As Is (current status)

B. Small Gap: Person does *not* see value in making a change.

Should Be (ideal situation)

As Is (current status)

Small Gap = little discomfort and probably no change is necessary

FIGURE 11.2.

cerned about purchasing a gym membership—in other words, there is a *small gap* between the "as is" and "should be" situation. However, if she feels bad because she doesn't like the way she looks, there's a very good chance that she will seriously begin to consider doing something that will result in her looking and feeling better—that is, there is a *large gap* between the "as is" and "should be" situation (see Section A of Figure 11.2).

Recognition of these gaps can be caused either *internally,* by the individual herself,

"How can it be empty?"

"I'm never going back here."

FIGURE 11.3. A Stimulus leads to a response.

or *externally*, as a result of marketing influences. Here are some examples of the kind of incidents that would cause **internal recognition**, defined as an increase in awareness that originates within the individual: (1) Don runs out of breakfast cereal, or realizes the heels on his shoes are badly worn; (2) Lynette buys a new eyeliner or tries a new restaurant and is not satisfied with either; (3) Nicole dyes her hair and then realizes she also needs a color-preserving shampoo.

On the other hand, it is the job of marketers to create **external recognition**—stimulation that guides people toward the recognition of a "problem" that can be solved with a new or different product or service. Marketers do this by using various advertising, sales, promotional, or public relations initiatives. For example, Rachel sees a four-color magazine ad for jeans with new details that she loves. The ad has caught her attention and touched her emotionally; she feels the desire to buy the jeans because she thinks her wardrobe needs a little more "spice" and the jeans will add it.

2. Collect Information or Data about Alternative Solutions

After identifying the problem, the next step involves collecting information about ways to eliminate the problem, thereby easing the discomfort. **Information collection** includes the search for and selection of information that provides alternative foundations for making good decisions. Therefore, we identify some alternatives and determine which ones are suitable. A person considering an expensive purchase may devote more time to thinking about the purchase and collection information (high involvement), whereas someone making an inexpensive choice may spend little time and effort (low involvement).

The search for information takes place both internally and externally. An internal search is simply thinking about prior purchase experiences to remind ourselves what was good or bad about each. Consumers today also rely heavily on external information sources such as the media, reference guides, friends, expert sources, or just shopping at various stores. We collect data whether we actively look for information, consider our past experiences, or remember advertising we previously heard or saw when we weren't really looking for a particular product or service (marketers refer to this last type as "low-dose" advertising[4]). What happens next? **Information filtering**—sorting through all the collected data, then prioritizing and selecting that which best meets our needs. For example, Rachel reviews magazine photos, talks to her friends, and considers other information before deciding which jeans to buy.

Note that a person's information search and ultimate decision includes influence (guidance and/or pressure) from the same sources mentioned in Chapter 8: people or groups with lifestyles above us, below us, or at our same level. Another factor that plays a role in the decision-making process is the element of risk (the

Table 11.1.   External Information Sources

Traditional	Internet-based
Co-workers	www.ask.com
Doctors	www.census.gov
Family	www.dogpile.com
Friends	www.google.com
Libraries	www.hoovers.com
Media	www.lycos.com
Schools	www.yahoo.com

chance of loss). People handle risk—or the perception of risk—differently. Some people have personalities that process risk more comfortably; others struggle with it constantly.

Perceived risk is the risk a customer believes exists in the purchase of goods or services from a specific retailer, whether or not a risk actually exists.[5] The following five risk areas are of particular concern to consumers in relation to the purchase of goods and services:

- *Functional.* Does it work / perform as expected?
- *Monetary.* Is there a higher value than cost to me for using this product or service?
- *Physical.* What kind of safety or harm concerns are related to using this?
- *Psychological.* How accurately does this product or service reflect my self-image?
- *Social.* How harmful will this be to my way of life?

Perceived risk is generally low when a consumer doesn't really know too much about potential problems that might arise when using the product or service. Conversely, when consumers mentally exaggerate potential problems, the associated risk is perceived to be high.

Effective marketing campaigns address consumer perceptions of potential problems, showing customer benefits (return policy if not satisfied), or demonstrating how one brand, not another, provides the best solution. Marketers help us "see" the logical and emotional benefits associated with a specific product or service as a way of reducing the perception of risk. Nevertheless, consumers are still concerned about risk. For example, before buying a pair of stilettos, Mary considers the potential foot problems (physical) associated with wearing them. Dustin decides to buy a high-end watch because it presents the "correct" self-image (psychological). Lindsey selects a purse but wonders if it will hold up to the wear-and-tear during her typical day. How did Mary, Dustin, and Lindsey work through their respective concerns? They first identified some alternatives, and then weighed the benefits associated with the various choices. At this point there are some viable alternatives that will probably

off the mark.com   by Mark Parisi

SOON ALL PANTS WILL COME
WITH BUILT-IN LAPTOPS

FIGURE 11.4. Perceived Risk: "Should I really experiment with some new or untried product or service?"

help bridge the gap between what we have (our "as is") and what we want (our "should be"). If we now take the time to consider the pros (why it will work well) and cons (why it won't work well) of the various choices, we'll probably make a more informed and successful selection.

Let's Talk
How do you handle risk? Do all of your friends handle it the same way? Why do you think some people handle risk differently?

3. Review/Evaluate the Alternatives

The review and evaluation process consists of three steps:

1. Figuring out the standards or guidelines on which to base a decision
2. Determining the importance of each standard or guideline
3. Prioritizing (ranking) the alternatives

For example, you want to go to dinner with your significant other, and you have to decide where to go. You have already suggested four or five places. Using the three-step process mentioned above, your conversation might sound like this:

"How are we going to decide which restaurant we should go to tonight?" (The standards or guidelines under consideration might include ambience, convenience, dress code, entertainment, type of food, location, price, promotional coupons, and service.)

"OK, how important are each of these to you?" (The guidelines are then ranked as very important, not so important, completely unimportant.)

"Let's figure out our top two choices and then discuss them." (The alternatives are prioritized.)

If it's too difficult to evaluate the importance of each standard or guideline (the second of the three-step process mentioned above), consumers might revert to brand equity, the "added value a brand name/identity brings to a product or service beyond the functional benefits provided."[6] And if none of the alternatives meets or exceeds expectations, consumers might decide to not purchase the product or service at that time. What role do marketers play in this process? They try to educate consumers about which standards or guidelines should be used, or guide them in the ranking or prioritizing of these guidelines. (See Special Focus 11.1.)

〉〉〉 SPECIAL FOCUS 11.1: THE HOME-VIDEO MARKET: WHO RENTS, WHO BUYS, AND WHY 〈〈〈

When the door to a TLA Entertainment video store swings open, the primary question facing most consumers shuffling inside is relatively simple: "What movie will I take home tonight?"

But to Wharton marketing professor Jehoshua Eliashberg and Wharton doctoral candidate George Knox, the key question surrounding the burgeoning $12 billion home-video market goes at least one step further: Which consumers will rent their movie of choice tonight, and which consumers will *buy*?

In a study entitled, "The Consumer's Rent vs. Buy Decision: The Case of Home-Video," Eliashberg and Knox present a new model that they say accurately predicts the consumer's decision to rent or buy a particular movie at a video store. Using data collected from a home-video store over a six-month period, these marketing experts believe that the results could have a significant impact on how retailers can ultimately influence viewers to buy movies, which, from the retailers' point of view, is more profitable than renting.

In addition, Eliashberg says, the study's results could also have implications for marketing to consumers far beyond the parameters of the home-video market. The principles used to analyze the video industry, he notes, could be applied "to any situation where consumers face two options: Option One, whether to pay a flat fee for unlimited consumption *or* Option Two, whether to pay at each time of consumption."

Industries where flat-rate and pay-per-use options already exist include health clubs, spas, ski resorts, telephone calling plans, movie theaters, and drama and musical theater subscriptions. Even Weight Watchers, the dieting program, now offers flat-fee or pay-per-use options. "We chose to work on this because it has implications in other areas, not just in the buy-rent decision for home videos. The model we developed here will address these expanded concerns," Eliashberg says.

More DVD Players, Lower Video Prices
The two researchers began their study by noting that while "there has been a growing interest in research and modeling issues related to the entertainment

industry in general and the movie industry in particular," less attention has been paid to the home-video market and its related consumer decision-making process. And yet the topic is clearly ripe for analysis for one obvious reason: growth.

In 2003, the $12 billion home-video market represented 52% of the revenue of a major motion picture release, compared to just 1% only eight years earlier. Eliashberg credits the growth to two key factors: the expanding use of DVD players and home theaters, and the affordable pricing of videos for sale. Both, he says, "have made the home video market grow faster than expected in the last few years. While studios understand that aggregate drivers of success in the home video market are different from the box office, *how consumers decide whether to buy or rent a particular movie title is relatively unknown both to entertainment executives and academics.*"

Eliashberg and Knox developed and tested two models designed to capture how a consumer might choose between buying or renting. The two models reflect a basic premise that "at the heart of any decision to buy or rent is an estimate of how much value the consumer anticipates he or she will derive over subsequent movie viewings." In short, how do consumers determine value, and how does this affect their buying vs. rent decision?

In the first model, which is based on the real options literature in economics, "the consumer understands that the value of watching a movie diminishes over time and treats the problem of how many times he should watch the movie as an optimal stopping problem." Part of the value the consumer "attaches to buying is the flexibility" he or she has in "choosing when to stop watching . . . the movie."

Ultimately, the buyer compares the "expected utility of buying with a one-shot value from renting, and chooses the option that maximizes expected utility." In the second model, based primarily on cognitive psychology principles, the consumer is "concerned with the number of times a movie is watched, not value or utility." Eliashberg notes that in this model, the consumer calculates a threshold level of viewings, based on the costs of renting and buying the title. "If the consumer's anticipated number of viewings is greater than the so determined threshold level, the consumer's decision is to buy the home video. Otherwise, he will rent it."

The main difference between the two models and their subsequent equations, Eliashberg says, "is that in model one, the consumer anticipates decay in enjoyment. He will enjoy it less after watching it the first or second time. With model two, there is no such anticipation. The decision he makes is based on arithmetic— *How many times will I watch the movie?—and is the ratio beneficial to buy?*"

To collect data used to calibrate both models, Eliashberg and Knox turned to

TLA Entertainment Group, a home-video retail chain that operates six stores in Philadelphia and New York City and was ranked 15th in revenue across the country for specialty stores in 2002, according to the report. Eliashberg and Knox chose to collect data from the largest TLA store in Philadelphia during the last six months of 2003; of the 75,000 transactions recorded during this period (covering 9,000 movies and 5,000 members), the study focused exclusively on 24,000 DVD transactions from 4,276 customers for 76 of the most popular movies, available for both renting and buying with the store. These 76 movies included such selections as *Anger Management, Bend It Like Beckham, Bowling for Columbine, Bringing Down the House, Die Another Day, Gangs of New York, Holes, Jerry Seinfeld Comedian, Just Married, Lord of the Rings: The Two Towers, Malibu's Most Wanted, Narc, Punch-Drunk Love, Shanghai Knights* and *View from the Top.*

Why study DVDs and not VHS movies? Two reasons, the study noted. DVDs are priced to sell in the $10 to $25 range compared to VHS tapes, which can cost as much as $100. And "given the scenario we model, both options—renting and buying—have to be available at the same time for the choice to be legitimate. DVDs are most commonly released for rental and purchase simultaneously, whereas VHS tapes are more often released sequentially."

To obtain useful implications from the models, Eliashberg and Knox introduce what they call "relevant parameters"—namely, factors that, once estimated, can be employed to make inferences about the "rent/buy behavior of individuals and the rentability/purchasability of movies." For instance, they consider whether the consumer balances the cost of watching the same movie again with the future possibility of positive value—which could be seeing some favorite scenes again. And while price explains part of the process used to determine renting vs. buying, niche appeal accounts for many customer purchases.

R-rated Action Films

Several clear patterns eventually emerged. Confirming what the authors call "industry intuition," the study documents that the TLA store's customers are more likely to buy action movies that did well at the box office and have an R-rating. And when it comes to predicting who will buy and who will rent, a movie's value, represented most clearly by the authors' first model, had a clear advantage. "We find that accounting for diminishing value of the video adds significant predictive power . . . to the model," the authors write.

The results also indicated that basing the prediction solely on the box office gross could not explain why a movie like *How to Lose a Guy in 10 Days* (with receipts of $106.1 million) inspired one buy out of 41 transactions, whereas a cult favorite like *About Schmidt* ($65 million) saw seven buys out of 54 transactions.

"Conventional wisdom holds that a movie can correct for a bad showing at the box office by subsequent DVD sales, because DVD releases provide more of a 'level' playing field to all movies being released than at the theater, where only a handful of movies at any given time are seen as being successful."

The purpose of the study, Eliashberg cautions, is not to determine which variable "can strongly predict rental and purchase sales across the entire home video market." Rather, the marketing experts propose that retailers such as TLA can use the equations related to price, rental options and different purchasing patterns to predict which consumers will buy a movie—and then generate customized purchase prices for consumers that take these histories into account. The goal? To create an option that is so attractive that a customer will buy rather than rent a movie, a more profitable transaction for the retailer. Noted Eliashberg and Knox: "We are interested in a particular retailer's prediction problem, given its own customer base, in order to customize its prices or manage its inventory."

Which means, in the future, that the home-video consumer who walks into a TLA store could soon be subject to the same price-discrimination practices that many consumers already face when buying airline tickets or browsing online product stores. For instance, say a prospective renter of one "purchasable" movie title— i.e., a movie whose value does not diminish rapidly over time—has a previous pattern of buying or renting similar movies, data which TLA has collected. When he goes to rent, TLA punches the consumer data into the Eliashberg-Knox equation or model, and comes up with a tempting movie purchase price offer of $12.50.

But when renter No. 2 enters and picks up the same "purchasable" movie but doesn't exhibit a previous pattern of buying, the result from the rent vs. buy model might force the retailer to sweeten the offer a bit.

Based on the variables, she is offered the movie for $10.50.

By collecting information about consumer spending habits and purchase predictability, retailers already offer various consumers the same product at different prices. Eliashberg thinks the home-video market—and any market that offers flat fee vs. pay-per-use options—is ready for the same scenario.

"How many times have I found myself sitting next to someone else, and he or she has made me feel like a sucker, or I made him feel like a sucker, for going to the same destination on an airline but paying more for the ticket?" Eliashberg noted. "Price discrimination has become acceptable. It is very micro marketing."

And, he added, "our model is also very applicable to websites. In fact, in the introduction to the paper, we talk about different types of home-video business models on the web. There are those like Columbia House that allow you only to buy, and those like Netflix that allow you only to rent, and then those like Wal-Mart that allow you to either buy or rent. Our model will tell you in advance which movies are particularly rentable and which ones are buyable. And the customized pricing options are definitely applicable and able to be used by those websites offering both options for their customers."

The paper cautions that "these results represent the clientele of TLA and may not be representative of the home video market as a whole." And Eliashberg did admit that choosing to base his study on a particular video store in downtown Philadelphia could result "in a very idiosyncratic preference for movies, one that should be taken into account. I have seen that also in movie theaters. If you [compare] what movies people like in downtown Philadelphia as opposed to the suburbs, that could have an affect on the study."

The paper also notes that the dataset does not allow the authors to observe day-to-day availability of a movie title. "To the extent that consumers substitute across titles given unavailability, we would not expect this to bias our results. However, if consumers substitute renting for buying the same movie or vice versa because the movie is unavailable in one format, we would expect our results to be biased . . . We can only partially control this by choosing movies that TLA stocks heavily."

As far as the study's ability to predict trends, Eliashberg suggests that "stores such as TLA will continue to make business mainly from the rental activity unless they take seriously our customized pricing accommodations. And then they can generate, through price discrimination, more profit for themselves by offering the clientele the opportunity to buy."

>>> Source: Knowledge@Wharton. "The Home-Video Market: Who Rents, Who Buys and Why." February 8, 2006. Retrieved August 31, 2007, from http:// knowledge.wharton.upenn.edu/index.cfm?fa=printArticle&ID=1377.

Let's Talk
In Special Focus 11.1, what influences consumers to buy or rent videos? Why will consumers pay a flat monthly fee or a fee per individual transaction? How can other industries use this consumption model? But many people do not buy at the first store they visit; they like to comparison shop before making a purchase. The Internet has made the process of shopping around for alternatives much easier.

Comparison shopping today is easier or more complicated, depending on the consumer's tolerance for stimulation, desire for information, and ability to process the information. According to Barron's *Dictionary of Business Terms*, *comparison shopping* is a process whereby a consumer gathers as much information as possible about particular products and services for comparison before purchasing them. This

FIGURE 11.5. Too Many Choices

activity consists of doing the necessary research, which includes going to the stores offering the merchandise, comparing point-of-purchase displays (eye-catching floor displays that provide product or service information), looking at competitive advertisements, Web sites, and so on.

How can a consumer make this process more organized and efficient, without getting overwhelmed by modern technology? One way is to use a *cybermediary*, an online intermediary that does just that.[7] Consumers can find these types of services by typing "comparison-shopping online" into a computer search engine. These online agents/intermediaries, or "shopbots," help in transforming passive search and retrieval engines into active, personal assistants.[8] Their job is to make the search and evaluation process more efficient.

Aside from the technology-related tools that make this evaluation process work more smoothly, there are also simple mental rules of thumb (methods based on common sense) that help people make decisions more quickly. Because we don't always make decisions rationally or objectively, we use these rules of thumb or mental generalizations, termed **heuristics**, to help in weighing our choices and alternatives.

Examples.

1. Maribel, who wants to buy a car, tells her friend that she will not buy one from a used car dealer because her past experiences lead her to believe that it's really better to go directly to the dealer or buy one through the Internet.

2. Graham, who wants to buy a single-family house, remembers how difficult it was for a friend of his to buy a condo by himself, not using the services of a real estate agent. After three months, the friend hired a real estate agent, who reduced the stress associated with making an offer, keeping the deal together, and finally closing and taking possession of the property.

How do we choose the best alternative solution? What kind of decision guidelines, technological tools, or influences from others direct us to select one item over another?

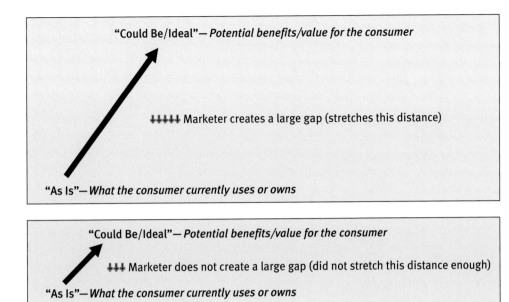

"Could Be/Ideal"—*Potential benefits/value for the consumer*

↓↓↓↓↓ Marketer creates a large gap (stretches this distance)

"As Is"—*What the consumer currently uses or owns*

"Could Be/Ideal"—*Potential benefits/value for the consumer*

↓↓↓ Marketer does not create a large gap (did not stretch this distance enough)

"As Is"—*What the consumer currently uses or owns*

FIGURE 11.6A and B.

4. Choose the Best Alternative

The next step in the decision-making process is the evaluation of key points that differentiate the choices. Michael Solomon, a well-known consumer behavior scholar and author, calls these choice features *determinant attributes* and suggests that a marketer's job done well frequently results in the education of consumers or selection of key choice factors to be used in the decision-making process.[9] Once we select the major criteria or features we think will provide the greatest amount of benefits, we can move forward with the best alternative choice.

Marketers create advertising and promotional campaigns designed to emphasize the existence of a large gap between the customer's "as is" situation (what is currently owned or used) and the "should be" status (the ideal—the total benefits when using the product or service). If the marketer has done a good job (by creating a large gap), the consumer's best alternative is to buy the marketer's product or service.

The consumer generally selects the alternative that has made the strongest impression; that is, the marketer has created the widest distance between the "as is" and the "should be." When the marketer makes it easy for the consumer to (1) understand the differences among competing brands, (2) relate to and visualize the sizable improvements gained, and (3) minimize the difficulty in decision making, the consumer can select much more easily, and then buy the product or service. (This last step is referred to as "purchase behavior.") For example, a computer salesperson demonstrates added features that

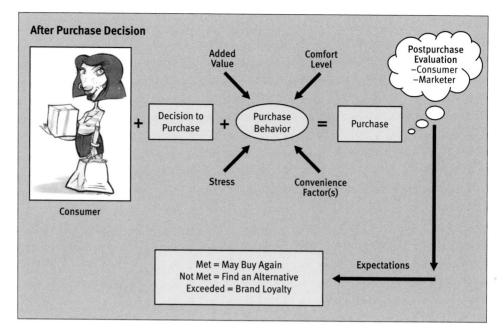

FIGURE 11.7.

significantly improve productivity, efficiency, and the "fun factor" between a customer's current computer and a new one.

5. Evaluate the Decision or Purchase

Obviously, both the consumer and marketer want the end result of the purchase behavior and post-purchase evaluation to be very positive. Have you ever had good or bad feelings about a purchase you just made, or decided you needed to buy something else to go with your initial purchase? For example, you buy a pair of boots and then realize how well a particular belt would go with them. Or perhaps you're buying furniture for your living room and feel that a new HD flat-screen, wall-mounted TV would work nicely there as well. And then there's the experience of feeling guilty about what you just bought and thinking that maybe you should not have purchased it. This sense of uneasiness is known as buyer's remorse or post-purchase dissonance (also discussed in Chapter 4).

During post-purchase evaluation the consumer will judge the product or service to have met, exceeded, or not met his or her expectations. Situations such as the ones described above can lead to either additional purchases or reconsideration of the purchase decision. The marketer's objective in either scenario is to anticipate and address these common kinds of thoughts after the purchase. This is done to increase the purchaser's long-term satisfaction and customer loyalty and reduce product returns. The savvy marketer addresses the potential post-purchase issue by finding ways to positively reinforce the value and benefits attached to its products. For example, a sales associate e-mails or mails an article to a client who just purchased an item; this article reinforces how others are enjoying and benefiting from a similar purchase. Repeat purchases signal that the customers' experiences have been positive.

Types of Decision Making

Although this chapter has presented a common method for decision making, there is really no single way to make decisions. If you use more logically based, left-brain thinking to process information and carefully review the pros and cons, you are using what researchers call the **rational perspective**. Marketers who understand how rational perspective consumers learn, retrieve, collect, analyze, and process information can implement strategies into marketing campaigns that appropriately target this type of analytical consumer. Stanford University marketing professor Itamar Simonson suggests that consumers who consciously choose specific store environments and experiences are more likely to consciously process a marketer's strategy—in other words, it is not lost in the "noise" of a typical store.[10]

On the other hand, actions consumers have learned in response to specific stimuli are collectively called the **behavioral perspective.** (Also see the discussions in Chapter 3 about behavioral learning conditions and Chapter 4 about rational versus emotional motives.) Study of decision-making behaviors at Duke University and Stanford University, among others, suggests that this type of specific learned response to stimuli provides the framework of habitual or automatic responses that people use to make or improve judgments or choices.

Low-involvement decision making in fashion-oriented purchases is sometimes referred to as "impulse buying." Marketers can use store design, product placement, even scents, to trigger impulse purchases. Richard L. Petersen, M.D., a Stanford University neuroeconomics research scientist, noted that "when someone views a potential gain in the environment the brain's cycle of reward approach motivation is set into action." This all leads to the choice selection.[11]

Finally, someone using the **experiential perspective** (explained by gestalt psychology,[12] discussed in Chapter 3 and the ABCs of attitude covered in Chapter 5) considers the overall experience, not just a particular point or the "how" of the situation.[13] These are the metaphorical "lenses" in the consumer's glasses that incorporate

FIGURE 11.8. How Did You Make that Decision?

the values, beliefs, behaviors, and domestic and global views that influence that person's decisions. (See TORA described in Chapter 5.)

Modern technology can also provide solution alternatives. For example, you can walk into some retail stores, input data on a computer system about your buying preferences, and then get a printout listing products that reflect your preferences. Special Focus 11.2 describes how one company uses proprietary software to help learn about consumers' feelings regarding a brand or marketing campaign. Consumers can also use technology to preprogram their decisions; examples of this include the use of the home entertainment service TiVo to record television programs, and software features (such as filters) that can help detect computer-based problems such as *spam* (unsolicited and unwanted commercial advertising) and *phishing* (e-mail fraud scam conducted for the purposes of information or identity theft).

〉〉〉 SPECIAL FOCUS 11.2: GROUP M UNVEILS AUDIENCE ENGAGEMENT MEASUREMENT TOOL 〈〈〈

From iPods to cellphones to the web and old-fashioned TV, the plethora of media channels used to reach consumers has exploded. That's led to a heated debate on how best to measure consumers' reception to an ad message, what the industry has started referring to as engagement. Group M is rolling out a research and communications-planning tool that it says can identify, define and measure consumer engagement.

Proprietary Software

The tool, called Connections, collects qualitative and quantitative data on consumer preferences about advertising and brands, which are then analyzed using a proprietary software program. The outcome: a host of data about a particular marketing campaign or issue that includes consumers' feelings about the brand or campaign. It is now in use at Group M agencies, which include WPP Group's media agencies Maxus, MediaCom, Mediaedge:cia and MindShare.

"By being able to measure that engagement, whether it be emotional or behavioral, I think we are able to take a strong step forward," said Bob DeSena, the newly hired director–active engagement, Mediaedge:cia.

Numerous industry executives, including Mr. DeSena, have for years been debating how best to move beyond traditional measures of reach and frequency, said Bob Barocci, CEO-president, Advertising Research Foundation, which participates in a task force on the matter. "Many agencies are working on this because advertisers want it."

$2 million to Develop

Group M spent nearly $2 million to develop Connections, which comprises some borrowed elements—for instance, two products used to gather data, Channel Connect and Demand-and-Activation, come from WPP sibling company Millward Brown—and some that are built from scratch, such as the new software program.

"We've collaborated at the Group M level with Millward Brown, but each agency interprets the findings in its own way," said Stephan Bruneau, regional director, MED MediaLab, in Europe, Middle East and Africa. "At Mediaedge we customize the communications plan using our in-house process, called Navigator." MindShare and MediaCom adapt the tool to their planning programs.

But within the agencies, Connections is used to create customized reports for particular clients. Each report is designed to solve a particular question or issue, such as: How best can an automaker reach an 18- to 24-year-old male? Using what media channel? Or, how can a brand with strong brand preference among consumers translate that advantage into higher sales? The agency might design a study using Connections to investigate what motivates consumers to buy.

>>> Source: Lisa Sanders, "Group M Unveils Audience Engagement Measurement Tool," *Advertising Age*, June 27, 2006, http://adage.com/print?article_id =110187.

Consumer Effort Expended

How much effort do we put into making a decision—not much, a moderate amount, or a lot? Consumer behaviorists use the terms "routine," "limited," and "extensive," respectively, to describe the various levels of effort expended by consumers in decision making.

Naturally, each category is relative to the individual's situation and personality; for example, one person buying a car may see it as an extensive decision-making process, while another person might view it as requiring limited effort. We can characterize **routine** or **habitual decision making** as an autopilot mechanism; we don't really give it too much thought (for example, buying the daily newspaper). **Limited decision making** involves some thought, but frequently involves general rules of thumb we've learned or borrowed from others (for example, buying a purse with cleats already on the bottom of the bag). When **extensive** consideration is needed, we weigh the pros and cons, along with the perceived risks and benefits (for example, selecting a college).

Market Habits

Consumers often behave in certain patterns with regard to their purchases; these are known as "market habits." In addition to heuristics (previously defined as men-

Table 11.2. Effort Exerted in Making Purchase Decisions

Type of Effort	Purchase Time Line	Cost	Search Effort	Example
Routine	Frequent	Low	Minimal	Junk Food Grocery Staples Handbags
Limited	Periodic	Moderate	Moderate	Sunglasses Designer Fashions
Extensive	Not Very Often	High	High	Graduate School

tal generalizations that help us make decisions more quickly), people also use other decision-making methods that are considered less sophisticated than the models discussed earlier in the chapter. Customers with an **inertia habit** frequently buy the same brand because it takes little or no energy; thus any competitor that makes the purchase of a similar product even easier may win over a customer. A brand-loyal person sticks with the same product or service brand frequently due to both logical and emotional reward preferences (benefits received) learned through past experiences. For example, a person repeatedly watches a particular TV news station, buys a specific brand-name soup, or purchases the same make of shoes because he has had both objective (what others have thought) and subjective (personal preferences) user criteria met. And finally, another group of consumers with a distinguishable market habit are those who prefer to keep consumption choices that belong and relate specifically to their own culture; this is called **ethnocentrism**. (Also see discussion of culture in consumer behavior in Chapters 9 and 15.)

Because many factors are involved with and influence an individual's decision-making process before, during, and after a purchase decision, it's very important that marketers understand consumer concerns associated with this process. So customer feedback from both those who bought and didn't buy is important to marketers for crafting successful campaigns.

The next question is, "Where and how do consumers buy fashion products?" Chapter 12 explores these issues.

"Heuristics, you're looking for the easiest choice. And, Inertia Habit, you're quoting ideas your father told you about buying things. Now, Brand Loyal, you told us you'd never change brands, no matter what. And Ethnocentric, you sound like you pre-judge everything."

FIGURE 11.9.

Let's Talk
How have you given marketers your feedback about your level of anxiety or satisfaction regarding a purchase or something you were thinking about buying? In person? In groups? Via the Internet? Which method did you prefer and why?

Summary

Decision making is a multistep process that is influenced by both internal and external forces. These forces can play a role before, during, or after the decision is made. The five-step decision-making process helps consumers identify, evaluate, and feel satisfied about the results of their decision. The Problem Awareness Model depicts the gap (distance) between the "as is" and "could be" or "ideal" situations in response to stimuli. Marketers, on the other hand, try to stretch this gap when it is small and use various media to alert, educate, and persuade consumers to accept a particular point of view. When consumers perceive this added value (that is, when the gap is large and the product or service will help close that gap) and judge a perceived risk to be manageable, the decision to buy is usually the result. Technological tools called cybermediaries can help consumers filter through abundant information; another method is the use of simple, mental rules of thumb (heuristics) to help make searching for and evaluating information more efficient.

Some important decision-making factors that marketers try to address in advance are (1) the amount of energy expended in making a decision, (2) how consumers perceive the benefits expected from a purchase, and (3) the level of stress associated with the decision. If a customer's expectations are met, a repeat purchase might happen; if expectations are not met, consumers might decide to consider a substitute product or service. Marketers who anticipate and exceed customer expectations often create brand loyalty, whereby customers continue to make positive buying decisions about specific products or services.

Key Terms

Behavioral perspective	Information filtering
Ethnocentrism	Internal recognition
Experiential perspective	Limited decision making
Extensive decision making	Problem awareness
External recognition	Perceived risk
Heuristics	Rational perspective
Inertia habit	Routine/habitual decision making
Information collection	

Questions for Review

1. Why are marketers thought of as problem solvers, and how can marketers create wants?
2. What are the five steps in the decision-making process? Which of these steps is the most important?
3. How does the Problem Awareness Model relate a large gap versus small gap to the probability of success in a marketer's attempt to influence a consumer decision?
4. What are the differences between actual and perceived risk, and why are these ideas important to consumers and marketers?
5. How do the rational, behavioral, and experiential perspectives in decision making differ?

Activities

1. Name a product and a service you are going to purchase in the next three to ten weeks. Use each of the terms noted in the Problem Awareness Model (for example, "as is," "should be," "stimulus"), and specifically identify and relate them to your actions and thoughts as you become aware of your "problem."
2. Identify two fashion products or services and two different media stimuli sources that guided you to recognize a "problem."
3. Illustrate the concept of information filtering, and relate it to your purchase of a fashion product or service you have bought during the last 12 months.
4. Create and explain a table of data that identifies two positive and two negative reasons that someone would consider after purchasing an item that was clearly more expensive than originally anticipated.
5. Interview several consumers who recently purchased a product or service primarily based on choices that related specifically to their own culture.

Mini-Projects

Teaming with two other class members, identify a product or service that each team member recently purchased using either routine, limited, or extensive decision making. (Note: Each team member should select a different decision-making category so that each one is discussed.) Then:

1. Describe your purchase and explain the type, purchase time line, cost, and search effort used (that is, how you got your information).
2. Discuss the major factor(s) that influenced your decision making (for example,

value, comfort level, convenience, and/or stress issues). Rank these factors in order of importance.

References

1. Tim Malloy, "Fill 'Er Up: Alternative Fuel Station Provides Look at Options." Associated Press. Retrieved from http://autos.aol.com/article/hybrid/hub/_a/fill -er-up/20060620165709990001 on June 20, 2006.

2. Lars Perner, *The Psychology of Consumers: Consumer Behavior and Marketing.* "Decision Making." Retrieved from www.consumerpsychologist.com/#Decision on August 31, 2007.

3. Nessim Hanna and Richard Wozniak. *Consumer Behavior: An Applied Approach* (Upper Saddle River, NJ: Prentice Hall, 2001).

4. Girish Punj, "Presearch Decision Making in Consumer Durable Purchases," *Journal of Consumer Marketing* 4 (Winter 1987).

5. Melody Vargas, Retail Glossary of Terminology. Retrieved from http:// retailindustry.about.com/library/terms/p/bld_perceivedrisk.htm on August 31, 2007.

6. Jacob Jacoby and Leon B. Kaplan, "The Components of Perceived Risk," *Advances in Consumer Research* 3 (1972): 6–10 and 382–383.

7. MSN Encarta, "Cybermediary" entry, www.encarta.msn.com/dictionary _561546803/cybermediary.html.

8. First Monday Web site. "Using an Intelligent Agent to Enhance Search Engine Performance, www.firstmonday.org/issues/issue2_3/jansen/.

9. Michael Solomon, *Consumer Behavior: Buying, Having and Being* (Upper Saddle River, NJ: Prentice Hall, 2007), p. 321.

10. Itamar Simonson, "In Defense of Consciousness: The Role of Conscious and Unconscious Inputs in Consumer Choice," *Journal of Consumer Psychology* 5, no.3 (2005).

11. Howard Greenfield, "Neuromarketing: Unlocking the Decision-Making Process." Retrieved September, 7, 2004, from www.marketingprofs.com/4/greenfield1.asp on.

12. M. P. Driscoll, *Psychology of Learning for Instruction* (Needham Heights, MA: Allyn & Bacon, 1993).

13. Clare Torrans and Dr. Nada Dabbagh, "Gestalt and Instructional Design," George Mason University, March 8, 1999.

Additional Resources

Berman, Barry, and Joel R.Evans. *Retail Management A Strategic Approach*, 10th *ed.* Upper Saddle River, NJ: Prentice Hall, 2007.

BPlans.com. Glossary of Business Terms. www.bplans.com/g/index.cfm.

SearchSecurity.com. Glossary. http://searchsecurity.techtarget.com/glossary/0,294242, sid14,00.html.

Wolff, David. "Exactly What Is 'Experiential Marketing'?" January 12, 2005. Retrieved August 31, 2007, from http://agelessmarketing.typepad.com/ageless_marketing/ 2005/01/exactly_what_is.html.

CHAPTER 12

How Fashion Consumers Buy

Carrying the last of the shopping bags in from the car, Jackie breathed a sigh of relief. With her 19-year-old daughter Emma's discerning eye (and friendly assistance from the boutique's attentive sales associate), she had picked out a stunning designer dress for the gala awards dinner she had to attend for business the following month. The dress was expensive, but worth it, since she wanted to look her best in front of important clients and business associates. And if she couldn't wear it again, maybe she could sell it at the local consignment shop. Besides, although Emma had been a little bored, Jackie always found it such an indulgence to shop at that boutique. The décor was lovely and the merchandise easy to browse. There was always classical music playing softly in the background, and the staff was helpful without being pushy, even offering tea or coffee to sip while shopping. Now she just needed to decide whether to wear shoes she already had in her closet or buy new ones to go with the dress. She decided to do an online search later to see if anything grabbed her attention.

The other errands they'd done that day had gone equally smoothly, Jackie thought. As a "thank you" to Emma for going along, they had stopped at the Metropark store that had recently opened, and she had bought her daughter a pair of jeans—even though the price seemed awfully high for denim, and the music videos flashing on wall-mounted plasma TVs were a little loud for Jackie's taste. After that, they'd gone to Target to look for sheets for Emma's dorm room, since she would need an extra set when she headed back to campus. There was a sale and the price was so good, they ended up buying two sets, as well as a fun, funky bracelet that caught Emma's eye and cost less than $10. Their final stop had been Costco, to stock up on household basics like detergent and dog food. While they were there, Jackie noticed a pair of Giorgio Armani sunglasses that looked a lot like a pair her husband had lost and not yet replaced. At the warehouse club price, she knew the designer shades were a bargain compared to other stores, so she added them to her cart before zipping through the checkout and heading home.

Changes in Fashion and Fashion Consumption

Where and how people buy products is as much a part of consumer behavior as what they buy and why, especially with today's wealth of shopping options. As we've seen in previous chapters, many factors come into play whenever consumers need (or want) to purchase something. Similarly, how they go about shopping and buying can depend on everything from what item they're seeking, to how much time they have, and even what mood they're in on a given day. When it comes to fashion merchandise, the purchasing process also depends on what kind of fashion consumer a person is—that is, how the individual relates to products within the fashion life cycle.

Fashion Leaders and Followers

As you can tell from observing people, both in your own surroundings and on television and in other media, some people are fashion leaders and some are fashion followers. As discussed in Chapter 6, fashion leaders—also known as fashion innovators—are those people who seek out new fashion and wear it before it becomes generally accepted. The evolution of style seems to come instinctively to them. In fact, a recent Lifestyle Monitor report by Cotton Incorporated found that nearly two-thirds of fashion innovators trust their instincts and buy clothing on impulse.[1]

The majority of people are **fashion followers**, those who adopt a look only after they are sure of a fashion trend. There are several reasons why consumers might be fashion followers. They may not have the time, money, or interest to spend on fashion pursuits; or they may be insecure about their own tastes, so they look to others to determine what is acceptable and appropriate, including imitating people they admire. They might follow to keep pace with neighbors or to be accepted by their peer group, or they might simply need to be exposed to new styles for a while before accepting them.[2] Whatever their reason, fashion followers are crucial to the fashion industry because they, as much as fashion leaders, contribute greatly to the ebb and flow of styles known as the fashion life cycle.

The Fashion Life Cycle

All products have a life cycle, and fashions are no different. A **fashion life cycle** is the length of time a given look or style is popular. Whether a fashion look begins in a designer's runway show or on the streets of a city, its life cycle consists of five stages: introduction, rise, peak, decline, and obsolescence or rejection. That cycle is generally represented by a bell-shaped curve, as shown in Figure 12.1.

Introduction

The **introduction phase** of the fashion life cycle is when a new style first appears. Many times, that will be at the launch of a new designer collection for the coming season, where only a few garments are produced and their prices are at a high level. Only a small number of consumers can afford this couture apparel, and its availability is limited to a handful of exclusive ateliers. Some styles are rejected outright by the public, which may include retailers and the media, and never make it past the introduction stage. But if a style catches on and is wanted by consumers, it enters the next phase.

Rise

The **rise phase** is the period when a look is growing in popularity. Early in this stage, a style that started at the couture level will generally spread first to the higher-end

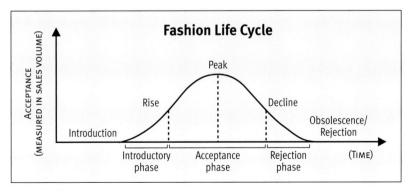

FIGURE 12.1. Fashion life cycle.

department and specialty stores, such as Neiman Marcus or Saks Fifth Avenue. In time, the style will be copied at a wider range of price levels and appear in mainstream department and specialty stores such as Macy's and The Limited.

The rise phase of the fashion life cycle is dependent on **knock-offs**, the industry term for copies of the original styles. Some apparel makers specialize in copying high-fashion apparel; one of the best known is designer Victor Costa, who at one time was called the "Copy-Cat King." Knock-offs can be exact duplicates of an original designer garment, referred to as "line-for-line copies." At other times, knock-offs modify or reinterpret the style, incorporating certain key features of the original such as a certain neckline or sleeve treatment; these are known as "adaptations."

You might think that apparel knock-offs would be illegal, but under current U.S. copyright law, they are not. A rule within the law states that copyright does not protect the design of "useful" articles like clothing, since their aesthetic features are not separable from their utilitarian function—in this case, covering the body. However, fashion accessories such as handbags are protected by copyright law, so knock-offs of those items are considered counterfeit and are illegal to produce or sell. (Counterfeits are discussed in greater detail in Chapters 15 and 16.)

Some people in the fashion industry are pushing to extend copyright protection to apparel designs, but others believe that copying is actually good for the industry, accelerating the fashion life cycle and stimulating greater interest in and development of new fashions.[3] Even renowned designer Karl Lagerfeld said, about being imitated, "[Coco] Chanel called it flattery. For me, it's good because it pushes me to things they can't copy."[4]

FIGURE 12.2. At the peak phase of the fashion life cycle, a style can be seen seemingly everywhere.

Peak

A style that is in the **peak phase** of its life cycle is at the height of its acceptance and popularity. At this stage, it is widely available at all price ranges and may be found in a wide variety of store types, including popularly priced department and chain stores such as JCPenney and Kohl's, and discount stores such as Target and Kmart.

Decline

Once a style has saturated the market, people begin to tire of it and the most fashion-conscious consumers have already turned their attention to newer looks.

At that point, the style is in the **decline phase**, experiencing decreasing sales and availability only in the lower price ranges. Retailers will not order any new garments in the style and will try to sell any leftover inventory at sale or clearance prices.

Obsolescence or Rejection

The **obsolescence** or **rejection phase** marks the end of a style's life cycle, indicating that the look is out-of-date and no longer being sold, except perhaps in thrift stores. From time to time, an obsolete style will be revived and reintroduced in an updated version. For example, bell-bottom pants (first popular in the 1960s) were reborn in the late 1990s as boot-cut or flare-leg trousers.

> *Let's Talk*
> *Can you think of a fashion look that is currently in the rise phase of the life cycle? How about one in decline? What local stores might be carrying each of those?*

Length of Fashion Cycles

The basic progression of a fashion life cycle is the same for all looks and styles, although the length of time from introduction to rejection can vary dramatically and

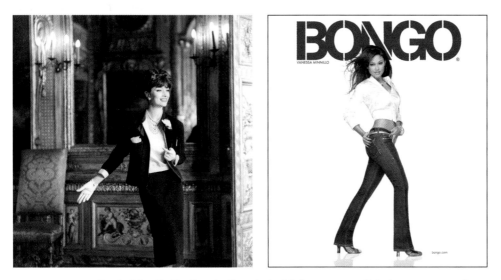

FIGURE 12.3A AND B. Classic styles, like the Chanel suit, can be in style for many years. Fads, however, are popular for only a short time.

a certain style may drop out of the fashion life cycle at any time. A **classic style**, for example, is one that is characterized by a simplicity of design that keeps it from becoming easily dated, and therefore it has an extended life cycle that may last many years, with occasional modifications to keep it fresh and current. Examples of fashion classics include the Chanel suit, Keds sneakers, and turtleneck sweaters.

A **fad**, on the other hand, is a short-lived fashion that bursts onto the scene, is wildly popular among a target group of consumers, then disappears, sometimes in a year or two, sometimes in a single season. A fad may reflect some cultural phenomenon of its time, and in general, either its concept is too extreme or it does not have strong enough design elements to ensure long-term acceptance. Some fads over the years have included poodle skirts in the 1950s, pet rocks in the 1970s, and stirrup pants in the 1990s. Recent fads that you might remember are Beanie Babies and Furby toys, platform shoes (repeating a 1970s fad), low-riding jeans, and cause-related wristbands.

Fast Fashion

The twenty-first century has seen a dramatic acceleration of the fashion life cycle, made possible in part by advanced technology and instant global communications, which can give consumers immediate exposure to new fashion looks from anywhere in the world. The use of digital photography, streaming Internet video, text messaging, and the like means that a new style seen on a fashion show runway can be transmitted almost immediately to a knock-off producer's factory—and the knock-off might actually arrive in stores *before* the original! This rapid dissemination of fashion information has spawned a new breed of retailers that practice "fast fashion." **Fast fashion** is the term for offering consumers the latest fashions as quickly as possible. Because the apparel is also designed to be very affordable, it has also been called "disposable chic" or "cheap chic" (a phrase also applied to Target's trendy, inexpensive apparel).

One of the best-known fast-fashion retailers in the United States is Sweden-based H&M , which, because of its direct relationship with more than 700 manufacturers worldwide, can move a new design from the studio to the store in as little as six weeks, as compared to traditional department stores that sometimes place orders with major apparel companies six months or even a year in advance.[5, 6] Zara, a fast-fashion retail chain that originated in Spain, moves even more quickly, taking a design from the drawing board to the store shelf in just *two* weeks.[7] Other retailers taking a fast-fashion approach include Forever 21, Charlotte Russe, and British chain Topshop, which opened its first U.S. stores in 2007.

In addition to its speed to market, another aspect of fast-fashion apparel is that it is generally produced in small quantities, so that some of the most popular items

FIGURE 12.4A and B. Retailers like H&M take a "fast fashion" approach to get new looks to consumers within weeks of their introduction.

might arrive in stores and be sold out less than a week later. That perceived scarcity of hot items contributes to the stores' appeal to their target customers, since consumers who are eager for the latest look feel the need to grab a new style quickly before it's gone.

Retail Marketing of Fashion

The emergence of fast fashion is a current illustration of the fact that retailers have always sought ways to provide consumers with the products they want and need, when they want and need them. From the first enterprising pioneer who set up a general store to sell necessities to frontier farmers and homesteaders, to the first Internet entrepreneur who saw a way to sell products through cyberspace, the retail industry has continually adapted to meet constantly shifting consumer lifestyles, desires, and behaviors.

Where Consumers Buy Fashion

During the last few decades, many once-famous stores, such as Gimbels, B. Altman, and Venture, faced insurmountable obstacles—some with a dwindling customer base, some unable to adapt their merchandise assortment to meet evolving consumer needs, others with real estate or other issues—and disappeared from the retail landscape. Today's fashion retailers face even greater challenges, with instant, global communication bringing new information to consumers, and changing economic, lifestyle, and fashion influences coming into play. As retailers meet those challenges, they give consumers a wider choice of places to buy fashion goods than ever before.

Store Retailing

According the research firm NPD Group, 90 percent of all U.S. apparel shopping dollars are spent in "brick-and-mortar" retail venues—that is, in physical stores. Within that overall category, consumers' shopping options range from large department stores, to specialty shops, to discount stores, boutiques, designer outlets, and more.

Department stores remain a top choice for fashion purchases, as documented by a recent "Where America Shops" study commissioned by *Women's Wear Daily*. The survey found that more than two-thirds (68 percent) of women regularly shop at department stores for clothes for themselves.[8] While the number of individual department store companies has shrunk over the past two decades (and particularly after a major merger in 2005 that converted a number of other retail names to Macy's), department stores still attract shoppers who want a wide selection of better-quality fashion merchandise. At the higher price levels are retailers such as Neiman Marcus, Nordstrom, Saks Fifth Avenue, and Bloomingdale's, which cater to an upscale clientele, carry designer and upper-tier labels, and tend to offer more customer service. Mid- and lower-price department stores are less known for service than they used to be, but offer a strong assortment of national brand, designer, and their own private label fashions. Among the most prominent department store names in this category are Macy's, JCPenney, Kohl's, Dillard's, and Sears.

> > > **POINT OF VIEW 12.1: WHEN IT COMES TO SHOPPING,
> > > MEN AREN'T LIKE WOMEN** < < <

Comedian Rita Rudner has a line, "When I eventually met Mr. Right, I had no idea that his first name was Always." Face it. Men have been getting bashed for years. But they've gotten the respect they deserve from a Packaged Facts study that's all about men—as consumers.

Entitled "The U.S. Men's Market," the study stated that with the blurring of traditional gender differences, and more men helping to rear kids and do household chores, the way companies market to men should evolve. Among the report's interesting facts:

- Men, particularly older men, shop only when they have to. Only a quarter of men, compared to half of women, enjoy shopping when they don't have something to buy.
- Men are more likely than women to enjoy shopping with the opposite sex; 27 percent of men compared to only 16 percent of women agreed with that one.

- Men are doing more of their own shopping. In 1985, women were responsible for 60 percent of men's apparel purchases. Some 20 years later, the number dropped to 30 percent.
- Men are less likely than women to wait until things go on sale, shop for bargains, and travel to a factory outlet store.

>>> Source: Adapted from David Morse, "It's a Man's World," *RetailWire*, March 30, 2005, http://retailwire.com/Discussions/Sngl_Discussion.cfm/10552.

Discount stores have taken a bigger portion of consumers' fashion dollars in recent years, as they have raised the fashion level of their merchandise while maintaining prices that are affordable to most consumers. In fact, the same survey previously mentioned found that 65 percent of women regularly shop at discounters for their clothes, almost the same percentage as for department stores. Leading the pack of discounters is Target, whose on-trend assortment of "cheap chic" apparel became so popular that it led to other discounters, notably Wal-Mart, adding more upscale fashions to their merchandise mix. While discount stores generally carry a mixture of national brands and private label apparel, Target has also offered exclusive apparel collections by designers such as Isaac Mizrahi.

Specialty stores are another important channel for consumers shopping for fashion goods. According to the *Women's Wear Daily* survey, 45 percent of women shop for their own apparel at small specialty store chains, while 14 percent shop at large specialty stores. As the name implies, specialty stores focus on a relatively narrow segment of apparel or other goods to attract a specific target consumer. Within the apparel category, there are specialty stores that carry clothing for children, for teens, for men, for plus sizes, and many other target groups. Some stores limit their offerings to a lifestyle category such as active sportswear or career wear, or to a particular price range.

FIGURE. 12.5. More than two-thirds of women consumers shop for apparel in department stores.

FIGURE 12.6. Talbots targets petites within its selection of women's apparel.

There are also specialty stores that focus on non-apparel fashion goods, such as jewelry, accessories, home furnishings, footwear, and luggage and leather goods. Talbot's, Casual Male, Victoria's Secret, Foot Locker, Claire's, and Bed Bath & Beyond are all examples of specialty stores.

In many cases, an existing specialty store company sees an opportunity with a different consumer segment and launches a new retail venture. One company using this strategy is American Eagle, which developed Martin + Osa to offer sportswear for men and women ages 25 to 40, an older demographic than the typical American Eagle customer; the retailer also launched a chain called Aerie, which sells intimate apparel. Other examples include Aeropostale, a retailer that targets shoppers ages 11 to 18 and opened Jimmy'Z, which is geared to a slightly older (18- to 25-year-old) consumer, as well as Ann Taylor Stores, known for career wear, which created Ann Taylor Loft to sell lower-priced casual clothes.

In addition, a growing number of apparel brands and designers have been setting up their own retail stores, giving consumers an opportunity to buy a full range of merchandise under a single label. Among the companies operating their own retail locations are Ralph Lauren, Liz Claiborne, Coach, Jones New York, and Lacoste.

The Internet

It might be hard to believe, but in 2000, many people thought Internet retailing—which was still in its infancy—was already dying. Some thought that consumers would only buy products they could touch first or see in person, or wouldn't want to wait for their purchases to arrive; others believed concerns about the security of personal information and credit card details would keep consumers away. Clearly, that was not the case, and as retailers got better at their presentation and logistics, consumers became more comfortable with the idea of clicking to buy. According to Forrester Research, by 2003, online sales in the United States (not including travel) passed the $100 billion mark, and between 2003 and 2006, they more than doubled, to nearly $220 billion. Of that total, approximately $14 billion was spent on apparel, accessories, and footwear.[9]

Online retailing was initially dominated by "dot-coms," or retailers that sold only on the Internet, and there are still numerous "pure-play" e-tailers (as Internet retailers without a physical store are called). Amazon.com, Zappos.com, and Bluefly.com are three examples. Many brick-and-mortar retailers, however, are also using the Internet as an additional outlet to supplement their in-store business; this two-pronged approach has been nicknamed "click-and-mortar." Most of these retailers feature full online sales and support of their merchandise offerings—in fact, retailers frequently offer a wider selection of products on their Web sites than they can physically stock in their stores. Sometimes the extended selection includes a greater breadth of items from a particular brand or designer, or it may include sizes outside the most common range, for which there is less in-store demand. Even luxury goods are increasingly being sold online, both by upscale retailers such as Nordstrom and Bergdorf Goodman, and by Internet-only companies like Net-a-porter.com and Yoox.com.

❯❯❯ SPECIAL FOCUS 12.1: ATTENTION SHOPPERS: MERCHANDISE FOUND ONLINE ISN'T ALWAYS IN THE STORE ❮❮❮

Heather Fullerton often goes window shopping online, printing out pictures of clothes she likes at Web sites run by high-end retailers before visiting the stores to try them on. The trouble is, she sometimes discovers that the stores don't stock items she sees on their Web sites.

A growing number of retailers have started displaying a different—and sometimes trendier—mix of merchandise online than they offer in stores. Click on handbags at Neiman Marcus and you'll see a $620 "sleek leather shoulder bag" from Bulga, a label that celebrities like Jessica Simpson are carrying. But don't try buying the bag at a Neiman Marcus store; it's available only online, as are maternity clothes, furniture, and certain gift items during the holiday season.

While the reasons are sometimes logistical—stores don't have room to stock everything they carry online—retailers are now using exclusives to try to attract shoppers who don't frequent their stores. Saks Fifth Avenue says it puts some trendier items on its Web site because its average online customers, at 38 or 39 years old, are 10 years younger than the average shopper at its stores, and roughly a third of them don't shop at Saks stores.

>>> Source: Adapted from Rachel Dodes, "The New Web Exclusives," *Wall Street Journal*, April 1, 2006, http://online.wsj.com/article/SB114383552389513769.html.

For fashion consumers, shopping online offers both advantages and disadvantages. On the negative side, consumers can't touch and examine the products before buying, and in the case of apparel, they obviously can't try on the clothes before purchasing them. The social aspect of shopping is also missing. Some consumers are uncomfortable using a credit card over the Internet, and others don't like to pay the shipping costs. On the positive side, shopping online gives fashion consumers access to a far wider selection of retailers and merchandise than is available in their local shopping area. Online tools such as product search and price comparisons can also help them to find the right item at the best price.

Let's Talk

What products would you consider purchasing online? Are there any items you'd prefer to buy in a physical store? Why or why not?

Catalogs

With the growth of the Internet and online shopping, many people thought printed catalogs would become obsolete. But that has not been the case; U.S. sales from catalogs have actually risen in recent years, topping an estimated $152 billion annually.[10] Of the more than 11,000 catalogs produced in the United States, some 750 are devoted to apparel and accessories.[11]

Catalog shopping has some of the same advantages and disadvantages of online shopping, including the benefit of being able to purchase from a retailer without a nearby location, as well as the downside of not being able to try on apparel before buying. Catalogs, however, may be preferred by consumers who are not computer-savvy or who feel uneasy about giving credit card information online—or who simply like the personal contact of speaking to someone on the phone to place their order.

Some companies that began their business as catalog-only, such as Norm Thompson (which sells men's and women's apparel, home décor, and gourmet foods), have translated their catalog to a complementary Web site sales operation. Others, such as upscale women's apparel retailer Coldwater Creek, have gone online and also added physical stores. On the other hand, illustrating the continued viability of catalogs, some traditional store retailers are publishing catalogs for the first time; Bath & Body Works, for example, recently followed the launch of its retail Web site with the launch of a print catalog.[12] The use of catalogs, stores, and the Internet in a coordinated marketing plan is known as **multichannel retailing**—a significant trend that we'll discuss later in this chapter.

Table 12.1. Where Consumers Shop

A *Women's Wear Daily* survey found that discounters follow closely behind department stores as the top places that women regularly shop for clothes for themselves:

Where Do You Regularly Shop for Clothes for Yourself? (pick up to five)

Department stores	68%
Discounters	65%
Small specialty chains	45%
Internet/catalog	38%
Independent boutiques	20%
Large specialty stores	14%
Dollar stores	5%

Source: Women's Wear Daily, "Where America Shops" survey, June 20, 2005.

Other Ways to Buy Fashion Goods

Department, discount, and specialty stores, the Internet, and catalogs may be the primary places where consumers shop for fashion, but they are not the only places. Outlet stores, which traditionally were viewed as selling only discontinued or defective merchandise, are increasing in number as some companies seek ways to enhance awareness

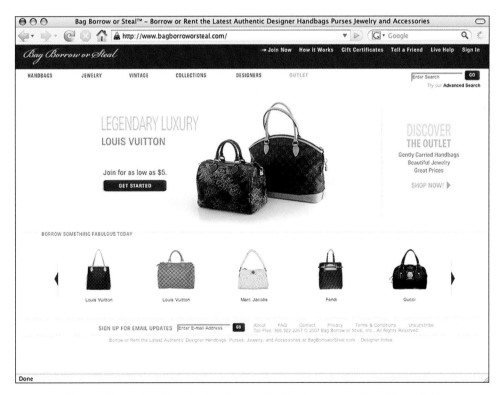

FIGURE 12.7. Some retailers, such as the online Bag Borrow or Steal, allow consumers to rent luxury fashions.

and sales of their brand. Brooks Brothers, as well as Coach and Gap, for example, even design some merchandise exclusively for their factory and outlet stores.[13]

Television shopping, via channels such as QVC and HSN, is not new, but with advances in interactive technology, "t-commerce" is poised to expand even further.[14] Already a hit in Europe and spreading to the United States, the updated TV shopping mode will allow consumers to order products they see on the screen (even on a regular program) with their TV's remote control. Imagine: press a few buttons on the remote and the Gap shirt you're admiring on the *American Idol* contestant is yours! Cell phones are also well on the way to becoming a shopping outlet for consumers. A recent promotion by *Lucky* magazine illustrates one approach, where readers could send text messages to buy merchandise from companies such as Liz Claiborne, L'Oréal, and Target.[15] Another approach comes from a company called GPShopper, which lets consumers enter the name of the product they want and their ZIP code into their cell phone, and up will pop a photo and description of the item along with a list of local stores that carry it, and even a map to locate those stores.[16]

Consumers can also shop for fashion merchandise via the direct sales method, such as through Avon Products, which sells apparel and accessories in addition to its signature cosmetics and skin care products; and via house parties, where consumers can socialize while buying products ranging from lingerie, to cosmetics, to shoes, and more. And for fashion consumers whose pocketbook can't keep up with their tastes, there are a number of retailers, both online and off, that will let customers rent luxury products (from a Chanel handbag, to a Vera Wang necklace, to a Zac Posen gown) for a fraction of the price of buying them. One of the best known is the Internet company Bag Borrow or Steal, which operates in a manner similar to the movie rental company Netflix. For a monthly fee, members can borrow the handbag or jewelry of their dreams, and then exchange it for another when they're ready for a new look.

Some fashion consumers also enjoy bidding for items in online auctions, such as at eBay, or browsing in thrift shops, consignment shops, and vintage clothing stores, perhaps searching for a bargain on a gently used designer item or hunting for a one-of-a-kind treasure to enhance their wardrobe or their home décor. Those shopping venues can also become a source for consumers who are ready to part with fashion items. Unless an item is ripped, stained, or otherwise too worn to be reused, many consumers donate their clothing or home fashions to a charity or thrift shop. For better items in good condition, they might decide to resell them online or through a consignment shop, where the shop takes a percentage of the sale price.

Influence of Shopping Environments

As discussed in Chapter 11, a variety of conscious and unconscious techniques are involved in consumers' decision making, including the choice of where to shop for a particular product. Rational aspects, such as a store's general price range or its prox-imity to the consumer, will enter into the decision, as will emotional aspects, such as how previous purchases there made the shopper feel or how prestigious the retailer is with the consumer's peer group. The store's atmosphere, services, and product mix are also important, and retailers focus heavily on these areas in their planning and marketing in order to win consumers' interest and loyalty.

Physical Surroundings

A recent IBM survey found that 46 percent of shoppers said they tend to stay away from retailers that look and feel the same as other retailers, and about a third avoid stores that are disorganized.[17] What do those numbers tell us? They confirm that the appearance and ambience of a store are very important to consumers in deciding where they want to shop.

The physical features of a store are often what give consumers their first impres-sion of a retailer, so most stores devote considerable effort to designing a look and atmosphere that will create a favorable impression as well as differentiate them from other stores. That mind-set applies to the store's exterior as well as its interior. Archi-tectural details and meticulously designed display windows are frequently used to capture the style and essence of a store's merchandise—and catch the eye of target consumers. But a few mall-based stores have recently taken an opposite approach, differentiating themselves by doing away with the traditional floor-to-ceiling glass storefront. For example, the storefronts of Ruehl No. 925 (the new Abercrombie & Fitch chain targeting college students) instead feature a brick façade that looks like the front of a townhouse, hiding the merchandise inside and drawing customers in to find out what's there. Similarly, Hollister (Ruehl's sister store aimed at high schoolers) has an exterior that mimics a beach shack with wooden shuttered win-dows.[18]

A store's interior is designed to both accentuate the merchandise and appeal to the store's target consumers. Retail-ers scrutinize everything from color schemes and lighting to the size and comfort of dressing rooms when plan-ning a store's layout and look. When Barneys New York opened a new Boston store, it was designed to reflect the retailer's luxe image, with décor that includes an elegant staircase, huge

FIGURE 12.8. Retailers devote much effort to cre-ating a store ambience that will appeal to their target consumers. Metropark's design includes plasma TVs show-ing music videos, as well as a selection of street-inspired art.

skylight, and a women's shoe department with chic sofas and banquettes and a fireplace.[19] At its New York flagship store, Bloomingdale's recently renovated the entire floor devoted to bridge lines (high-priced apparel that's a step below designer), incorporating mirrored arches on the back perimeter walls, crystal chandeliers, Tibetan carpet, and other luxurious touches to appeal to the department's upscale consumers.[20] By contrast, retailers that target a younger, hipper consumer design their stores to reflect the likes and lifestyles of those customers. The growing Metropark chain mentioned in this chapter's opening scene, for example, attracts young adults not only with its trendsetting apparel but with music videos, street-inspired art, and live DJs on weekends.[21] Big-box stores such as Home Depot and Sam's Club, on the other hand, use a purposely spartan décor to emphasize their extensive selection and low prices.

〉〉〉 SPECIAL FOCUS 12.2 THERE'S ART—AND SCIENCE—IN STORE DESIGN 〈〈〈

Under certain conditions, a citrus smell–oranges with a hint of lemon–seems to magically open the pocketbooks of shoppers and increase their desire to spend. But only if the store is not too crowded or too empty.

That's just one example of how retailing has become a science that uses psychology and anthropology to find what shapes consumer behavior.

Take the effect of music. Parents dragged into Abercrombie & Fitch to buy jeans and sweaters for their kids probably complain of a headache, but to teens, the pulsing sounds of Moby are a shopping stimulant that gets their heart racing and their nervous system aroused. And several years back, retailers such as Banana Republic and J. Crew began using wooden tables because they are associated with touch, prompting shoppers to pick up that polo knit or pair of khakis, in turn making it more likely they will buy it.

Many retailers turn to Paco Underhill, author of *Why We Buy* and a well-known retail consultant, for advice. Among his research findings is the "butt brush" theory, which postulated that if shoppers, especially women, were touched from behind as they browsed merchandise, they would probably get irritated and move. The lesson: Never put products that require more than cursory inspection in a narrow aisle.

>>> Source: Adapted from Douglas Sams, "Retailers Look at What Triggers Consumers to Spend their Money," *Gwinnett* (Ga.) *Daily Post*, July 30, 2006, http://www.gwinnettdailypost.com/index.php?s=&url_channel_id=35&url_subchannel_id=&url_article_id=17778&change_well_id=2; and Richard Morin, "Citrus

Smell Makes Cents, Study Finds," *Seattle Times*, March 1, 2005, http://seattletimes.nwsource.com/html/nationworld/2002193078_smell01.html.

Service and Amenities

As retail consultant Anthony Stokan, author of *Naked Consumption: Retail Trends Uncovered*, recently pointed out, modern consumers expect more than mere satisfaction from retailers. They want to be delighted, so that they will feel passionate about the retailer.[22] In many cases, that means retailers must go above and beyond providing the right merchandise in the right setting by also offering exceptional service—and sometimes additional "extras."

Obviously, good customer service means different things to different shoppers, but it is at least somewhat important to a whopping 99 percent of consumers when deciding to make a purchase, according to a national survey conducted by the NRF Foundation and American Express. In the survey, two-thirds of shoppers said it was extremely important for retail employees to be courteous, and 61 percent found it important that employees be available to ask for help. For online shoppers, good customer service translated to on-time deliveries for 73 percent of respondents, while 74 percent wanted the retailer to handle questions and requests quickly.[23]

Some retailers are turning to technology to help improve their customer service. Casual Male Retail Group, for one, allows sales associates at the store to review and update database information about a customer, such as collar size or style preferences, in order to provide more personalized service.[24] La-Z-Boy Furniture Galleries implemented a color technology system that lets consumers scan a throw pillow, paint chip, drapery panel, or other item from home that they want to match and instantly receive a range of coordinating fabric from the more than 1,500 textiles in the La-Z-Boy library.[25]

FIGURE 12.9. Customer service is important to consumers, who at the very least want sales staff to be courteous and available to answer questions.

Online retailers are also stepping up their service levels, with enhancements to the "live chat" options that allow consumers to ask for help in real time. Designer clothing e-tailer Bluefly, for instance, introduced a new chat service in which, if a customer searches for more than three items in five minutes (which presumably indicates more than just casual browsing), a pop-up window appears featuring a friendly face offering help. In addition, if customers are idle on the checkout screen for more than a minute, a Bluefly customer service representative will initiate a dialog.[26]

As retailers face ever-stiffer competition for consumers' time and money, many are expanding their service efforts and offerings, and implementing customer amenities that range from play areas for children, to WiFi access, to special events and entertainment. Bed Bath & Beyond and The Container Store, for example, have both created model dorm rooms at college campuses to give students (and their parents) ideas on how to make their own room more comfortable and organized.[27] Club Libby Lu offers fantasy makeover parties for 5- to 13-year-old girls, in themes including Sparkle Princess and Drama Queen.[28] And as part of its efforts to become more "customer-centric," consumer electronics retailer Best Buy trained its sales personnel to identify soccer-mom-type customers who might be intimidated by technology, helping them find what they were looking for, guiding them to special checkout aisles, and even escorting them to or from their cars with umbrellas on rainy days.[29]

Let's Talk
What service do you expect to receive from stores where you shop? Do you expect more attention from a clothing store than a drug store? Does the level of service influence whether you'll shop there again?

Product Mix

Even the most wonderful ambience and outstanding service will not satisfy consumers if they can't find the products they want at a given store. So retailers must continually adjust their merchandise to meet the needs and expectations of their target customers, as well as work closely with manufacturers to make sure that products are available when consumers want them.

Despite the fact that all retailers have a defined group of target consumers, offering the right mix of merchandise requires constant attention to what customers are looking for, since needs can change. Plus-size consumers, for instance, have told retailers that they are interested in more fashion-forward apparel and, as a result, stores including Ann Taylor and Banana Republic, as well as designers including Eileen Fisher and Dana Buchman, are offering fashions in larger sizes.[30] Similarly, Gap recently introduced its women's products in petite and tall sizing, although the sizes are available only on the retailer's Web site.[31]

Changing Trends in Consumer Shopping

Just as fashion is constantly evolving, so are the ways that consumers shop for fashion. What is right for retailers today might not work next month or next year, but there are two key trends that are likely to continue shaping the way consumers buy for the foreseeable future.

Shopping Up and Shopping Down

One of the big differences in the way consumers buy today is that their income does not automatically translate to where they will shop or how much they will spend. Jackie, in the opening scene of this chapter, is a perfect example: She splurged on a designer dress for an important occasion, but then went to a discount store for bargains on sheets. Lois Huff, senior vice president at research and consulting firm Retail Forward, referred to this phenomenon as "bipolar purchasing," in which shoppers "can go down and get some great fashions at the lower prices, but then they also go up and get something that really satisfies the ego."[32]

This new-millennium trend is also documented in *Treasure Hunt: Inside the Mind of the New Consumer*, whose authors see the end of only the rich buying expensive goods, the middle class buying mid-priced products, and the poor buying cheap merchandise. Instead, consumers at all income levels are shopping at lower-priced stores such as Wal-Mart, Target, and Costco—partly because they don't want to overpay for an item, but also because getting a bargain on one purchase gives them more money to splurge on a luxury or indulgence.[33] That growing tendency of consumers to cross-shop is even changing the tenant mix in many malls, which are rethinking the conventional formula of department store anchors supporting a blend of smaller specialty stores. Some malls now feature discounters such as Target next to high-end department stores such as Neiman Marcus, along with other stores, such as Best Buy and Bed Bath & Beyond, which were not traditionally found in malls.

FIGURE 12.10. Higher-income consumers are increasingly "shopping down" to obtain a bargain.

Shopping through Multiple Channels

As previously mentioned, another key trend is multichannel retailing, in which retailers are treating their physical store and their Web site, plus their catalog if they have one, as integral parts of a marketing whole. That trend is based largely on new patterns of consumer behavior, whereby consumers might research a product online and then purchase it at a store (or vice versa), or select items from a catalog and then order it online.

The fact that consumers are increasingly using brick-and-mortar stores, the Web, and catalogs interchangeably was documented by a report by Adjoined Consulting, a technology consulting and implementation company. The study asked 5,000 consumers to rate 25 leading retailers' ability to meet their emotional and rational desires, and found that consumers expect all aspects of a retailer's business to "work seamlessly with each other in order to deliver a single, united customer experience," according to an Adjoined executive.[34] As more retailers refine their approach, it will in turn drive consumer behavior even further toward multichannel shopping, where consumers order online from an in-store computer, return a catalog purchase to a store, and other options—some not yet even imagined.

In the next chapter, we'll look beyond the individual fashion consumer to see how organizations are involved in the use of fashion goods.

Summary

Where and how consumers buy fashion products is an important aspect of consumer behavior. Consumers are either fashion leaders or fashion followers, depending on how they relate to products within the fashion life cycle. All fashion products follow the same cycle of introduction, rise, peak, decline, and rejection or obsolescence, although the length of time from introduction to rejection can vary tremendously. The rise phase of the cycle is characterized by knock-offs, which are lower-priced copies of an original style. Getting the latest fashions to consumers as quickly as possible is termed "fast fashion," and practiced by retailers including H&M and Zara.

Consumers have many choices for purchasing fashion, although 90 percent of apparel purchases are made in brick-and-mortar stores. Fashion consumers shop most frequently in department stores, followed by discount stores and specialty stores. Specialty retailers target a narrow consumer group or specific style or price range, and sometimes create new retail concepts to address a different target market. A growing number of consumers are shopping for fashion goods on the Internet, and "pure-play" e-tailers have been joined online by store retailers adding Web sales to their brick-and-mortar operations. Catalogs remain another important shopping source for fashion consumers, who have additional shopping options including outlet stores, television shopping, and even luxury rental stores.

Consumers are influenced in their shopping choices by a store's physical features and atmosphere, which retailers design to enhance their merchandise and to attract their target consumers. Service is also important to shoppers, who increasingly expect additional amenities from retailers, such as entertainment or personalized assistance. Other factors affecting where consumers shop are the retailer's assortment of merchandise and the availability of products consumers are seeking. Two key trends in current shopping behavior are the tendency of consumers to shop either up or down from their traditional income level and their use of stores, Internet, and catalogs interchangeably, as more retailers offer multichannel retailing.

Key Terms

Classic style	Introduction phase
Decline phase	Knock-offs
Fad	Multichannel retailing
Fashion followers	Obsolescence or rejection phase
Fashion life cycle	Peak phase
Fast fashion	Rise phase

Questions for Review

1. What are the five phases of a fashion life cycle? Describe what occurs in each phase.
2. Name three types of stores where consumers can make fashion purchases, and give an example of each.
3. What are some of the advantages of shopping for fashion goods on the Internet or from a catalog? What are some of the disadvantages?
4. What are three key aspects of a shopping environment that influence consumers' desire to shop at a particular store?
5. What are two important trends that are shaping the way consumers shop in the twenty-first century?

Activities

1. Look through a variety of magazines or store circulars, or browse online, and find an example of a style at each phase of the fashion life cycle. Make a note of where you found each example. How does the source help you determine whether the style is in the first half or second half of its cycle? Can you find multiple examples of a peaking style at different prices or offered by retailers at different price tiers?
2. Think of a fashion product or style that is currently or has recently been a fad. List the attributes of the item, including the gender(s) and age group(s) it appeals

to, where or how it began (for example, from a movie or celebrity, etc.), and how long it was or has been popular. In your opinion, why do you think the item caught on? Why do you think it won't remain popular? Survey your classmates for their view.

3. Pick two different specialty stores to visit and compare how their store environments are designed to appeal to their target customer. Make note of elements, including the storefront, the style of merchandise sold and the way it is displayed, the lighting and music, the appearance of the sales associates, and so on, and how those elements contribute to the total ambience. How successful are the stores in conveying an immediate image? If they are targeting a similar consumer, how do their approaches differ? How are they similar? Present your findings to the class.

4. Pretend you are planning to buy a particular item of clothing. Choose three different retailers that sell apparel online, and browse their Web sites. How easy or difficult is it to search each site? Can you find size and color information easily? What tools does each e-tailer provide to help you find your item and/or any similar styles? Do any of the sites pop up suggestions for complementary or alternative items? Do they let you know whether the item is available in your size, or whether it's available for pick up at a nearby bricks-and-mortar store? Make a chart comparing the features and ease of use of the three sites.

5. Visit a local thrift store or consignment shop or go to an online auction site (such as eBay) and browse through a selection of the clothing for sale. How much appears to be recently at the end of its fashion life cycle, and how much would be considered vintage styles? Do you see any current styles? If you're looking online, find two or three items that are drawing multiple bids, and see how they are described, whether new or used, vintage, and so on. If you're in a shop, see if you can speak to the owner or manager, and find out what criteria he or she has for accepting items for sale and what types of items seem to sell fastest.

Mini-Project

Imagine you are going to open your own apparel store. Remembering all the factors that influence consumers as they shop and buy, write a full description of what your store would be like, including customers you'd target, types of merchandise you'd carry, price ranges of the merchandise (low, medium, high), features of the store ambience (for example, styles of lighting, displays, music, etc.), level of customer service you'd offer, whether you'd include online sales, and so forth. Present your "store" to the class.

References

1. "Basic Instinct: Fashion Innovators Trust their Inner Style Voices," Cotton Incorporated Lifestyle Monitor, http://cottoninc.com/lsmarticles/?articleID=516 on.

2. Gini Stephens Frings, *Fashion from Concept to Consumer*. 4th ed. (Englewood Cliffs, NJ: Prentice Hall, 1994), p. 61.

3. Chris Sprigman, "Fashion's Piracy Paradox," University of Chicago Law School Faculty Blog, http://uchicagolaw.typepad.com/faculty/2006/11/fashions_piracy.html on November 13, 2006.

4. Marion Hume, "If You've Got It, Flaunt It," *Time*, March 28, 2005, www.time.com/time/magazine/article/0,9171,1039713,00.html.

5. "H&M: It's the Latest Thing—Really," *BusinessWeek*, March 27, 2006, www.businessweek.com/magazine/content/06_13/b3977004.htm.

6. "Speed Demons: How Smart Companies Are Creating New Products—and Whole New Businesses—Almost Overnight," *BusinessWeek*, March 27, 2006, www.businessweek.com/magazine/content/06_13/b3977001.htm.

7. Rachel Riplady, "Zara: Taking the Lead in Fast-Fashion." *BusinessWeek*, April 4, 2006, www.businessweek.com/print/globalbiz/content/apr2006/gb20060404_167078.htm.

8. Sharon Edelson, "The Big Shift," *Women's Wear Daily*, July 10, 2006, Section II, p. 4.

9. National Retail Federation and Forrester Research, Inc., "Online Clothing Sales Surpass Computers, According to Shop.Org/Forrester Research Study," news release, May 14, 2007.

10. Ann Meyer, "Niche Retailers Find Catalogs Can Bring in New Audiences," *Chicago Tribune*, June 14, 2005, www.dminsights.com/inTheNews.cfm.

11. Chantal Tode, "Online Only Catalogs Nearly Double," *DM News*, April 17, 2006, www.dmnews.com/cgi-bin/artprevbot.cgi?article_id=36464.

12. Melissa Dowling, "Bath & Body Works Goes Direct," *Multichannel Merchant*, May 1, 2006, http://multichannelmerchant.com/mag/bath_body_works_05012--6/.

13. "Retailers Eye Outlet Stores for Growth," Reuters, January 28, 2006, http://asia.news.yahoo.com/060127/3/2eu3z.html.

14. Lorrie Grant, "Networks Hope Remote-Control Shopping Clicks," *USA Today*, May 24, 2005, http://usatoday.com/money/industries/retail/2005-05-24-t-commerce-usat_x.htm.

15. Stuart Elliott, "Shopping by Phone, on the Move," *New York Times*, July 10, 2006, www.nytimes.com/2006/07/10/technology/10adcol.html?ex=1184558400&en=8348135b361c1506&ei=5070.

16. Susan Reda, "Seven Predictions for '07," *Stores*, December 2006, www.stores.org/archives/2006/12/cover.asp.

CHAPTER 13

The Use of Fashion Goods by Organizations

Coco Chanel said: "Fashion fades but style remains."

Napoleon said: "Victory belongs to the most persevering."

Each of these quotes can be adapted to individuals and organizations as they buy, use, and dispose of goods or services. This chapter explores how organizations use fashion, and how both for-profit and not-for-profit operations use consumer behavior principles to survive and thrive in competitive environments.

Organizations

An **organization** is a group of individuals who have joined together for the purpose of accomplishing a common goal. The word comes from the Greek "organon," meaning "tool."[1] Essentially, an organization can do what individuals cannot achieve alone. Organizations exist at all levels of society. Your circle of friends, classmates, as

FIGURE 13.1 A, B, and C. Organizations: Friends, Family, and Classmates.

well as faculty and student clubs are all groups of people working together to achieve something (for example, weekend activities or a presentation).

A basic organization that is familiar to everyone is the family, which exists to ensure the survival of its members. The leader(s) of this group has goals in mind for each individual, and at the same time determines how each individual's accomplishments will contribute to the overall success of the family. (The influence of the family is discussed in Chapter 7.)

If you are reading this book for a class, you are doing so to prepare for membership in an organization—perhaps a company involved in the field of design. Maybe your goal is to become part of an organization that will allow you to do what you love (and get paid for it!). As a member, you will learn the group's expectations, the rules you need to follow, whom to report to, and what part you'll play in helping to achieve the organization's goals.

Types of Organizations

If an organization's objectives become more complex, its members become more organized and task specific. For the purposes of this discussion, there are two kinds of organizations. The first is the **for-profit business**, one that is established, maintained, or conducted for the purpose of making a profit and developing human resource potential.

The second is composed of charitable and institutional groups, which are also both structured and focused on specific goals, but are not businesses (as we know them); they are **nonprofit organizations**, also called not-for-profit organizations, formed for the purpose of achieving a specific socially responsible goal while sustaining a profitable position.

First, we will be examining the different perspectives of for-profit organizations, their history and methods, and how they fit into the realm of design.

FIGURE 13.2A and B. Organizations: Macy's—for profit/Salvation Army—nonprofit.

Organizational Levels

A business is an organization with ultimate goals of making a profit and developing its human resource capital (employees). It is through the application of the **organizational hierarchy**, successive levels with each one superior to the one below it, that the group is able to organize itself and direct its members' talents and assets toward the end result. What is the organizational hierarchy? How does it make an organization work? People need direction and purpose. The group dynamic and hierarchal structures both create and support the purpose-driven action for and of its members.

Non-Business Entities versus Profit Organizations

There can also be a **profit motive**, the incentive to work in order to gain something. The need to survive or be promoted sparks and sets the group in motion.

As Figure 13.3 illustrates, a hierarchy is a pyramid-like model of leadership, with the leader and final decision maker at the peak, and vice presidents, managers, support staff, and workers filling in the rest of the pyramid. In our personal lives we are free to think and act in accordance with our own values and beliefs. However, organizations are not designed to benefit the individual, but rather to benefit the group as a whole; therefore, someone has to be in charge, and someone has to follow orders or the group will not function efficiently, if at all.

Think of a large clothing manufacturer. There are very likely many designers, working with a certain degree of autonomy (independence), who are expected to come up with innovative ideas that are in keeping with the design philosophy/direction of the company. At the top of the pyramid is the creative director. He or she gives the designers a focus by conveying the fashion "story" or concept that the company intends to present for a particular season. Although the designers will assist when it comes to developing that concept, choosing fabrics, creating the collection, and so on, it is the creative director who must make the final choices as to what and how much

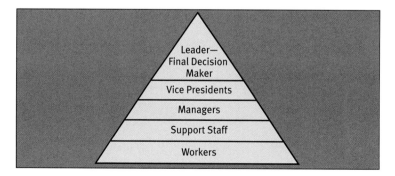

FIGURE 13.3. Pyramid Model of Leadership

will actually be produced—and who is ultimately responsible for the success or fail-ure of the line. The designers make the industrial fabric purchases for the company, and must provide the director with clothing designs that are saleable in order to be useful to the organization. Individual achievement is crucial to the success of the or-ganization as a whole and is, therefore, rewarded.

Non-Business Entities versus Nonprofit Organizations

There are many goal-oriented organizations that can be defined as **non-business entities**. These organizations have well-defined goals and structured methods of achieving their objectives. They are organizations without clearly defined owners, such as public works or governments. Other examples include schools, religious groups, and political parties. All have agendas and measurable results; however, although they may be run like a business, they are not classified as businesses. These groups do not measure their successes in the number of products sold, but in the cre-ation of ideas, the graduation of students, the spread of ideology, and any number of intangible results. It's important to differentiate the non-business entity from the nonprofit organization.

Specifically, a "non-business entity" is any group (of two or more individuals), cor-poration, association, firm, partnership, committee, club, or other organization that

1. Is not primarily concerned about making a profit.
2. Received more than 10 percent of its revenues the prior year from contributions, gifts, or membership fees.[2]

On the other hand, as mentioned earlier in the chapter, a "nonprofit" is in practice and appearance an organization that gives its earnings to a cause or converts them to a specific use. The Council of Fashion Designers of America, Inc. (CFDA) is a not-for-profit trade association with group members working in various areas of the fash-ion industry. Members of this organization meet to network, to discuss trends and innovations, to assist each other, and so on. One of the organization's stated interests is raising monies for breast cancer awareness.[3] Another example of a nonprofit is ASID, the American Society of Interior Designers. This organization "strives to advance the interior design profession and, in the process, to demonstrate and cele-brate the power of design to positively change people's lives."[4] Most successful non-profits are nearly identical in all respects to large corporations. Massive international nonprofit organizations like the United Way and the Red Cross rely on marketing an image as much as, if not more so, than any for-profit company.

Nonprofits are selling an idea or a cause and therefore must convince members and potential donors of how their organizations serve the community, add value to the representation of a cause, and benefit others (directly and indirectly) without having an actual physical product. In other words, they also engage in marketing. Today's nonprofit organizations also understand that market research is just as important for them as it is for profit-driven businesses, because of the intense competition in the marketplace. After all, their members and donors are their customers. (See Special Focus 13.1.)

〉 〉 〉 SPECIAL FOCUS 13.1: SELLING A CAUSE? BETTER MAKE IT POP 〈 〈 〈

With competition fierce, charities are finding that savvy marketing is a must.

The Empire State Building will glow red for an evening in February. Niagara Falls will run red for a day. And on February 3 newscasters will don red dresses. It's all part of a grassroots campaign to remind women of heart disease risks that has drawn employees at thousands of companies to hand out Red Dress pins plugging the American Heart Assn.'s National Wear Red Day. Backed by marketing hustle worthy of a new car rollout, recognition of the pin could come to rival awareness of the pink ribbon as a symbol for breast cancer research.

With big-name endorsements and flashy events, the "Go Red for Women" effort will use all the tricks of a big ad campaign for a shampoo or an SUV. Increasingly, nonprofits are finding it's a game they must play. Amid an explosion of causes competing for attention, even trusted charities like American Heart have had to rewrite their fund-raising playbooks to cut through the din.

A decade ago marketing was a foreign term to most nonprofits. Donors judged a group's success by how much of its budget went to good works vs. fund-raising. The Susan G. Komen Breast Cancer Foundation changed the landscape, positioning itself as a favorite marketing partner of big companies from General Motors Corp. to Whirlpool Corp., driving annual revenues to $180 million in 2005. But many nonprofits have been slow to follow. "The M-word was not considered a good thing," says Tom Peterson, vice-president for marketing at Heifer International, an anti-poverty group that lets you send animals to the needy via catalog. It recently landed an appearance for one of its goats on NBC's The West Wing. Says Peterson: "It was as if we were losing our soul."

That view is changing now that there are more than 1.2 million nonprofits, spurring stiff competition for support. Not even the 82-year-old AHA can depend on its name recognition to survive. At American Heart, fund-raising had long been a grassroots activity. Volunteers organized walks, and folks raised money from neighbors. Then, eight years ago, Wall Street veteran M. Cass Wheeler became

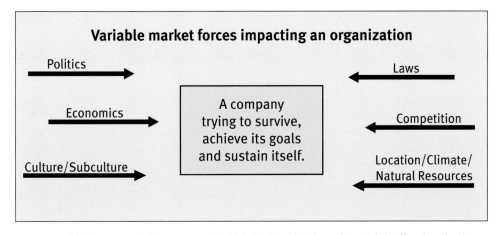

FIGURE 13.4. This diagram symbolizes a company that is trying to achieve its goals, sustain itself, and survive the challenges it faces.

CEO of the Dallas-based group. Armed with consumer research, he woke the place up to marketing. "People trusted [that] we did what we did well, but they were not sure exactly what we did," recalls Wheeler. Moreover, while women walked and raced and cooked to fight breast cancer, few understood it was heart disease that was more likely to kill them.

Wheeler cut the 56 field offices to 12 and built a marketing department. The AHA had previously relied on free public service announcements. But competition for the shrinking pie of free ads has become fierce. So, starting in 2003, Wheeler invested $12 million with ad agency Campbell-Ewald Co., best known for handling Chevy cars and trucks. TV ads, posters, and pamphlets with folks who had lost loved ones to heart disease were wrapped around a new slogan, "Learn and Live," replacing the ossified "Fighting heart disease and stroke." Says Campbell-Ewald President Jeff Scott: "It's more of a call to action."

Spending money to advertise has paid off. Public support for American Heart reached $540 million in 2005, up from $326 million in 1998. In two years, some 366,833 people have logged on to the Learn and Live quiz (at americanheart.org), which helps people identify heart attack risks. Meanwhile, Wheeler hired marketing agency Cone Inc. to design the "Go Red" campaign. With about $1.5 million behind it over two years, it has returned $40 million in contributions and drawn activists from more than 9,500 companies.

Of course, nonprofits considering big branding initiatives walk a tightrope. While they need to get noticed and show marketing savvy to companies whose support they seek, good causes can't appear too slick. Nonprofit umbrella group Independent Sector found that charities operating too much like businesses turn off potential donors. Ruth A. Wooden, president of nonprofit think tank Public Agenda, says organizations need to adopt what she calls the Pier 1 strategy. "It's got to look modern and hip," she says, "but it can't be too expensive."

>>> Source: Jessie Hempel, "Selling a Cause? Better Make It Pop. *BusinessWeek*. February 13, 2006. Retrieved on August 31, 2007, from www.businessweek .com/magazine/content/06_07/b3971109.htm.

Let's Talk
What have you seen nonprofit organizations do to market their cause? What types of media have they used in these efforts? From your perspective, how effective was their marketing effort?

Outside Influences

Both for-profit and nonprofit organizations are driven by **market forces**, external forces that impact the organization's ability to achieve its goal and provide services or products to its customers.

According to Michael Porter, a Harvard Business School professor, there are five market forces. Four of these—the bargaining power of customers, the bargaining power of suppliers, the threat of new entrants, and the threat of substitute products—combine with other variables to influence a fifth force: the level of competition in an industry.[5] To successfully market any product, service, or cause, an organization must (among others things) be in touch with the zeitgeist, the spirit of the times, and be willing and able to use that spirit in order to further the goals of the organization. It is in this utilization of society's moods and tastes that fashion enters the equation. How do organizations use fashion to market their products and services to other businesses? Do organizations such as schools, churches, governments, and charities use fashion to promote themselves?

Yes!

The following example describes in detail how a large corporation was able to interweave its marketing strategy with current times. In November 2005 AT&T merged with SBC Communications to form one of the largest communications brands in the world. The challenge facing the newly formed company would be to attract new customers while keeping the current ones. The purpose of a merger is to join the strengths and resources of two companies, but this new strength also causes dilemmas. How do you let your existing customer base know that you have not changed or forgotten them, while simultaneously telling the rest of the world that you have, in fact, merged into a new company?

"We had some work to do repositioning the company. We had to reassure our existing customers that everything they liked about the old companies would remain," says Wendy Clark, AT&T's vice president for advertising.[6] **Repositioning** is revising the marketing strategy for a product or a company in order to increase sales. AT&T needed to find out from its customers what they wanted and expected from the new company.

Understanding the Market

AT&T conducted a qualitative (understanding the why or motivation of the buy) and quantitative (understanding the who and what of the buy) research study (see Chapter 10 for a detailed discussion of research) of both existing and prospective customers to find out what they wanted. Of the 2,000 respondents included in the qualitative research, half were businesses and the other half were consumers. The study focused on the brand drivers of a communications company. The **brand drivers** are the aspects of a brand that attract and retain consumers. AT&T found through a quantitative study of 15,000 respondents that there was an 85 percent overlap of brand drivers as ranked by business customers and consumers. "It was astounding to find such a strong correlation between B2C [business-to-consumer] and B2B [business-to-business] customers," Clark says. Innovation, fairness, and promises kept were the top three communications brand drivers among both consumers and business customers. How did AT&T use this information?

The tagline "Your World Delivered." was developed and used as the focus of the visual (magazines, newspapers, and events) ad campaign. Remember our definition of fashion: It applies to anything that's of the moment and subject to change; it's anything that members of a population deem desirable and appropriate at a given time. There isn't much that changes faster than technology! With the desires of their consumers (innovation, fairness, and promises kept) in mind, AT&T created an ad campaign that imparted messages of trust, commitment, and giving.

The campaign featured TV, print, online, outdoor, events, and sponsorships, and kicked off on New Year's Eve 2005 during Dick Clark's annual broadcast. The TV spot, titled "Eclipse," featured images of earth juxtaposed with shots of people around the world communicating, while an eclipse (two celestial bodies merging into one—get it?) formed the new logo of AT&T. A hit song at the time, "All Around the World," by the band Oasis, was the soundtrack for the spot. The message of the ad was "AT&T is looking out for you. We are strong and we are present in your world." In tune with the zeitgeist, mainly the worldwide tension created by the Iraq War, AT&T offered security, stability, familiarity, and protection to its customers, while at the same time reinventing itself. The company then narrowed its focus to

FIGURE 13.5. The interior of new McDonald's incorporates neutral colors, unlike older McDonald's, which used bright reds and yellows.

further target the business segment by running ads in *BusinessWeek, Forbes, Fortune, Fortune Small Business, CIO*, and many other business-related publications.

AT&T estimates that its brand awareness increased threefold, by being in step with the moment. The company produced an ad campaign that has reached both residential and business consumers successfully.[7] This example (case study) demonstrates that the marketing techniques, including capitalizing on the issues of the times, used in B2B fields are remarkably similar to those used in the B2C realm. Nonprofit and non-business entities, depending on their budgets and the audience they need to reach, employ the same general strategies and methods in promoting themselves and also communicating their messages.

AT&T defined its target market and did research in order to identify the benefits needed to satisfy that target market. It then took into account the prevailing zeitgeist and created a strategy that would effectively attract and retain customers.

Fashion Combinations

How does fashion meld with business, and how important is it to both consumers and other businesses in today's marketplace? In fall 2006 the *Wall Street Journal* thought it important enough to create a bureau for covering this $200 billion fashion industry.[8] The following sections describe how the worlds of fashion and business benefit each other; can you think of specific examples from your life that illustrate this as well?

Fashion and the Business World

In modern U.S. society it's easy to see the effects of fashion in the business world. Consider McDonald's, for example. You might remember when the interiors of most McDonald's restaurants were in a bright red and yellow color palette. This color scheme originally served to stimulate the "fast" portion of the fast-food equation. Research shows that red and yellow encourage movement and action. At its inception,

McDonald's aim was to sell food that was prepared quickly and eaten quickly. There-fore, it was to the advantage of the restaurants to "turn tables" (have a steady stream of diners arriving and leaving) quickly; hence the firehouse color scheme. Over the years, however, McDonald's noticed a shift in the habits of many customers. As more families began to dine out together in fast-food places, the company realized it would be beneficial to encourage customers to linger a bit. It was at that point in the early 1990s that McDonald's began to redecorate its restaurants with more relaxing earth-tone shades and homelike fixtures. The company had recognized the change in the zeitgeist, the behavior of its customers, and, most importantly, the necessity to adapt to the moment.

❯ ❯ ❯ SPECIAL FOCUS 13.2: MCDS FRANCHISEE HOPES UPSCALE LOOK MAKES CUSTOMERS SMILE ❮ ❮ ❮

A growing number of McDonald's customers in the Dallas area are enjoying their Big Macs and fries surrounded by the elegance of Ralph Lauren wallpaper, crystal chandeliers, and classical music.

"I think the entire system is looking very closely at what we are doing," said Ed Bailey, a McDonald's operator with more than 30 stores in the Dallas area. But a more highly stylized decor is not a new venture for Bailey, who was one of only 10 U.S. operators and 25 worldwide to be honored in April at McDonald's franchisee gathering with the prestigious Golden Arch Award, recognizing all-around opera-tional excellence.

"The store outperformed the company's first-year sales projections by about 25 percent," said Bailey, whose company is called E.L.B. Enterprises Manage-ment. "It was the first store of its kind in Dallas, and it got so much positive feedback that I felt like we had something special. From that point forward we have used the same concept." In addition to driving sales growth, Bailey said a more deluxe decor package has other benefits as well, such as increasing staff retention in today's tight labor market. Bailey explained that his average man-agement turnover this year is about 10 percent and crew turnover is 55 percent, which compares with McDonald's average crew turnover of about 130 to 135 percent.

"Relative to staffing, we have very low turnover, and we attribute at least a part of that to the upscale environment," Bailey said. "The crew feels proud to work in this type of ambience. We think there is a direct correlation between our low turnover rate and the ambience of our restaurants. The store was done with an Old English country look." Some of the most dramatic elements include oil paintings with ornate frames, a stately grandfather clock, moldings made from oak-stained mahogany wood, antique cabinets used as condiment centers, 10 wall sconces and seven chandeliers, of which four are crystal and three are brass.

The restaurant is divided into three distinct areas, each featuring different patterns of Ralph Lauren wallpaper and fabric, as well as distinct ceiling and floor treatments, such as a tile pattern arranged to look like an Oriental rug near the front counter.

Dismissing the notion that a fancy decor could intimidate some customers, Bailey insisted he has received only positive feedback from his guests, and he added that he believes the restaurant's design enhances the perception of value.

"It is like flying first class for the price of coach," Bailey explained. "There are two aspects to value. One is price, and another major piece of value is experience. There is absolutely no question that when people enjoy the ambience they are in, they will come back more often." Bailey, attesting to the universality of his design concept, said he has incorporated the look into nearly all of his stores, not just the ones located in more upscale suburbs. "We have had zero vandalism and a very positive reaction in all of our restaurants, even those in lower socioeconomic areas," he says.

Jon Kelley, director of operations for E.L.B. Enterprises, said he finds that customers are more "protective" of these stores, and they also tend to clean up after themselves more often than they do in traditional-looking units.

The cost of the decor package in the Piano restaurant was about 40-percent higher than that of a typical McDonald's, according to Bailey, who declined to disclose exact dollar amounts on costs or average unit volumes. But Bailey pointed out that his stores generate 20- to- 25-percent higher yearly volumes than McDonald's U.S. system-wide average, which exceeds $1.5 million, according to the NRN Top 100 report. Bailey added that he keeps costs to a minimum by creating the designs in-house and by establishing relationships with suppliers, such as Ralph Lauren's Polo Shop.

>>> Source: Amy Zuber, "McDs Franchisee Hopes Upscale Look Makes Customers Smile." Nation's Restaurant News. September 11, 2000. Retrieved on August 31, 2007, from FindArticles.com, http://findarticles.com/p/articles/mi_m3190/is_37_34/ai_65297388.

Architectural/engineering design firm Haag Muller, Inc. redeveloped one of the McDonald's sites to "provide for a safer and more pedestrian-friendly environment.

The design incorporates a theme of 'marketplace appearance' . . . and colors from the rich burgundy blend of the brick . . . , fabric awnings, and gooseneck style light fixtures, subdued color schemes, flat-screen TVs and Wi-Fi Internet access—a classier look than before."[9]

We know that for-profit companies aggressively use marketing and fashion tools to position themselves, but what about the nonprofits? What kind of fashion-directed marketing efforts do nonprofits use, and why is it important?

Fashion and the Nonprofit Organization

It might seem that hospitals do not need to attract customers or repeat business, but this is not always the case. With nearly 6,000 hospitals nationwide, patients have a variety of facilities to choose from for acute inpatient care. Fewer than 800 hospitals are for-profits, but these organizations tend to offer fewer services in order to keep costs down. The majority of health care organizations are nonprofits. In fact, because the financial factors that determine efficiency and productivity, as well as the cost of medical care, are rising, the number of U.S. hospitals steadily declined between 11 percent to 16 percent from 1996 to 2002, based on data collected from 1,400 hospitals in the 100 largest U.S. cities, according to the American Hospital Association.[10]

Although we frequently don't have the option to select medical facilities for emergency treatment, people who need long-term care or elective procedures do have the option of "shopping around." Because research suggests that the condition of our surroundings can have a great impact upon how we feel, modern hospitals are reconsidering the traditional "institutional" look of their facilities in favor of surroundings that rival the ambience of luxury hotels. An excellent example of a nonprofit hospital that incorporates current interior fashions with the natural beauty of its location is the Carson-Tahoe Hospital of Carson City, Nevada.

An obvious aesthetic extends throughout the hospital waiting areas and treatment facilities, an example of which can be seen in one of the examination rooms. In addition to its medical equipment (the mere sight of which might intimidate some patients), the room features tiny lights on the ceiling that mimic a starry

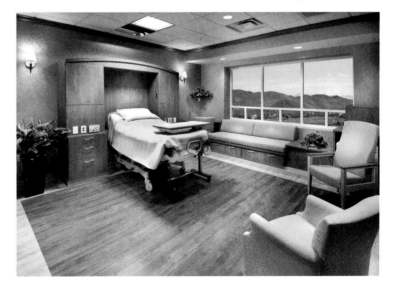

FIGURE 13.6. Large, private rooms with oversized windows and beautiful cabinetry "mask" intimidating medical equipment. Features include guest pull-out beds and soothing colors.

night, to help relax patients during an exam. The lobby is open and inviting, giving patients the impression of visiting a mountain resort.

Let's Talk
What changes have you seen in the last five years regarding how hospital rooms or other medical facilities are decorated? Where do you think these decorating ideas start? What sources would such facilities use to plan for such accessorizing? As the consumer (patient), what types of design features would you like to see?

So rather than feel anxious about checking in for medical treatment, patients can experience the current taste for luxury that seems to be everywhere today, even in nonprofit health care facilities. Hospitals are now advertising on television and in magazines, a practice unheard of in the past, but like any other organization in a competitive marketplace, hospitals must create brand equity (a group of strong assets that include value, esteem, and worth—intangibles that help create satisfaction, retention, and demand in the marketplace) for themselves. Hospitals do have an advantage, though, because most people eventually need their services.

But what about other nonprofits, such as charitable organizations that don't operate hospitals? Are they market-driven as well? Think about the last charity or cause that you or your family donated to. In 2005, Hurricane Katrina relief was a major concern; there now seems to be less and less of a call to action for Hurricane Katrina victims in the mainstream media, though there is still much to be done. Charitable causes come and go—they go in and out of fashion. Why? The media and the public have a short attention span. When a consumer buys a product, she consumes it, uses it, experiences the product in some way. On the other hand, should she donate to a particular cause, there is a degree of separation; the check may be written and mailed, and then the cause may be forgotten. Aside from giving blood, how often do people make repeat donations to the same cause? It is for this reason that charities frequently include fashion spokespeople in their marketing campaigns.

Many American film and television stars have historically avoided doing TV commercials or print ads, but many actively and visibly support their favorite organizational or charitable causes (see Special Focus 13.3). Their advocacy frequently does legitimate good in the world—the star power of someone like Bono can increase the number of contributions to a charity or cause exponentially—while improving their image.

❭ ❭ ❭ SPECIAL FOCUS 13.3: ASHLEY JUDD TAKES ON TEEN NUTRITION ❬ ❬ ❬

Teens, with their penchant for burgers and fries and other fast foods, aren't necessarily model citizens when it comes to nutrition. And what do they drink to wash down their unhealthy fare? According to one report, at least three or more soft drinks daily, which adds up to more than nine pounds of pure sugar a month and 108 pounds in a year in just soda alone.

Those scary stats mobilized actress Ashley Judd to do something to raise awareness about sugar intake by teens. The dark-haired beauty partnered with American Beauty, the new skincare and cosmetics line from Beauty Bank—a division of Estée Lauder—YouthAIDS and Population Services International to start NutritionAID, a charity that looks to educate teens in underserved areas about the necessity of proper nutrition and fitness.

Nutrition Aid's first major initiative is a communications toolkit for select schools due this fall filled with healthy eating and physical activity guidelines, and event-planning tips for students and communities. The toolkit will roll out nationally in 2006. To celebrate NutritionAID's launch, American Beauty created a special lip palette that will be available at Kohl's in October. The palette retails for $15, with a portion of sales going to support NutritionAID.

"This is a really critical time for this country," Judd said. "Sixty percent of Americans are obese, and they're passing along the same bad habits to their children. It's time to educate the kids."

❭❭❭ Source: Sandra O'Loughlin, "Ashley Judd Takes On Teen Nutrition," Brandweek, April 25, 2005, Vol. 46, Issue 17, p. 38.

Fashion Celebrities and Nonprofit Organizations

The AIDS crisis is an example of how stars use their fame for good. In the early stages of this epidemic (the 1980s), it was not a crisis in the eyes of many Americans until a famous actor named Rock Hudson died from the disease. Actress Elizabeth Taylor and many others then became involved, and the amount of public attention given to the disease erupted; soon everyone was wearing red ribbons to show their support. That is *branding*. The cause of AIDS research was given a face and a symbol with great success. At the risk of appearing cynical, it can be said that the popularity of this cause waned as the public's interest moved on to the next crisis or tragedy. Causes and charitable organizations go through the same process of the **product life cycle,** the succession of stages a product goes through: development, introduction, growth, maturity, and decline.

During her life, Princess Diana actively supported charitable organizations and frequently donated to charities the proceeds from the sale of her beautiful gowns. In honor of their mother, Princes William and Harry organized the "Diana Charity Concert" in July 2007 at Wembley Arena in London, and asked performers (for example, Kanye West, Sir Elton John, Nelly Furtado) to autograph three guitars that would be auctioned on eBay for charitable causes.[11]

Many nonprofits (local, national, and international) stage fashion shows as part of their annual fund-raising efforts.

During the past 25 to 30 years, numerous humanitarian causes have temporarily captured the American consciousness, as well as that of the rest of the world. How many of these issues are still fresh in your mind?

- AIDS
- The Gulf War
- Livestrong wristbands
- 9/11
- The second Iraq War
- Tsunami in Southeast Asia
- Hurricane Katrina

Now think about those nonprofit charitable organizations that your parents trust without hesitation, such as the Red Cross or UNICEF. The Red Cross affiliated itself with governments worldwide nearly a century ago and is an internationally recognized symbol (brand) of nonpartisan care for all in need.[12] The Red Cross responds to manmade and natural disasters, providing a range of supplies and services for those affected. UNICEF (United Nations International Children's Emergency Fund, founded in 1947) is the charitable arm of the United Nations. Though many people have strong opinions about U.N. politics, few protest the efforts of UNICEF or accuse it of being an unworthy cause. In addition to the work done by its representatives throughout the world, UNICEF has long employed one of the most effective marketing tools: the celebrity endorsement. Audrey Hepburn, a beloved Academy Award winning actress and fashion icon of the 1950s, 1960s, and 1970s, was UNICEF's goodwill ambassador (celebrity advocate) from 1989 until her death in 1993. Other ambassadors have included soccer player David Beckham, tennis player Roger Federer, martial artist Jackie Chan, and actress Angelina Jolie.[13]

This practice had been dubbed "**charitainment,**" celebrity do-gooderism. But entertainers have always been called upon to help drive attendance at benefits. (For example, Live Aid and Live 8 concerts featured pop music's biggest stars.) Celebrity endorsements exemplify how nonprofits apply fashionable faces to their organizations to garner attention and support for their cause (see Special Focus 13.4). However, some people claim these celebrities only partner with charities for the media spotlight, "face time" with the cameras. Perhaps some do, but if this marketing tool helps an organization whose ultimate goal is helping those in need, isn't that enough?

These organizations have obviously applied fashion to their causes with great success, suggesting that there might be little difference between

FIGURE 13.7. Angelina Jolie, a UNICEF celebrity endorser.

nonprofit and for-profit marketing. While nonprofit organizations can find great success when taking advantage of the methods and marketing tools utilized by their for-profit counterparts, the reverse is becoming true as well. Modern corporations have learned the value of societal marketing, attaching themselves to socially responsible causes by mimicking the image and message-based marketing of charities. Ben Cohen, cofounder of Ben & Jerry's Ice Cream, as well as Ben & Jerry's Foundation, and a societal marketing trailblazer, shares his philosophy succinctly: "Business has a responsibility to give back to the community."[14] In 2006 General Electric launched its "ecomagination" campaign, an environmentally focused series of ads and Web sites that, instead of attempting to sell a particular product, aimed to portray the industrial giant as a group of forward-thinking environmentalists developing ideas and solutions for the future of the planet.[15] (Social responsibility is discussed in detail in Chapter 15.)

❯❯❯ SPECIAL FOCUS 13.4: THE YEAR OF CHARITAINMENT ❮❮❮

At Manhattan's Supper Club, Angelina Jolie—humanitarian, Oscar winner, erstwhile wearer of a vial of Billy Bob Thornton's blood—is scheduled to speak about Sierra Leone. It's a benefit dinner for Witness, a group that has been chronicling abuses in the war-torn African country—slaughter, rape, the drafting of child soldiers. So, naturally, a swarm of cameras are there to get her take on the big issue of the day: Isn't she, like, totally excited that Brad Pitt has decided to adopt her two kids?

Jolie is just a woman of her time. 2005 will go down as the year of charitainment. The networks broadcast celebrity telethons for both tsunami and Hurricane

Katrina aid. Bono and Bob Geldof organized the Live 8 concerts with the help of screenwriter Richard Curtis (Love Actually), who wrote HBO's The Girl in the Café, the world's first romantic comedy about African debt relief. (As propaganda goes, it was at least a better date flick than Triumph of the Will.) Even celebrity cartoons were pressed into service. UNICEF blew the Smurfs into little blue smithereens for a commercial intended to raise money for the rescue of child soldiers.

It is easy to say that people don't help others because they're unaware of what's going on in the world. But maybe the problem is that they're too aware. In a world of endless woes, you can be overwhelmed into inaction. Or you can make, at some level, an arbitrary choice. That is where celebrities come in, because there is no phenomenon more arbitrary than celebrity. They are attention filters, the human equivalent of throwing a dart at a map. A pretty face and a famous name are a convenient excuse to focus on one problem in the midst of a thousand equally unignorable others. To give to Tibet and not Africa may seem callous. But to pick Richard Gere over Bono—that's just show biz.

Source: Excerpted from James Poniewozik, "The Year of Charitainment," *Time*, Monday, December 19, 2005. Retrieved on August 31, 2007, from http://www .time.com/time/magazine/article/0,9171,1142281,00.html.

Fashion Companies and Nonprofit Organizations

Gucci's creative director, Frida Giannini, designed 15 holiday items, *Flora Joy* (flora print motif on velvet handbags and oversize silk scarves), that were sold through 200 Gucci stores worldwide for a special charity program of the United Nations Children's Fund for December 2006; 20 percent of the proceeds from the sale of the Gucci pieces were directed to the fund to support educational programs and services for children in Mozambique.[16]

Creating unique products for, or in other ways lending their name and resources to, charitable causes can create positive name recognition for fashion companies, as well as pecuniary benefits. Buying a product the proceeds of which will be donated to a charity, and that they also really like, can make consumers feel better about spending money. The end result can be effective marketing of the cause to the consumers, increased donations to the charity, and positive name recognition for the fashion company. If it gives consumers, designers, and the public at large a hand in helping someone else, charitable organizations would be wise to accept this type of free advertising graciously.

As discussed in the previous section, nonprofits are taking cues from the corporate world in order to achieve their charitable goals. Stores like Macy's and Neiman

Marcus are famous for their store windows and displays, but have you ever been stopped in your tracks by the merchandise at a local thrift shop? By using the same marketing techniques employed by successful for-profit retailers, one New York based nonprofit organization—Housing Works—created "dazzling display windows in its six thrift stores that have helped the non-profit organization sell goods and raise more than $800,000 as of July 2006," according to *The Chronicle of Philanthropy Fund Raising.* Apparently responding to consumers' need for variety, Emily Hull Martin, the charity's full-time visual designer, entirely redresses ten display windows in the six Housing Works stores approximately twice a month.[17]

And the list of proactive, fashion-related nonprofits is growing. In response to Hurricane Katrina, the nonprofit company Fashion Delivers was organized in September 2005 to provide products from fashion and related industries to victims of natural disasters; board members of this organization include high-profile fashion industry luminaries Sean Combs (Sean John) and Russell Simmons (Phat Fashions).[18] The organization helped mobilize manufacturers to donate more the $3 million in merchandise to victims of both Hurricane Katrina and Hurricane Rita.

The connection between the fashion world and the business world is strong, whether it's in service of the missions of for-profit or charitable organizations. What's more, the world of fashion reaches all around the globe and touches people everywhere; we examine this topic in Chapter 14.

Let's Talk
What do you do to improve your community? How are you helping others who are less fortunate than you? Who do you know that actively contributes his or her time to an organization that benefits others?

Summary

Nonprofit and for-profit organizations have somewhat parallel characteristics. For-profits exist to make money and develop the potential of their employees. Nonprofits need money to survive, but the success of these organizations is not measured by profit, but instead by fulfillment of their purpose or mission. For-profits and nonprofits are structured and operated using similar, if not identical, business models—including the aspect of marketing. It is in these marketing strategies that fashion has an impact. A charity must be able to gauge the public interest in a particular cause with just as much accuracy as a designer interprets upcoming trends. Regardless of their for-profit or not-for-profit status, every organization must be able to tap into the zeitgeist, that intangible feeling and knowledge of the moment that is necessary connecting with both donors and consumers in modern society.

Key Terms

Brand drivers

Charitainment

For-profit organization

Market forces

Non-business entity

Nonprofit organization

Organization

Organizational hierarchy

Product life cycle

Profit motive

Repositioning

Questions for Review

1. Define the term "organization," and discuss one consumer behavior principle that it uses to survive and thrive in today's marketplace.
2. What are the differences and similarities between for-profit and nonprofit organizations? Provide examples of both and compare their mission statements.
3. Why is an organizational hierarchy important for both profit and nonprofit companies? How do they differ? Show examples.
4. What are three market forces that impact organizations? Cite one company and explain how the market forces have influenced that organization.
5. How do fashion celebrities or fashion organizations help to promote charitable causes? Give an example of such a cause and connection that has been promoted during the last six months.

Activities

1. Create a list of organizations to which you belong, directly or indirectly. How are they similar? How many other people also belong to more than one of these same groups? Why do you think that's the case? Do they play similar roles in each group?
2. Search the Internet for visual examples illustrating how the décor, colors, and fixtures in one of your favorite retail stores or fast-food restaurants has changed during the last five years. List three reasons for these modifications.
3. Scan current newspapers or magazines, and cite three examples of businesses that have improved their fashion image during the last three years. Why do you think these changes have been made?

4. Develop a list of four charitable organizations, and select one that interests you. Note its purpose, mission statement, and history of accomplishments. Explain why you would consider contributing your time or money to this organization.

Mini-Projects

1. Assemble a team of three class members. Have each member select either a celebrity, organization, or fashion designer connected to a charity. Then have each member lead an in-class panel discussion on how that individual or company partners with a charitable organization.

2. Visit a retail store, office, or restaurant, and note the fashion accessorizing that has been done. Then create your own list of suggested improvements, including justification of why you would make such changes. Report your findings in class.

References

1. *Webster's New World Dictionary*, 3rd ed. New York: Simon and Schuster, 1988.

2. Department of the State of Idaho. "Statement by a Nonbusiness Entity." www.idsos.state.id.us/elect/finance/forms/c_6.pdf.

3. Council of Fashion Designers of America Web site, www.cfda.com.

4. American Society of Interior Designers Web site, www.asid.org/about/.

5. Michael Porter, "How Competitive Forces Shape Strategy," *Harvard Business Review* (March/April 1979)

6. BtoBonline.com, "Integrated Marketing Success Stories: AT&T," August 14, 2006, http://ctstage.sv.publicus.com/apps/pbcs.dll/article?AID=/20060814/FREE/608140734.

7. Ibid.

8. BtoBonline.com, "'The Wall Street Journal' Creates Bureau for Fashion Coverage," September 12, 2006,http://ctstage.sv.publicus.com/apps/pbcs.dll/article?AID=/20060912/FREE/609120710&SearchID=7.

9. www.haagmuller.com/restaurants.htm

10. "Number of Public Hospitals Declining." www.medicalnewstoday.com/medicalnews.php?newsid=29297//. Also, Dennis P. Andrulis and Lisa M. Duchon, "Hospital Care in the 100 Largest Cities and Their Suburbs, 1996-2002: Implications for the Future of the Hospital Safety Net in Metropolitan America," August 2005, www.rwjf.org/files/research/Andrulis%20Hospitals%20Report-final.pdf.

11. http://jollypeople.com/blog/2007/07/03/princess-diana-charity-auction. American Red Cross, A Brief History of the American Red Cross, www.redcross.org/museum/history/brief.asp.

12. American Red Cross, *A Brief History of the American Red Cross*, www.redcross.org/museum/history/brief.asp.

13. Unicef Web site, www.unicef.org.

14. Ben and Jerry's Web site. http://benjerry.com/our_company/about_us.

15. General Electric. "Advertising: Ecoimaginiation," www.ge.com/company/advertising/ads_eco.html and www.ge.ecomagination.com.

16. *Women's Wear Daily*, October 11, 2006 ; The Fashion Spot message board for "Gucci's Gianni Makes Holiday Items for UNICEF," www.thefashionspot.com/forums/f60/gucci-xmas-unicef-49699.html.

17. Alison Stein Wellner, "Creating Eye Candy for Charity," *Chronicle of Philanthropy*, http://philanthropy.com/free/articles/v18/i19/19002601.htm.

18. Fashion Delivers Web site. Press kit. www.fashiondelivers.org/press.html.

Additional Resources

Berman, Barry, and Joel R. Evans. *Retail Management: A Strategic Approach,* 10th ed. Upper Saddle River, NJ: Prentice Hall, 2007.

Department of the State of Idaho. "Statement by a Nonbusiness Entity." www.idsos.state.id.us/elect/finance/forms/c_6.pdf.

Granger, Michele, and Tina Sterling. *Fashion Entrepreneurship.* New York: Fairchild Publications, 2003.

Institute for Strategy and Competitiveness, www.isc.hbs.edu/.

Levy, Sidney, and DennisRook. *Brands, Consumers, Symbols, and Research.* Thousand Oaks, CA: Sage Publications, 1999.

Liss, David. "Nonprofits and Associations." June 25, 2004, *Washington Post.* www.washingtonpost.com/wp-dyn/articles/A61316-2003Apr30.html.

Live 8 Web site. "The Story So Far." www.live8live.com/whathappened.

Moon, Youngme. "Break Free from the Product Life Cycle." *Harvard Business Review* (May 2005).

Poniewozik, James. "The Year of Charitainment." *Time.* December 19, 2005. www.time.com/magazine/article/0,9171,1142281,00.html.

Roberts, Kevin. *Lovemarks: The Future Beyond Brands.* New York: Powerhouse Books, 2004.

Salamone, Gina. "Where They Are Now: Diana's Dresses—Auctioned in '97—Have Made Quite a Journey." *New York Daily News*, July 2, 2007.

www.nydailynews.com/lifestyle/2007/07/02/2007-07-02_where_they_are_now.html.

Solomon, Michael R. *Consumer Behavior: Buying, Having and Being,* 7th ed. Upper Saddle River, NJ: Prentice Hall, 2007.

Stinson, Lashonda. "Diana's Gowns Exhibit to Raise Money for Cancer." www.ocala .com/article/20070615/NEWS/206150378/1054/Features03&template=storyde-tails.

12Manage Web site. "Five Competitive Forces (Porter)." www.12manage.com/ methods_porter_five_forces.html.

Maddox, Kate. "Smaller Industry-specificwww.btobonline.com August 14, 2006. http:// btobonline.com/apps/pbcs.dll/frontpage.

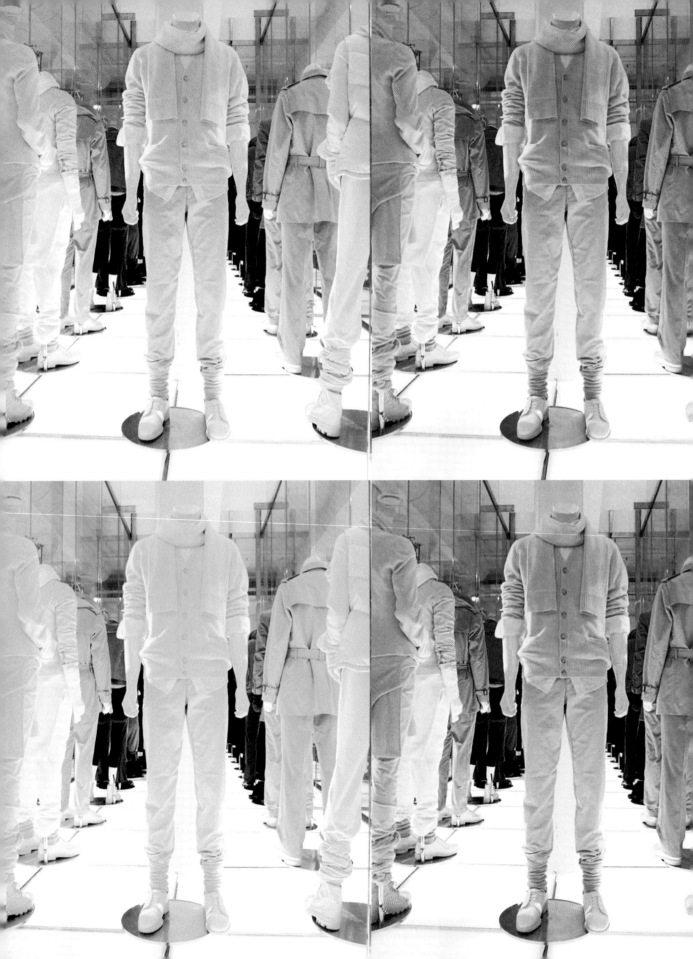

CHAPTER 14

Global Consumers of Fashion and Design

From Japan to Jakarta and from Nevada to North Carolina, purchasing habits appear to be both quite similar and quite different. What human beings need, what we desire, and what we value definitely vary from country to country and culture to culture; yet many appear to be universal.

Are We All Alike?

To be successful, marketers need to understand how people differ from place to place, especially in today's interconnected world. In the United States alone, people of different nationalities, religions, locations, political parties, and social classes have beliefs and customs that are unique. Can they all want the same products?

FIGURE 14.1. The opulent BurJuman shopping mall in Dubai is known for its architecture and its assortment of high-end retail shops.

Subcultural Differences Influence American Buying Habits

The United States is composed of a multitude of subcultural groups, groups within a society/culture, such as persons of the same age, political ideology, ethnic group, social class, sexual orientation, and so on, that possess distinct beliefs, goals, interests, and values that differentiate them from the dominant culture. Hispanic, Italian, Irish, Polish, Indian, and Arab people compose some of the many ethnic subcultural groups that are living, working, and raising families in the United States. However, while they all might call this country "home," researchers have learned that members of these groups do not necessarily share the same preferences when it comes to consumer goods. Additionally, these differing

FIGURE 14.2. Do consumers the world over want the same things?

preferences are much more complex than simply favoring Thai food over Chinese or straight-leg jeans over boot-cut jeans, and they must be studied and understood if marketers are to address and appeal to the varied interests and desires of U.S. shoppers.

❯❯❯ POINT OF VIEW 14.1: THREE STUDIES: DIFFERENCES IN THE SHOPPING HABITS OF AMERICAN SUBCULTURAL GROUPS ❮❮❮

African-American college students demonstrate high levels of media consumption enthusiastically embrace technology and are active consumers. Black collegians also are socially conscious and highly motivated to achieve professional goals and to continue their education beyond the baccalaureate level. Favorite shopping sites, Old Navy (40 percent), Gap (28 percent) and Victoria's Secret (25 percent), were visited in the past month. In fact, 44 percent of all females shopped at Victoria's Secret in the past month. More than 3 in 4 (77 percent) purchased jeans in the past 6 months, and about 6 in 10 (59 percent) purchased athletic shoes or sneakers. Nearly 6 in 10 females purchased cosmetics, spending an average of $28.30. Nearly 3 in 4 females (72 percent) purchased fragrance spending an average of $48.

> ❯❯❯ Source: Eric Weil. "Study Looks at Habits of African-American Students as Consumers." *Target Market News*, www.targetmarketnews.com/ storyid07210602.htm.

Hispanic shoppers are far less satisfied with supermarkets, drug stores and other high-frequency retail outlets than the general population—and while they shop at supercenters much less than the general population, they prefer big-box stores when they're available, according to data from a new study released today by Unilever. Results of the study in four major Hispanic markets—New York, Los Angeles, Houston and Miami—also found Hispanic shoppers are highly resistant to using frequent-shopper cards because of privacy concerns, reported AdAge.com. Though 51 percent of Hispanic consumers in the study had frequent-shopper cards, only 44 percent of those who had them used them. This is despite the fact that Hispanic consumers are more value-conscious and prone to buy products on promotion than the general population, suggesting they're losing considerable savings because of fear of sharing personal data, according to the study.

> ❯❯❯ Source: www.csnews.com/csn/search/search_results_taxo.jsp?id= 1162675540736.

Compared to the average American consumer, Asian Americans are more frequent shoppers, more driven by bargains, and more likely to pay attention to advertising. They over-index in credit cards, allocate more of their budgets to designer clothing, are health conscious about food and have a preference for prescription medicine carrying a brand name. Not surprisingly, Asian Americans are big consumers of electronics, and are far more likely than the average consumer to say they keep up with developments in technology. The median income of Asian American households is 26 percent higher than the average. Still, there are disparities between different Asian groups, i.e. Japanese, Filipinos, Pakistanis, Vietnamese, etc.

>>> Source: David Morse, President and CEO, New American Dimensions, LLC (-www.newamericandimensions.com); www.retailwire.com

Marketing to Diversity

Diversity is a concept that is of great interest to the modern businessperson. **Diversity** is that which makes us dissimilar or different from one another. Americans are a diverse bunch, made up of people who've come to the United States from all over the world and who live their day-to-day lives in very different ways.

off the mark.com   by Mark Parisi

offthemark.com

AMERICAN GOTH

FIGURE 14.3.

Although we may have in common our respect for the ideals of freedom and independence (even though exactly *what* those ideals mean to each of us probably differs), our unique orientations can't help but influence our behavioral (including consumer) patterns.

Adding to the issue of diversity are the regional consumption behaviors and preferences that exist in various geographic locations in the United States. People living on the far northeastern coast need cold-weather clothes for at least half the year, while those living in the deserts of the Southwest might not even own coats. Marketers need to recognize such differences (in this example, weather-influenced behavior) so they can tailor strategies to meet the needs of the marketplace, whatever they might be.

Diverse lifestyles also have a place in the subcultural mix. A lifestyle is an individual's distinctive way of living—a pattern that influences a person's choices in all areas of life, from how one spends his or her time to how one spends his or her money. (See Chapter 9 for information on psy-

FIGURE 14.4. The United States is a geographically large country where many subcultures coexist, sharing some values but differing in many others.

chographics.) Consumer researchers continuously identify, track, and study emerging and alternative lifestyles, knowing that distinctive lifestyles often produce new kinds of buyers with new and specific needs. And, as we know, new needs create new opportunities for products and the marketing of those products.

⟩ ⟩ ⟩ SPECIAL FOCUS 14.1: METROSEXUALS: A WELL-GROOMED MARKET? ⟨ ⟨ ⟨

Metrosexuals, identified and named in the early twenty-first century, are men who are part of an emerging lifestyle for which new products have been created.

Since the advent of metrosexuality, companies have realized that they have a new market to capitalize on—men who spend their money on grooming and appearance supplies. Walk through the aisles of any U.S. drugstore, and you'll notice an abundance of male-targeted personal grooming products, such as anti-aging eye-creams, shower gels and formula facial cleansers, slowly monopolizing the shelves.

"With men becoming more involved with their grooming habits and the explosive growth in the men's segment (dollar volume +49 percent in 2005), we saw a huge opportunity to introduce the male consumer to a new proposition in skincare," says Carol J. Hamilton, president of the L'Oréal Paris division of L'Oréal USA, Inc., whose Men's Expert line was among the first to hit the mass market a few years ago.

According to L'Oréal Paris' 2005 annual report, men's skincare—with its 11 percent growth in sales—was L'Oréal Paris' fastest growing sector. And it's not just a U.S.-based trend. There are numbers that quantify this as a global trend. The same report states only 4 percent of European men used a skincare product in 1990, compared to a whopping 20 percent in 2003.

The numbers do not lie. Younger men are clearly more interested in taking care of themselves than their fathers or even their older brothers. But is it because metrosexuality has become more widely accepted by the masses or simply because of their generation's habits?

Young or old, metrosexuals apparently are here to stay.

>>> Source: Adapted from Vivian Manning-Schaffel, "Metrosexuals: A Well-Groomed Market?" BusinessWeek Online. May 24, 2006. http://businessweek .com.

Let's Talk
Are subcultural behaviors passed down from generation to generation, or are they transmitted in other ways? Do you think we inherit them, learn them, adopt them? Are you a member of a subculture? If you think you are, how did you come to understand the behaviors that are expected of you?

Clearly, there are many kinds of people who are part of this country; this makes the United States a **multicultural** society, with a dominant culture that includes many subcultures. We all consume goods, but do so in different ways.

As varied as our buying behavior is, however, there are certain products and items, as well as consumption activities, that communicate connectedness, and are symbols that tell observers we all belong to the same culture. Eating turkey on Thanksgiving, wearing baseball hats with our favorite team's name, wearing jeans, and using American slang are all signals that some degree of acculturation has occurred. **Acculturation** is the process of adapting to a new primary or main-stream culture. Those who are born into a culture go through the much easier pro-cess of **enculturation**, whereby humans learn about and act according to the expectations of their own culture from birth on. Although most people living in the Unites States identify, at least somewhat, with the ethnic and religious groups into which they were born, or the countries where their relatives came from, many make at least some effort to adapt to the predominating culture in an attempt to identify with those around them (an example could be learning to speak and read English). Such adaptation allows for a certain degree of comfort, security, and convenience.

Consumption Mirrors Cultural Values

As discussed in an earlier chapter, a value is something we consider important, something that matters to us. A **value system** is "a learned organization of principles and rules to help one choose between alternatives, resolve conflicts, and make decisions."[1] Every culture has certain values that its members share, and although it seems that some values change over time, it's probably more accurate to say that the methods or symbols used to express the values are what actually changes. Therefore, marketers must be careful not to misuse these methods and/or symbols, since misinterpretation can lead to misunderstanding. For example, Jean Paul Gaultier, the avant-garde French couturier, is famous for what is referred to as **cultural borrowing**, the use of symbols that are meaningful to other cultures. But borrowing these symbols does not necessarily mean they are truly understood by the users, or are properly used. Why not? For the simple reason that they've been taken out of their original context. In one of Gaultier's collections, he created clothing based on the traditional dress of Hasidim, the ultra-orthodox sect of the Jewish religion, which included dark gray or black gabardine suits, oversized long suit jackets, and wide-brimmed, fur-trimmed hats. This caused numerous debates and articles about whether Gaultier went "too far" or showed a lack of respect for the religion he used as his inspiration.

Marketers agree that in most situations, it's best not to use certain religious or cultural images or symbols unless their exact meanings and proper usages are understood, in order to avoid misinterpretations. Another factor marketers must acknowledge when targeting multiple cultures is that in each value system, the values are ranked differently. For example, speed and efficiency are high priorities in some cultures, while in others it is patience that's considered crucial. Additionally, some values are culture-specific. Individualism for example, is one of the most prized American values, whereas in Japan, the focus is on fulfilling one's obligations, which is viewed as a far greater achievement than serving the self.[2] Obtaining a state of self-assurance and independence would not be something to aim for in Japanese culture; instead, one's efforts should go toward the creation of harmony and consideration for what is in the best interest of the group to

FIGURE 14.5. The symbolic value of a tailored Ralph Lauren Purple Label suit, as sported by rapper Jay-Z on the Academy Awards red carpet, goes beyond the cost of the suit itself.

which one belongs. Japanese-Americans also tend to rank obligation and harmony high, but convey them in a way that is "acceptable" in the United States.

Belonging and achievement are important goals for members of cultures that value individualism (see Maslow's Hierarchy of Needs, Chapter 4). One way for cultures and subcultures to attain these goals is through the purchase of similar items, especially those that are fashion and/or design related. This is because the possession of designed goods is largely symbolic; owning/wearing certain products is a way of conveying social status, letting others know you understand what a given culture values, and clarifying your own position in that culture. Thus, when Japanese people become part of American culture, they are likely to choose products that help them express a combination of values from both countries. For example, a Japanese-American might serve dinner to his guests on red lacquer plates with antique ivory chopsticks, but have the guests sit at his chrome-and-glass dining room table, rather than on floor cushions.

In the 1970s, researcher Jonathan Gutman explored the role that cultural values play in influencing purchase behavior. His **means-end chain** is a structure that links a consumer's knowledge about a product's attributes (benefits or risks) with the desired cultural value state the person wants to achieve. In other words, the means = the product, the end = the desired value/outcome.[3] Thus, an impeccably tailored suit by Ralph Lauren (an example of a highly symbolic product) would be a means by which a consumer could enjoy a positive consequence, be it status, a feeling of belonging, or any positive experience. When marketers are trying to attract the attention of multicultural consumers, they must be continuously aware that the portrayal of a product and how it's presented and positioned is frequently more important than its functionality or utility.

Marketers have a challenging task in today's mobile and global world, where so many cultural influences must be studied and understood. How do marketers determine which product attributes (product properties and the benefits they provide) are most meaningful to so many consumers in so many cultural groups? They identify the beliefs (values) that are important to the society/group that's being targeted, focus on the ones that are most heavily weighted, develop products that are innovative and well designed (while continuously referring to those beliefs), and devise the marketing stimuli most likely to appeal to each group. To do this, modern marketers have turned to revisit an old field of study. **Anthropology**, the study of human cultural characteristics that include habits, customs, and relationships, is no longer only about studying the artifacts left behind by past peoples; rather, in its newer incarnation, it has become an aid to the understanding of what members of varying cultures want today. **Cultural anthropology** focuses on the common symbols, values, and beliefs of social groups and institutions.

››› POINT OF VIEW 14.2: CULTURAL ANTHROPOLOGY IS ESSENTIAL TO SUCCESSFUL MARKETING ‹‹‹

For marketing purposes, cultural anthropology might be applied to studying teenaged consumers, soccer moms or corporate executives.

Crack the Code

A big part of cultural anthropology involves identifying the codes and symbols people use to communicate value and meaning. Crack the code and find the right symbol, and you're halfway to reaching the target audience in a meaningful, attention-grabbing way. Miss the symbols or interpret them wrongly and your message falls on deaf ears. After all, more than 80% of communication between humans is nonverbal.

If one of the definitions of design is to invent, then cultural anthropology helps ensure that what is invented will resonate with the core audience. Cultural anthropology helps marketers create designs—or inventions—that communicate the brand to every core audience at every touch point or interaction they have with that brand, and makes sure those "interactions" are meaningful experiences that add value to the brand.

In other words, if you get the design wrong, you get the message wrong as well. The design is the message. And no amount of clever words in an ad will override a bad design that communicates an irrelevant symbol.

›› Source: Emma Gilding. "Anthropological Marketing Insights: Why Non-Verbal Cues Are Crucial to Advertising Strategy and Design." www.AdAge.com. March 6, 2006.

Marketers consider the importance of all of these factors in their development of sound marketing strategies. Marketers also use ongoing research about emerging design trends in the multicultural marketplace compiled by **trend forecasting services**, which provide advisories formulated by professional observers of cultural shifts that contain calculated predictions about the likely direction in which design preferences are moving. (See Chapter 1 for additional information about trends and forecasting.)

Awareness of the direction in which trends are moving is crucial to the efforts of anyone planning a marketing strategy, whether it's for a global or local audience. Former staff writer for *Time* magazine, AOL executive, and frequent contributor to the *New York Times,* Guy Garcia offers some astute observations in his book, *The New*

Table 14.1. Forecasting Companies Specialize in All Areas of Design

Site	Review
Trendstop	Trendstop.com is an exciting, visual, and inspiring trend information service online. Trendstop is dedicated to constantly providing fast, focused, and accurate fashion forecasts and global trend information. Trendstop's global team identifies all key trends fast. It shows you how to translate trends into successful products in order to outsmart your competition. You can even download editable trend silhouettes for Illustrator and other design programs. Trendstop gives you the edge you need.
PromoStyl	PromoStyl is a global trend forecasting agency with headquarters in Paris and a network of agents worldwide. Centering on lifestyle trends, PromoStyl gives adaptations for all markets with color and silhouette direction with a balance of creativity and commercial viability. Around for almost 40 years, PromoStyl works with major companies in all fields: apparel, beauty, automotive, consumer products, and more.
Peclers Paris	Peclers Paris, a trend forecasting agency, offers a line of trendpublications that preview and decipher consumer expectations for the fashion, interior, and industrial design fields. Founded 30 years ago, Peclers Paris offers both consulting services and trend forecasting publications internationally. With an office in New York and agents in Los Angeles, Miami, and Canada, Peclers Paris adds extensive knowledge of the North American market to its expertise in the European and Asian markets.
SnapFashun	BGA/SnapFashun, after 25 years, remains one of the world's leading retail trend analysts, covering the U.S. and European markets. Its CD services, EyeSpy Europe and USA, are renowned for their innovative and sharply focused reporting style. Beside photos each CD includes SnapFashun Adobe Illustrator sketches. EyeSpy is an essential tool for those clients requiring immediate direction for current seasons or for product development. SnapFashun supplies fashion trend information and software to manufacturers and educational institutions. The group does business with the likes of MGM, Lee Jeans, JCPenney, and FIT, as well as a host of other manufacturers, schools, and retailers.
Pantone Inc	Nice presentation and easy navigation. Pantone provides color systems and technology across a variety of industries. They have products such as "Color Matching System" a book of standardized color in fan format. It is the reference for selecting, specifying, matching and controlling colors in color critical industries, including textiles, digital technology and plastics. You can buy everything online.
Tobé Report	Tobé is an international fashion and retail consulting service. Their clients depend on them for reality-based strategies and utilize them as a senior-level management tool. Tobé clients include top-line department and specialty stores, mass merchants, and chain stores. Tobé provides in-depth fashion and retail analysis, trend forecasting, product and brand development, merchandising and strategic planning, and market news. Tobé was acquired by Doneger in October, 2005.
Worth Global Style Network	A great site! WGSN's extensive news and information service covers every facet of fashion industry. This subscription-based business-to-business site offers its subscribers fast access to all aspects of international style information. Find free daily news on WGSN everyday. Offices in London, New York, Los Angeles, Madrid, Frankfurt, and Tokyo.

Table 14.1. *(continued)*

Site	Review
Color Association of the United States	Beautiful colors with cool graphics. CAUS is the oldest color forecasting service in the US. Since 1915, it has provided color forecasting information and its relation to various industries from apparel, accessories, textile, and home furnishings. In addition, assorted industry professionals comment on where they find inspiration and how it influences the direction of color. You've got to become a member to get information.
Le Book	A good sourcebook for trends and inspiration for fashion designers, cosmetic companies, advertising agencies, art directors, magazines, photographers, fashion stylists, makeup artists, and hair stylists. It is for sale on the Web site. There are also great listings of contact names.
Color Portfolio	Color Portfolio is a full-service color, trend, and communications marketing company. You can buy its color presentation cards online. It offers offline service, if you are looking for personalized design and concept development.
Carlin Group	Carlin Group includes over 40 people dedicated to trends and a network of agents throughout five continents.
Henry Doneger Associates Inc.	Doneger Associates is the largest fashion consulting company in the United States. It offers extensive market research and analysis, product recommendations, and trend forecasting to members through its online site.

Source: Adapted from "Top Trend Forecasting Services," © 2007 InfoMat Inc. Accessed on August 31, 2007, from www.infomat.com/publications/infpu0001576.html.

Mainstream: How the Buying Habits of Ethnic Groups Are Creating a New American Identity, pointing out that products today are endorsed by a variety of individuals who, not that long ago, would have been considered "outsiders" rather than the celebrities they are now. Chinese basketball players, African-American golf champions, and Latino film stars, all of whom demonstrate the new kind of socioeconomic power in the United States, are reflecting the changing demographic and consumer makeup of the country. The United States has evolved from a "melting pot" to a "salad bowl" of all kinds of people with different interests, experiences, and orientations, and these groups have become a new and influential multiethnic block of tastemakers and trendsetters.[4]

Fashion and Design as Unifying Forces

In addition to studying the differences among the members of our diverse population, marketers also have discovered that the purchase and ownership of fashion-related goods can bring people together in many ways. Many people interested in fashion and design are curious about how others around the world view, wear, and create designed goods. The designed items we choose are regarded by many researchers as an unspoken language that can communicate information about our universal similarities and function as a unifying device (see Special Focus 14.2).

❯❯❯ SPECIAL FOCUS 14.2: FASHION COMMUNICATES ACROSS THE GLOBE ❮❮❮

Patricia Handschiegel, a Chicago native living in Los Angeles, founded My Style Diary online (mystylediary.net) two years ago. Since then, more than 10,000 people have posted more than 100,000 photos of what they wear and what they buy. The site attracts more than 4 million viewers a month.

[Handschiegel] explains that looking at the perfect ensemble in *Vogue* or an expertly coordinated outfit in Lucky is entertaining, like visiting a contemporary art museum. But outfits with six-figure price tags are hard to mimic when your entire wardrobe costs somewhere in the five-digit range.

While peeking inside closets all over the world, it's most surprising that so many of us are plagued by the same fashion dilemmas and sometimes the same wardrobe items.

Handschiegel, who can be seen under the user name "absentminded," said, "Trends are more global because people are exposed to everything. It's pretty amazing to see." She said that when peasant skirts hit a peak earlier this year, they weren't just popular in Chicago or New York; she saw them in Japan, India, and Africa as well.

One world united by fashion? Maybe.

❯❯❯ Source: Debra Bass, "Fashion Communicates across the Globe," *St. Louis Post-Dispatch*, August 17, 2006.

We Are the World

A dominant issue for many companies in the modern marketplace is **globalization**, the ability to offer and market a product any place in the world where a demand for it exists. Continuing to grow and increase profits is a common business objective, and today many businesses do that by entering foreign markets and expanding their customer bases.

❯❯❯ POINT OF VIEW 14.3: ABERCROMBIE & FITCH TO EXPAND IN EUROPE ❮❮❮

Abercrombie & Fitch Co., New Albany, Ohio, announced plans to expand its retail presence throughout Europe. The company is in the process of securing locations in Italy, France, Germany, Spain, Denmark and Sweden, and plans to identify additional key locations in the United Kingdom. "We have been evaluating European markets for some time and it is clear that the demand for the Abercrombie & Fitch brand is very strong," said Mike Jeffries, CEO and chairman of the board of Abercrombie & Fitch. "We believe that now is the ideal time for us to execute our international growth strategy with expansion throughout Europe." The expansion follows the opening of the first Abercrombie & Fitch flagship in Europe at 7 Burlington Gardens in London. Abercrombie & Fitch operates 355 stores, 182 Abercrombie stores, 409 Hollister Co. stores and 17 RUEHL stores in the United States.

❯❯❯ Source: "Abercrombie & Fitch Expand in Europe." July 13, 2007, DDI, www.ddimagazine.com/displayanddesignideas/search/article_display.jsp?vnu_content_id=1003611452

The United States is one of the biggest *importers* of fashion-related goods. **Imports** are those goods and services, provided by foreign producers, that are purchased and brought into a country. An **export** is any good or commodity, transported from one country to another country in a legitimate fashion, typically for use in trade. Exported goods or services are provided to foreign consumers by domestic producers. To be considered legitimate, all trading must be done in accordance with **tariffs** and **duties**, additional monies or taxes on imports imposed by the country receiving those goods, and **quotas**, limits on the quantities of certain goods that can be brought into a country. Both are ways that a country can protect its own producers, as both usually result in increased demand for products made within the country. Many people don't want to pay extra for foreign goods.

Let's Talk
If you wanted a product from another country, but discovered that 20 percent to 30 percent of the price was actually the result of import taxes, would you be willing to pay the price? Why or why not?

When a country imports more than it exports, it creates a **trade deficit**. Conversely, when a country exports more than it imports, it creates a **trade surplus**. During the first decade of the new millennium, a combination of factors (including expired trade agreements and lower prices offered to American companies by overseas manufacturers of a variety of goods) left the United States with a significant trade deficit.

››› POINT OF VIEW 14.4: CENSUS BUREAU FIGURES FROM 2006 REFLECT THE U.S. TRADE DEFICIT ‹‹‹

The U.S. Census Bureau and the U.S. Bureau of Economic Analysis, through the Department of Commerce, announced that total August exports of $122.4 billion and imports of $192.3 billion resulted in a goods and services deficit of $69.9 billion, $1.9 billion more than the $68.0 billion in July, revised. August exports were $2.7 billion more than July exports of $119.7 billion. August imports were $4.6 billion more than July imports of $187.7 billion.

In August, the goods deficit increased $2.1 billion from July to $75.5 billion, and the services surplus increased $0.2 billion to $5.7 billion. Exports of goods increased $2.5 billion to $88.0 billion, and imports of goods increased $4.6 billion to $163.5 billion. Exports of services increased $0.2 billion to $34.4 billion, and imports of services decreased $0.1 billion to $28.8 billion. In August, the goods and services deficit was up $11.1 billion from August 2005. Exports were up $14.4 billion or 13.4 per cent, and imports were up $25.5 billion, or 15.3 percent.

››› Source: "USA: US International trade in goods and services August 2006." www.fibre2fashion.com/news/daily-textile-industries-news/newsdetails .aspx?news_id=24675.

These factors, plus many more, have combined to make marketing U.S. products globally critical for many companies. World trade has exploded, fueled by peoples' frequent exposure to other cultures and their practices. Exchanging information about lifestyles and products through media, music, travel, and the Internet has become the norm, resulting in widespread interest in foreign products by people around the world. There are obviously tremendous opportunities beyond our borders, and as consumers from overseas market segments have shown, they are just as interested in acquiring international products as Americans are.

Global business expansion continues to grow at a remarkable pace. Estée Lauder products are sold in Russia, Nike is popular in Vietnam, and Starbucks has opened coffeehouses in India. Similarly, merchandise from European companies such as IKEA, H&M, and Topshop are now in many American homes. Becoming active and competitive in the global marketplace has become the key to ongoing success for many companies. And maintaining a more equal balance between a country's imports and exports, referred to as a **balance of trade**, would appear to be advantageous, although there is some disagreement among experts as to whether or not this is actually true.

The United States has posted a trade deficit since the 1970s, and it has been rapidly increasing since 1997. Interestingly, this trend indicates that the trade deficit increases most rapidly during times of economic expansion, and slowly during times of contraction.[5]

Some economists, including Milton Friedman, Ph.D., 1976 winner of the Nobel Prize in Economics, have taken the position that a large trade deficit (importation of goods) actually signals that the currency of the recipient country is strong and desirable. To them, a trade deficit simply means that consumers get to purchase and enjoy more goods at lower prices; conversely, a trade surplus implies that a country exported goods that its own citizens did not get to consume and enjoy, and that they paid higher prices for the goods that were consumed. According to Friedman, "A fallacy seldom contradicted is that exports are good, imports bad. The truth is very different. Our gain from foreign trade is what we import. Exports are the price we pay to get imports; the citizens of a nation benefit from getting as large a volume of imports as possible in return for its exports or, equivalently, from exporting as little as possible to pay for its imports."[6]

Others, like Paul Krugman of the *New York Times*, feel that a trade deficit indicates America is living beyond its means, spending far more than it earns. The trade deficit, Krugman predicts, will eventually have to become smaller as a decline in the foreign exchange value of the dollar is inevitable; when this happens, consumers will be unable to continue buying as many products from other countries. Furthermore, Krugman anticipates that American workers, especially those with less formal educations, will see their jobs shipped overseas, or find their wages decreased, as others with similar qualifications crowd into their industries looking for employment to replace the jobs they lost to foreign competitors[7] who charge lower prices to produce many items.

Regardless what school of economic thought one subscribes to, one trend is clearly emerging—consumers everywhere are more interested than ever in goods from outside their own countries. And, of course, overseas companies are also taking advantage of the boom, making their way to the U.S. marketplace.

> > > SPECIAL FOCUS 14.3A: THESE COUNTRIES, AMONG OTHERS, ARE WELCOMING FOREIGN BUSINESSES. < < <

India

After more decades of socialist deprivation, when consumer goods were so limited that refrigerators were given pride of place in living rooms, they have ever more wares to spend it on: cellphones, air-conditioners and washing machines; Botox, sushi and Louis Vuitton bags; and, perhaps the biggest status symbol of all, cars.

>>> Source: Amy Waldman. "In Today's India, Status Comes with Four Wheels." December 5, 2005. www.nytimes.com.

China

Hope of joining China's growing middle class drove Xiang Jun Mei, a poor rice farmer's daughter, to hawk Mary Kay products door-to-door and to everyone she met. China is the company's fastest-growing and second-largest market, and it is expected to surpass the United States in sales in the next 10 years. Growing ranks of Chinese women are donning the Mary Kay uniform of tailored suits, reading Ash's books translated into Mandarin, holding skin-care classes and professing the blond matriarch's go-getter philosophy.

>>> Source: Julia Glick. "Mary Kay Cosmetics finds a growing middle class market—Pink-collar work a hit in China." August 3, 2006. Accessed as www .houstonchronicle.com, Business Section.

England

Claudio Del Vecchio is bringing an icon of American retailing to London. Brooks Brothers—the preppy New York-founded chain that formally opens the mahogany and brass doors of its first 11,000 sq ft British flagship store this week—is as much a part of the fabric of America as baseball, Cadillacs and apple pie.

The oldest American retailer has dressed American presidents, including Abraham Lincoln, John F. Kennedy and Bill Clinton, business leaders, notably Bill Gates, sportsmen and actors, including Brad Pitt, Katharine Hepburn, Will Smith and Nicolas Cage. Now Del Vecchio wants Britons to wear the American dream.

>>> Source: John Arlidge, "Suits You, Brooks Brothers," (London) Times Online, September 10, 2006, http://business.timesonline.co.uk/article/0,,9074 -2350241,00.html.

Mexico

Guess Inc. has entered into a joint venture agreement for the manufacture, wholesale distribution and retail sale of the company's clothing in Mexico with an affiliate of Grupo Axo, a Mexican company that helps the development of international brands. The first Guess retail store under the joint venture opened in May in Mexico City and the second one opened in Cancun in July. The move into Mexico is part of an overall international expansion strategy, according to Paul Marciano, co-chairman and co-CEO of Guess.

>>> Source: Bob Howard, "Guess Expands in Mexico," September 26, 2006. www.globest.com/news/732_732/retail/157930-1.html.

>>> SPECIAL FOCUS 14.3B: SUCCESSFUL RETAILERS FROM OTHER COUNTRIES ARE DOING BUSINESS IN THE UNITED STATES AND THROUGHOUT THE WORLD <<<

Spain

It's fast, it's fashionable, and it's out to conquer the world from a remote corner of northwestern Spain. Inditex, parent of cheap-chic fashion chain Zara, has transformed itself into Europe's leading apparel retailer over the past five years, and is now aiming to rev up growth in Asia and the U.S. But as Chief Executive Pablo Isla maps out plans for global expansion, some are wondering whether Inditex is moving a little too fast for its own good. . . . Too fast? No way, says Isla. "We think we can keep up the pace of expansion without endangering profits," he says.

Zara's nerve center is an 11,000-square-foot hall at its headquarters in Arteixo, a town of 25,000 in Galicia. That's where hundreds of twentysomething designers, buyers, and production planners work in tightly synchronized teams. It is there that the company does all of its design and distribution and half of its production. The concentrated activity enables it to move a dress, blouse, or coat from drawing board to shop floor in just two weeks—less than a quarter of the industry average.

>>> Source: Kerry Capell, Marina Kamenev, and Nichola Saminthar. "Fashion Conquistador." September 24, 2006, http://businessweek.com.

England

Tesco's unusually stealthy US expansion strategy is about to take it to Las Vegas, one of the fastest growing cities in the US, in addition to its previously reported plans to open stores in the Los Angeles and Phoenix areas next year.

The US expansion comes as the UK's biggest supermarket chain, which already takes £1 in every £8 spent on the British high street, powers ahead in its home market. Verdict Research, the retail analysts, predict it will become Britain's biggest non-food retailer by the end of the year, overtaking Argos Retail Group.

The US push is part of a double-pronged effort to expand in its domestic market and abroad.

>>> Source: John Birchall and Elizabeth Rigby, "Tesco Plans to Open Las Vegas Supermarket," $August 9, 2006, www.ft.com/cms/s/bf4e64a0-2743-11db-80ba-0000779e2340.html?CFID=1721349&CFTOKEN=89925011.

Japan

Uniqlo, which has blanketed Japan with inexpensive sportswear sold in 720 stores, is making an expensive bet that American consumers have not already overdosed on the "cheap chic" designs intended to bring a sense of style to retailers from Kohl's to Wal-Mart (with) a mammoth New York flagship in SoHo. . . . the Japanese retailer . . . whose arrival could further reshape the American clothing industry with its promise of high-quality cashmere sweaters for $99 or less . . . will be the largest single-brand fashion store in the retail-saturated Manhattan neighborhood, putting its competitors on notice that the company has aggressive plans for the United States (see Figure 14.6).

>>> Source: Alex Kuczynski. "Service with a Motto: A Japanese Chain Arrives." October 6, 2005. Accessed at www.nytimes.com.

FIGURE 14.6. The interior of the Uniqlo store in New York City.

Understanding and Accommodating the Global Consumer

More and more, companies are incorporating global thinking into the design of their marketing strategies. But how does one think globally when accustomed to only "thinking locally"? After all, thought processes are influenced by experiences, and those processes are based on a one-country experience or what's been called a "domestic mind-set."[8]

For marketers, developing a global way of thinking involves closely examining and analyzing the forces at play within the targeted country—physical forces (location, natural resources, climate), financial/economic forces, sociocultural forces, and historic and political forces. Those wishing to really participate in the global market must also assess competitive forces, production capabilities, and labor practices.

Obviously, the global marketplace is both large and complex. So, how can a marketer determine where specific opportunities are? Research and experience show that the largest markets for U.S. goods are in countries with the following:

- A sophisticated infrastructure
- A large industrial base
- A stable financial basis
- A transportation network

Also, they are already doing their own importing and exporting of products.

Developing countries present different kinds of opportunities, including specific demand patterns and economic needs that have to be met in accordance with their limited financial resources. However, the marketplace of each nation is fluid, and the possibility exists that interest in fashion goods could develop anywhere (see Special Focus 14.4). Therefore, in-depth examination and assessment of a country's market attractiveness is a prerequisite to sound selection of potential trading partners.[9]

❯❯❯ SPECIAL FOCUS 14.4: APPAREL SPENDING AND BRAND APPEAL STRONGEST IN DEVELOPING COUNTRIES, NEW RETAIL FORWARD STUDY REPORTS ❮❮❮

Consumers in developing countries—particularly China, India, Russia, Mexico and Brazil—are buying and paying more for well-known or familiar apparel brands, a recently released study by Retail Forward reports.

The Global Softgoods Shopper Update also finds that the beneficiary of the robust apparel spending in developing a market is clothing specialty stores more so than department stores, hypermarkets and supercenters. The study was based on surveys conducted for Retail Forward by Global Market Insite Inc. (GMI).

The impact of new shopping alternatives—notably hypermarkets and supercenters from Carrefour, Wal-Mart and Tesco for example—is being felt primarily in certain countries and categories. The impact of online and non-store retailers in the apparel sector appears to be strongest in France, Germany, Japan and the United Kingdom. Despite the new alternatives, however, the study finds that shopping frequency at clothing specialty stores and traditional department stores appears to be holding up in most countries.

Retail Forward's *Global Softgoods Shopper* Update report is based on the GMIPoll online Omnibus™ survey of 1,000 consumers in 13 select countries. Retail Forward's report analyzes the responses of those consumers to questions about their shopping frequency, behavior and attitudes related to shopping for apparel.

"Our research indicates that shoppers are buying more apparel—more often higher quality apparel—from apparel specialty stores and to a lesser extent from traditional department stores," states Frank Badillo, author of the *Global Softgoods Shopper Update* and Manager of the *Global Retailing Program of the Retail Forward Intelligence System™*. "Conversely, demand for apparel at hypermarkets and supercenters is less robust in less developed retail markets."

Consumers surveyed in less-developed retail markets also indicated a strong interest in buying and paying more for well-known or familiar clothing brands than shoppers in more well-developed markets. At the same time, a high share of shoppers surveyed across most countries is willing to try an unfamiliar clothing brand if it is recommended by someone or if the price or style is right. Among the findings from the Shopper Update report:

Clothing and department stores remain favored, but face challengers. Clothing, specialty and department stores are holding up well across most countries as the store types where most consumers prefer to buy clothing and accessories most often. But alternative formats—most notably hypermarkets and supercenters in Japan, the United Kingdom and the United States—are making competitive inroads. The pressure is most evident in teen and children's clothing. Also feeling the impact are women's and men's casual clothing and shoes.

Shopping frequency shifts evident in developed markets. Despite the growing impact of hypermarkets and supercenters, shopping frequency at clothing and other specialty stores is holding up well in less developed retail markets and some European markets. Slippage at traditional department stores is evident primarily in the developed markets of Japan, the United Kingdom and the United States.

Online and non-store apparel retailing is strongest in Europe and Japan. Consumer interest in online apparel retailers—and more broadly in non-store apparel retailers including catalogs and personal selling—is strongest in France, Germany, Japan and the United Kingdom. Non-store retailers in the European countries, particularly France and Germany, have benefited from regulations that limit store hours and store development. Canada is among the laggards in terms of interest in online and other non-store retailers. The United States is between the extremes.

>>> Source: Katharine R. Clarke. "Apparel Spending and Brand Appeal Strongest in Developing Countries, New Retail Forward Study Reports." October 4, 2005. www.retailforward.com.

But remember, when a company does decide to expand globally, it's not enough to simply transfer a product that's been well received to another country, no matter how many consumers have responded favorably to it. Although that's certainly a solid reason to begin exploring expansion options, it's not a guarantee of success. As previously stated, the key to success in the global business world is understanding the setting (cultural, environmental, economic, political) in which the company will be operating and then designing a strategy that will connect with people in the host culture. The ever-changing dynamics of today's marketplace are providing a wealth of exciting opportunities due to numerous factors, including the intertwining of cultures in both the United States and abroad.

Finally, it's essential that global marketers not only develop global information systems but that they also develop *themselves*, personally, by learning a language other than English and by making genuine efforts to consider noncritically the practices of people from countries with which they're unfamiliar. Traveling abroad can be both educational and helpful in developing personal connections with people from other countries. To successfully reach and service consumers, understanding and addressing both universal and diverse human values and needs is at the core of the process. Only then can marketers begin to create business relationships that truly span the globe.

Today, successful businesspeople have to surmount many challenges, whether marketing products locally or abroad. Demonstrating social responsibility, adhering to quality standards, and supporting fair treatment of workers are just some of the ethical issues that we will address next in Chapter 15.

Summary

Although people from different parts of the world differ in many ways, research and observation have shown that, despite these differences, we are all very interested in goods and services from other countries. Additionally, sharing products and practices tends to foster relationship building and increase acceptance, both of which grow from recognizing our similarities and appreciating our differences.

Whether targeting subcultural groups within the United States or those in foreign countries, consumer behaviorists know that understanding and respecting diverse cultures, lifestyles, and values are key factors in the growth of any business, no matter who the customers are or where they live. Entering any new market requires the assessment of needs, preferences, and potential buying power of that culture prior to expansion. It's also imperative that marketers consider the meanings of cultural symbols in order to avoid their misuse. Using cultural anthropology as a basis for analysis of preferences can be helpful, as can information from trend forecasting services and research firms that track the needs and wants of diverse market segments.

Globalization efforts must be carefully planned and conducted. As long as accurate information is obtained, trade agreements are understood and enforced, and appropriate marketing strategies are used, the import and export of goods and services can be beneficial and rewarding.

Key Terms

Acculturation	Imports
Anthropology	Means-end chain
Balance of trade	Multicultural
Cultural anthropology	Quotas
Cultural borrowing	Tariffs
Diversity	Trade deficit
Duties	Trade surplus
Enculturation	Trend forecasting service
Exports	Value system
Globalization	

Birchal, Jona
markets."
-0000779e
Capell, Kerry
Septembei
Chaney, Lilli
3rd ed. Up
Ferraro, Gary
dle River, l
Fibre 2 Fashic
ber 13, 20(
.aspx?new
Gilding, Em
Crucial to
Glick, Julia. "
.HoustonC
Harrell, Gilt
River, NJ:
Howard, Bol
archives/n
Hoyer, Wayr
Houghtor
Manning-Sc
24, 2006.
Sherwood, S
section.
Verjee, Neel:
business.t
Waldman, A
with Four
Wilson, Eric
York Tim
www.csnews
www.ddima
e3i1b179
www.infom:
www.retailw
www.targetr

Questions for Review

1. Define "subculture." How can subcultural differences affect consumer purchases?
2. What is a lifestyle? How are subculture and lifestyle related? Make a list of specific products that could be termed "lifestyle products," and explain your reasons for choosing those products.
3. Explain cultural borrowing and how it might be misinterpreted if used without sufficient research. Discuss the importance of understanding cultural values when using this technique.
4. How can marketers benefit by using trend forecasts? Give examples that relate to marketing designed goods.
5. Define "globalization." List three specific considerations that should be addressed by any business seeking to introduce a new product to another country.

Activities

1. Watch the film *Monsoon Wedding* with a classmate. Discuss how the buying behavior of the bride's father reflect both the Indian culture and the universal desires of fathers of brides everywhere. Submit a written summary of your conclusions.
2. Interview a student from another country. Ask him or her to describe the shopping habits, product preferences, and availability of designed goods in his or her culture. How do they differ from those of Americans? Do the marketing practices also differ? Present your findings in a three- to five-minute report to the class.
3. Choose a group within the United States that practices an alternative lifestyle. Investigate the value system, customs, shopping habits, and product preferences of its members, and discuss your findings with classmates and their implications for marketers.
4. Choose an American product that is currently being sold in another country, and determine how it and/or the accompanying marketing strategies have been modified for the host culture. Discuss possible reasons for the modifications with classmates.
5. The majority of fashion goods in the U.S. are now made outside of this country. Choose an American apparel designer/manufacturer that has its goods produced overseas. In class, lead a discussion about the fashion industry's reasons for using foreign labor rather than keeping jobs within the United States.

Mini-Projects

1. The North American Free Trade Agreement virtually eliminates tariffs and quotas on imports and exports among Canada, Mexico, and the United States. In a

PART V

Fashion Consumers and Responsible Citizenship

Just like any other industry, the fashion business functions within the greater framework of society, subject to the rules and standards of behavior that govern both individual and corporate entities—some of which will be examined in Part V.

Ethical issues as they relate to fashion marketing and consumption are explored in Chapter 15, along with a look at the social and environmental responsibilities of fashion and other businesses. Chapter 16 describes the role of the government and private-sector organizations in regulating or monitoring products and marketing programs, with the goal of protecting consumers from harm.

CHAPTER 15

Ethics and Social Responsibility

Barry had had an amazing time in New York City, visiting his aunt and uncle, taking in a couple of Broadway shows, and even getting to a Major League ball game. Before heading home to the Midwest, though, he wanted to pick up a gift for his girlfriend, Laura, who hadn't been able to take time off from work to join him on the trip.

Strolling the streets of the city, Barry passed dozens of department stores, shops, and boutiques, checking out their window displays to judge whether the merchandise inside might be interesting. One store had some pretty, colorful tops that caught his eye, but once inside, he noticed a mannequin prominently displaying a dyed fox jacket and hat, and decided not to shop there, since both he and Laura strongly opposed the use of animal fur in clothing.

Back outside, Barry noticed a group of people milling around a table on the sidewalk. He went over to take a closer look and saw that the table was covered with what looked like designer handbags—even he recognized the distinctive Coach logo on many of them. Amazingly, though, the prices were much lower than those he had heard his sister and Laura discussing for similar bags. "This is perfect," Barry said to himself, scanning the selection to see which of the many styles to buy. Just then, however, he overheard two women who were walking away and saying something about "fakes" and "if the police catch them," and he stopped short. If they could recognize the bags as fakes, perhaps Laura would, too, and that would ruin the whole surprise—not to mention the fact that he might be breaking some law by buying a counterfeit.

Feeling a little discouraged, yet determined to find the right gift, Barry continued on his quest. Halfway down the next block, his eyes lit up: A sign in the window of a small boutique touted the shop's selection of "organic and eco-friendly" clothing. Knowing Laura was an avid environmentalist, he was sure he'd hit the jackpot. Inside, a friendly sales associate helped him pick out a soft, tangerine-colored hooded sweatshirt and white V-neck jersey made of bamboo and organic cotton. He was sure Laura would be thrilled—even more so when he noticed a tag on the tops that mentioned the manufacturer was donating 5 percent of its profits to rainforest preservation efforts.

Defining Ethics

As we've discussed throughout this book, many conscious and unconscious factors go into each and every purchase decision consumers make. In Barry's situation, his decision making hinged in large part on ethical considerations. **Ethics** is a system of moral values, or a set of principles that define right and wrong. In some cases, ethical standards are established for an entire culture or profession; medical ethics, for example, prescribe that physicians shall provide competent medical care, with compassion and respect for human dignity and rights, and shall support access to medical care for all people. Individuals also have their own personal ethical standards, formed by a combination of upbringing, experiences, and beliefs, such as the "golden rule" of treating others as you would want to be treated. Barry's personal ethics told him that creating apparel out of animal fur was wrong, since obtaining the fur generally involved cruelty to the animals, and he had been a lifelong animal lover. Laws are generally based on ethics—for example, in the United States, it is both illegal and unethical to plagiarize someone else's work. Other ethical standards are not actually law, even if they are commonly accepted. For instance, most people would agree that it is unethical to cheat on a test, even though it is not a crime.

Going hand in hand with ethics is social responsibility. **Social responsibility** refers to the principle that everyone is responsible for making the world a better place for all its inhabitants. In business, the concept means that companies should contribute to the welfare of society and not be solely devoted to maximizing profits. When a company provides free child care to its employees, or organizes a recycling program for its used products, it is being socially responsible. On an individual level, social responsibility can take the form of a charitable act, such as donating a still-good winter coat to a homeless shelter to benefit someone less fortunate, or driving a hybrid car to reduce greenhouse gases. The company that made the clothing Barry bought was exhibiting social responsibility both in its use of bamboo, which is renewable and grown in an environmentally friendly way, and in its donation to help save the rainforests.

In this chapter, we will explore how ethics and social responsibility come into play in the fashion world, examining their effect both on the way fashion marketers do business and on the way consumers behave.

Consumer Theft

One of the most obvious breaches of ethics is stealing; and it is a crime in every country in the world. Yet, as you know, not everyone obeys the law, and **inventory shrinkage**—a term that includes employee theft, shoplifting, vendor fraud, and administrative error—is an enormous problem, costing U.S. retailers more than $41 billion a year, according to an annual survey conducted by the University of Florida. That number represents about 1.6 percent of retailers' total annual sales, with employee theft, known as "pilferage," accounting for the largest losses. Shoplifting, however, has been growing in recent years, and accounts for about one-third of losses.[1]

Shoplifting

Shoplifting is not only a crime, but a consumer behavior that is often not based on need. There have been instances over the years of famous and presumably wealthy people stealing from stores, perhaps simply for the "thrill" of it. Notably, actress Winona Ryder made headlines with her arrest in 2001 for taking more than $5,500 worth of merchandise from a Saks Fifth Avenue store. Most shoplifting is on a smaller scale, and some people might try to rationalize the theft of a candy bar or lipstick as being inconsequential. But even those "small" crimes contribute to an overall

FIGURE 15.1. Retailers employ a variety of security measures to combat theft by both employees and shoplifters.

problem that hurts both retailers and consumers. In an effort to thwart both employee theft and shoplifters, retailers spend millions of dollars on security, ranging from uniformed or undercover security guards to often cumbersome security systems, such as the bulky plastic tags that have to be removed from apparel and accessories once consumers pay for them. Even then, retailers generally are forced to raise their prices to make up for sales lost to theft—a solution that affects the store's entire customer base. Should losses become too high, a retailer might close the store or lay off workers in order to remain profitable.

Let's Talk
What would you do if you were in a store and noticed someone shoplifting? Would you notify store personnel? Discuss why or why not.

In recent years, a new breed of thieves has compounded the problem. Their crime is called **organized retail theft (ORT)**, also known as "boosting," and it usually involves multiple shoplifters working together to steal larger quantities of products, which are stolen not for personal use, but to resell through fencing operations (individuals or groups that receive and dispose of stolen goods) or perhaps at flea markets.[2] The average loss per ORT incident is now more than $46,000,[3] and investigators estimate that a single shoplifter operating as part of an organized group can steal as much as $200,000 worth of merchandise in one weekend.[4] ORT has grown so significantly in the past decade that retail industry groups, government, and law enforcement are all looking at ways to specifically address the problem. In 2004, retailers formed the National Retail Federation (NRF)/FBI Intelligence Network in an effort to better share information and identify active ORT operations around the country. In addition, legislation passed in 2006 established an Organized Retail Theft Task Force at the FBI.

Fraudulent Returns

A related issue involves people who make dishonest returns to stores. Have you ever known someone who bought an expensive dress, wore it to a party or other event with the tags tucked inside, and then returned it to the store as new? Not only is that highly unethical, it is just one type of fraudulent return that costs U.S. retailers more than $16 billion each year.[5]

Other examples of fraudulent returns include people trying to return an item to a store where they did not buy it, or shoplifting merchandise and then returning it for cash or store credit. In some cases, individuals sell actual store receipts that have not expired, and the buyers shoplift identical merchandise that they then "return" to the store for credit in the form of a gift card. Some thieves who have obtained store gift cards for fraudulent returns then try to sell the cards online, a tactic that in 2004 led eBay to begin limiting sellers to one gift card auction per week, with a maximum value per card of $500.[6]

Taking preventive measures even further, some retailers are partnering with The Return Exchange, a company that uses software to help client retailers identify customers who make fraudulent returns. Retailers using the system require customers to present identification, such as a driver's license, when returning purchases. That information is checked against The Return Exchange's database to track the frequency of returns, dollar amounts, and other variables.[7] The resulting reports give retailers tools to either tighten their return policies or, in some cases, refuse to take back merchandise from customers who have made more than an ordinary number of returns or exchanges at a specific store.

Counterfeiting

It is a classic comedy scene: A man approaches a stranger, whips open his trench coat to reveal the lining dotted with wristwatches, and asks, "You wanna buy a watch—cheap?" In real life, however, selling fake designer or brand-name products is not funny, and the problem goes far beyond Rolex watches and lone individuals hiding them in a trench coat. Counterfeiting today is a sophisticated, global operation that the FBI estimates costs U.S. businesses as much as $250 billion a year.[8]

Counterfeit goods are unauthorized copies of designer or branded products, designed to mimic the authentic goods (down to the detailing, logo, and even the label). Their appeal to consumers is clearly that they look like the real thing, yet cost only a fraction of the price of the original. Counterfeit goods are not the same as apparel knock-offs, which are considered an integral part of the fashion life cycle (see Chapter 12); fashion-related counterfeiting falls more in the categories of handbags, shoes (especially athletic shoes), and watches. Selling counterfeit merchandise is against the law; and while it is not illegal to purchase fake goods (as Barry feared in the chapter's opening scenario), it is unethical to knowingly do so. Special Focus 15.1 describes how to spot a fake product.

〉〉〉 SPECIAL FOCUS 15.1: HOW TO SPOT A FAKE 〈〈〈

Is the price too good to be true? If it seems too good to be true, it probably is. For sale and discount pricing, familiarize yourself with the usual sale price range. Sale prices that are still too good to be true might mean that the product is not "the real deal."

Where is the product usually sold? Authentic branded products are not usually available at flea markets, "purse parties," in mall kiosks, in New York's Chinatown neighborhood or Santee Alley in Los Angeles, or on auction Web sites. If you purchase branded products in any of these places, the risk of being defrauded is highly likely.

Is the packaging neat and clean? Examine the packaging closely. Is the shrink-wrap tight around the product, or loose and sloppy? If it does not look packaged in a quality way, it may mean the product is not authentic.

Are there misspellings in the fine print? If you are about to purchase something from a vending site that is out of the norm for the product or the price is deeply discounted, examine the front AND back of the packaging for misspellings (for example, does it say "Calvin Kline" instead of "Calvin Klein"?)

Does the vendor engage in cash-only transactions and not charge sales tax? If the vendor does not charge sales tax or take credit cards, it signals an illegal transaction. You could even be contributing to the vendor's tax evasion.

Is it legal? Just because a vendor has a city vending license does not legalize the sale of illegal counterfeited or pirated products.

Does it need assembly? If the vendor is asking you to choose the type of famous logo or brand name to place on a product, assume the vendor has no legal right to it.

>>> Source: The International AntiCounterfeiting Coalition.

Because counterfeiting has become such a huge issue in the marketplace—worldwide, the manufacture and sale of fake goods is a $650 billion-a-year industry[9]—businesses are taking unprecedented steps to combat it. Brands such as Fendi, Gucci, Yves Saint Laurent, and Bottega Veneta are sewing holograms into the lining of their handbags, boots, and even mink coats, with encrypted codes that allow police and customs officials to authenticate the products with a special magnifying device.[10] Some companies are also hiring private investigators to track down counterfeit merchandise and are then suing those selling it. Actions taken in recent years include the following:

- LMVH Moet Hennessy Louis Vuitton filed suit against eBay, claiming that the online marketplace had allowed sales of fake Louis Vuitton handbags and Dior Couture products by its sellers. LVMH's lawsuit said that of the 300,000 Dior-branded items and 150,000 Vuitton bags offered on eBay during one 6-month period, 9 out of 10 were fakes.[11]

- Abercrombie & Fitch hired a former FBI agent to help crack down on poor-quality copies of its polo shirts, jeans, and other apparel being sold around the world. The company had discovered fake A&F storefronts in Korea, and at one point intercepted 300,000 pairs of counterfeit jeans being shipped from Hong Kong.[12]
- Coach Inc. filed suit against Target, accusing the retailer of selling counterfeit Coach-style bags, featuring the signature "C" pattern and complete with a hangtag that said "Coach." The luxury handbag company has also sued Kohl's for infringing on its trademarks.[13]
- Luxury jean maker 7 For All Mankind hired as senior vice president and general counsel an attorney who had spent more than 20 years combating counterfeiters for other fashion companies, including Kate Spade, Calvin Klein, and Ralph Lauren. Within six months, the executive was blocking an average of 10,000 online auctions of fake "Sevens" every month, and also discovered a woman selling counterfeit versions of the jeans at Tupperware-style house parties.[15]
- Wal-Mart stores was facing charges by LVMH Moet Hennessy Louis Vuitton for selling counterfeit Fendi brand bags and wallets in its Sam's Club stores. The giant retailer had previously settled similar lawsuits brought against it by Tommy Hilfiger, Nike, Nautica, Polo, and the Fubu group at Inter Parfums.[16]

FIGURE 15.2. Street vendors are one potential source of counterfeit goods, but even reputable retailers have been accused of selling fakes.

In addition to businesses' efforts to fight back against counterfeiters, government and law enforcement are also playing a stronger role by passing tougher laws and cracking down on sellers, shippers, and even landlords who rent to businesses marketing fake goods. (The role of government is discussed in greater detail in Chapter 16.) The concern is not only because the legitimate companies stand to lose business and sales, but also because of other consequences of counterfeiting. For example, manufacturers of counterfeit products do not pay taxes, which hurts the economy for everyone, nor is it likely that they pay fair wages or benefits to workers, who might even be children if the goods originate in countries without strict

Top Five Counterfeited Brands	Top Brands Counterfeited by Classification
1. Louis Vuitton	Clothing & Accessories: Louis Vuitton
2. Nike	Computer Equipment & Supplies: Canon
3. Microsoft	Entertainment & Software: Microsoft
4. Gucci	Food & Alcohol: Nestle
5. Adidas	Jewelry & Watches: Chanel
	Other Goods: Titleist
	Perfume & Cosmetics: Christian Dior
	Toys & Sports Equipment: Disney

FIGURE 15.3 A AND B.
Source: International Chamber of Commerce / BASCAP (Business Initiative to Stop Counterfeiting and Piracy)

labor laws. There is also evidence that the sale of some counterfeit goods might fund terrorist groups such as Al Qaeda. Designers and other legitimate manufacturers hope that by making the public more aware of all those factors, consumers will choose to act ethically and pass up the next "great deal" they see on a branded or designer product, thereby making it less profitable for counterfeiters to stay in business.

Let's Talk
Have you ever bought something you knew was a counterfeit? Knowing all the negative effects that counterfeits have on legitimate businesses and the economy, would you buy one in the future? Would you discourage a friend from buying one? Discuss your reasons.

Business Ethics

While counterfeiting is a clear-cut violation of ethics and the law, there are many decisions that legitimate businesses make every day that involve ethical considerations. In some cases, making a decision that is unethical leads to committing an illegal act. News headlines in the first years of this century were dominated by ethics scandals at corporate giants Enron, Tyco, and Adelphia, to name some of the most prominent, in which business and accounting rules were bent and/or broken, resulting in enormous losses for the companies' employees and shareholders, as well as prison terms for key executives involved in the criminal actions. In other cases, the line between unethical and illegal is not as clearly defined, and company executives must rely on their own sense of right and wrong to reach a decision. Sometimes, listening to their customers can help them determine the best course of action, particularly when dealing with an issue that consumers feel strongly about and make their opinions known. Let's examine a few of those areas that affect the fashion industry.

〉 〉 〉 SPECIAL FOCUS 15.2: PHILANTHROPY BECOMES "BUSINESS AS USUAL" FOR RETAILERS 〈 〈 〈

After decades of treating charity as an afterthought—and using cheap trinkets as an incentive for shoppers to give—retailers are putting philanthropy at the center of their product lines, whether it is clothes, books, or shoes. In the process, stores are transforming charity from a crush of donation requests every season into a sustainable, year-round business model.

Retail executives say that consumers, shocked by a series of high-profile business scandals, are putting greater value on corporate citizenship. So in a weak retail climate, philanthropy, and the image it projects, has suddenly become a competitive advantage. As a result, retail executives and philanthropy experts said, charity is no longer an option — it is a requirement for stores. Said Michael Gould, chief executive of Bloomingdale's, "Intimate apparel and sportswear defines you for a moment in time, but this defines you forever."

Source: Adapted from Michael Barbaro, "Candles, Jeans, Lipsticks: Products with Ulterior Motives," *New York Times*, November 13, 2006.

Consumer Privacy

Consumers have always viewed certain personal information—for example, their tax returns and medical records—as being private. With modern technology, however, those and other personal records are no longer simply stored on paper in a filing cabinet, but very well could be on computers, discs, or other electronic media that are potentially vulnerable to theft or to hacking (unauthorized computer access). If key information, such as a person's social security number, falls into the wrong hands, it can lead to identity theft, in which a criminal obtains credit and spends sometimes-massive amounts of money using another person's identity, leaving the innocent person responsible for clearing his or her name. As a result, protecting consumers' privacy has become a serious ethical issue for marketers who gather and retain customers' personal data.

For example, many retailers use **loyalty programs**, which offer a reward or an

FIGURE 15.4. Store credit cards provide benefits to consumers through their loyalty programs, but they also gather personal information that raises privacy issues.

incentive to keep shoppers returning to their store. One of the most common forms of loyalty programs is the "frequent shopper card" that supermarkets, drugstore chains, and other retailers offer to customers who fill out a simple registration form. The card is then scanned at the register each time customers make a purchase at that store, often to give an instant discount on certain items. In other cases, a retailer may use its store credit card as a "reward" card, tracking the dollar amount of a customer's purchases and offering special sale prices, exclusive sale days, or other rewards for shopping at the store.

While loyalty programs offer benefits for consumers, they also benefit retailers, enabling them to collect purchasing information that can help them identify trends and fine-tune their merchandise assortment. In some cases, customers' previous purchases are used to identify other products that the store might market to them. Some consumers fear that the amount of information stores gather about them could become intrusive or be misused, or worry that the retailer might sell the information to another company that in turn might misuse it or not keep it safe. One study found that the information shoppers find most acceptable to give retailers include their name (89.8 percent), e-mail address (78.1 percent), and street address (60.7 percent); less than half (46.8 percent), however, found it acceptable for retailers to collect information on past transactions.[17]

Online shopping raises additional privacy issues and concerns. Despite the rapid growth of e-commerce, nearly half of American consumers polled as recently as 2005 said they avoid shopping on the Internet out of fear that their personal information will be stolen.[18] For those who do shop online, many consider retailers' cookies a threat to privacy. As discussed in Chapter 10, online merchants download those small pieces of software onto consumers' computers so they can track how often consumers visit their Web sites, what they do on the sites, and often what they do before and after visiting the sites. Because of privacy concerns, however, some consumers block cookies from being accepted on their computer, and over half of online shoppers delete cookies at least once a week or once a month, according to one study.[19]

Privacy concerns also surround the emerging use of RFID (radio-frequency identification) tags on merchandise. Considered a boon to manufacturers and retailers, the inexpensive chips, which are often smaller than a grain of sand, can be embedded in virtually any merchandise—from a piece of apparel to a pack of gum—and read by a wireless device from several yards away, providing a cost-effective way to automate inventory levels and track merchandise all the way from factory to store checkout. But because each chip has a unique ID code, there are concerns that they could also be used to track consumers themselves as they carry or wear products with embedded chips.[20] That is an ethical issue that privacy watchdogs and some lawmakers are urging industry to address even before the RFID tags are in widespread use—requesting, for example, that the tags be permanently disabled once an item has been purchased.

Ethical Advertising

Numerous aspects of advertising can raise questions of ethics. One of the most basic is the long-standing question of whether advertisers try to create a need where none exists. In the fashion world, one could argue that clothes generally do not wear out after one season, and therefore trying to convince consumers that they need to buy a new wardrobe that reflects the newest styles could be considered unethical. Today's consumers, however, have grown up surrounded by advertising and, for the most part, understand its intent; in general, they are not easily manipulated by an ad's pitch. In addition, advertisers who make outright false or misleading claims are subject to prosecution under the truth in advertising laws enforced by the Federal Trade Commission (FTC). (Chapter 16 provides detailed information on government legislation.)

Of greater concern to some consumers is the content of some advertising. Obviously, the purpose of advertising is to get a product or brand noticed. But what if it is attracting attention by featuring scantily clad models, subtle or not-so-subtle sexual innuendoes, or other elements that

FIGURE 15.5. Victoria's Secret has pushed the boundaries with its sexy ads, which entice some consumers but offend others.

push the envelope of good taste? Because marketers are competing for consumers' attention amid an increasing array of media and messages, they may sometimes use questionable taste to try to break through the "clutter." What's more, since taste is subjective, advertising content that one audience finds acceptable may be offensive to another audience. Fans of American Apparel's hip clothing, for example, may enjoy the company's racy ads (such as one that pictured a woman in a see-through shirt in a shower[21]), while others might find it sexist and in bad taste.

There are occasions when advertisers take the initiative to counteract what some consider objectionable content or images, as Dove did in using "real" women with real-life shapes in an ad campaign for its body-care products. (See Chapter 6, Special Focus 6.1.) At other times, if an ad is offensive to enough people, it can cause a consumer backlash against the company, which can result in the ad being discontinued. That is especially true if the advertising is directed at children or teenagers. Retailer JCPenney, for example, found itself barraged by angry letters from parents when one of its back-to-school sales circulars featured a selection of T-shirts adorned with Budweiser and other alcohol brand logos. As a result, the retailer repositioned them within the men's department.[22] Similarly, a Macy's store in Portland, Oregon, came under fire for a back-to-school ad that featured a T-shirt emblazoned with "Beer Pong," a drinking game, as well as for T-shirts with other beer-related slogans on display in the store's teen section. After complaints from a local substance-abuse prevention group and a TV news report spotlighting the controversy, Macy's parent company announced it was removing the shirts from all its Macy's and Bloomingdale's stores across the country.[23]

> > > POINT OF VIEW 15.1: "GIRLCOTT" PROTESTS OFFENSIVE T-SHIRTS < < <

There's nothing unusual about a boycott, but how about a "girlcott?" That's what a group of Allegheny County, Pennsylvania, teenage girls called for in their campaign against Abercrombie & Fitch's "attitude T-shirts," which the girls found to be demeaning to young women. The offending shirts featured such slogans as "Who needs brains when you have these?" and "Blondes are adored, brunettes are ignored."

The protest by two dozen or so girls began with a local news conference and rally at Chatham College in Pittsburgh; the girls also began e-mailing their friends, who in turn e-mailed more friends. Before they knew it, the story was picked up by the national media and featured on NBC's Today show and CNN, among others. In addition to encouraging young women not to buy the controversial shirts, the girls were asking those who agreed with their stance to contact Abercrombie & Fitch to let them know they didn't think the T-shirts were "cool" anymore.

This was not the first time Abercrombie & Fitch had been taken to task for edgy product lines. Earlier, parents and anti-drug and alcohol advocates pressured the retailer into removing shirts they said glorified drinking; and before that, the company outraged parents by selling thongs for girls as young as 10, some of which had the words "eye candy" printed inside a tiny heart. The company also sparked protests over T-shirts that featured racial caricatures of Asians, and caught flak for a catalog that featured provocatively posed, nearly nude teenage-looking models. Negative publicity forced the retailer to pull the catalogs.

And what happened with the "girlcott?" Abercrombie & Fitch pulled several of their "attitude" T-shirts—and executives of the company met face-to-face with some of the original protesters to hear their pitch for alternative T-shirts featuring positive messages.

>>> Source: Adapted from Monica Haynes, "Bawdy T-shirts Set Off 'Girlcott' by Teens," *Pittsburgh Post-Gazette*, November 3, 2005, http://www.postgazette .com/pg/pp/05307/599884.stm; and Monica Haynes, "'Girlcott' Organizers Meet with Abercrombie & Fitch Execs over T-shirts," *Pittsburgh Post-Gazette*, December 6, 2005, http://post-gazette.com/pg/pp/05340/617917.stm.

Fur and Animal Testing

One of the most emotional topics for those discussing ethics in fashion involves the use of animal fur in apparel. People who oppose cruelty to animals believe that using fur in clothing and accessories is both unethical and immoral—recall that Barry in the opening scenario felt so strongly about it that he would not even shop in a store selling fur garments. Some particularly aggressive anti-fur activists have been known to throw red paint (symbolizing blood) on women wearing fur coats, although the ethics of such behavior could certainly themselves be called questionable. Less violent protests have been organized by various groups, notably People for the Ethical Treatment of Animals (PETA), a global animal rights group. Celebrities sometimes help raise the visibility of the anti-fur message, as when actress Pamela Anderson stripped down to a G-string in a London shop window on behalf of PETA, under a banner that read "Rather bare skin than wear skin."[24]

Another memorable protest took place in New York City's Times Square, where a man and woman lay naked in cardboard coffins to protest the torture and inhumane killing in China of dogs and cats for their fur.[25] The use of dog and cat fur in apparel has been banned in the United States, Australia, France, Italy, and several other countries, but because the fur is very difficult to identify, it is sometimes dyed and/or purposely mislabeled and passed off as fur from other animals. Most of the fur of domestic

FIGURE 15.6. Some designers and apparel manufacturers still use real fur in their lines, despite the fact that many consumers find it unethical.

animals comes from China, but a Humane Society investigation found that the Czech Republic and other Eastern European countries also contribute to the more than 2 million dogs and cats estimated to be killed each year for their fur.[26]

Because many consumers oppose the use of fur in fashion, and because there are many alternatives, including high-quality fake fur, a number of designers and apparel marketers have discontinued using real fur in their lines. Clothing retailer J. Crew announced in 2005 that it would no longer sell products made with fur, stating that the decision was made for business reasons and not due to a PETA campaign that had targeted the company. In 2006, Polo Ralph Lauren said it was eliminating fur from all of its apparel and home collections, the first major design house to do so since the mid-1990s, when Calvin Klein discontinued its use of fur.[27]

A related ethical issue involves the use of animals in testing the safety of cosmetics and cosmetics ingredients. Many consumers believe it is wrong to deliberately harm animals in the development of new beauty and personal care products, and go out of their way to purchase from companies that maintain a no-animal-testing policy. Some individuals or groups even **boycott** companies that test on animals, that is, consumers make the conscious decision not to purchase any of the companies' products as a protest and moral statement. The Coalition for Consumer Information on Cosmetics, a group of animal-protection organizations that encourages consumers to purchase products that have not been tested on animals, launched in 1996 a uniform "Corporate Standard of Compassion for Animals" that manufacturers are encouraged to adopt. The coalition also offers a list of companies that comply with the standard (such as Mary Kay, The Body Shop, and Kiss My Face), helping shoppers choose products from manufacturers that share their belief.[28]

Labor Practices

Over the past several decades, American manufacturers—including fashion companies—have moved an increasing proportion of their production to countries where it costs less to manufacture the goods. In some cases, those countries may not have or enforce laws to protect workers from unsafe conditions or to ensure they are paid a living wage. Such workplaces are often referred to as **sweatshops**, or factories where workers are obliged to work long hours, under poor conditions, for very little pay. In fact, despite numerous labor laws, sweatshops still exist in the United States. A report issued by the United States Government Accountability Office in 1994 (the most recent on this topic) found that there were thousands of them in this country, using as the definition of a sweatshop any "employer that violates more than one federal or state labor law governing minimum wage and overtime, child labor, industrial homework, occupational safety and health, workers' compensation, or industry registration."[29]

In 1996 actress and TV celebrity Kathie Lee Gifford faced intense criticism when it was discovered that her Kathie Lee clothing line, sold by Wal-Mart, was made by sweatshop workers in Honduras and in New York City. The publicity from this case helped raise awareness of the prevalence of sweatshops and harsh working conditions in the fashion industry, which in turn has led to public pressure on companies to verify that the products they sell have been manufactured according to ethical labor practices. Some companies are actively addressing the issue. In 2004, a group of retailers, manufacturers, and industry associations including Federated Merchandising Group, Reebok International Ltd., The Wet Seal, and the National Retail Federation jointly formed a nonprofit organization called the Fair Factories Clearinghouse (FFC) to create a global database of information on factories and workplace conditions. The information can be easily shared among participants, enabling manufacturers and retailers to make informed decisions as they source (find suppliers for) merchandise and to improve factory workplace conditions around the world.[30]

The movement toward ethical labor practices has also spread to other companies in the apparel industry. For example, manufacturers including Nike and Tommy Hilfiger have formalized codes of conduct for their factories, prohibiting child labor and requiring that legal minimum wages be paid.[31] Wal-Mart increased its inspections of thousands of foreign factories from which it buys clothes, shoes, toys, and other products, although critics have maintained that the chain is still not doing enough.[32] Yet other compa-

FIGURE 15.7. A growing fair-trade movement has spawned new apparel companies that operate with ethical labor practices and use organic materials in their clothing, such as this outfit from Edun.

nies are being founded specifically for the purpose of creating apparel according to **fair-trade practices**, or standards for working conditions, environmental responsibility, and fair pricing that are based not only on ethical labor practices but also on the intent to provide opportunity to disadvantaged workers and help alleviate poverty.[33] Originally limited to commodities such as coffee, tea, fruits, and cotton, the concept of fair trade has recently begun to enter into the clothing marketplace. In 2005, Bono, the U2 lead singer and activist, introduced Edun, a fair-trade line of apparel made from organic materials, which has been sold through high-end stores including Saks and Nordstrom.[34] More recently, a group of former Lands' End executives launched Fair Indigo, consisting of a Web site, catalog, and stores offering their own line of fair-trade apparel.[35] The selection is designed for mainstream consumers and includes men's and women's apparel, as well as accessories, jewelry, and gift items.

⟩⟩⟩ POINT OF VIEW 15.2: CONSUMERS RAISE AWARENESS OF "BLOOD DIAMONDS" ⟨⟨⟨

Monica Gibson says she is not particularly political, but when she heard about conflict diamonds on an episode of *The Oprah Winfrey Show* featuring the cast and director of the movie *Blood Diamond*, she looked down at her engagement ring and thought not of love but of wars and violence.

With interest in the origin of diamonds fueled by the Hollywood movie that denounces the practices of the diamond industry, customers like Ms. Gibson are asking more questions about the iconic symbol of eternal love. The terms "conflict diamonds" or "blood diamonds" refer to gems that have been used by rebel groups to pay for wars that have killed and displaced millions of people in Africa, the source of an estimated 65 percent of the world's diamonds.

While many consumers remain unaware of the issue, others are doing research and reacting accordingly. Some jewelers said people have made it clear they want only conflict-free diamonds and have asked where the stones sold at retail were mined. Some customers are shunning diamonds from Africa in favor of diamonds from Canada, antique diamonds, or synthetic stones.

Source: Adapted from Mireya Navarro, "Diamonds Are for Never?" *New York Times*, December 14, 2006.

Social Issues
Anyone who reads or watches the news cannot help but be aware of challenges that affect the entire planet, such as global warming or dependency on fossil fuels, as well

as more localized problems, including poverty and natural disasters. Individuals and companies that work to address some of those challenges—whether or not the hardships directly affect them—are taking social responsibility and acting in an ethical manner.

Environment

Some people consider protecting and preserving the environment to be one of the most serious ethical issues of our time. Countless scientific studies have demonstrated the toll that modern human activities are taking on the earth and its atmosphere, and an increasing number of people are looking for ways to lessen their own impact on the environment. As a result, numerous companies in the fashion industry have been exploring ways of doing business that are more environmentally friendly.

For example, Timberland, the outdoor clothing manufacturer, has made a strong commitment to lessening the environmental impact of its manufacturing, including efforts to reduce its use of harmful chemicals and increase its use of more-sustainable natural resources. In 2002, the company began exploring ways to reduce its carbon emissions and decided on a multifaceted plan that included building a wind farm in the Dominican Republic, installing solar panels at one of its distribution centers in California, and purchasing power generated by renewable resources. By 2006, the company had cut its emission of greenhouse gases by 17 percent and set a goal of becoming "carbon-neutral" by 2010 by adding more renewable or alternative energy sources to offset its emissions.[36]

Milliken Carpet, which manufactures carpet and area rugs, is another company that has implemented policies to make its operations more environmentally friendly. A division of Milliken & Company, the company over the years has adopted procedures to dramatically reduce paper and cardboard waste, and has certified its factories to some of the highest environmental standards.[37]

A number of retailers have also taken steps to be more environmentally conscious. Nordstrom, for example, committed to printing its catalogs, internal company newsletter, and annual report on paper stock certified to contain 30 percent post-consumer waste.[38] Recreational Equipment Inc. purchased 10 million kilowatt hours of green power, including wind, landfill gas, and solar-generated electricity, to provide power for 17 of its 82 stores.[39] Wal-Mart has begun multiple initiatives to become more eco-friendly, including reducing excess packaging on its private-label toys, switching packaging for some grocery items from petroleum-based plastic to corn-based plastic, and installing auxiliary power units on its trucks to eliminate wasting fuel through idling.[40, 41] The giant retailer has also opened test stores incorporating a host of features designed to save energy and natural

FIGURE 15.8A and B. Wal-Mart is among the retailers and manufacturers that are addressing environmental issues through better energy efficiency, eco-friendly packaging, and other initiatives.

resources[42] and plans to cut energy use by 30 percent at its more than 7,000 stores worldwide by 2013,[43] among other projects. Taking environmental commitment even further is a new mega-mall scheduled to be built in Syracuse, New York, called Destiny USA. According to plans, the mall will include 1,000 shops and restaurants, plus hotels, theaters, and a 200-acre recreational "biosphere"—all powered strictly by renewable energy.

> *Let's Talk*
> *Have you noticed changes in environmental awareness in any of the retailers you regularly shop or brands you regularly buy—such as stores offering reusable cloth bags or manufacturers reducing their excess packaging? Would changes such as these influence your shopping decisions?*

Concern for the environment is also extending to fashion products themselves, as an increasing number of consumers seek products that they know are made in an eco-friendly manner. Manufacturers and designers are meeting that demand with apparel made from a variety of sustainable and environmentally sound fabrics, such as organic cotton, soy, corn, and bamboo, and even material made from "repurposed" (recycled) fur, leather, and denim or blended of cotton and recycled plastic soda bottles.[44]

Organic cotton, which is grown using no chemical fertilizers, pesticides, or herbicides, is one of the fastest-growing eco-friendly fabrics, with annual sales topping $275 million in the United States.[45] Jeans maker Levi's began offering organic cotton versions of its most popular styles in 2006, with additional organic products planned to follow. Organic cotton's use in home textiles is also blossoming, with companies including Welspun and Anna Sova Luxury Organics creating towels, sheets, and blankets from the fabric.[46] Bamboo is also increasingly finding its way into apparel and home textiles products, and is appreciated for the fact that it is highly renewable, can grow a foot or more in a day, and can grow to heights of 80 or 90 feet, making its fiber plentiful.[47] Soy is another renewable fabric source that is increasing in importance in fashion. The company 2(x)ist even offers a line of soybean fiber blend men's underwear, T-shirts, and socks.

❯❯❯ SPECIAL FOCUS 15.3: HOME FURNISHINGS WITH A HEART ❮❮❮

What if a retailer created a home furnishings line that brought an unexpected twist to familiar objects, tested new and environmentally sound materials, reflected multicultural influences, and had heart? That's the idea behind IKEA's PS collection, which incorporates the "themes of global thinking, the environment, and social issues," according to Mats Nilsson, creative director for North America for IKEA.

Included in the collection are wall storage cones made of recyclable paper and plastic, as well as cushion covers designed by women in Uttar Pradesh, India, where child labor is customary. The women are paid to hand-embroider the covers with materials that are supplied by local carpet vendors. The program, which reflects IKEA's partnership with UNICEF, enables these women to boost their earning power and allow their children a better opportunity to go to school.

❯❯❯ Source: Adapted from Barbara Thau, "IKEA's Innovative PS Home Line Asks: 'What If?' " *HFN*, October 17, 2005, p. 12.

Causes and Charitable Giving

In addition to concern for the environment, social responsibility can encompass a wide variety of direct actions to help people who are sick, hungry, poor, or homeless. Socially responsible companies also support charitable organizations that work to alleviate problems challenging people and societies. This trend is growing in the fashion business, as in other industries. While there were only a handful of retailers in the 1990s that were socially active—ice cream maker and retailer Ben & Jerry's is a prominent example—the number has grown dramatically in recent years. As Tracy Mullin, president and CEO of the National Retail Federation, the world's largest retail trade association, states, "As our shoppers vote with their wallets, retailers are recognizing that

FIGURE 15.9. Fashion marketers sometimes create products specifically to help support a cause. Gap designated a portion of the profits from its Project Red apparel to be donated to the Global Fund to Fight AIDS.

customers want them to make a difference."[48] At upscale women's clothing designer and retailer Eileen Fisher Inc., the corporate commitment to social responsibility is so strong that there is an executive with the title of "Manager of Social Consciousness."

One way that companies can express social responsibility is through cause-based or cause-related marketing, in which—you'll recall from Chapter 2—they identify a charity or other cause to which a specified portion of profits from one or more products in their line will be donated. By mentioning the donation in the product's marketing materials, such as in ads and on packaging or hangtags, companies can often influence consumers who support the cause to purchase those items over another product. In some cases, marketers designate an exclusive product for a limited time for a cause-based program. Dressbarn, for instance, offered a limited-edition stuffed toy lamb in support of National Breast Cancer Awareness month and donated all net profits from the sale to the American Cancer Society[49]; and Bath & Body Works sold a scented candle from which 10 percent of each sale was donated to the Elton John AIDS Foundation.[50] See Chapter 13 for more information about how the fashion industry partners with charities.

In other instances, companies make a longer-term commitment to a cause. Mobile Edge, for example, continuously contributes 10 percent of sales of its Caring Case collection of handbag-styled notebook computer carrying cases to the Susan G. Komen Breast Cancer Foundation. British fashion designer Katharine Hamnett launched a new "ethically made" collection of clothing and accessories in 2007, with 15 percent of the net profit designated to go to a new charity Hamnett was creating to help cotton farmers in developing countries switch to organic methods, among other socially conscious activities.[51] In yet another example, a joint effort initiated by U2's Bono called Project Red saw companies including Gap, Motorola, Converse, Apple, and others creating special red products from which a portion of profits would be donated to the Global Fund to Fight AIDS.

Natural disasters and other crises also provide manufacturers and retailers with an opportunity to act in a socially responsible manner by donating money and/or products to help people in need. After Hurricane Katrina devastated New Orleans and the Gulf Coast in 2005, many companies, including Wal-Mart and Best Buy, stepped forward to assist. Wal-Mart rushed to reopen stores that had been closed by the storm, enabling victims to buy much-needed supplies, and also gave approximately $5 million in emergency cash to affected employees. Best Buy offered cash advances to its displaced employees and also set up banks of computers with Internet connections in stores so that hurricane victims could contact family members and reach the Red Cross and other assistance agencies.[52]

One of the longest-running charitable programs within the fashion industry is Kids in Distressed Situations (K.I.D.S.), a global charity made up of leading retailers, manufacturers, and licensors of children's and youth products. For more than 20 years, K.I.D.S. has worked in partnership with major foundations to help improve the lives of children and their families who are ill, are living in poverty, or are the victims of natural disasters. After the tsunami disaster in Southeast Asia in December 2004, K.I.D.S. collected and distributed more than $4 million worth of children's clothing, shoes, and blankets donated by its members; in the aftermath of hurricanes Katrina and Rita, the organization delivered more than $9 million worth of products to families in the Gulf Coast region.[53]

Summary

Consumer behavior is sometimes influenced by ethics, a system of moral values or principles of right and wrong. Unethical actions are sometimes, but not always, illegal as well. One aspect of ethics is social responsibility, the principle that everyone is responsible for making the world a better place for all its inhabitants. Individuals as well as companies operate under their own ethical standards.

Consumer theft is both unethical and illegal; shoplifting is a prominent example. Organized retail theft is a growing problem in which teams of shoplifters work together to steal larger quantities of merchandise that is usually then resold. Fraudulent returns are also an issue of concern for retailers, some of which are now using software systems to track returns and try to identify dishonest customers.

Counterfeiting of designer or branded products is a huge, global problem. It is illegal to manufacture or sell counterfeit goods, but knowingly purchasing them is not illegal, only unethical. Businesses, government, and law enforcement are all increasing their efforts to find and stop counterfeiters, who may also break other laws, including labor laws, or help fund terrorist groups.

Businesses face ethical decisions in many aspects of their daily operations. Safeguarding the privacy of consumers is one ethical concern, since the increasing amount of personal information that is being gathered could be vulnerable to theft or computer hacking. Ethical considerations in advertising include the ads' truthfulness, as well as the appropriateness of their content, which can sometimes offend an audience. The use of fur in fashion and product testing on animals are two ethical issues that are highly emotional for many consumers, and a number of designers and manufacturers have eliminated the practices as a show of compassion. Marketers are also making efforts to avoid sweatshops in the production of their products and are implementing ethical labor practices that include safe workplace conditions and fair wages.

Many people see protecting the environment as one of today's most serious ethical issues, and a number of fashion manufacturers and retailers have taken steps to lessen the environmental impact of their operations. Fashion products themselves are increasingly being made with eco-friendly fibers and fabrics, such as organic cotton, bamboo, and soy. Fashion companies also address social responsibility through charitable giving, including cause-based marketing and other donations to charities or victims of disaster.

Key Terms

Boycott	Loyalty programs
Counterfeit goods	Organized retail theft (ORT)
Ethics	Social responsibility
Fair-trade practices	Sweatshop
Inventory shrinkage	

Questions for Review

1. What are two common types of consumer theft from retailers? How does organized retail theft differ from regular shoplifting?
2. What are some of the steps fashion marketers are taking to combat counterfeit goods?
3. Name three ways in which marketers might collect information about consumers that could raise concerns about privacy of personal data.
4. What unethical labor practices are being addressed by many companies and associations in the fashion industry?
5. Name at least three ways in which some retailers and manufacturers are working to make their operations or products more environmentally friendly.

Activities

1. Visit a local store and see how many security measures you can identify that the store is using to prevent theft. Make a list of both the visible deterrents (for example, locked cases, security tags on products, security guard) and more discreet techniques (for example, electronic device at exit, one-way glass from an office area). If you are able to, interview a store manager to learn which of the methods the store finds to be most effective.
2. Do an online search for sellers of "fake handbags" or "replica handbags." Choose a site and compare one of the fake items to a genuine product at that brand's own Web site. Do you think the differences are distinct enough for the item not to be

considered a counterfeit? See if the site selling the fakes has a disclaimer that tells consumers its products are not "the real thing."

3. Find an ad in a fashion magazine that you think some people might consider sexist, indecent, or otherwise offensive in some way. Show it to a variety of people of different ages and gender, and ask them for their reaction. Keep track of the responses and see whether the negative reactions come more from younger or older people, or more from males or females. Do any people feel so strongly about the ad that they would either boycott the company or, at the other extreme, make a point of buying the product being sold? Present your findings to the class.

4. Select one of your favorite designers or brands and go to the company's Web site. See if you can find information on causes that the company supports or ways in which it is socially responsible. Does the company give information on its efforts to be more environmentally friendly? Does its Web site discuss its labor practices or policies? Are you surprised by how much or how little the company is doing, based on its site? Does the information make you feel more or less favorable toward the company than you did before? Discuss your findings and reaction with the class.

Mini-Project

Create a questionnaire with 8 to 10 questions that will let you determine people's opinions on various ethical and social issues as they relate to fashion. For example, you could create attitude scales (see Chapter 10) asking questions such as how likely your respondents would be to shop at a retailer that sells apparel made with fur, how favorably they would view a designer who uses organic fabrics or actively seeks fair trade suppliers, or how likely they would be to purchase an item they knew or suspected was counterfeit. Survey at least 15 different people from different age groups, and write a report of your findings.

References

1. National Retail Federation, "Retail Losses Hit $41.6 Billion Last Year, According to National Retail Security Survey," News release, June 11, 2007.

2. Amy Fletcher, "Retailers Struggle with Problem of Organized Theft." *Denver Business Journal*, April 28, 2006. Retrieved August 22, 2007, from www.bizjournals.com/denver/stories/2006/05/01/story4.html.

3. ADT Security, "Retail Theft Increases for First Time in Four Years According to Annual Retail Security Survey," News release, November 22, 2006.

4. Jayne O'Donnell, "Stores Protect Turf from Gangs of Thieves," *USA Today*, November 17, 2006. Retrieved August 22, 2007, from www.usatoday.com/money/industries/retail/2006-11-17-retail-cover-usat_x.htm.

5. Christine Van Dusen, "Company Helps Stores Fight Dishonest Returns," *Atlanta Journal-Constitution*, June 16, 2005, p. H1.

6. Elizabeth Woyke, "Many Unhappy Returns for Retailers," *BusinessWeek*, August 5, 2005. Retrieved August 22, 2007, from www.businessweek.com/bwdaily/dnflash/aug2005/nf2005085_9756_db016.htm.

7. Van Dusen.

8. Erica Ryan, "Abercrombie Cracks Down on Counterfeiters," *Washington Post*, July 20, 2006. Retrieved August 22, 2007, from www.washingtonpost.com/wp-dyn/content/article/2006/07/20/AR2006072000117.html.

9. "Worldwide Market for Counterfeit Goods: $650 Billion," PPI *Trade Fact of the Week*, June 14, 2006. Retrieved August 22, 2007, from www.ppionline.org/ndol/print.cfm?contentid=253907.

10. Christina Passariello, "Holograms Tell Fake from Fendi," *Wall Street Journal*, February 22, 2006. Retrieved August 22, 2007, from http://online.wsj.com/article/SB113057680060579777.html.

11. Carol Matlack, "LVMH vs. eBay: A Counterfeit Suit." *BusinessWeek*, September 22, 2006. Retrieved August 22, 2007, from www.businessweek.com/globalbiz/content/sep2006/gb20060922_888836.htm?chan=globalbiz_europe_today's+top+story.

12. Ryan.

13. Vanessa O'Connell, and Kris Hudson, "Not Our Bag, Coach Says in a Lawsuit Alleging Target Sold Counterfeit Purse," *Wall Street Journal*, October 3, 2006. Retrieved August 22, 2007, from http://online.wsj.com/article/SB115981450811080264.html.

14. Heather Salerno, "Fighting the Fakes," *(NY) Journal News*, June 20, 2006.

15. Pallavi Gogoi, "Wal-Mart's Luxury Problem," *BusinessWeek*, June 13, 2006. Retrieved August 22, 2007, from www.businessweek.com/investor/content/jun2006/pi20060613_187965.htm.

16. Carol Matlack, "Fed Up With Fakes," *BusinessWeek*, October 9, 2006. Retrieved August 22, 2007, from www.businessweek.com/magazine/content/06_41/b4004060.htm.

17. National Retail Federation, "Shoppers Want Loyalty Programs, But Not at the Cost of Privacy, According to New NRF Foundation/Adjoined Consulting Research," News release, January 16, 2006.

18. Bob Sullivan, "Data Leaks Stunt E-Commerce, Survey Suggests," MSNBC.com, June 15, 2005. Retrieved August 22, 2007, fromwww.msnbc.msn.com/id/8219161/.

19. Linda Punch, "Crumbling." *Internet Retailer*, August 2005. Retrieved August 22, 2007, from http://internetretailer.com/article.asp?id=15635.

20. Rich McIlver, "RFID Privacy Issues: How RFID Will Impact Consumer Privacy," *RFID Gazette*, March 22, 2005. Retrieved August 22, 2007, from www.rfidgazette .org/2005/03/rfid_privacy_is.html.

21. Christopher Palmeri, "Living on the Edge at American Apparel," *BusinessWeek*, June 27, 2005. Retrieved August 22, 2007, from www.businessweek.com/magazine/ content/05_26/b3939108_mz017.htm?chan—z&.

22. Andrew A. Newman, "J.C. Penney Decides T-shirts with Beer Logos Are for Men," *New York Times*, September 26, 2005. Retrieved August 22, 2007, from www.nytimes.com/2005/09/26/business/26shirts.html?ex=1164085200&en= 05114b36db45003e&ei=5070.

23. Andrew A. Newman, "Overage Logos, Underage Market," *New York Times*, October 16, 2006. Retrieved August 22, 2007, from www.nytimes.com/2006/10/16/ business/media/16beer.html.

24. "Pamela Anderson Strips for Anti-Fur Protest," ExpoSay.com, June 29, 2006. Retrieved August 22, 2007, from www.exposay.com/pamela-anderson-strips-for -anti-fur-protest/v/2470/.

25. "Nude Anti-Fur Protest Held in Times Square," Associated Press/abc11.tv.com, November 23, 2005. Retrieved August 22, 2007, from http://abclocal.go.com/ wtvd/story?section=bizarre&id=3661604.

26. Sector, Charlotte, "Is Dog and Cat Fur Being Used in Coats?" ABC News, January 24, 2006. Retrieved August 22, 2007, from http://abcnews.go.com/International/ print?id=1533368.

27. "Polo Ralph Lauren to Remove Fur from Its Collections." *Wall Street Journal*, June 8, 2006. Retrieved August 22, 2007, from http://online.wsj.com/article/BT _CO_20060607_715582.html.

28. The Humane Society of the United States, "The Coalition for Consumer Information on Cosmetics," Retrieved August 22, 2007, from www.hsus.org/animals _in_research/animal_testing/the_coalition_for_consumer_information_on _cosmetics/.

29. U.S. General Accounting Office, "Garment Industry: Efforts to Address the Prevalence and Conditions of Sweatshops," November 1994. Retrieved August 22, 2007, from www.gao.gov/archive/1995/he95029.pdf.

30. Fair Factories Clearinghouse, www.fairfactories.org.

31. Bob Tedeschi, "A Click on Clothes to Support Fair Trade," *New York Times*, September 25, 2006. Retrieved August 22, 2007, from www.nytimes.com/2006/ 09/25/technology/25ecom.html?ex=1184558400&en=3f09deab7bbb1840&ei= 5070.

32. Marcus Kabel, "Wal-Mart Finds More Foreign Violations," Associated Press, September 27, 2006. Retrieved August 22, 2007, from www.msnbc.msn.com/id/15033280/.

33. IFAT: The International Fair Trade Association, "The 10 Standards of Fair Trade," http://ifat.org/ftrinciples.shtml.

34. Tedeschi.

35. Susan Chandler, " 'Fair-Trade' Label Reaches Retail Market," *Chicago Tribune*, October 8, 2006. Retrieved August 22, 2007, from www.chicagofairtrade.org/aboutFairTrade/clothing/IndigoChicagoTrib.

36. Jad Mouawad, "The Greener Guys," *New York Times*, May 30, 2006, p. C1.

37. Rosamaria Mancini, "Moral Fibers," *HFN*, March 28, 2005, p. 14.

38. Chantal Todé, "Nordstrom to Put Recycled Paper in Catalogs," *DM News*, March 8, 2007. Retrieved August 22, 2007, from www.dmnews.com/cms/dm-news/catalog-retail/40320.html.

39. "REI Committed to Green Power." *Outdoor Retailer*, March 28, 2006. Retrieved August 22, 2007, from www.outdoorretailer.com/or/news_display.jsp?vnu_content_id=1002237505.

40. Marc Gunther, "Wal-Mart Sees Green," CNNMoney.com, July 27, 2006. Retrieved August 22, 2007, from http://money.cnn.com/2006/07/25/news/companies/wal-mart-short.fortune/index.htm.

41. Harold Brubaker, "Wal-Mart Goes More Eco-Friendly," *Philadelphia Inquirer*, October 20, 2005, p. C01.

42. Barbara Thau, "Greening House," *HFN*, November 14, 2005, p. 6.

43. Mindy Fetterman, "Wal-Mart Grows 'Green' Strategies," *USA Today*, September 25, 2006. Retrieved August 22, 2007, from www.usatoday.com/money/industries/retail/2006-09-24-wal-mart-cover-usat_x.htm.

44. Laura Daily, "Eco-Fashion Goes Haute Couture," *USA Weekend*, March 3–5, 2006, p. 12.

45. Frank Green, "Going Au Naturel," *San Diego Union-Tribune*, May 25, 2006. Retrieved August 22, 2007, from www.signonsandiego.com/uniontrib/20060525/news_1b25organic.html.

46. Rosamaria Mancini, "A Natural Selection," *HFN*, September 26, 2006, p. 14.

47. Annie Groer, "Fine Bedding Turns to the Trees," *(NY) Journal News*, July 13, 2006, p. 1D.

48. Tracy Mullin, "An Awakened Conscience," *Stores*, August 2006. Retrieved August 22, 2007, from www.stores.org/archives/2006/8/President'sColumn.asp.

49. Dressbarn. "Dressbarn's Lela Is Back to Fight Cancer," News release, September 21, 2005.

50. Michael Barbaro, "Candles, Jeans, Lipsticks: Products with Ulterior Motives," *New York Times*, November 13, 2006, p. F33.

51. Tami Adbollah, "Look Good, Do Good: Stylish Products for a Cause," *Wall Street Journal*, August 18, 2006. Retrieved August 22, 2007, from http://online.wsj.com/article/SB115586146014338975.html.

52. H. J. Cummins, "Target, Best Buy Taking Care of Gulf Coast Workers," *Minneapolis Star Tribune*, September 18, 2005. Retrieved August 22, 2007, from www.cebcglobal.org/Newsroom/News/News_092005.htm.

53. Kids in Distressed Situations, "K.I.D.S. Milestones." Retrieved August 22, 2007, from www.kidsdonations.org/about/milestones.htm.

CHAPTER 16

The Role of Government

Patrice was overjoyed. Her older brother and his wife were adopting a two-year-old girl, and Patrice would be an aunt for the first time. She couldn't wait to go shopping for cute little outfits, cuddly stuffed animals, and new toys.

It was exciting, but Patrice also knew that a small child in the family meant important responsibilities. After all, the newspapers were continuously printing articles about children who had been injured by everyday items. She remembered reading a recent story mentioning drawstrings on children's hoodies; Patrice wondered if there was an actual law about that and decided to go online to double-check before shopping for any toddler outfits. She also wanted to make sure that any clothes she bought for the child could be easily laundered. "Thank goodness for the labels sewn into garments," she thought, knowing that she could not only verify that an outfit was machine-washable and dryable before buying it but could also look at the fiber content of the fabric, since she felt that natural fibers like cotton would be more comfortable against a small child's delicate skin.

In addition, because of the babysitter training class she'd taken back in middle school, Patrice knew that before buying a toy, she would need to look carefully at the toy's construction to make sure there were no sharp edges or small parts that could come loose and be swallowed by her little niece. "And I'd better also ask my brother how they feel about toys based on cartoon characters," she thought, knowing that her mother had often complained about some TV shows being like one long commercial for related products. It was a lot to consider—but all worth it, Patrice felt, as she smiled thinking about the little girl she would soon welcome into the family.

It is clear that Patrice is a very conscientious consumer, at least when it comes to shopping for her new niece. Not all consumers, however, are equally careful about researching their purchases and "reading the fine print" and unfortunately, as discussed in Chapter 15, not all companies follow strict ethical guidelines to ensure that everything about their products, their manufacturing, and their marketing is completely aboveboard. That is where government can play an important role, both in enforcing laws to ensure that products are safe and marketed truthfully, and in giving consumers the tools they need to make an informed purchase. What's more, there are a number of independent organizations that provide resources to help educate consumers and to help businesses better meet the needs of the public. In this chapter, we'll take a look at some of those agencies, regulations, and organizations to see how they affect the fashion industry and how they can influence consumer behavior.

Federal Agencies

Through the work of various agencies, the federal government provides oversight, creates standards, and enforces regulations designed to protect the public from unsafe products or unfair business practices. Those efforts may be supplemented with additional regulations implemented by individual state governments, and with the programs of industry associations, which sometimes take it upon themselves to adopt voluntary standards for their member companies to follow.

Consumer Product Safety Commission

When you think of fashion products, the issue of safety probably doesn't immediately spring to mind. But there are several areas where safety could be a concern if it were not for government oversight. Imagine your jeans bursting into flames if you accidentally dropped a lit match on them, or a small child choking on a decorative teddy bear appliqué that pulled loose too easily from his jacket. Fortunately, those are situations that are very unlikely to occur, thanks to the efforts of the **U.S. Consumer Product Safety Commission (CPSC).**

FIGURE 16.1 A AND B More than 15,000 different products, including toys and clothing, are monitored for safety by the Consumer Product Safety Commission.

Created in 1972 by Congress under the Consumer Product Safety Act, the CPSC has as its directive to protect the public "against unreasonable risks of injuries associated with consumer products." An independent agency—meaning it does not report to and is not part of any other department or agency in the federal government— the CPSC's staff of nearly 500 is responsible for monitoring the safety of more than 15,000 kinds of consumer products sold in the United States, ranging from air fresheners, beds, and carpet to sunglasses, toys, and windows, and much more. Since 1972, the work of the CPSC has contributed to a 30 percent decline in the rate of deaths and injuries associated with consumer products.[1]

Flammable Fabrics Act

One of the specific areas the CPSC monitors is the flammability of clothing and household furnishings, using the guidelines set forth in the federal **Flammable Fabrics Act**. Passed in 1953, the Flammable Fabrics Act was written initially to regulate the manufacture of highly flammable clothing, such as brushed rayon sweaters. But Congress amended the act in 1967 and expanded its coverage so that it now regulates the flammability not only of clothing but also of home furnishings as well as paper, plastic, foam, and other materials used both in apparel and interior furnishings. Responsibility for administering the Flammable Fabrics Act was transferred to the CPSC when that agency was created in 1972.

The CPSC has established mandatory flammability standards for clothing textiles, vinyl plastic film used in clothing, carpets and rugs, children's sleepwear, and mattresses and mattress pads. **Mandatory standards** mean that all manufacturers, retailers, importers, and distributors must ensure that the products they are selling meet specific safety criteria that the agency has set forth. The federal mandatory standards for fabric flammability are based on how quickly and how intensely a given material burns when exposed to a small open flame. Based on the fact that certain fabrics have consistently met the standards, they are exempt from testing and considered safe for use in apparel. Among those are fabrics made entirely of acrylic, modacrylic, nylon, olefin, polyester, and wool. Other fabrics must be guaranteed to have passed the flammability tests before being used in apparel.

Because children can be particularly vulnerable, there are even more stringent safety rules for children's sleepwear flammability. The Standard for the Flammability of Children's Sleepwear: Sizes 0 through 6X became effective in 1972, and the Standard for the Flammability of Children's Sleepwear: Sizes 7 through 14 took effect in 1975. The two standards are nearly identical and prescribe a test requiring that specimens of the fabric, seams, and trim from children's sleepwear garments self-extinguish after exposure to a small open flame. The standards target sleepwear because statistics show that children are most at risk from burn injuries that result from playing with matches, candles, stove burners, and other fire sources just before bedtime and just after rising in the morning.[2]

In 1996, after a review of the circumstances surrounding children's burn injuries, the CPSC amended the flammability standards for children's sleepwear to exclude garments sized for infants nine months of age or younger, and to exclude tight-fitting sleepwear garments. The amendments were based on the premise that those categories do not present an unreasonable risk of burn deaths and injuries, and by revising the rules, the agency would enable consumers to have a greater selection of sleepwear for children while still being protected by safety standards. As a result, children's sleepwear that is not flame-resistant is permitted as long as it fits the child snugly. To alert shoppers to the potential danger of loose-fitting children's sleepwear not made of flame-resistant fabric, the CPSC issued a new requirement in 2000 that children's snug-fitting sleepwear made of cotton or cotton blends must carry a hangtag or permanent label reminding consumers that it must fit snugly for safety.

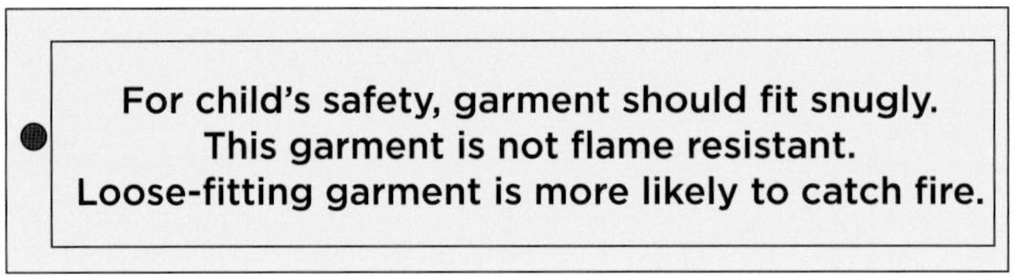

FIGURE 16.2. The CPSC requires children's sleepwear that is not flame-resistant to carry a yellow hangtag like this one, or to include a permanent label sewn into the neck of the garment that says, "Wear snug-fitting. Not flame resistant."

**For child's safety, garment should fit snugly.
This garment is not flame resistant.
Loose-fitting garment is more likely to catch fire.**

››› SPECIAL FOCUS 16.1: SMOKESCREEN SURROUNDS
FIRE SAFETY STANDARD FOR UPHOLSTERY ‹‹‹

After waiting in vain for more than a decade, the National Association of State Fire Marshals renewed its call for a national fire safety standard for upholstery, and implored the furniture industry to "let people come before profits." Watchdog group Citizens against Government Waste has also pushed for a standard, saying that the federal Consumer Product Safety Commission has delayed a decision on a national standard for years.

The furniture industry, hoping to head off piecemeal legislation by individual states, backed a 2004 federal proposal to impose a flammability standard covering open-flame ignition sources such as lighters and candles, as well as cigarettes. CPSC gave preliminary approval, but the legislation went into limbo when CPSC staffers made changes to it.

According to CPSC statistics, fires originating in upholstered furniture account for 20 percent of all fire-related deaths in the United States and kill an average of 10 people a week. The petroleum-based foam often used in upholstered furniture creates thick, black, toxic smoke that can overpower consumers very quickly.

The American Home Furnishings Alliance has said the industry has "made great strides in reducing the flammability risks associated with its products," but does support an Upholstered Furniture Action Council program that includes a set of voluntary construction guidelines that most upholstered furniture makers follow.

››› Sources: Gary Evans, "CPSC Blasted for Delay on Upholstery Open-Flame Standards," *Furniture Today*, September 20, 2006; and Susan M. Andrews, "Fire Marshals Call for Upholstery FR Standard," *Furniture Today*, October 31, 2006.

Other Product Hazards

Flammability of clothing and home furnishings is an important safety issue, but there also are many other areas in which the CPSC monitors and regulates safety. The agency frequently issues specific safety alerts when it identifies a potential hazard; alerts in recent years have included such topics as the danger of strangulation from cords of window coverings and the risk of bunk bed mattresses falling if not properly supported. In many cases, the CPSC works closely with industry to develop voluntary safety standards. To improve the safety of cribs, for instance, the CPSC has worked with the Juvenile Products Manufacturers Association, which administers a voluntary program to certify cribs meeting specific standards. The toy industry has also actively collaborated with the CPSC and other testing organizations to develop voluntary standards for concerns such as small parts that could become a choking hazard if swallowed by a young child.

Despite the variety of mandatory and voluntary standards, products that pose a potential hazard can still occasionally find their way into the marketplace. When that happens, and it is brought to the attention of the CPSC, the result is generally a recall. In a **recall**, announcements are issued to the public alerting them to the danger, urging them to stop using the product immediately, and providing them with further information on what to do with the product or how to contact the manufacturer. If the problem is something that can be fixed, the recall notice will provide instructions on how to consumers can have the problem repaired. If it cannot be fixed, consumers are usually notified of the ways they can get a replacement product or a refund.

The volume of product recalls in the fashion industries is relatively small, but there have been a number of them in recent years. Discount store Target voluntarily recalled about 6,000 men's hooded, zip-up sweatshirts[3] and Victoria's Secret Direct (the catalogue and online division of Victoria's Secret) voluntarily recalled about 500 silk kimono tops,[4] in both cases because the garments failed to meet mandatory standards for fabric flammability. About 92,000 chamois blankets were voluntarily recalled by Pottery Barn in cooperation with the CPSC because the decorative stitching on the blanket's edge could come loose, allowing a child to become entangled in the yarn, posing a strangulation hazard to young children.[5] Also, thousands of necklaces, bracelets, earrings, and hair accessories were recalled by American Girl Place,[6] and 300,000 children's charm bracelets were recalled by Reebok,[7] both recalls due to the products' high lead content, which would pose a serious health hazard if ingested.

Remember that Patrice at the beginning of this chapter was wondering about drawstrings on hooded garments for her new niece. She was surely thinking of the numerous recalls over the past decade of certain children's outerwear items, such as jackets and sweatshirts, which included a drawstring at the neck or waist. Those drawstrings had been known to get caught on playground equipment, in bus doors, or on other objects, with sometimes deadly results. So while there is not a mandatory requirement, the CPSC has issued guidelines regarding the length of the drawstring, how it is attached to the garment, and other criteria to minimize the danger of injury. Those guidelines were incorporated in 1997 into a voluntary standard that is followed by most manufacturers and retailers of children's apparel.

Let's Talk
Do you think manufacturers would be as careful about product safety if there were no government agency monitoring the issue? Why or why not?

U.S. Food and Drug Administration

While the CPSC monitors the safety of thousands of types of products, there are other product categories over which the agency has no jurisdiction. One of those categories is cosmetics, which is regulated by the **U.S. Food and Drug Administration (FDA)**. The FDA was established in 1930 and is now part of the U.S. Department of Health and Human Services. As described by its mission statement, the FDA "is responsible for protecting the public health by assuring the safety, efficacy, and security of human and veterinary drugs, biological products, medical devices, our nation's food supply, cosmetics, and products that emit radiation."

The need for a government entity to monitor food and drugs became clear in the early part of the twentieth century, when journalists and others began uncovering and publicizing serious problems in the processing of meat and other foods, and exposing the fact that some companies were including dangerous ingredients in their patent medicines (trademarked, nonprescription drugs). That reporting led to the Food and Drug Act of 1906, and later to the establishment of the FDA, initially to ensure the safety specifically of food and drug products. In 1938, however, the FDA's authority was extended to cover the cosmetics industry when the Federal Food, Drug, and Cosmetic Act was passed.

Federal Food, Drug, and Cosmetic Act

One of the two most important laws covering cosmetics marketed in the United States, the **Federal Food, Drug, and Cosmetic Act (FD&C Act)** prohibits the marketing of adulterated (contaminated) or misbranded cosmetics in interstate commerce (business conducted between parties in different states). As defined by the act, the term "cosmetic" means "articles intended to be rubbed, poured, sprinkled, or sprayed on, introduced into, or otherwise applied to the human body or any part thereof for cleansing, beautifying, promoting attractiveness, or altering the appearance," as well as components of such articles, excluding soap. If that sounds like it covers a lot, it does: The FDA estimates that more than 40,000 different cosmetic product formulations are being marketed in the United States, incorporating more than 7,000 different cosmetic ingredients and 4,000 fragrance ingredients.[8] To help manage the vast number and variety of products under its umbrella, the FDA maintains six product-oriented centers that carry out its mission. Cosmetics are monitored by the Center for Food Safety and Applied Nutrition, known as CFSAN.

Although the FDA has legal authority over cosmetics, that authority is somewhat different from other products it regulates. Pharmaceutical drugs, for example, must undergo a stringent and lengthy testing and approval process by the FDA before they're allowed on the market. But with the exception of color additives, the FDA does not test or give approval to cosmetic products or ingredients before they go to market. In other words, it is up to cosmetic firms to substantiate the safety of their products

FIGURE 16.3. A wide range of personal care products, including skin moisturizers, perfumes, lipsticks, fingernail polishes, face makeup, shampoos, hair colors, toothpastes, and deodorants, are regulated by the Food and Drug Administration.

and ingredients before marketing them to the public. That includes not only ensuring that the product and its ingredients are safe but that the product has been prepared, packed, handled, and shipped in a way that prevents it from becoming adulterated.

The FDA can and does, however, inspect cosmetic manufacturing facilities to ensure product safety and accurate branding and, as part of that plant inspection, collects product samples for examination and analysis. The agency may also conduct research on cosmetic products and ingredients to address safety concerns, and as a follow-up to any complaints of adverse reactions from a product. One ingredient that was being studied for safety in recent years, for example, is phthalates (pronounced "thallets"), a group of chemicals found in hundreds of products ranging from toys and wall coverings to personal care products, such as nail polish, hair sprays, soaps, and shampoos. Some research indicates that phthalates might affect sexual development in humans,[9] but the FDA had not yet determined a definitive risk that would warrant banning the chemicals. To help avoid problems regarding safety, manufacturers are encouraged to register their companies and file Cosmetic Product Ingredient Statements with the FDA's Voluntary Cosmetic Registration Program (VCRP), although there is no requirement to do so.

Fair Packaging and Labeling Act

The FD&C Act goes further in permitting the FDA to take action against companies selling cosmetics that are improperly labeled or deceptively packaged. Under the act, a cosmetic is considered to be misbranded if its labeling is false or misleading in any particular, or its label does not include all the required information, among other stipulations. Those requirements are defined further by the **Fair Packaging and Labeling Act**, which was passed in 1966. Under this act, all cosmetics products must list their ingredients in descending order of predominance (as illustrated by the example in Figure 16.4) and the packaging must give the net quantity of contents—for example, the actual weight of the face powder without the compact case, or the volume of mascara minus the tube and wand. Cosmetics that do not comply with the Fair Packaging and Labeling Act regulations are considered misbranded under the FD&C Act, and subject to enforcement by the FDA.

FIGURE 16.4. FDA labeling rules require ingredients in cosmetics to be listed in order of predominance. How many ingredients do you recognize?

Both the Federal Food, Drug, and Cosmetic Act and the Fair Packaging and Labeling Act, along with their related regulations, are intended to protect consumers from health hazards and deceptive practices and to help them make informed purchase decisions. If the FDA has information that a cosmetic product is adulterated or misbranded, it can pursue action through the federal court system to remove that product from the market and/or initiate criminal action against the violator. In the case of a cosmetic product that represents a hazard or is somehow defective, the FDA is not authorized to require a recall, but it does monitor manufacturers or distributors that initiate a voluntary recall of a product. The agency, like the CPSC, also issues alerts, warnings, and informational publications to let the public know about possible safety issues. For instance, one such notice warned consumers of possible allergic reactions to the color additives in temporary decal-type tattoos, and the agency has recommended specific labeling for products containing alpha hydroxy acid (AHA) to make consumers aware that use of the product could increase their skin's sensitivity to the sun and the possibility of sunburn.[10]

〉〉〉 POINT OF VIEW 16.1: ARE MANICURES HAZARDOUS TO YOUR HEALTH? 〈〈〈

When it comes to the $20 billion-a-year manicure industry in the United States, consumers are more likely to fear foot fungus, not the beauty products themselves. That despite the fact that the nail industry uses 10,000 chemicals in its products, 89 percent of which have not been safety tested by any independent agency, according to a report by the National Asian Pacific American Women's Forum. That's got advocates worried not only for consumers, but nail salon workers.

Currently, the U.S. Food and Drug Administration does not safety-test ingredients used in cosmetic or personal-care products before they hit the market. That research is carried out by an industry-funded group. Consumers are left to sift through the tiny typeface listing ingredients on the back of the bottle.

Efforts to reach out to nail salon workers and owners on health and safety are sprouting up across the United States. Along with education and research, advocates are also pushing for reforms at the industry and governmental level on chemical policy.

〉〉〉 Source: Adapted from Ngoc Nguyen, "The Beauty Industry's Ugly Secret," *Inter Press Service*, September 20, 2006. Retrieved August 22, 2007, from http://ipsnorthamerica.net/news.php?idnews=436.

Federal Trade Commission

Another U.S. government agency that helps protect consumers is the **Federal Trade Commission**, or **FTC**. Even if you don't think you know anything about the FTC, you are certainly familiar with some of its work. Every time you check the care label on a shirt before throwing it in the wash, or trust a TV ad to be truthful about what a product can do, or enjoy a quiet dinner without interruptions from telephone sales calls, you are benefiting from some of the rules and laws enforced by the FTC.

The FTC, an independent agency of the U.S. government, was created by the Federal Trade Commission Act of 1914 to prevent unfair methods of competition in commerce, as part of a campaign of "trust-busting." The term **trust** refers to large business entities that succeed in controlling a market, in essence becoming a monopoly. Over the years, Congress has passed additional laws giving the FTC greater authority to police anticompetitive practices beyond just antitrust measures. Among those is the Wheeler-Lea Amendment, passed in 1938, which includes a broad prohibition against "unfair and deceptive acts or practices," and the Magnuson-Moss Act, passed in 1975, which gives the FTC authority to adopt trade regulations that define unfair or deceptive acts in particular industries.

The FTC divides its wide-ranging work among the Bureau of Consumer Protection (whose mandate is to protect consumers against unfair, deceptive, or fraudulent practices), the Bureau of Competition (which is the FTC's antitrust arm, seeking to prevent anticompetitive mergers and other anticompetitive business practices in the marketplace), and the Bureau of Economics (which helps the FTC evaluate the economic impact of its actions). Let's look at some of the specific areas in which the FTC has an impact on the fashion industries and consumer behavior.

Textile Products Labeling

Among the FTC's most visible mandates are the laws that require specific labeling of most clothing as well as textile products commonly used in a household. These labels must include key pieces of information, including the fabric's fiber content, care instructions, manufacturer identification, and country of origin. Depending on what a product is made of, it may be covered by one or more of several different laws and official guidelines.

Textile Fiber Products Identification Act.   The **Textile Fiber Products Identification Act**, also known as the Textile Act, states that any company that advertises or sells clothing or fabric household items must label its products to accurately reflect their fiber content. Enforced by the FTC, the Textile Act covers fibers, yarns, and fabrics, as well as an array of household textile products made from them, such as clothing and accessories, draperies, towels and washcloths, bedding, cushions—even

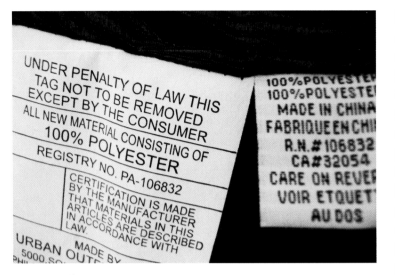

FIGURE 16.5. Fiber content labels such as these must be permanently affixed to virtually all clothing and household items made of fabric.

ironing board covers and umbrellas. Any product that is covered by the act must include a fiber content statement that lists the generic name of each fiber in order of predominance, and the percentage of the product's weight represented by each fiber. For example, a T-shirt might be labeled "100% Cotton," or a throw "65% Silk, 20% Nylon, 15% Angora." Fibers that represent less than 5 percent of the item's weight must be listed simply as "other fiber(s)." However, if the fiber has a functional significance, even in small amounts, it may be listed. For instance, spandex might be present as only 4 percent of a garment's weight, but without it, the garment would offer no elasticity, so the manufacturer may list it by name on the label.

The Textile Act includes additional stipulations for manufacturers in their fiber content labeling, covering issues such as fiber trademarks, which can be used but only if they appear immediately next to the generic fiber name. Lycra, for instance, is a trademark for a specific type of spandex made by Invista, so its use in a garment cannot be stated on the label simply as "Lycra," but must say "Lycra Spandex." Other requirements are meant to ensure that labeling is not deceptive. For example, if the base fabric of a towel is made of upland cotton and the loops are of pima cotton, a label stating "100% Pima Cotton" would not be acceptable—but the manufacturer could label the towel "100% Cotton, Pima Cotton Loops" or "100% Cotton, 100% Pima Cotton Loops," without misleading consumers. Similarly, if a printed advertisement for a product mentions its fiber content, the ad must also do so in a way that is not false, deceptive, or misleading.

Wool Products Labeling Act. While the Textile Act covers most apparel and fabric home furnishings items, products that contain any amount of wool are subject to the specific requirements of the **Wool Products Labeling Act**, also known as the Wool Act. Under the rules of the Wool Act, even if wool accounts for less than 5 percent of the weight of the product, it must be listed on the label.

The Wool Act addresses the use of specialty wool fibers—such as cashmere, camel hair, mohair, alpaca, llama, and vicuna—as well as the more common sheep or lamb's wool in apparel and home goods. A garment made of any of those fibers individually or in combination may be called simply "100% Wool" or "All Wool," assuming it has no other fiber content; or if it were made only of cashmere, it could be called "100% Cashmere." However, a sweater or blanket made half of wool and half of cashmere would have to be labeled either "100% Wool" or "50% Cashmere, 50% Wool," and to avoid misleading consumers, the product's hangtag or other packaging could not simply say "Fine Cashmere Garment." The same holds true for any printed advertising descriptions, as with the Textile Act rules.

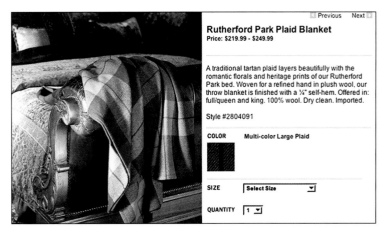

Previous Next

Rutherford Park Plaid Blanket
Price: $219.99 - $249.99

A traditional tartan plaid layers beautifully with the romantic florals and heritage prints of our Rutherford Park bed. Woven for a refined hand in plush wool, our throw blanket is finished with a ¼" self-hem. Offered in: full/queen and king. 100% wool. Dry clean. Imported.

Style #2804091

COLOR   Multi-color Large Plaid

SIZE   Select Size

QUANTITY   1

FIGURE 16.6. Catalogs and Web sites must give accurate fiber content information, since shoppers cannot look at the products' labels in person. This blanket has been clearly identified by the online seller as "100% wool."

Let's Talk

Do you check the fiber content label whenever you're buying clothes? Does the fiber content influence your purchase decision? If so, how?

Fur Products Labeling Act.   Garments made of fur must follow similar but distinct rules and regulations as set forth in the **Fur Products Labeling Act**. Under this act's rules, garments made either entirely or partly with fur must have a label disclosing, among other things, the type of animal; if the fur is used or damaged; and if the fur product is composed in whole or substantial part of pieces, such as paws, tails, bellies, scraps, heads, and so on. The label must also disclose if the fur is pointed (meaning that separate hairs are inserted into the fur, often either to repair damaged areas or to simulate other furs), dyed, bleached, or artificially colored; or if those treatments don't apply, the fur must be labeled "natural." In addition, the label must provide the textile or wool content of the product.

While the FTC's fur labeling guide provides a list of animals whose fur could be used in a garment, just because an animal name appears on the list does not mean it is necessarily legal to sell that fur in the United States. If the animal is an endangered species, for instance, the sale of its fur is prohibited by the Endangered Species Act of 1973. Similarly, the Dog and Cat Protection Act of 2000 prohibits the distribution, importation, or sale of any products made with dog or cat fur. Under the Fur Products Labeling Act, it is also illegal to label a fur with the name of any animal other than the animal that produced the fur, or to use invented or fictitious animal names.

› › › SPECIAL FOCUS 16.2: IS THAT FIDO IN YOUR FUR COAT? ‹ ‹ ‹

You might think the fur trim on your jacket is fake, but Fido may disagree. An investigation by the Humane Society of the United States turned up coats—some with designer labels, some at higher-end retailers—with fur from man's best friend.

The Humane Society said it purchased coats from reputable outlets, such as upscale Nordstrom, with designer labels including Andrew Marc and Tommy Hilfiger, and found them trimmed with fur from domestic dogs, even though the fur was advertised as fake. The investigation began after the society received a tip from a consumer who bought a coat with trim labeled as faux fur that felt real. The coats were tested by mass spectrometry, which measures the mass and sequence of proteins, to determine what species of animal the fur came from. Of the 25 coats tested, 24 were mislabeled or misadvertised. Most of the fur came from China.

Importing domestic dog and cat fur was outlawed in 2000. Intentionally importing and selling dog fur is a federal crime punishable by a $10,000 fine for each violation. Mislabeling fur is a misdemeanor punishable by a $5,000 fine or a year in prison. Fur valued at less than $150 is not required to be labeled.

In response to the investigation, Tommy Hilfiger stopped selling the fur-trimmed garment from its line. Nordstrom gave consumers who had bought the fur-trimmed vests in question the opportunity to return them and stopped buying fur-trimmed products from the vendor that had supplied them and marketed them as faux fur.

Other fashion companies that have faced issues with mislabeled fur products include JCPenney, Macy's, Burlington Coat Factory, Lord & Taylor, Donna Karan's DKNY, Michael Kors, and Oscar de la Renta. In addition, Sean "Diddy" Combs stopped producing and selling coats from his Sean John line and rapper Jay-Z pulled coats from his Rocawear label, both because the coats featured fur from raccoon dogs—a nondomestic animal that looks like an oversized, fluffy raccoon. Importing raccoon dog fur is not illegal, but activists argue that they are still a type of dog.

>>> Source: Adapted from Kasie Hunt, "Is Your Fur Fake, or Is It Fido?" The Associated Press, February 23, 2007. Retrieved August 22, 2007, from http://www.msnbc.msn.com/id/17298301/.

Down, Leather, and Jewelry Products Guidelines.   While there is not a separate law regarding the labeling of products made with down or feathers, up until the late

1990s the FTC did have official Down Guides for manufacturers to follow. They were rescinded in 1998, however, since the FTC believed that some of the stipulations were based on outdated manufacturing capabilities, and actually promoted inaccurate labeling and advertising. The International Down and Feather Testing Laboratory and Institute (IDFL) has since published its own labeling standards for the industry.[11] The FTC still offers a brochure of guidelines for manufacturers, since the overall rules of the Textile Act remain applicable to down and feather items, along with general FTC rules regarding deceptive advertising.

General guidelines for the labeling and advertising of leather and simulated leather products are also available from the FTC. In addition, the agency publishes Jewelry Guides that cover advertising claims made for gold, silver, platinum, pewter, diamonds, gemstones, and pearls, and define how certain common terms may be used in ads. For example, the guides explain when a product can be called "gold-plated" or when a diamond can be called "flawless."

Country of Origin and Manufacturer Identification. In addition to fiber content and other labeling requirements, products covered by the Textile and Wool Acts, as well as the Fur Products Labeling Act, must include the product's country of origin on the label. A special rule for socks, requiring that the country of origin be placed on the front of the packaging, took effect in March 2006. Imported products must identify the country where they were processed or manufactured; products made entirely in the United States of materials also made in the United States must be labeled "Made in U.S.A." or an equivalent phrase. In some cases, a garment or other product is partially made in another country but finished in the United States, or is manufactured in the United States from imported materials. In either situation, the label must identify the originating country for both the materials and the manufacture.

When clothing is being sold over the Internet, its country of origin must be stated in the product description, since consumers cannot examine a label before buying the garment. Occasionally, the FTC must take action to enforce the rule, as in a 1999 complaint against Bugle Boy Industries[12] and another against retailer Gottschalks[13] for selling certain textile products online without disclosing whether they were made in the United States, imported, or both.

Product labels must also include identification of the manufacturer, importer, or other firm that may be marketing, distributing, or otherwise handling the product. This can be either the full company name or the company's Registered Identification Number (RN), as issued by the FTC to U.S. companies.

Care Labeling Rule. In this chapter's opening scene, Patrice was planning to shop for toddlers' clothes that she knew could be machine-washed and dried. She, and all consumers, can verify the proper way to care for a garment thanks to the FTC's **Care Labeling Rule**, which requires manufacturers and importers to attach care instructions to their garments. As the FTC notes in its guide for businesses, "Clothes Captioning: Complying with the Care Labeling Rule," care labels are often a deciding factor when consumers shop for clothing, since many consumers prefer the economy of laundering clothes by machine, while others think that dropping off clothes for dry cleaning is more convenient. Either way, the FTC Care Labeling Rule lets consumers make the choice that is best for them.

The Care Labeling Rule covers all textile apparel with a few exceptions, such as shoes, gloves, hats, belts, and neckties. Piece goods, or lengths of fabric sold for making apparel at home, are also covered. On the label for each garment, manufacturers must provide complete instructions about regular care, or provide warnings if certain procedures would harm the product. For example, consumers would assume that a pair of pants labeled safe for washing would also be able to be ironed; so if ironing could harm the pants, the label should state, "Do not iron." In addition, manufacturers must ensure that the care labels are easily seen or found by consumers at the point of sale, and that they will remain attached and legible throughout the useful life of the product.

Since 1997, the FTC has permitted manufacturers to use specified care symbols instead of written instructions on garment labels (as shown in Figure 16.7). The symbols are intended to allow companies to include the same care labels on garments being sold in Canada or Mexico, as well as the United States. A minimum of four symbols are required for laundering instructions—washing, bleaching, drying, and ironing—with one symbol required for dry-cleaning instructions. Manufacturers may and often do use additional symbols or words, or both, to clarify the instructions for consumers; but fortunately for those who cannot decipher the symbols, if there is no clarification on the label, there are numerous Web sites (including the FTC's) that provide a translation.

Violations of the Care Labeling Rule are subject to enforcement actions by the FTC and penalties of up to $11,000 for each offense. Two of the largest penalties paid in recent years involved Tommy Hilfiger and Jones Apparel, each of which paid $300,000 in penalties. In the Hilfiger case, the garments in question were labeled with a washing instruction that, when followed, resulted in dye bleeding from one portion of the garment to another.[14] In the Jones Apparel case, some garments faded when dry-cleaned, while with other garments that featured flocking (a raised design), the flocking disappeared when the garments were dry-cleaned according to instructions. The complaint against Jones Apparel also included some cashmere sweaters that were labeled "dry clean only" but that could actually be safely hand-washed.[15]

FIGURE 16.7. The FTC has permitted the use of these symbols on fabric care labels since 1997. Do you know what they mean without an explanation?

Let's Talk
How carefully do you think most consumers follow the care labels on their cloth-ing? Do you follow the label more closely when an item is new? When it's more expensive? Why?

Truth in Advertising

As part of its mandate to protect consumers against unfair, deceptive, or fraudulent practices, the FTC devotes considerable resources to enforcing the nation's **truth-in-advertising laws**. These laws require advertisers—whether in newspapers or maga-zines, on television or radio, on the Internet or in any other medium—to create advertising that is truthful and to be able to support any claims about a product with reliable, objective evidence.

According to the FTC's Deception Policy Statement, an ad is deceptive if

- It contains a statement or omits information that is likely to mislead consumers acting reasonably under the circumstances.
- The information is "material"—that is, important to a consumer's decision to buy or use the product.

Injections?

Chemical peels?

Neutrogena
HEALTHY SKIN®

ANTI-WRINKLE CREAM
SPF 15

A Retinol
Facial Treatment with
Multi-Vitamins

**There is another way
to see fewer wrinkles.**
• #1 wrinkle fighter-Retinol, essential for skin cell regeneration*
• #1 Dermatologist Recommended*
• #1 Selling anti-wrinkle cream*

Neutrogena®
www.neutrogena.com

DERMATOLOGIST RECOMMENDED

FIGURE 16.8. Advertisers must be able to prove any claims they make—whether the claims are express or implied.

Similarly, the FTC's Unfairness Policy Statement deems an ad or business practice unfair if

• It causes or is likely to cause substantial consumer injury that a consumer could not reasonably avoid.
• It is not outweighed by the benefit to consumers.

To determine whether an ad is deceptive, the FTC looks at it from the point of view of a "reasonable" or typical consumer, taking the entire ad in context to judge what it conveys to consumers, and what it fails to say that could leave consumers with a misleading impression about the product. The FTC also looks at both express claims and implied claims in an ad. **Express claims** are those that are made literally; for example, "ABC Mouthwash prevents colds." **Implied claims** are those that are made indirectly or by inference; for example, "ABC Mouthwash kills the germs that cause colds." Although the second example does not literally say the mouthwash will prevent colds, it would be reasonable for a consumer to conclude from the statement, "kills the germs that cause colds," that it will prevent colds. Under the law, advertisers must have proof, such as research results, to support both express and implied claims in their ads.

With the increased consumer interest in purchasing "green" products, the FTC issued Environmental Guides (often referred to as "Green Guides") in 1992 that specifically address environmental advertising and marketing claims within the context of truth in advertising. The guides, which were updated in 1998, cover how words like "biodegradable," "recyclable," and "environmentally friendly" can be used in ads, and reinforce the requirement for all claims to be fully substantiated.

Let's Talk

Do you remember seeing advertising that made you wonder about how truthful the advertiser's claims were? Do you think advertisers sometimes try to bend the rules to make their point, without technically breaking the law? Do you think this is a question of ethics?

Price Fixing

As part of its regulation of anticompetitive business practices, the FTC enforces federal laws against price fixing. **Price fixing** occurs when business competitors make an agreement to set the price for which their products will be sold in a given market. The result of price fixing is generally higher prices for the consumer and higher profits for the companies fixing their prices. The laws against price fixing are the reason many products are marked with a "manufacturer's suggested retail price," since by a long-standing law, companies were not permitted to give retailers a minimum or specific price at which they must sell their products. In 2000, women's shoe company Nine West Group agreed to settle charges with the FTC and individual states that it engaged in resale price fixing with certain retailers. The company was accused of fixing retail prices for its shoes as well as restricting when retailers could hold sales and promotions.[16] However, a 2007 Supreme Court ruling (in *Leegin Creative Leather Products, Inc v. PSKS, Inc.*) stated that manufacturers may sometimes set minimum prices for their products; the effects of that ruling are likely to have an impact in the marketplace for fashion as well as other products in the years to come.

Other FTC Regulations

There are many other areas in which the FTC is involved in enforcing federal rules and regulations. The agency gives particular focus to advertising and marketing directed to children, since they are more vulnerable to certain kinds of deception, and reviews those ads from a child's perspective rather than an adult's. The FTC also enforces the Children's Online Privacy Protection Act, a federal law requiring Web sites to obtain verifiable parental consent before collecting, using, or disclosing personal information from children.

Catalog marketers and Internet retailers are subject to the FTC's oversight when it enforces laws including the Mail or Telephone Order Merchandise Rule, which requires companies to ship purchases when promised (or within 30 days if no time is specified), or give consumers the option to cancel their order for a refund. Under the conditions of the Do Not Call Registry, established by the FTC in 2003, telemarketers are prohibited from calling consumers who have placed their phone number on the list—although companies with which a consumer has already done business can still call, unless directly requested not to.

Consumer credit and financial privacy are also areas where the FTC wields its power. The agency is responsible for enforcing the Truth in Lending Act, which requires creditors to disclose in writing certain cost information, including annual percentage rate, before consumers enter into a credit agreement. The FTC also enforces the Fair Credit Reporting Act, which ensures the accuracy and privacy of information kept by credit bureaus and other consumer reporting agencies, and gives consumers the right to know what information about them is filed in their reports. To further promote informed consumer choice, the FTC maintains the Web site www.consumer.gov in partnership with the FDA, CPSC, and other agencies; this site features links to many other sources of consumer information.

Federal Anti-Counterfeiting Programs

As discussed in Chapter 15, counterfeit goods are increasingly prevalent in the marketplace, and the federal government is working to combat that trend on several fronts. The first line of defense is the U.S. Patent and Trademark Office, an agency within the Department of Commerce. By registering trademarks, the agency helps businesses protect their intellectual property investments and promote their goods and services, and helps safeguard consumers against confusion and deception in the marketplace. Those trademarks are further protected by the Lanham Act of 1946, also known as the Trademark Act, which gives trademark users exclusive rights to their marks; as well as by the Trademark Counterfeiting Act of 1984, which makes intentional use of a counterfeit trademark a federal offense.

Other agencies working to stop the marketing of counterfeit goods include Customs and Border Protection, part of the Department of Homeland Security, which devotes substantial resources to intercepting and seizing shipments of counterfeit goods crossing U.S. borders. The Federal Bureau of Investigation (FBI) investigates cases of criminal counterfeiting, and the Department of Justice prosecutes intellectual property crimes on behalf of the United States.

To further coordinate the effort, a new government initiative was announced in October 2004, called the **Strategy Targeting Organized Piracy (STOP!)**. STOP! brings together all the key agencies in a comprehensive initiative to "fight global piracy where it starts, block bogus goods at America's borders, and help American businesses secure and enforce their rights around the world." In March 2006, the anti-counterfeiting laws were strengthened even further with the signing of the Stop Counterfeiting in Manufactured Goods Act. While the shipment and sale of counterfeit goods was already illegal, the new legislation closed a loophole that had permitted the shipment of fake labels or packaging, which counterfeiters could then attach to fake products. The new law also requires courts to order the destruction of all counterfeit products seized in an investigation; it also toughens the penalties for convicted counterfeiters, requiring them to turn over their profits and any equipment used in their operations, and to reimburse the legitimate businesses they exploited.

FIGURE 16.9. Real Louis Vuitton—or fake? Shipment of counterfeit labels, even when not yet attached to a product, is illegal under the Stop Counterfeiting in Manufactured Goods Act.

Other Government Programs

There are many other federal laws and agencies that play a role in the way fashion products are marketed and sold, and that can influence the behavior of consumers.

The Equal Employment Opportunity Commission enforces the nation's **Equal Employment Opportunity (EEO)** laws, which prohibit discrimination in hiring based on race, color, religion, sex, national origin, or disability, and which protect men and women who perform substantially equal work in the same establishment from sex-based wage discrimination, among other things. For example, a retailer may break the law in trying to maintain a certain "look" for its sales staff that it believes will attract cus-

FIGURE 16.10. Automatic door openers are one way retailers comply with the Americans with Disabilities Act.

tomers or entice them to buy. In late 2004, a class action suit under the EEO laws was settled by Abercrombie & Fitch for $40 million after a group of Black, Asian, and Latino employees alleged that the retailer was hiring a disproportionately white sales force, favoring white employees for the best positions, and discouraging minorities from applying for jobs.[17]

The **Americans with Disabilities Act (ADA)**, which is enforced by the Department of Justice, further protects the rights of people with disabilities not only in equal employment opportunities but in equal access to public transportation, public buildings, and other places and activities. To comply with the requirements of this law, retailers and other companies must ensure that their places of business have doorways, hallways, and aisles wide enough to accommodate a wheelchair, and that wheelchair-accessible ramps or elevators are available in addition to stairs.

Many states, counties, and local governments also have their own laws that supplement the federal laws, and state or local agencies that enforce them. All states have a consumer protection or consumer affairs department or agency; sometimes safety rules on the state level are even more strict than the equivalent federal regulations. California, for example, has a flammability requirement for upholstery, even though there is not a federal rule. Generally, states also have their own laws regarding advertising, which can impose restrictions above and beyond those of the federal government.

Both federal and state governments provide a wealth of resources for consumers and businesses seeking more information about a particular law, or who want to file a complaint about a safety issue or deceptive business practice. Web sites for the individual agencies offer extensive information, much of which is also available in print format, often at no charge.

Independent Agencies and Services

Outside of government, there are a number of independent agencies and business groups that work to educate consumers and promote ethical business practices. One of the most widely recognized is the **Better Business Bureau (BBB)**, a private, not-for-profit organization. There are local or regional Better Business Bureaus and branches in over 150 locations across the country, all of which fall under the umbrella of the Council of Better Business Bureaus, which was founded in 1912. The umbrella organization is supported by more than 300,000 local business members nationwide, and is "dedicated to fostering fair and honest relationships between businesses and consumers, instilling consumer confidence, and contributing to an ethical business environment."

The BBB is best known for its Reliability Reports on local businesses. These reports, which are accessible to anyone making an inquiry, include information such as whether there are unresolved disputes or consumer complaints against the business. The BBB also offers dispute resolution services, as well as materials and resources for businesses and consumers on numerous topics, two of which are identity theft and online shopping. It also promotes truth in advertising, encouraging self-regulation of advertising claims by its business members.

Another important organization is the **National Consumers League**. Founded in 1899, the league is a nonprofit membership organization working for health, safety, and fairness in the marketplace and workplace. Among the areas the league monitors are consumer fraud, food and drug safety, fair labor standards, child labor, health care, e-commerce, financial services, and telecommunications. The league promotes consumer education through outreach to high school students and provides information to consumers through publications, media outreach, and multiple Web sites.

To give the public easy access to the variety of consumer information available, the Federal Citizen Information Center of the U.S. General Services Administration offers a broad listing of national consumer organizations in its free *Consumer Action Handbook*; the information is also available online at the Consumer Action Web site at consumeraction.gov.

Summary

The federal government plays an important role in creating and enforcing laws that protect the public and help consumers make informed purchase decisions. There are also laws and government agencies on the state and local level that supplement federal regulations, and independent groups that promote consumer education and fair business practices.

The Consumer Product Safety Commission protects the public against unreasonable risk of injury from a wide variety of products. The CPSC administers the Flammable

Fabrics Act, which establishes mandatory standards of flammability for textiles used in clothing and many home furnishings. Even more stringent standards apply to the flammability of children's sleepwear. Other safety issues monitored by the CPSC include strangulation and choking hazards and lead content. When unsafe products on the market are identified, the agency works with the company responsible to issue a recall.

The Food and Drug Administration is responsible for protecting the public's health and the safety of products in categories that include food, drugs, and cosmetics. It enforces the Federal Food, Drug, and Cosmetic Act, which prohibits the marketing and sale of adulterated or misbranded cosmetics, as well as the Fair Packaging and Labeling Act, which requires that specific information about ingredients be given on the product labels of cosmetics.

The Federal Trade Commission works to protect consumers from unfair or deceptive practices and to prevent businesses from engaging in anti-competitive practices. The FTC enforces laws regarding labeling of textile products, including the Textile Fiber Products Identification Act, which requires clothing and many textile household products to be labeled with their fiber content, country of origin, manufacturer identification, and directions for proper care. It also upholds the nation's truth-in-advertising laws, as well as regulating mail-order and Internet retailing, consumer credit and financial privacy, and other issues.

Federal agencies involved in the government's anti-counterfeiting efforts include the U.S. Patent and Trademark Office, Customs and Border Protection, and the Federal Bureau of Investigation. Helping to coordinate the work of the various agencies is the Strategy Targeting Organized Piracy (STOP!) initiative. The Stop Counterfeiting in Manufactured Goods Act recently strengthened the law even further.

Other government regulations affecting fashion commerce and consumer behavior include the Equal Employment Opportunity laws and Americans with Disabilities Act. Outside of government, there are many additional resources for business and consumer information, including the nationwide Better Business Bureau system.

Key Terms

Americans with Disabilities Act (ADA)

Better Business Bureau (BBB)

Care Labeling Rule

Consumer Product Safety Commission (CPSC)

Equal Employment Opportunity (EEO) laws

Express claims

Fair Packaging and Labeling Act

Federal Food, Drug, and Cosmetic Act (FD&C Act)

Federal Trade Commission (FTC)

Flammable Fabrics Act

Food and Drug Administration (FDA)

Fur Products Labeling Act

Implied claims

Mandatory standards

National Consumers League
Price fixing
Recall
Standard for the Flammability
   of Children's Sleepwear
Strategy Targeting Organized
   Piracy (STOP!)

Textile Fiber Products
   Identification Act
Trust
Truth-in-advertising laws
Wool Products Labeling Act

Questions for Review

1. Explain the purpose of the Consumer Product Safety Commission, and give three examples of the types of hazards the agency monitors that relate to fashion products.

2. How does the Food and Drug Administration regulate cosmetics, and how does that regulation differ from other products under its jurisdiction, such as drugs?

3. What information must be included on the label of clothing or fabric home furnishings, according to the Textile Fiber Products Identification Act? What does the Care Labeling Rule require?

4. What criteria does the Federal Trade Commission use to judge whether an advertisement is truthful?

5. Name two laws that are designed to protect people from discrimination in either the workplace or in access to public places.

Activities

1. Go to the Web site for the Consumer Product Safety Commission (www.cpsc.gov), and review the product recall announcements for three different months. How many recalls were there in total? How many were related to apparel or fashion? For the fashion-related recalls, make a list of the hazards the products posed, and indicate how many recalls there were for each. What were the remedies for consumers who had bought the products?

2. Go to a drugstore or other retailer that sells cosmetics and toiletries, and choose two brands of a similar item, such as lipstick or toothpaste. Compare the list of ingredients for the two brands. Are there some of the same ingredients in both? Are they in the same relative position in the list of ingredients, indicating their predominance in the formula? Write down the names of two or three ingredients that you are unfamiliar with, and research them to find out what they are and what they do. Share your results with the class.

3. Browse through the apparel in your closet, and find the labels identifying the fiber content. Select five items that have different fiber content from each other, and compare the look and feel of the fabric. Would you have known what the fab-

ric was without looking at the label? Now find the care labels for each and compare how they differ based on the fiber content. Make a chart showing the fabrics and their care, and describe what you think might happen to each garment if you did not follow the care instructions given.

4. Look through a magazine or watch TV to find four or five examples of advertisements for fashion-related products. Write down what the product is and what claim (or claims) the ad is making about the product. Indicate whether the claims are express claims or implied claims.

Mini-Project

Alone or with a group, choose a current fashion item (apparel, accessories, footwear, or cosmetics), and imagine you are in charge of marketing that item to consumers. Determine the product's key selling points, and create two versions of copy for an advertisement—one version that makes express claims about the product and one that makes implied claims. Describe the kind of proof you think you would need to support each claim.

References

1. U.S. Consumer Product Safety Commission, "CPSC Overview," http://cpsc.gov/about/about.html.
2. U.S. Consumer Product Safety Commission, "New Labels on Children's Sleepwear Alert Parents to Fire Dangers," News release, June 26, 2000.
3. U.S. Consumer Product Safety Commission, "CPSC, Target Corp. Announce Recall of Men's Sweatshirts," News release, November 19, 2002.
4. U.S. Consumer Product Safety Commission, "CPSC, Victoria's Secret Direct Announce Recall of Silk Kimono Tops," News release, February 23, 2006.
5. U.S. Consumer Product Safety Commission, "CPSC, Pottery Barn Kids Announce Recall of Chamois Blankets," News release, January 24, 2005.
6. Rummana Hussain, "Lead Fears Force Recall of American Girl Jewelry," *Chicago Sun-Times*, March 31, 2006, p. 20.
7. U.S. Consumer Product Safety Commission, "Reebok Recalls Bracelet Linked to Child's Lead Poisoning Death," News release, March 23, 2006.
8. eMedicineHealth.com, "FDA Overview." Retrieved August 22, 2007, from www.emedicinehealth.com/fda_overview/page6_em.htm.
9. Waldman, Peter, "From an Ingredient in Cosmetics, Toys, A Safety Concern." *Wall Street Journal*, October 4, 2005. Retrieved August 22, 2007, from http://online.wsj.com/public/article/SB112838975847059205.html.

10. U.S. Food and Drug Administration, "Labeling for Topically Applied Cosmetic Products Containing Alpha Hydroxy Acids as Ingredients," January 10, 2005. Retrieved August 22, 2007, from www.cfsan.fda.gov/~dms/ahaguid2.html.

11. International Down and Feather Testing Laboratory, "USA Labeling Standards—Down and Feather Products," January 2005. Retrieved August 22, 2007, from www.idfl.com/articles/IDFL%20USA%20Labeling%20Standards %20(Jan%202005).pdf

12. Federal Trade Commission, Docket No. C-3871, "In the Matter of Bugle Boy Industries, Inc.," June 2, 1999. Retrieved August 22, 2007, from www.ftc.gov/os/ 1999/06/bugleboycmp.htm.

13. Federal Trade Commission, Docket No. C-3878, "In the Matter of Gottschalks, Inc." June 3, 1999. Retrieved August 22, 2007, from www.ftc.gov/os/1999/06/ gottschalkscmp.htm.

14. Federal Trade Commission, "Tommy Hilfiger U.S.A., Inc., Agrees to Pay $300,000 Civil Penalty to Settle FTC Charges of Violating Care Labeling Rule," News release, March 17, 1999.

15. Federal Trade Commission, "Jones Apparel Group Agrees to Pay $300,000 Civil Penalty to Settle FTC Charges of Violating the Care Labeling Rule," News release, April 2, 2002.

16. Federal Trade Commission, "Nine West Settles State and Federal Price Fixing Charges," News release, March 6, 2000.

17. CBS News, "The Look of Abercrombie & Fitch," November 24, 2004, retrieved August 22, 2007, from www.cbsnews.com/stories/2003/12/05/60minutes/ main587099.shtml.

GLOSSARY

absolute threshold The lowest level at which our senses can recognize a stimulus (ch. 3).

acculturation The process of adapting to the primary or mainstream culture (ch.14).

activation The process by which information can be retrieved in our memory networks (ch. 3).

actual self In self-concept theory, who we think we are (ch. 6).

affective element The portion of our attitudes that is made up of our emotions toward an attitude object (ch. 5).

ambush marketing Strategy of identifying venues where the placement of unique marketing materials is sure to attract consumer and media attention (ch. 1).

Americans with Disabilities Act (ADA) Law that protects the rights of people with disabilities in equal employment opportunities, as well as in equal access to public transportation, public buildings, and other places and activities (ch. 16).

anthropology The study of human cultural characteristics that include habits, customs, relationships, and so on (ch. 14).

approach–approach A motivational conflict in which a choice must be made between two desirable options (ch. 4).

approach–avoidance A simultaneous desire to engage in a certain behavior and to avoid it (ch. 4).

archetypes According to Carl Jung, shared memories of the past that become the basis for present culture and are sometimes personified by characters (ch. 6).

aspirational groups Groups to which we do not actually belong but wish we did (ch. 8).

associative groups Groups to which we belong and identify, such as a volleyball team or professional association (ch. 8).

attention The focusing of our thoughts on a certain stimulus (ch. 3).

attitude Our settled opinion—either positive or negative—about people, ideas, places, or objects (ch. 5).

attitude objects In consumer behavior, those things about which we form attitudes and opinions (ch. 5).

attitude scales Research questionnaire tool through which respondents can indicate their level of favorable or unfavorable opinion across a range of answers (ch. 10).

avoidance–avoidance A motivational conflict in whiich a choice must be made between two undesirable options (ch. 4).

balance of trade The relationship between a country's imports and exports (ch. 14).

balance theory Theory stating that people want to maintain harmony or balance in their attitudes (ch. 5).

behavioral element The portion of our attitudes that determines how we intend to act toward an attitude object (ch. 5).

behavioral learning Theory that states learning takes place after exposure to external stimuli. Two types of behavioral learning are classical conditioning and instrumental conditioning (ch. 3).

behavioral perspective The use of actions that consumers have learned in response to specific stimuli as a basis for decision making (ch. 11).

Better Business Bureau (BBB) Umbrella organization for more than 300,000 local business members nationwide that are dedicated to fostering fair and honest relationships between businesses and consumers, instilling consumer confidence, and contributing to an ethical business environment (ch. 16).

birthrate The number of babies born in a year (ch. 9).

boycott Action in which consumers make the conscious decision not to purchase a product as a protest and moral statement (ch. 15).

brand The total of all that is known and felt about a product, service, or organization, from its recognizable name, logo, slogan, and packaging to the power it holds in people's minds (ch. 1).

brand drivers The aspects of a brand that attract and retain consumers (ch. 13).

brand equity The accumulation of brand image and brand loyalty that results in consumer satisfaction, retention, and demand (ch. 1).

brand image The deliberate, consistent way a product's qualities and essence are communicated to the public (ch. 1).

brand loyalty Repeat purchase behavior exhibited by customers who have strong connections to a favorite brand (ch. 1).

brand personification The characteristics, related to human personality traits, that advertisers give to certain brands (ch. 6).

buyer's market Situation in which there are more sellers than buyers; a consequent excess of supply over demand results in lower prices for consumers (ch. 2).

buyer's remorse *See* post-purchase dissonance.

buzz The tongue-wagging and word-of-mouth chatter about a product set in motion by marketers, particularly public relations and advertising experts. *See also* ambush marketing; guerilla marketing; viral marketing (ch. 1).

Care Labeling Rule   Law that requires manufacturers and importers to attach care instructions to their garments (ch. 16).

cause-based marketing or cause-related marketing   The public association of a for-profit company with a nonprofit organization, often involving the donation of a specified portion of profits to the nonprofit charity or cause (ch. 2).

charitainment   Celebrity do-goodism (ch. 13).

chunking   The capacity of our memories to amass large amounts of encoded information on a topic by adding on and linking to what we already know (ch. 3).

classic style   A style or fashion that is characterized by a simplicity of design that keeps it from becoming easily dated (ch. 12).

classical conditioning   Creating change in behavior by teaming an artificial stimulus with a natural one, with the goal of gaining a response from the artificial stimulus alone (ch. 3).

cognitive element   The portion of our attitudes that comes from what we have seen, read, or experienced concerning an attitude object; it forms the basis of our beliefs about that object (ch. 5).

cognitive learning   A problem-solving process where individuals seek out information in order to make an informed decision (ch. 3).

collective selection   A process by which a mass of people formulate certain collective tastes reflected by the goods and services they choose, and their selections illustrate the beliefs and values of the group's social system (ch. 1).

competitive advantage   The delivery of benefits that exceed those supplied by the competition, making it the best choice for the customer and the most profitable for an organization (ch. 1).

compliance   Response to social influence that occurs when we choose to do something because someone else asked us to do it (ch. 8).

compulsive buying behavior   Indiscriminate purchasing of goods; a form of neurosis (ch. 6).

conflict   Situation requiring a choice between two actions or behaviors that might result in equally desirable or equally undesirable outcomes (ch. 4).

conformity   A response to social influence that occurs when we behave like others in order to be accepted or feel like "one of the group" (ch. 8).

conscious motive   Reason for an action that we know and understand; we are aware of what we are doing and why (ch. 4).

consumer behavior   The actions and decision-making processes of buyers as they recognize their desire for a product or service, and engage in the search, evaluation, purchase, use, and disposal of that particular commodity (ch. 1).

consumer confidence   How consumers feel about the state of the economy (ch. 9).

consumer decision-making process   Purchase process that includes: need recognition, information search, evaluation of alternatives, purchase, post-purchase evaluation (ch. 4).

Consumer Product Safety Commission (CPSC)   An independent government agency whose directive is to protect the public against unreasonable risks of injuries associated with consumer products (ch. 16).

consumerism   (1) The movement protecting consumers by requiring honest packaging and product guarantees. (2) The theory that the greater consumption of economic goods is beneficial. (3) The attachment to materialistic values and possessions (ch. 9).

consumption   The using up of a resource by the person who has selected, adopted, used, and discarded or recycled it (ch. 1).

consumption roles   The expected or prescribed behaviors of consumers within a household; includes information gatherers/influencers, gatekeepers, decision makers, purchasers, and users (ch. 7).

count   Observational research method whereby an observer or team of observers keeps a written tally of the category being studied (ch. 10).

counterfeit goods   Unauthorized, illegal copies of designer or branded products (ch. 15).

cultural anthropology   The study of the common symbols, values, and beliefs of social groups and institutions (ch. 14).

cultural borrowing   The use of symbols that are meaningful to other cultures (ch. 14).

culture   All the shared beliefs, values, and traditions learned and practiced by a group of people, who may live close to each other, all of whom are focused on a common quest (ch. 1).

customization   The integration of individual requirements into a product (ch. 2).

decider/decision maker   The person who ultimately determines, with or without input from members of a group, which items will be considered and purchased, and how they will be used and discarded (ch. 7).

decline phase   Stage in a fashion's life cycle when it is experiencing decreasing sales and availability only in the lower price ranges (ch. 12).

demand   The level of desire among consumers for a particular product and the price that people are willing to pay to obtain it (ch. 4).

demographics   The measurable statistics concerning a population, particularly its size, composition, and distribution (ch. 9).

depth interview   A qualitative research method that involves one participant offering thoughts and opinions to a researcher (ch. 10).

design   A creative process, driven by a need, that leads to an invention of some sort, be it practical or artistic, functional or simply attractive, devised to enhance life in some way (ch. 1).

desire A yearning or longing for something (ch. 4).

differentiation The way companies attempt to make their products seem unique when compared to similar products by competitors (ch. 1).

direct (primary) influencers Groups or people with whom we have the most contact, such as family or close friends, and whose opinions are very powerful (ch. 8).

direction In evaluating the motivation behind a consumer purchase, what the customer wants from a product in terms of features or benefits (ch. 4).

disassociative groups Groups that do not interest us and of which we may disapprove (ch. 8).

discretionary income The amount of money consumers have after meeting all expenditures for necessities (ch. 9).

disposable income The amount of money, after taxes, that people have left for necessities such as food, shelter, utilities, and transportation (ch. 9).

diversity Variety or variation that which makes us dissimilar or different from one another (ch. 14).

downward flow (trickle-down theory) Movement of fashion in which styles adopted by upper classes trickle down the social ladder and are later adopted by the mainstream (ch. 8).

duties Additional monies and taxes on imports imposed by the country receiving those goods (ch. 14).

ego The conscious component of personality, our sense of ourselves; it reacts to reality in a socially acceptable way, serving as a mediator between the desires of the id and the restraint of the superego (ch. 6).

emotional needs Purchase motivation based on nonrational behavior and reasoning (ch. 4).

encoding The way we select visual images or words in short-term memory to represent what we want to store in long-term memory (ch. 3).

enculturation The process through which humans learn about and act according to the expectations of their own culture from birth on (ch. 14).

Equal Employment Opportunity (EEO) laws Federal laws that prohibit discrimination in hiring based on race, color, religion, sex, national origin, or disability, and which protect men and women who perform substantially equal work in the same establishment from sex-based wage discrimination, among other things (ch. 16).

ethics A system of moral values, or a set of principles that define right and wrong (ch. 15).

ethnocentrism Situation in which individuals make consumption choices that relate specifically to their own culture (ch. 11).

exchange A transfer or trade for something of value (ch. 2).

experiential hierarchy An attitude formation during the purchase process by which consumers are interested in enjoying a product, its symbols, and emotional meanings before learning about its features and benefits; the basis for consumption that is hedonic (ch. 5).

experiential perspective Use of the overall experience as opposed to a particular decision criterion in decision making (ch. 11).

exports Goods or commodities transported from one country to another country in a legitimate fashion, typically for use in trade (ch. 14).

exposure Situation that occurs when we encounter a stimulus through our senses: seeing, hearing, smelling, touching, or tasting (ch. 3).

express claims Advertising assertions about a product's benefits that are made literally (ch. 16).

extended family Family group that includes grandparents, aunts, uncles, and other relatives beyond the nuclear family (ch. 7).

extended self Self-identification that represents the relationship between ourselves and our possessions (ch. 6).

extensive decision making Decision-making process in which the consumer weighs the pros and cons, along with the perceived risks and benefits (ch. 11).

external recognition Awareness of a need or "problem" that is stimulated by others, such as marketers (ch. 11).

external (social) factors Elements of motivation derived from outside influences (ch. 4).

extroverts People who are outgoing and mainly concerned with external matters (ch. 6).

fad A short-lived fashion that bursts onto the scene, is wildly popular among a target group of consumers, and then disappears (ch. 12).

Fair Packaging and Labeling Act Law that states all cosmetics products must list their ingredients in descending order of predominance and the packaging must give the net quantity of contents (ch. 16).

fair-trade practices Standards for working conditions, environmental responsibility, and fair pricing that are based not only on ethical labor practices but also on the intent to provide opportunity to disadvantaged workers and help alleviate poverty (ch. 15).

false need The desire for something to which we attribute more value than it is actually worth (ch. 4).

family A group of individuals who live together and are related either by blood, adoption, or marriage; the unit that teaches each member the skills needed to function in society (ch. 7).

family life cycle   The emotional and intellectual stages and relationships through which people pass as they age (ch. 12).

fashion   Whatever is of the moment and subject to change; anything that members of a population deem desirable and appropriate at a given time (ch. 1).

fashion diffusion   The spread of a fashion throughout different societal groups (ch. 8).

fashion followers   People who adopt a look only after they are sure of a fashion trend (ch. 12).

fashion influentials   People who recognize and endorse what fashion innovators are wearing and doing (ch. 6).

fashion innovators (fashion leaders)   People who buy the earliest and are the first visual communicators of the season's styles (ch. 6).

fashion life cycle   The length of time a given look or style is popular (ch. 12).

fast fashion   Term for offering consumers the latest fashions as quickly as possible (ch. 12).

Federal Food, Drug and Cosmetic Act   Law that prohibits the marketing of adulterated (contaminated) or misbranded cosmetics in interstate commerce (ch. 16).

Federal Trade Commission (FTC)   Independent agency of the U.S. government created by the Federal Trade Commission Act of 1914 to prevent unfair methods of competition in commerce (ch. 16).

Flammable Fabrics Act   Law that regulates the flammability of clothing and home furnishings, as well as paper, plastic, foam, and other materials used both in apparel and interior furnishings (ch. 16).

Food and Drug Administration (FDA)   Federal agency that is responsible for protecting the public health by assuring the safety, efficacy, and security of human and veterinary drugs, biological products, medical devices, the nation's food supply, cosmetics, and products that emit radiation (ch. 16).

focus group   Qualitative research method that gathers a small group of consumers with a moderator to discuss and offer opinions about a product, service, or other marketing-related topic (ch. 10).

for-profit organization   A business maintained or conducted for the purpose of making a profit and developing human resource potential (ch. 13).

forecasting   A creative process used by industry professionals to predict future trends (ch. 1).

functions of attitude   Daniel Katz' theory of the four classifications of attitudes that serve to help us achieve balance in life: (1) utilitarian, (2) value-expressive, (3) ego-defensive, and (4) knowledge (ch. 5).

Fur Products Labeling Act   Law stating that garments made either entirely or partly with fur must have a label disclosing the animal name; if the fur is used or damaged; and if the fur product is composed in whole or substantial part of pieces, among other information (ch. 16).

gatekeeper   A knowledgeable individual who controls access and information flow to followers, and influences them to act in specific ways (ch. 7).

geodemographic system   A consumer-measuring technique combining geography and demographics, first devised by Claritas Corp (ch. 9).

gestalt psychology   The phenomenon of coming to a conclusion after seeing the total picture or pattern; the "aha" experience (ch. 3).

globalization   The ability to market a product anywhere in the world that a demand for it exists (ch. 14).

goal   A particular outcome or end desired by an individual or organization (ch. 4).

group   Two or more people who share similar values and beliefs and communicate interdependently (ch. 8).

guerilla marketing   A term coined by Jay Conrad Levinson to describe unconventional marketing tactics designed to get maximum results from minimal resources (ch. 1).

habitual or routine decision making   Situation in which not much thought is needed to reach a decision (ch. 11).

hedonic consumption   A part of the emotional aspect of our relationships to products that comes from the ways we respond to stimuli (ch. 3).

heuristics   Simple mental rules of thumb that help us make decisions more quickly (ch. 11).

hierarchy of effects   The series of steps—feelings, beliefs, actions—that we go through in forming our attitudes (ch. 5).

high-involvement hierarchy   An attitude formation problem-solving process consumers use to reach a buying decision about a product that is usually an important purchase (ch. 5).

horizontal flow (trickle-across theory)   Movement of fashion in which influences among peer groups with similar demographic or psychographic profiles are what determine a style's adoption (ch. 8).

household   Any single person or a group of persons who live together in a residential setting, regardless of whether they are related (ch. 7).

hype   A set of activities set in motion prior to the actual introduction of a new product or service that helps create a supportive marketing environment and a spontaneously infectious kind of person-to-person image spinning (ch. 1).

id (libido)   Unconscious personality component that controls our biological drives of hunger, sex, and self-preservation; it is with us from birth, and its impulses require immediate gratification (ch. 6).

ideal self   In self-concept theory, who we would like to be (ch. 6).

ideal social self-image   In self-concept theory, how we would like others to see us (ch. 6).

immigration   The influx of people into a country from another country (ch. 9).

implied claims   Advertising assertions that are made indirectly or by inference (ch. 16).

imports   Goods and services provided by foreign producers that are purchased and brought into a country (ch. 14).

incentive   To move the consumer from an actual state to a desired state; a reason to buy (ch. 4).

income   The money and other assets that people typically receive in a year from their work, property, and other investments (ch. 9).

indirect (secondary) influencers   Groups that are not in our immediate circle of friends and family and therefore do not have a strong influence on our decision making (ch. 8).

inertia habit   Act of completing a consumption activity or buying the same brand because it takes little or no energy (ch. 11).

influencer   A person who provides information/guidance to other members of a group about products and services; also referred to as "information gatherer" (ch. 7).

information collection   The search for and selection of data that provide an adequate foundation for making good decisions (ch. 11).

information filtering   The process of sorting through collected data, then prioritizing and selecting that which best meets our information objectives (ch. 11).

information overload   The condition of being bombarded with more information than we can process or store in our memories (ch. 3).

informational influences   Facts, figures, data, and so on from professionals who are familiar with a specific subject or brand that have an effect on our decision making (ch. 3).

informational social influences   Factors that cause us to copy the behavior of others because they directly or indirectly offer information to assist in our decision making (ch. 8).

innovation   Something that is new to the person seeing or experiencing it (ch. 1).

instinct   An innate drive that we are born with and that is largely physiological (ch. 4).

instrumental conditioning   Creating change in behavior by making choices that result in rewards and avoid punishment (ch. 3).

integrated marketing system (IMS)   The continuous, efficient sharing of information and ideas among all participants in an organization, with a goal of organized, effective communication with the desired audience (ch. 1).

intensity   In evaluating the motivation for a consumer purchase, the level of a customer's interest in a product (ch. 4).

internal (nonsocial) factors   Elements of motivation that come from within a person (ch. 4).

internal recognition   Awareness of a need or "problem" that originates within an individual (ch. 11).

introduction phase   Stage of the fashion life cycle when a new style first appears (ch. 12).

introverts   People who choose to turn inward, rather than concern themselves with external matters (ch. 6).

inventory shrinkage   Retail term for losses that includes employee theft, shoplifting, vendor fraud, and administrative error (ch. 15).

just noticeable difference (j.n.d)   The ability of our senses to distinguish between two closely similar stimuli, such as popular music and jazz (ch. 3).

knock-offs   Fashion industry term for copies of the original styles (ch. 12).

learning   The process of changing behavior through experience (ch. 3).

life expectancy   The length of time people will live, and how long they can be productive in an economy and in society (ch. 9).

lifestyle   An individual's distinctive way of living; a pattern that influences a person's choices in all areas of life, from how to spend time to how to spend money (ch. 9).

Likert scale   Quantitative research tool that presents a statement and asks consumers to select a degree of agreement or disagreement with the statement (ch. 10).

limited decision making   Process of decision making that involves some thought, but frequently involves general rules of thumb we've learned or borrowed from others (ch. 11).

long-term memory   The part of memory that stores information we want to keep for permanent use and recall at will (ch. 3).

low-involvement hierarchy   An attitude formation purchase process in which the purchase is insignificant, the consumer does not prefer one brand over another, and does not form a firm like or dislike until after using the product (ch. 5).

loyalty programs   Retail marketing programs that offer customers a reward or an incentive to keep them returning to the store (ch. 15).

magalogs   Shopping magazines, such as *Lucky*, featuring fashion, and *Domino*, showcasing home décor (ch. 10).

mandatory standards   Government rules requiring all manufacturers, retailers, importers, and distributors to ensure that the products they are selling meet specific criteria, usually for safety (ch. 16).

market forces External variables that impact an organization's ability to achieve its goal and provide services or products to its customers (ch. 13).

market research The collecting of information about the marketplace that results in planned marketing activities and that helps generate revenues (ch. 2).

market segment A homogeneous group of buyers displaying like needs, wants, values, and buying behaviors (ch. 1).

market segmentation A method for dividing markets into smaller homogeneous units in order to more effectively reach potential customers who reflect similar characteristics, wants, and needs (ch. 2).

marketing A process that includes the communication of all information sellers want to share with consumers, from the time a product or service is an idea, through its purchase, use, evaluation, and disposal by the customer (ch. 1).

marketing concept A design that focuses on a company's knowing its clients, satisfying their needs, and doing so more effectively than its competitors at a profit (ch. 2).

marketing research The process of analyzing a given marketing opportunity or problem and finding solutions through understanding the behaviors and preferences of the market's consumers (ch. 10).

mass marketing The distribution and promotion of the same product to a broad base of all potential customers (ch. 1).

materialism The importance that we attach to the things we own (ch. 9).

means-end chain (MEC) A structure that links a consumer's knowledge about a product's attributes (benefits or risks) with the desired cultural value state the person wants to achieve; the means = the product, and the end = the desired value/outcome (ch. 14).

memory The process of storing and retrieving the knowledge we have learned (ch. 3).

motivate To impel, incite, or move a person into action (ch. 4).

motivation The result of forces acting either on or within a person to initiate or activate certain behavior (ch. 4).

motivational research Field of research that studies the effect of the unconscious id and the superego on motives in purchasing behavior (ch. 6).

motives Reasons that impel us to act. Categories include conscious vs. unconscious, internal vs. external, positive vs. negative, rational vs. emotional (ch. 4).

multi-attribute model Fishbein's model stating that a combination of consumers' beliefs, derived from their knowledge of the attributes of a product, reveals their overall attitude toward the product (ch. 5).

multi-channel retailing The use of catalogs, stores, and the Internet in a coordinated marketing plan (ch. 12).

multicultural Term used to describe a group of people belonging to a dominant culture but who have diverse cultural backgrounds (ch. 14).

multiple selves   The many roles we each take on in our self-concept (ch. 6).

National Consumers League   A nonprofit membership organization working for health, safety, and fairness in the marketplace and workplace (ch. 16).

need   An internal state of discomfort that calls for a solution. Types include acquired, primary vs. secondary, stability vs. variety (ch. 4).

need for achievement   A personality trait shown by people who want to stand out from the crowd or do better than others (ch. 6).

need for affiliation   A personality trait demonstrated by people who place an emphasis on gaining friends, maintaining close relationships, and belonging to groups (ch. 6).

need for cognition (NC)   A personality trait indicating the desire for knowledge (ch. 6).

need for power   A personality trait shown by people who want to influence or control others (ch. 6).

need satisfaction   The experiencing of pleasure when a need has been addressed (ch. 4).

negative motivation   Impetus for an action that is based more on dissatisfaction with a current situation than on the benefits the action would bring (ch. 4).

neurosis   A mental disorder with emotionally painful symptoms that can surface as anxiety, compulsion, and depression (ch. 6).

non-business entity   An organization without clearly defined owners, such as public works, governments, and nonprofit organizations (ch. 13).

nonprofit organization   A company formed for the purpose of achieving a specific socially responsible goal while sustaining a profitable position (ch. 13).

nontraditional family   Family group that may include single parents, step-relatives, unmarried partners, and so on (ch. 7).

nontraditional family life cycle   *See* twenty-first-century family life cycle (ch. 7).

normative beliefs   The opinions of other people who matter to us (ch. 5).

normative social influence   Form of pressure that requires a person to conform to the expectations of others (ch. 8).

nuclear family   Family group that includes parent(s) and children living together (ch. 7).

obedience   Response to social influence that occurs when one strictly obeys an order from an authoritative person or group (ch. 8).

objectives (for research)   The specific information marketers want to learn through a research study (ch. 10).

obsolescence or rejection phase   Stage that marks the end of a style's fashion life cycle, indicating that the look is out-of-date and no longer being sold (ch. 12).

opinion leader   Individual who is highly regarded by his peers and serves as a credible source or a liaison, who transmits and translates information from mass media to those seeking advice (ch. 8).

optimal stimulation level (OSL)   Concept that people have different needs for stimulation, most preferring moderate stimulation over high stimulation (ch. 6).

organization   A group of individuals who have come together for the purpose of accomplishing a common goal (ch. 13).

organizational hierarchy   Successive levels of an organization with each one superior to the one below it (ch. 13).

organized retail theft (ORT)   Multiple shoplifters working together to steal larger quantities of products, which are stolen not for personal use, but to resell (ch. 15).

peak phase   Stage of the fashion life cycle when a style is at the height of its acceptance and popularity (ch. 12).

per capita personal income   Total income of a prescribed area divided by the total population (ch. 9).

perceived cost   The balance between the bundle of benefits received and a competitor's comparable cost (ch. 2).

perceived risk   The risk a customer believes exists in the purchase of goods or services whether or not a risk actually exists (ch. 11).

perception   The process of interpreting our surroundings through our senses (ch. 3).

perceptual mapping   A graphics technique enabling marketers to visualize consumers' attitudes toward their products and those of their competitors (ch. 5).

personality   The individual psychological characteristics that routinely influence the way people react to their surroundings (ch. 5).

positioning   Creating a certain perception or image about a product in the minds of consumers that differentiates it from the competition (ch. 1).

positive motivation   Impetus for an action that is based on recognition of the action's benefits (ch. 4).

post-purchase dissonance ("buyer's remorse")   Situation in which doubt about making a purchase decision follows the actual purchase and creates tension or a state of dissonance; also known as "cognitive dissonance" (ch. 4).

primary (basic) needs   Basic physiological requirements for all humans, including food, clothing, shelter, sleep, etc. (ch. 4).

primary data   Original information that is collected firsthand via personal interviews, focus groups, and surveys (ch. 2).

price fixing   Situation in which business competitors make an agreement to set the price for which their products will be sold in a given market (ch. 16).

primary research   An original study designed to address a company's specific objectives (ch. 10).

PRIZM NE (Potential Rating Index by ZIP Code—New Evolution)   A geodemographic method of segmenting markets by ZIP codes, and then combining demographics (such as income and education) with lifestyles, thus identifying areas of similar consumer behavior throughout the United States (ch. 9).

problem awareness   State in which a consumer perceives an imbalance between his or her current ("as is") situation and an ideal ("should be") situation (ch. 11).

product differentiation   Strategy by which companies attempt to make their product seem unique when compared to similar products by competitors (ch. 1).

product life cycle   The succession of stages a product goes through: development, introduction, growth, maturity, and decline (ch. 13).

profit motive   The incentive to work or accomplish something in order to gain something (ch. 13).

psychology   The study of individual behavior (ch. 4).

psychoanalytic theory   Sigmund Freud theory stating that many of our behaviors and dreams come from our unconscious, where thoughts, of which we are largely unaware, are stored (ch. 6).

psychographics   The study of consumer personality and lifestyle (ch. 9).

purchaser   One who secures/buys product(s) (ch. 7).

purchasing power   The amount of goods and services the dollar will buy (ch. 9).

qualitative research   Research that is subjective, focusing on people's opinions and attitudes toward a product or service (ch. 10).

quantifying   Measuring and expressing a result as a number equivalent (ch. 2).

quantitative research   Research that is objective, focusing on collecting numbers and facts that can be analyzed statistically (ch. 10).

quota   A limit on the quantity of goods that can be imported into a country (ch. 14).

rational needs   Purchase motivation based on reasoning and logic (ch. 4).

rational perspective   The use of logically based, left-brain thinking to process information and carefully review the pros and cons of a decision (ch. 11).

recall   The removal of an unsafe product from the marketplace, involving public announcements about the danger and providing information on what to do with the product or how to contact its manufacturer (ch. 16).

reference group   Any person or group serving as a point of comparison or frame of reference for an individual when that individual is forming his own beliefs and behaviors (ch. 7).

repositioning   The act of revising a marketing strategy for a product or a company in order to increase sales or counteract negative perceptions (ch. 13).

response   Reaction to a stimulus (ch. 11).

retrieval   The process we go through to use information stored in our memories (ch. 3).

rise phase   The period in the fashion life cycle when a look is growing in popularity (ch. 12).

role   The behavior expected of a person in a given setting (ch. 7).

secondary (acquired) needs   Needs that are learned in accordance with the values of a person's specific culture and which are met only after primary needs are fulfilled (ch. 4).

secondary data   Information that has been collected from other studies or sources such as textbooks, magazines, the Internet, and other published materials (ch. 2).

secondary research   Locating data from existing sources that meets a study's research objectives (ch. 10).

selective perception   Paying attention to the stimuli that connect to our needs (ch. 3).

self-concept   An individual's perception of his or her own characteristics and attributes (ch. 6).

self-concept theory   Theory stating that in addition to the personality having multiple selves, we envision ourselves both privately and in relation to others (ch. 6).

self-esteem   Our positive and negative opinions of ourselves and our estimate of our self- worth (ch. 6).

self-image   The actual self, who we think we are (ch. 6).

selling concept   Business approach that focuses on trying to sell what a company has already made, not what the customer wants (ch. 2).

seller's market   Situation in which there are more buyers than sellers; increased demand and low supply result in higher prices (ch. 2).

semiotics   The study of symbols and their meanings (ch. 6).

sensory memory   The part of our memory where sensory stimuli are briefly stored (ch. 3).

short-term memory   The part of our memory where we hold for a limited time the sensory stimuli we decide to record (ch. 3).

social class   Groups of individuals belonging to different levels of society; social classes are hierarchical and, for the most part, depend on levels of prosperity and opportunity, and at times on inheritance (ch. 8).

social impact theory   Theory stating the probability of influence increases depending on the number of people involved and the importance and proximity of the influencers (ch. 8).

social influence   The information or pressure that an individual, group, or type of media presents or exerts on consumers (ch. 8).

social self-image   In self-concept theory, how others see us (ch. 6).

social responsibility The principle that everyone is responsible for making the world a better place for all its inhabitants (ch. 15).

socialization Process of preparing children for the future by teaching them the skills, attitudes, and general knowledge necessary to effectively integrate into society (ch. 7).

societal marketing concept The idea that companies should balance profits with customer wants, competitors' actions, and society's long-term interests (ch. 2).

sociology The study of group behavior (ch. 4).

stability Constancy; a need that can motivate people not to take a new action (ch. 4).

stakeholder A person or persons with an interest in seeing a company succeed (ch. 2).

Standard for the Flammability of Children's Sleepwear Federal regulations that prescribe a test requiring that specimens of the fabric, seams, and trim from children's sleepwear garments self-extinguish after exposure to a small open flame (ch. 16).

stimulus An energizing force that causes a state of tension or arousal (ch. 4).

strategic marketing plan A business road map that identifies a specific target market, the preferences of that market's members, and specific ways to connect with and keep them (ch. 2).

strategy A plan that addresses how to respond to consumers and competitors in the marketplace (ch. 2).

Strategy Targeting Organized Piracy (STOP!) Government initiative that brings together key agencies in a comprehensive initiative to fight global piracy and counterfeiting (ch. 16).

subculture A smaller group within a large society/culture (such as persons of the same age, political ideology, ethnicity, social class, sexual orientation) who possesses distinct beliefs, goals, interests, and values that differentiate them from the dominant culture (ch. 8).

subjective norms Influences on our decision making that include our normative beliefs, plus the extent to which we are motivated to go along with others' opinions (ch. 5).

subliminal perception The perception of stimuli by our senses below our level of conscious awareness or absolute threshold (ch. 3).

superego Component of personality that acts as a conscience, promoting acceptable standards of behavior and restraining the impulsive id by creating feelings of guilt to punish misconduct, real or imagined (ch. 6).

supply chain The organizations and related activities associated with the manufacture and delivery of a service or product. It represents the work flow from supplier to manufacturer to wholesaler to retailer to the end user, the consumer (ch. 2).

sweatshops Factories where workers are obliged to work long hours, under poor conditions, for very little pay (ch. 15).

target market Group of potential customers that share similar lifestyles and preferences, on which a company intends to focus its marketing efforts (ch. 1).

target marketing Defining a specific segment of the market and making it the strategic focus for the business or marketing plan (ch. 2).

tariffs Taxes on imports imposed by the country receiving those goods (ch. 14).

Textile Fiber Products Identification Act (Textile Act) Federal law stating that any company that advertises or sells clothing or fabric household items must label its products to accurately reflect their fiber content (ch. 16).

theory of cognitive dissonance Theory explaining consumers' discomfort due to conflicting attitudes concerning an attitude object, often a recent significant purchase (ch. 5).

theory of reasoned action (TORA) Theory stating that in addition to the affective, cognitive, and behavioral components of attitude, subjective norms including our normative beliefs (others' opinions) plus the extent to which we're motivated to go along with those opinions play a part in reaching a buying decision (ch. 5).

trade deficit Situation in which a country imports more than it exports (ch. 14).

trade surplus Situation in which a country exports more than it imports (ch. 14).

traditional family life cycle The historically typical stages in relationships through which people pass as they age. Phases include bachelorhood, honeymoon, full nest, empty nest, dissolution (ch. 7).

traits Distinct characteristics that differentiate us from others and contribute to our behavior (ch. 6).

trend The direction in which something (such as fashion) is moving (ch. 1).

trend forecasting services Services that offer advisories formulated by professional observers of cultural shifts that contain calculated predictions about the likely direction in which design preferences are moving (ch. 14).

trunk show Fashion event in which a designer or representative of a manufacturer brings an entire line to a local store for customers to see and buy (ch. 10).

trust Large business entities that succeed in controlling a market, in essence becoming a monopoly (ch. 16).

truth-in-advertising laws Regulations enforced by the Federal Trade Commission that require marketers to create advertising that is truthful and to be able to support any claims about a product with reliable, objective evidence (ch. 16).

twenty-first-century family life cycle An updated equivalent of the traditional family life cycle, the phases of which include child/teen, single/independent, new couple/partnership, mid-adulthood, empty nest, dissolution (ch. 7).

unconscious motive   Reason for an action in which we are not aware of why we are acting in that particular way (ch. 4).

unsought goods   Products or services that consumers do not actually seek or plan to buy, such as items that are purchased without advance need recognition (e.g., an umbrella for a sudden downpour) (ch. 4).

upward flow (trickle-up theory)   Movement of fashion in which a new fashion idea starts among the lower echelons of society or on the "street" and works its way up (ch. 8).

user   One who consumes/uses a product or service (ch. 7).

utilitarian influences   Factors that cause an individual to yield to another person's or group's influence to gain recognition and reward or avoid punishment (ch. 8).

VALS   A psychographic system developed by SRI International that many marketers employ to find out why customers make certain buying decisions based on psychological traits, motivation, and resources (ch. 9).

value   Tangible or intangible attributes that improve the desirability of a product or service (ch. 2).

value expressive influences   Motivational factors that address core values or the values people believe they should possess, which would enhance their image in the eyes of others (ch. 8).

value system   A learned organization of principles and rules to help one choose between alternatives, resolve conflicts, and make decisions (ch. 14).

values   The ideas one considers important in life; an individual's set of principles for behavior (ch. 9).

variety   Changeability; a need that can motivate people to make a change or do something different (ch. 4).

viral marketing   The passing on of a marketing message to others, much like passing a virus from one person to another (ch. 1).

wants   Desires that are not necessities nor required for survival (ch. 4).

Weber's Law   Theory that states the more intense a first stimulus, the stronger the next stimulus must be in order for people to distinguish it as different (ch. 3).

Wool Products Labeling Act (Wool Act)   Federal rules requiring that, even if wool accounts for less than 5 percent of the weight of a product, it must be listed on the label (ch. 16).

word-of-mouth marketing (WOM)   The passing along from person to person of a marketing message or opinions about a product, which can happen either spontaneously or as a result of a marketer's strategy (ch. 1).

zeitgeist   The spirit of the times, experienced by many people simultaneously (ch. 1).

CREDITS

Chapter 1
1.1 PRNewsFoto/Sam's Club
1.2 Jeff Vespa/WireImage
1.3 © Anthony Jenkins for Fairchild Publications, Inc.
1.4 JEAN-PIERRE MULLER/AFP/Getty Images
1.5 Time Magazine/Wrights Reprints LLC
1.6 CartoonStock. www.CartoonStock.com
1.7 © Anthony Jenkins for Fairchild Publications, Inc.
1.8 © Anthony Jenkins for Fairchild Publications, Inc.

Chapter 2
2.1 © Anthony Jenkins for Fairchild Publications, Inc.
2.2 (left) PRNewsFoto/Pitney Bowes Inc/(right) PRNewsFoto/First National Bank Omaha
2.3 © Anthony Jenkins for Fairchild Publications, Inc.
2.4 © Anthony Jenkins for Fairchild Publications, Inc.
2.5 Courtesy of Fairchild Publications, Inc.
2.6 Courtesy of Motorola
2.7 Cartoon copyrighted by Mark Parisi, printed with permission.
2.8 © Anthony Jenkins for Fairchild Publications, Inc.
2.12 © Anthony Jenkins for Fairchild Publications, Inc.

2.13 © Anthony Jenkins for Fairchild Publications, Inc.

Chapter 3
3.1a Courtesy of Fairchild Publications, Inc.
3.1b Courtesy of Fairchild Publications, Inc.
3.1c Courtesy of Fairchild Publications, Inc.
3.2 © Anthony Jenkins for Fairchild Publications, Inc.
3.3a Courtesy of Fairchild Publications, Inc.
3.3b Courtesy of Fairchild Publications, Inc.
3.4 The Advertising Archives
3.5 © Anthony Jenkins for Fairchild Publications, Inc.
3.6 Courtesy of Fairchild Publications, Inc.
3.7 ® Coach, the Coach Tag, the Coach Lozenge, and the Coach Signature C design are registered trademarks of Coach.
3.8 The Advertising Archives

Chapter 4
4.1 © Anthony Jenkins for Fairchild Publications, Inc.
4.2 Cartoon copyrighted by Mark Parisi, printed with permission. Visit offthemark.com.
4.3 The Advertising Archives
4.4 Brad Barket/Getty Images for JCPenney

Chapter 5
5.1 © Anthony Jenkins for Fairchild Publications, Inc.

5.2	© 2007 GlaxoSmithKline. Reproduced with permission.
5.3	Business Wire
5.4	The "Art. Ask for More." advertisement is provided courtesy of Americans for the Arts, 2007.
5.5a	Courtesy of Nordstrom
5.5b	The Advertising Archives
5.5c	Courtesy of Payless ShoeSource
5.6a	Courtesy of Not Your Daughter's Jeans
5.6b	Reproduced with permission of Cotton Incorporated
5.7a	Courtesy of L.e.i. jeans
5.7b	The Advertising Archives
5.8	Courtesy of Fairchild Publications, Inc.
5.9	© The New Yorker Collection 2005 Barbara Smaller from cartoonbank.com. All Rights Reserved.
5.10	PRNewsFoto/Rocawear

Chapter 6

6.1	The Advertising Archives
6.2	© Warner Bros/Courtesy Everett Collection
6.3	Courtesy of David Barton
6.4	Image Courtesy of Celestial Seasonings, Inc. © 2007
6.5	© Anthony Jenkins for Fairchild Publications, Inc. Adapted from Atomic Dog
6.6	CATHY © 2007 Cathy Guisewite. Reprinted with permission of UNIVERSAL PRESS SYNDICATE. All rights reserved Universal Press Syndicate.
6.7	Courtesy of Stefani B
6.8a	The Advertising Archives
6.8b	The Advertising Archives
6.9	Courtesy of Fairchild Publications, Inc.
6.10	Courtesy of Merrel
6.11	Courtesy of Eileen Fisher
6.13	Courtesy of Hummer

Chapter 7

7.1	© Anthony Jenkins for Fairchild Publications, Inc.
7.2a	Photoedit
7.2b	© Mark Karrass/Corbis
7.2c	© Ariel Skelley/CORBIS
7.3a	© Bart Geerligs/Getty
7.3b	© Big Cheese Photo LLC/Alamy
7.3c	Bill Bachmann/PhotoEdit Inc.
7.4	© Anthony Jenkins for Fairchild Publications, Inc.

Chapter 8

8.1	Courtesy of Fairchild Publications, Inc.
8.2	© Anthony Jenkins for Fairchild Publications, Inc.
8.4a	Courtesy of Fairchild Publications, Inc.
8.4b	Courtesy of Fairchild Publications, Inc.
8.4c	Courtesy of Fairchild Publications, Inc.
8.4d	Courtesy of Fairchild Publications, Inc.
8.5	© Anthony Jenkins for Fairchild Publications, Inc.
8.6	© Anthony Jenkins for Fairchild Publications, Inc.
8.7	© Anthony Jenkins for Fairchild Publications, Inc.
8.8a	© Jason Horowitz/zefa/Corbis
8.8b	© Tim Pannell/Corbis
8.8c	© Image Source/Corbis
8.9a	copyrighted by Mark Parisi, printed with permission. Visit offthemark.com
8.9b	Cartoon copyrighted by Mark Parisi, printed with permission. Visit offthemark.com
8.10a	Courtesy of Fairchild Publications, Inc.
8.10b	Dave Hogan/Getty Images
8.10c	Courtesy of Fairchild Publications, Inc.

Chapter 9

9.1a–c	Courtesy of Target
9.2	istock photo

9.3   Courtesy of Fairchild Publications, Inc.

9.4   © Bill Bachmann/Alamy

9.5   AP Photo/Jennifer Graylock

9.6   Source: U.S. Bureau of Economic Analysis

9.7   Melanie Stetson Freeman/The Christian Science Monitor via Getty Images

9.8   © Frank Herholdt/Stone/Getty Images

9.9   Courtesy of Svedka

9.10   © ACE STOCK LIMITED/Alamy

9.11   Getty Images/Blend Images

9.12   Courtesy of Fairchild Publications, Inc.

Chapter 10

10.1   © Big Cheese Photo LLC/Alamy

10.4   Spencer Grant/Photoedit Inc.

10.6   AP Photo/Vincent Yu

10.7a   and b Courtesy of Condé Nast Publications, Inc.

10.8a   PRNewsFoto/Vogue

10.8b   Courtesy of glam.com

Chapter 11

11.1   © Anthony Jenkins for Fairchild Publications, Inc.

11.3a   and b © Anthony Jenkins for Fairchild Publications, Inc.

11.4   Cartoon copyrighted by Mark Parisi, printed with permission. Visit offthemark .com

11.5   © Anthony Jenkins for Fairchild Publications, Inc.

11.7   © Anthony Jenkins for Fairchild Publications, Inc.

11.8a–c © Anthony Jenkins for Fairchild Publications, Inc.

11.9   © Anthony Jenkins for Fairchild Publications, Inc.

Chapter 12

12.2   Courtesy of Fairchild Publications, Inc.

12.3a   Henry Clarke/*Vogue* © Condé Nast Publications, Inc.

12.3b   PRNewsFoto/Iconix

12.4a   and b Courtesy of Fairchild Publications, Inc.

12.6   Courtesy of Fairchild Publications, Inc.

12.7a   Courtesy of Bag, Borrow, or Steal

12.8   Courtesy of Metropark

Chapter 13

13.1a   © Tokyo Space Club/Corbis

13.1b   © David P. Hall/Corbis

13.1c   © Ableimages/Getty Images

13.2a   © Erin Fitzsimmons

13.2b   AP Photo/Paul Sakuma

13.5   © 2007 Paul Hattem

13.6   Vancefox.com

13.7   AP Photo/Sukree Sukplang

Chapter 14

14.1   Chris Warde-Jones/The New York Times/Redux

14.2a–f Courtesy of Fairchild Publications, Inc.

14.3   Cartoon copyrighted by Mark Parisi, printed with permission.

14.4   © Anthony Jenkins for Fairchild Publications

14.5   Kevin Mazur/WireImage

14.6a   and b Courtesy of Uniqlo

Chapter 15

15.1   Dennis MacDonald/PhotoEdit Inc.

15.2   Courtesy of Fairchild Publications, Inc.

15.4   © Royalty-Free/Corbis

15.5   Courtesy of Victoria's Secret

15.6   Courtesy of Fairchild Publications, Inc.

15.7   Courtesy of Fairchild Publications, Inc.

INDEX

Note: figures and tables indicated with *f* and *t*

AARP (American Association of Retired People), 165
Abercrombie & Fitch (retailer), 42, 314, 383, 425
    Ruehl and, 313, 361
    offensive T-shirts of, 388–89
absolute threshold, 63, 431
abundance, economics of, 34
Accenture Technology Laboratories, 67
acceptance, 194, 301
accessories, 96
    dogs as, 5–6
    See also handbags
acculturation, 354, 431
    See also under culture
achievement, 240, 356
    need for, 145–46
ACNielsen studies, 227, 252, 254
acquired (secondary) needs, 85–86
activation, of memories, 74, 431
activities, interests and opinions (AIOs), 239, 240*t*
actual self, 137, 431
adaptability, 36–37
adaptations, 302. *See also* knock–offs
Adjoined Consulting, 318
Adler, Alfred, 134
adolescents. *See* teenagers
advergames, 164, 179
advertising, 7, 107
    attitude formation and, 115
    consumer reception to, 291–92
    emotional appeals in, 109
    ethical, 387–89
    gender factor in, 228
    ideal self and, 138–38
    little lies in, 95–96
    repetition in, 106

    sex in, 125, 387–88
    subliminal, 64
    testing approaches to, 260
    truth in, 387, 421–22
Advertising Age (magazine), 12
advertising agencies, 254
advertising campaigns, 333–34
Aerie (retailer), 308
Aeropostale (retailer), 308
affective element, 105, 106, 431
affiliation, need for, 145, 440
African-American college students, 351
age groups, purchasing behavior and, 161–70
    baby boomers, 19–20, 163, 164–65, 226–27
    "buy words" appealing to, 169*t*
    college (18-34 market), 9–10, 165, 225–26, 262, 351
    career age (35-54 generation), 58–59, 169
    generation X, 226
    millennials, 263–64
    online life of, 180–81, 264
    seniors (55-plus generation), 163, 169–70, 220, 227–28
    See also children; teenagers
aggressiveness, 135
AIDS research, 339, 396
alcohol, teens and, 95, 388
alternative fuels, 274–75
alternative lifestyles, 231–32
alternative shopping, 237
alternative solutions, 278–81, 287–88
ambience, 313–14
  hospital, 337–38
  restaurant, 335–36
ambush marketing, 11, 431
a.n.a. (A New Approach) private brand, 91–92
Anderson, Chris, 34
Andrews, Kenneth, 41

animal cruelty, 126, 389, 390. *See also* fur products
animal testing, 390
Ann Taylor Stores, 42, 308, 316
anthropology, 356, 431
anxiety, coping with, 135
Apple computers, 17, 151
approach-approach, 87
approach-avoidance, 87
archetypes, 134, 431
Armani, Giorgio, 110, 300
aromatherapy, 60
Asch, Solomon, 189
Asian Americans, shopping habits of, 352
aspirational groups, 201, 431
Association for the Advancement of Psycho-analysis, 135
Association of National Advertisers, 36
associative groups, 201, 431
AT&T, 332–34
attention, 65, 66, 276, 431
attitude, consumer, 103–27, 431
    affective element of, 105, 106
    behavioral element of, 106–7
    belief and, 118–23, 126
    buying behavior and, 118–23
    changing, 104
    cognitive dissonance theory and, 124–25
    cognitive element of, 105
    elements of, 105–7
    emotions and, 105, 106, 109–10
    family influences in, 116
    friends and peers, 116
    functions of, 112–13, 437
    hierarchy of effects and, 107–12
    influences in forming, 113–16
    Likert scales and, 256, 257t
    marketers and, 116–18, 123–24, 126
    methods used to change, 125–26
    multi-attribute model and, 120–21, 126
    personality and, 113–14
    positive, 104, 118, 123
attitude objects, 104, 106, 431
attitude scales, 256, 257f, 431
audience
    engagement measurement tool, 291–92
    finding, 13
automobiles, 125

advertising, 147f, 228
    design, 37f, 38, 41
avant-garde, 195
    See also fashion innovators
avoidance-avoidance, 87
Avon (cosmetics firm), 230, 312
awareness, 6
c
baby boomers, 163, 164–65
    buying behavior of, 19–20, 226–27
baby fashions, 171–72
Badillo, Frank, 368
Bag Borrow or Steal, 311f, 312
Bailey, Ed, 335, 336
balance of trade, 361, 431
balance theory, 119–20, 431
bamboo, in fabrics, 378, 379, 394
Barneys New York (retailer), 313
Barrett, Michael, 167
basic (primary) needs, 85
Bath & Body Works (retailer), 310
BBB (Better Business Bureau), 426, 432
B2B (business-to-business), 333, 334
B2C (business-to-consumer), 333, 334
Bed, Bath & Beyond (retailer), 233, 308, 316, 317
Beecher, Harriet Ward, 49
behavioral element, 105, 106–7, 431
behavioral learning, 69–71, 72, 432
    classical conditioning, 67, 68, 125
    instrumental conditioning, 67, 68–69
behavioral perspective, 289, 432
belief, and attitude, 118–23, 126
belief, normative, 121, 122t, 441
belonging, sense of, 145, 356
Bergdorf Goodman (retailer), 309
Best Buy (retailer), 316, 317, 396–97
Better Business Bureau (BBB), 426, 432
biodiesel fuel, 274
biogenic needs, 85
biological drives, 133
birthrate, 432
    in U.S., 219–20, 227
Bishop, Judy, 275
Blackberry (device), 73f, 145, 215
blind taste tests, 22
blogosphere (blogs), 202, 267
Bloomingdale's (retailer), 306, 314, 388

Bluefly (e-tailer), 316
blue jeans. *See* jeans
Bluetooth technology, 105
Bono (U-2 lead singer), 338, 342, 392, 396
Boorstin, Daniel, 80
"boosting" (theft), 380
Boston Consulting Group, 171, 230
boycott, 386–87, 432
BP "A+ for Energy" program, 275
Brain Reserve, 139
brand, 22, 432
    attitudes toward, 123–24
    color and, 151–53
    communication of, 357
    conditioned response to, 69, 71
    equity, 22
    fashion, 123–24
    human, 123, 124
    loyalty to, 22, 33, 293
    luxury (*See* luxury brands)
    personality, 149–53
    private, 91–92
    in public eye, 263
    in selling homes, 71
    stimuli and, 58*f*
    symbols (icons) of, 73
brand ambassadors, 268
brand awareness, 334
brand drivers, 333, 432
brand equity, 22, 338, 432
brand image, 22, 432
branding
    defined, 7
    up-branding, 15–17
Brand Keys (consulting firm), 123
brand loyalty, 22, 34, 293
brand personification, 149, 432
brand strength, 16
Brannon, Ellen, 188
Brazil, 214, 367
breast cancer research, 39, 330–31, 396
brick-and-mortar stores, 306–8, 309
Brickman, Marisa, 262
Brooks Brothers (retailer), 233, 312, 364
Bruneau, Steve, 292
Brunvand, Jan Harold, 205
Bureau of Competition, U.S., 415
Bureau of Consumer Protection, U.S., 415

Bureau of Economic Analysis, U.S., 254, 362, 415
Bureau of Labor Statistics, U.S., 162, 254
business ethics, 384–92
    in advertising, 387–89
    consumer privacy and, 385–87
    in fur and animal testing, 389–90
    labor practices and, 390–92
    social responsibility and, 378–79
business strategy, 41
business-to-business (B2B) customers, 333, 334
business world, fashion and, 334–35
"butt brush" theory, 314
buyer requirements, 32–36
buyer's market, 29–30, 432
buyer's remorse, 89, 288, 432
buying behavior
    compulsive, 142, 433
    culture and, 17–18
    See also consumer behavior
buying decisions, 80
    information in, 195–96
    technology and, 290–91
    See also decision making
buy-it-as-you-see-it fashion show, 93
buzz, 10, 12, 141, 167, 268, 432
By Design (Caplan), 5

Cadbury Schweppes, 38–39
CAD (compliance, aggressiveness, detachment) scale, 135–36
Campbell-Ewald Co. (ad agency), 331
Canada, 236, 369
cancer research, 37, 330–31, 396
capitalism, conspicuous consumption and, 94–95
career-age women, 58–59
Care Labeling Rule, 419–20, 421*f,* 432
Carlin Group, 359*t*
Carson-Tahoe (Nevada) Hospital, 337
Cartier (jeweler), 4
    fragrance by, 93–94
Casual Male (retailer), 315
catalog sales, 310, 417
cat fur, in apparel, 387–88, 417
cause-related marketing, 50, 330–32, 432
    social responsibility and, 395–97

celebrities, 106, 123, 263*f*
    anti-fur message and, 389
    charities and, 338, 340–42, 378
    dogs as accessories for, 5–6
    endorsements by, 37, 38–40, 119–20, 124
    fragrance marketing and, 60–61, 120
    hype and, 11
    nonprofit organizations and, 339–41
    observation of, 258
    as opinion leaders, 144
cell phones, 45, 263
    design of, 35, 36*f*
    shopping by, 45, 92–93, 312
    teens and, 165–66, 264
    text messaging by, 262, 264
    as timepiece, 165–66
Census Bureau, U.S., 171, 216, 254, 362
Center for Food Safety and Applied Nutri-
        tion, 411
Chanel, 123, 151
Chanel, Coco, 302, 325
Chanel suit, 303*f*, 304
charitainment, 340–42, 432
charities, 338
    cause-related marketing and, 47–48,
        330–32, 395–97
    celebrities and, 338, 340–42, 378
cheap chic, 304–5, 307, 365, 366
Chicago, market research in, 239
Chico's (retailer), 227
children, 224, 423
    alternative fuels and, 275
    baby fashions, 171–72
    Club Libby Lu, 136–37, 316
    family attitudes and, 116
    family influence on, 170
    family purchases and, 261
    K.I.D.S. program for, 397
    marketing directed at, 164, 179, 207, 386
    memory and, 74
    safe products for, 405–6, 408, 410
    sleepwear for, 405, 407, 408
    UNICEF, 340, 341*f*, 342
    See also teenagers
Children's Online Privacy Protection Act, 423
China, 214, 367, 390, 418
    Mary Kay cosmetics in, 364
Chong, Peggy, 206

The Chronicle of Philanthropy Fund Raising
        (Martin), 343
chunking, of information, 72, 432
cities, population of U.S., 216, 218*t*
    See also under urban
Citizens Against Government Waste, 409
Claiborne, Liz, 204, 205–6, 308
claims, deceptive ads and, 422
Clark, Wendy, 333
classical conditioning, 69, 125, 433
classic style, 303*f*, 304, 432
closure principle, 68
Club Libby Lu, 136–37, 316
Coach Inc., 383
Coalition for Consumer Information, 390
cognition, need for, 143, 440
cognitive dissonance, theory of, 124–25
cognitive element, of attitude, 105, 433
cognitive learning, 67, 71–72, 433
cognitive psychology, 282
cognitive research, 143
cognitive selection, 433
Cohen, Ben, 341
Cohen, Joel, 135
Cohen, Marshal, 37, 150, 166, 258
Coldwater Creek (retailer), 227, 310
collective selection, 15
college (18-34) demographic, 351
    buzz and, 9–10
    product seeding in, 262
    spending patterns of, 225–26
college education, 232
color
    brand personality and, 151–53
    in diamonds, 80
    forecasting trends in, 59, 152–53, 359*t*
    matching, 315
    palette, 64, 334
    in restaurant decor, 334–35, 337
Color Association of the United States, 57,
        153, 359*t*
Color Box, 57, 153
Color Marketing Group, 153
Color Portfolio, 359*t*
color scheme, 334–35, 337
Combs, Sean Jean, 34, 114–15, 343, 418
communications, 7, 179, 262
    buzz, 9–10, 11, 141, 167, 268

elements of, 263
    nonverbal, 357
    word-of-mouth, 9–11, 13*f*, 141, 267–68
community involvement, 7
comparison shopping, 285–86
competence, 149, 150
competitive advantage, 7, 45, 49, 362, 433
compliance, 135, 189, 433
compliance, aggressiveness, detachment
    (CAD) scale, 135–36
compulsive buying behavior, 142, 433
computers, replacement of, 96
The Concept of Corporate Strategy
    (Andrews), 41
conditioning, of behavior, 69–70, 125
Conference Board, 223
conflict, choices and, 86–88, 433
conformity, 189, 194, 433
Congo, Democratic Republic of, 4
connectedness, 354
    See also belonging
Connections (software), 291–92
conscience, 133
conscious motive, 84, 433
consciousness, 133
consistency, 138
conspicuous consumption, 95, 191
consume, desire to, 91. *See also* motivation
consumer
    decision making by (*See* decision making)
    empowerment of, 45
    inconsistency of, 14–15
    measuring engagement of, 291–92
    motivation of (*See* motivation)
    privacy of, 383–84, 423
    problem solving by, 65–66, 108 (*See also*
        cognitive learning)
    socialization process of, 207
Consumer Action, 426
consumer angst, motivation and, 95–96
consumer behavior, 3–22, 433
    collective selection in, 14
    cultural influences on, 17–18
    defined, 4
    family life cycle and, 176–77
    forecasting, 17–18
    inconsistency of, 13–14
    innovation and, 23

marketing and, 6–22
    quantifying responses, 34
Consumer Behavior and Marketing Strategy
    (Peter & Olsen), 189
consumer confidence, 223, 433
consumer engagement, 291–92
consumer information, 251–68
    focus group, 134, 238–39, 259–60
    loyalty programs and, 383–84
    market and marketing research,
        252–53
    online shopping and, 251–52
    research process, 253–61
    surveys, 252, 256, 306, 307, 311*t*, 368
consumerism, 95, 235–36, 433
consumer needs, creation of, 94–95
    See also needs
consumer privacy, 383–84, 423
Consumer Product Safety Commission
    (CPSC), 406–10, 433
consumer reaction, 262. *See also* feedback;
    focus groups
consumer research, 178
    blind taste tests and, 22
    focus groups, 134, 238–39, 259–60
    forecasting and, 18–19
    psychographics, 238–41
    See also research process
"The Consumer's Rent *vs.* Buy Decision"
    (study), 281–85
consumer theft, 379–80
consumption, 5, 433
    conspicuous, 95, 191
    cultural values and, 354–56
    democratized, 80
    emerging trends in, 230–31
    global inequalities in, 236
    hedonic, 62, 437
    values driving, 234–38
consumption roles, 178, 181*t*, 433
Container Store, 46–47, 316
control, 202
convenience, 92
"cookies," in online shopping, 259, 386
copyright law, 302
Cornerstone Promotion (marketing firm),
    262
corporate citizenship, 383

Corporate Standard of Compassion for Animals, 390
cosmetics industry, 312, 364, 411
    labeling in, 413
    male market and, 228, 230
    See also specific company
cost, perceived, 29, 441
Costa, Victor, 302
Costco (retailer), 103, 104, 233, 300, 317
cost *vs.* value, 30–32
cotton fabrics, 405
    organic, 378, 394–95
Coty (cosmetics firm), 61
Council of Fashion Designers of America, Inc. (CFDA), 329
count, in research, 259, 434
counterfeit goods, 381–84, 434
    federal programs to combat, 381, 424
    handbags, 302, 377–78, 382, 383, 424*f*
    listing of top brands, 384*f*
country of origin, on label, 419
couture. *See* haute couture
CPSC. *See* Consumer Product Safety Commission
Crate & Barrel (retailer), 120, 121
creative director, 328–29
creativity, 133
credible sources, 202
credit cards, store, 251, 259, 386
cross-shopping, 317
cultural anthropology, 356–57, 434
cultural borrowing, 355, 434
cultural memories, 134
cultural values, consumption and 354-356
culture, 190, 434
    buying habits and, 17–18
    ethnocentrism and, 293
    multicultural, 354, 357
    subcultural groups, 190, 350–52, 353*f*
    See also Hispanic market
customer loyalty, 48. *See also* brand loyalty
customer relationship
    building and maintenance, 7
customer research, 33
    See also consumer research; research; surveys
customers, scanners and, 44

customer satisfaction, 9, 48–50, 82
customer service, 30, 306, 315, 316
    See also under consumer
customization, 32–35, 36, 92, 227, 434
Czech Republic, fur from, 390

Daily News Record (DNR), 254
Deceptive Policy Statement, 421
decision making, consumer, 89, 273–94
    alternative solutions, 278–81, 287–88
    "as is" and "should be" gap in, 277, 287
    buyer's remorse and, 89, 288
    effort expended in, 292–93
    evaluation in, 280–81, 286
    family and household, 176–81
    five basic steps in, 276–81, 285–89
    information collection in, 278, 285–86
    limited, 292, 439
    market habits and, 292–94
    options in, 275
    post-purchase evaluation in, 288–89
    problem awareness, 276–78
    rent or buy, in home video market, 281–85
    types of, 289–91
decline phase, 302–3, 434
decor, 313–14
    restaurant, 334–37
De Feo, Michael, 12
Del Vecchio, Claudio, 364
demand, 434
    stimulation of, 94–95
demographics, 43, 214–38
    age (*See* age groups, purchasing behavior of)
    birthrate and, 219–20, 227
    defined, 215, 434
    education and occupation, 232–33
    gender, 228–32
    global, 214–15
    immigration, 220, 222
    income, 223–28, 230, 232
    life expectancy, 220
    population growth and distribution, 216
    population shifts, 233
    PRIZM NE (geodemographics), 242, 243*t*
    psychographics and, 238–41

spending patterns by age group, 224–28
urban growth, in U.S., 216, 218t
U.S. population and, 214–23
VALS framework, 240–41
values driving consumption, 233–38
department stores, 229t, 306, 311t, 368, 369
depth interview, 134, 260, 434
DeSena, Bob, 291
design
    consumer attitude and, 110–11
    defined, 5, 434
    leveraging, 16
    motivation and, 97
    social influences on, 190
    as unifying force, 359–60
designers, 106
    creative director and, 328–29
    Target and, 104, 106, 110–11
design purchases, uniqueness of, 5–6
desire, 83, 434
Desperate Housewives (TV series), 38–40
detachment, 135
determinate attributes, 287
developing countries, markets in, 367
    See also specific country
diamonds, 4, 419
    color of, 80
    origins of, 392
Dictionary of Business Terms (Barrons), 286
differentiation, 143, 434
digital age, 263–64
    See also online shopping
digital product integration, 266
direction, 90, 434
direct (primary) influencers, 200, 434
direct sales, 312
disassociative groups, 201–2, 434
discount retailers, 104, 229t, 231, 307, 311t
    See also Costco; Target; Wal-Mart
discretionary income, 223, 228, 434
Disney Company, 40, 165, 172
displays, interactive, 266
display windows, 313, 343
disposable chic, 304. *See also* cheap chic
disposable income, 223, 434
dissonance, post-purchase, 89, 288, 442
distribution channels, limiting, 16–17
diversity, 434

marketing to, 352–53
Dog and Cat Protection Act (2002), 417
dog fur, in apparel, 389–90, 417–18
dogs, as fashion accessories, 5–6
domestic mind-set, 364
Donegar Associates, 359t
Do Not Call Registry, 423
dopamine, 81
Dove, self-image issues and, 50, 139–38, 387
down guides for manufacturers, 418–19
downward flow (trickle-down theory), 191,
    434
Dressbarn (retailer), 396
Drolet, Mary, 136, 137
Drucker, Peter, 30, 48
duties, 361, 435

Eastern Europe, fur goods from, 390
EcoCenter for Alternative Fuel Education,
    275
ecological sustainability, 237
    See also environmental concerns
e-commerce, 386. *See also* online shopping
economic conditions, regional, 224–25
economic risk, consumer confidence and,
    223
economic theory, 34
economists, trade deficit and, 363
e-customization, 31
education, occupation and, 227
effects, hierarchy of, 107–12
e-gatekeepers, 202
ego, 133, 134, 138
    defined, 132, 435
ego-defensive function, 112–13, 114f
E.L.B. Enterprises Management, 335, 336
Eliashberg, Jehoshua, 281–85
Elizabeth Arden (cosmetics firm), 61, 151
e-mail, 179, 251, 264, 266
emotions, 125, 197, 313
    attitude and, 105, 106, 109–10
    motivation and, 88–90
employees. *See* people (employees)
empowerment, consumer, 45
empty-nest stage, of families, 173t, 176
encoding
    counterfeiting and, 382
    memory and, 73–74, 435

enculturation, 354, 435
       See also under culture
Endangered Species Act (1993), 417
energy conservation, 275, 393–94
England, 364
       Tesco in, 365–66
       See also United Kingdom
enhancements, to products, 96
environmental concerns, 79, 341, 393–95
       energy conservation, 275, 393–94
       green label, 17, 35, 422
       materialism and, 237
Environmental Guides, 422
Equal Employment Opportunity (EEO)
       laws, 425, 435
An Essay on Liberation (Marcuse), 94
EstÈe Lauder, 61, 69
e-tailing (e-commerce), 252
       "cookies" tracked in, 259, 384
       See also online shopping
ethics, 49, 50, 377–97
       in advertising, 387–89
       business ethics, 384–92
       consumer privacy and, 385–87
       counterfeit goods and, 377–78, 381–84
       defining, 378, 435
       fur and animal testing, 389–90
       in labor practices, 390–92
       social responsibility and, 378–79,
              392–97
       See also value system
ethnocentrism, 293, 435
Europe, 236, 361, 365, 369, 390
       See also specific country
evaluation, 122
       in decision making, 280–81, 286, 288–89
Evans, Karl, 274
excitement, 150
expected utility, 282
experience and information, 115
experience retailers, 136–37
experiential hierarchy, 108t, 110, 111–12,
              435
experiential perspective, 289, 435
experimental retailing, 92
exports, 361, 362, 363, 435
exposure, 435
       selective, 57, 66

express claims, 422, 435
extended family, 172, 435
extended self, 138, 435
       See also under self
extensive decision making, 292, 435
external recognition, 278, 435
external/social factors, 86
extroverts, 141, 435
e-zines, 266

fabric
       bamboo, 378, 379, 395
       content and care of, 67
       cotton, 378, 394–95, 405
       flammability of, 407–9, 410
       hand (feel) of, 57–58
       Spandex in, 105, 416
       wool, 416–17
Facebook, 13–14
fad, 304, 435
Fair Credit Reporting Act, 423
Fair Factories Clearinghouse, 391
Fair Packaging and Labeling Act, 413–14, 436
fair-trade practices, 392, 436
fake fur, 88, 390
fake goods. *See* counterfeit goods
false advertising, 385
false need, 94–95, 436
family
       attitudes and, 115–16
       changing needs of modern, 172
       consumer behavior and, 170–73
       decision making in, 177–81
       defined, 172, 436
       life cycle, 166f, 174–81
       nontraditional, 174, 441
       nuclear, 172, 441
       as organization, 326
       primary functions of, 174
       spending patterns in, 224, 261
family life cycle, 166f, 174–81
       consumer behavior approach, 176–77
       defined and redefined, 174, 436
       traditional, 174t, 176, 445
       twenty-first century, 175t
fashion
       baby boomers and, 18, 227
       business world and, 334–35

defined, 5, 37, 436
ideal self-image and, 138
marketing and, 35, 38
social influences on, 190
as unifying force, 359–60
fashion accessories. *See* accessories
fashion brands, 123–24
fashion communication, elements of, 263
fashion companies, nonprofits and, 342–43
fashion consumers, 299–319
changing shopping trends and, 317–18
as fashion followers, 126, 300–301
fashion life cycle and, 301–4
fast fashion and, 304–5, 307
multi-channel retailing and, 310, 317–18
retail marketing and, 305–18
shopping environments and, 312–16
fashion consumption, changes in, 300
Fashion Delivers (nonprofit), 343
fashion diffusion, 191–96, 436
theories of, 191–94
fashion followers, 126, 300–301, 436
Fashion Footwear Association of New York, 40
Fashion Forecasting (Brannon), 188
fashion influentials, 143–44, 436
fashion innovators (fashion leaders), 126, 143, 144, 300, 436
fashion life cycle, 301–4, 436
length of, 303–4
phases of, 301–3
fashion magazines, 264–65
fashion marketers, demographics and, 233
See also marketers
fashion purchases, uniqueness of, 5–6
fashion show, 263, 266
buy-it-as-you-see-it, 93
fashion solutions, 35
fast fashion (cheap chic), 304–5, 307, 363, 364, 436
FBI (Federal Bureau of Investigation), 380, 424
federal agencies, 406. *See also specific* agencies; bureaus
Federal Citizen Information Center, 426
Federal Food, Drug and Cosmetic Act (1958), 411, 414, 436
federal government, research by, 254, 255f

See also government
Federal Trade Commission (FTC), 415–23, 436
care labeling rule and, 419–20, 421f
price fixing and, 422–23
textile products labeling, 415–18
truth in advertising law and, 387, 421–22
feedback, 167, 293
customer satisfaction and, 9, 48
fiber content, on label, 416
55-plus generation (seniors), 163, 169–70, 220, 227–28
figure-and-ground concept, 68, 69f
Flammable Fabrics Act (1973), 407–9, 436
Fluevog, John, 235
foaf (friend of a friend), 205
focus group, 134, 238–39, 259–60, 436
folklore. *See* urban legends
Food and Drug Administration (FDA), 411–14, 436
Ford, Tom, fragrance line of, 61
Ford Motor Co., 41, 73, 275
forecasting, 18–19, 437
color trends, 57, 152–53, 359t
services for, 357, 358–59t
for-profit organization, 50, 327, 341, 437
Forrester Research, 180–81, 308
Forth & Towne (retailer), 19–20
fragrance, 60–61, 120
personalized, 92, 93–94
France, 214, 215, 368, 369
Franklin, Ben, quote from, 80
fraudulent returns, 380–81
frequent-shopper cards, 259, 351, 386
Freud, Sigmund, 132, 134
Friedman, Milton, 363
friend of a friend (foaf), 205
friends and peers, influence of, 116, 129
See also peer group
FTC. *See* Federal Trade Commission
functional foods, 79
functions of attitude, 112–13, 437
fur products,
animal testing and, 389–90
dog and cat, 389–90, 417–18
fake fur and, 88, 390
mislabeling of, 418

furniture, flammability of, 409
Fur Products Labeling Act, 417, 437

Gap, Inc., 19–20, 316
Garcia, Guy, 357
Garfield, Bob, 12
gatekeeper, 178, 181*t*, 202, 203*f*, 437
Gaultier, Jean Paul, 355
gay, lesbian, bisexual and transgender
        (GLBT) market, 231–32
gender, 228–32
    income equality, 230
    shopping habits and, 306–7
    See also men; women
General Electric (GE), 17, 69, 341
generation Xers (1985-2000), 226
geodemographic system, 242, 243*t*, 437
geographic region, 352, 353*f*
    income distribution by (U.S.), 224, 226*f*
Germany, 214, 215, 368, 369
Gernreich, Rudy, 14
Gersh, Bruce, 38
gestalt psychology, 67–68, 289, 437
Getches, Catherine, 32
Giannini, Frida, 342
Gibson, Monica, 392
Gier, Randy, 39
Gifford, Kathie Lee, 391
gift card fraud, 381
GLBT. *See* gay, lesbian, bisexual and trans-
        gender
Glimcher, Paul, 81
global consumer, understanding and accom-
        modating, 367–69
global inequality, 236
globalization, 360, 362–61, 363, 437
global marketing, 7
Global Market Insite (GMI) Inc., 368
global population, 214–15
Global Softgoods Shopper Update, 367–68
global trends, 360
goal, 82, 437
golf, 120, 233, 267
Gould, Michael, 383
government, 405–25
    anti-counterfeiting programs, 381, 424
    Consumer Product Safety Commission,
        406–10

Federal Trade Commission, 385, 415–23
Food and Drug Administration, 411–14
    labeling regulations, 413–19
    research by, 254, 255*f*
    safe products for children and, 405–6,
        408, 410
    state governments and, 425
    See also under Bureau
Government Accountability Office, U.S., 391
GPShopper, 312
graffiti and marketing, 11–12
gratification, 133
Graves, Michael, 106, 111
Gray, Taylor, 12
Greenburg, Hope, 258
green label, 17
green products, 34, 422
    See also environmental concerns
grooming products, for men, 228, 230, 353
group, 199–201, 437
Group M (ad agency), 291–92
Grupo Axo (Mexican firm), 364
Gucci, 240, 342
guerrilla marketing, 10, 11–12, 437
Guess (retailer), 364–65
guided consumer discussion. *See* focus group
Gutman, Jonathan, 356

Haag Muller, Inc., 336–37
habitual (routine) decision making, 292, 437
Hamilton, Carol J., 38, 40, 353
Hamnett, Katherine, 397
handbags, 37, 258, 311*f*, 312
    counterfeit, 302, 377–78, 382, 383, 424*f*
hand (feel), of textiles, 59–60
Handschiegel, Patricia, 360
Harley Owners' Group, 232
Haskelson, Mark, 192
haute couture, 4
    perfumes and, 60–61
health hazards, 410, 414
    See also Food and Drug Administration
hearing, sense of, 61–62
hedonic consumption, 62, 437
Heifer International (anti-poverty group),
        330
Henager, Kelsey, 10
heuristics, 286, 292–93, 437

hierarchy, low-involvement, 108–10
hierarchy, organizational, 328, 441
hierarchy of effects, 107–12, 437
hierarchy of needs, 84, 85, 194
high-involvement hierarchy, 107–8, 111–12, 437
Hilfiger, Tommy, 204, 206, 391, 418, 420
Hirsch, Alan, 149
Hispanic market, 222–23, 223*f*, 254, 351
H&M (retailer), 13, 120, 231, 362
    fast fashion and, 304
Hoff, Max Kale, 167
Hollister (retailer), 313, 361
Home Depot (retailer), 164–65, 314
home-related products, 216, 217*f*
home video market, decision making in, 281–85
horizontal flow (trickle-across theory), 192, 437
Horney, Karen, 135
Horsting, Viktor, 148, 231
hospitals, ambience in, 337–38
households, 173, 437
    consumption roles in, 178, 181*t*
    decision making in, 176–81
    evolution of, 172–73
    mass affluent, 162–63
    roles in, 177
Housing Works (nonprofit), 343
Huff, Lois, 317
human behavior, understanding, 80–82
    See also consumer behavior
human brands, 123, 124
human element, in consuming, 237
Humane Society, 390, 418
Hurricane Katrina, 224, 338, 343, 396–97
hype, as marketing tool, 11, 437

IBM survey, 313
Icky Baby (clothing retailer), 172
ideals and principals, 240
    See also values
ideal self, 137, 438
ideal social self-image, 137–38, 438
identification, manufacturer, 419
identity, fashion and, 227
identity (ID) tags, radio frequency, 45, 386–87

identity theft, 385
id (libido), 132–33, 134, 438
I Heard It Through the Grapevine (Turner), 204–5
IKEA (retailer), 103, 104, 105, 120–21, 362, 395
image promotion, 22, 111
    See also self-image
IMG Worldwide Inc., 266
Imitation of Christ (clothing line), 92
immigration, 219, 220, 222, 438
implied claims, 422, 438
imports, 361, 362, 363, 438
impulse buying, 81, 289
IMS. *See* integrated marketing system
incentive, 91, 438
income, 438
    discretionary, 223, 228, 434
    disposable, 223, 434
    distribution of, 223–24, 225*t*
        gender and, 228–30
        per capita personal, 224, 226*f*, 441
        spending patterns of age groups, 224–28
        in U.S., 223–32, 233
independence, 135
India, 214, 363–64, 367
indirect (secondary) influencers, 200, 438
individual, social responsibility of, 378–79
individualism, 355, 356
individuality, 70
Indonesia, 214
industry intuition, 283
inertia habit, 293, 438
"The Influence of Mere Social Presence in a Retail Context" (study), 196–98
influencer, 178, 181*t*
informational influences, 200, 438
informational social influences, 195–96, 438
information gatherers, 178, 181*t*
information overload, 74, 438
information pollution, 190
innovation, 23, 111, 438
    design and, 97
    and opinion leadership, 143–44
instinct, 83, 438
institutional look, 337
in-store marketing, 266
instrumental conditioning, 69–70, 438

integrated marketing system (IMS), 8–9, 22, 438
intensity, 90, 438
intent to buy, 121, 122t
interactive displays, 266
interactive name brand world, 164
interactive social influence, 197–96
internal/nonsocial factors, 86
internal recognition, 277–78, 438
International Color Authority, 153
International Down and Feather Testing
        Laboratory and Institute, 419
Internet, 190, 196, 266–67
    fashion shows on, 266
    gatekeeping on, 202
    millennials and, 263–64
    rentals on, 312
    retailing on, 308–9
    rumors on, 202, 204
    shopping on, 227, 311t, 386
    See also online shopping; Web sites
interpretant, symbol, 148
interview, depth, 134, 260
introduction phase (fashion cycle), 301, 439
introverts, 141, 439
inventory shrinkage, 379–81, 439
Isla, Pablo, 365

Japan, 214, 368, 369
    cell phone shopping in, 92–93
    group interests in, 355–56
    high incomes in, 215, 236
    Uniqlo (retailer), 366
JCPenney, 91–92, 92f, 306, 388, 418
jeans, 39
    counterfeit, 383
    marketing of, 21, 37, 262
    organic cotton, 394
Jeffries, Mike, 361
Jermyn, Leslie, 237
jewelry, guide for advertising, 419
    See also diamonds; Tiffany
Jimmy'Z (retailer), 308
John Deere (manufacturer), 71
Jolie, Angelina, 341
Jones Apparel (retailer), 420
Jones New York (retailer), 308
Jones Soda (beverage company), 235

Journal of Consumer Research, 196
Judd, Ashley, 339
Juicy Couture, 263
Julian, Alexander, 151
Jung, Carl, 134
just noticeable difference (j.n.d.), 63, 439
Juvenile Products Manufacturers Association, 409

Kaiser Family Foundation, 164
Kavovit, Barbara, 173
Kelley, Jon, 336
Kids in Distressed Situations (K.I.D.S.), 397
Klein, Calvin, 61, 390
knock-offs, 302, 439
    See also counterfeit goods
knowledge, desire for, 142–43
knowledge function, of attitude, 113, 114f
Knox, George, 281–83, 284
Kohler (manufacturer), 69
Kohl's (retailer), 306, 366
Krugman, Paul, 363

labeling regulations, 413–19
    care, 419–20, 421f
    for children's sleepwear, 405, 408f
    for cosmetics, 414
    country of origin, 419
    for down, leather and jewelry, 418–19
    manufacturer ID, 419
    for textile products, 415–18
labor practices, 390–92
LaCroix, Christian, 57
Lagerfeld, Karl, 231, 302
Lampel, Joseph, 30
Land's End (retailer), 119, 392
Lane Bryant (retailer), 308f, 316
Lanham Act (Trademark Act, 1966), 424
Lauren, Ralph, 60, 123, 138, 308
    fragrance line of, 61
    Polo, 55–57, 118, 336, 390
    tailored suits of, 355f, 356
Laurent, Mathilde, 94
La-Z-Boy Furniture Galleries, 315
learning, 68–72, 439
    behavioral, 69–71, 72
    cognitive, 69, 71–72, 433
    in selling homes, 71
    theories of, 68t

leather goods, 79
  labeling of, 419
Le Book, 359*t*
leisure class, 191
Levi-Strauss, 39, 151, 262, 394
  See also jeans
Lewis, Mike, 274, 275
libido. *See* id (libido)
life cycles. *See* family life cycle; fashion life
  cycle; product, life cycle
life expectancy, 219, 439
lifestyle, 352–53, 439
lifestyle research, 238, 239–41, 353
  VALS framework, 240–41
Likert scale, 256, 257*f*, 439
limited decision making, 292, 439
line-for-line copies, 302
Linley, David and Serena, 144
little lies, in advertising, 95–96
L.L. Bean (retailer), 118
Logo (cable TV) channel, 231
"The Long Tail" (Anderson), 34
long-term memory, 73–74, 439
Lopez, Jennifer, 120
L'Oreal Paris, 38, 40, 353
Louis, Tristan, 202
Louis Vuitton fakes, 382, 383, 384*f*, 424*f*
low-involvement hierarchy, 108–10, 439
loyalty, brand, 22, 33, 293
loyalty, of younger shoppers, 181
loyalty programs, 385–86, 439
luxury brands, 37, 134, 231, 234, 309, 338
  baby boomers and, 227
  counterfeiting of, 380, 381, 424*f*
  rental of, 311*f*, 312
  up-branding and, 15–17
  See also specific brand
LVMH Moet Hennessy Louis Vuitton, 382,
  383
Lycra Spandex, 105, 416

MacKenzie, Jack, 264
Macy's (retailer), 30, 233, 302, 306, 342,
  388
Madison, Eliza, 167
magalogs, 264–65, 439
Magnuson-Moss Act (1995), 415
Mail or Telephone Order Merchandise Rule, 423

mandatory standards, 407–8, 439
manicure industry, 414
manufacturers
  focus group and, 239
  identification of, 419
  suggested retail price, 423
  sweatshops, 390–91
mapping, perceptual, 117, 442
Marcuse, Herbert, 94
marketers
  attitudes and, 116–18, 123–24, 126
  brand personality and, 150–51
  cultural influences and, 356
  demographics and, 232–33
  message to consumers and, 262
  psychographics and, 238
marketers, motivation and, 87–88, 89–90, 97
  false needs and, 94–95
  See also motivation
market forces, 332, 439
marketing, 6–22
  ambush, 11, 431
  buzz, 10, 12, 141, 167, 268, 432
  cause-based, 50, 330–32, 395–97, 432
  child-directed, 162, 179, 207, 386
  coordinating efforts in, 8–9
  cultural anthropology and, 357
  customization and, 32–35
  defined, 440
  fashion and, 35, 38
  global, 7. *See also* globalization
  guerrilla, 10, 11–12, 437
  in-store, 266
  mass, 13, 440
  as problem solving, 19–20
  purchases influenced by, 6–7
  recent approaches to, 9–22
  target, 40–41
  tools, 42
  viral, 11
  word-of-mouth, 9–11, 13*f*, 141, 267–68
marketing components, 6–7, 8*t*
marketing concept, 48, 440
  societal, 49, 341, 444
marketing mix, 44*f*
marketing plan, 6, 36, 37*f*
marketing research, 252–53, 440
marketing strategy, 41

marketplace conditions, 29–30
market research, 48, 252–53, 439
    See also consumer research
market research firms, 254, 255*f*
market segment, 202, 439
    product placement and, 207
    urban uptowners, 242, 243*t*
    by ZIP code, 242, 243*t*
market segmentation, 13, 42–43, 116, 439
    categories, 43*t*
    by education and occupation, 232–33
    "funnel" approach to, 42
    See also age groups; demographics
Marshall Field's (retailer), 30
Martin+Osa (specialty store), 118, 308
Mary Kay cosmetics, 364
Maslow's hierarchy of needs, 84, 85, 194
mass affluent, ascent of, 162–63
mass marketing, 13, 440
materialism, 235, 236–37, 440
maternity wear, 164, 219
McCarthy, E. Jerome, 45
McCartney, Stella, 12–13, 14, 231
McClelland, David, 84–85
McDonald's restaurants, decor in, 334–37
McNeil, Patrick, 12
means-end-chain (MEC), 356, 440
media
    access to information and, 179
    fashion communication and, 263
    measuring response to, 291–92
    new, 266–67 (*See also* Internet)
    short attention span of, 338
    traditional, 264–66
    See also television; *specific media*
media planning, 7
membership influences, 201–2
memory, 72–74, 440
    cultural, 134
    long-term, 73–74, 439
    retrieval and activation of, 74
men
    gay market, 231–32
    grooming products for, 228, 230, 353
    metrosexuals, 353–54
    shopping habits of, 306–7
    spa services for, 229–30
    See also gender

"me too" products, 117
Metropark (retailer), 300, 314
metrosexuals, 353–54
Mexico, 4, 364, 367
Microsoft, 10
middle class, 214
millennials, 263–64
Mizrahi, Isaac, 111, 123, 126, 307
moral values. *See* ethics; values
motivate, 82, 440
motivation, 77–96, 240, 440
    complexity in, 86–87
    conflict and, 86–88
    conscious *vs.* unconscious, 84
    consumer angst and, 95–96
    design and, 97
    desire to acquire and, 91
    emotion used in, 88–90
    fashion consumer and, 77–96
    human behavior and, 81
    marketers and, 87–88, 89–90, 94–95, 97
    needs *vs.* wants, 82–83, 86
    need theories, 84–86
    power of, 90–91
    rational *vs.* emotional, 88–89
    reward approach, 289
motivational research, 134, 240–41, 440
motives, 440
Motorola cell phone, 37*f*, 38
Mullin, Tracy, 395–96
multi-attribute model, 120–21, 126, 440
multi-channel retailing, 310, 317–18, 440
multicultural, 354, 440
multicultural marketplace, 357
multiple selves, 136, 440
Murray, Henry A., 84
MySpace.com, 166–67
My Style Diary online, 360

*Naked Consumption: Retail Trends
    Uncovered* (Stokan), 315
Napoleon, quote from, 325
Narita, Kuniko, 93
National Asian Pacific American Women's
    Forum, 414
National Association of State Fire Marshalls,
    409
National Center for Health Statistics, 171

National Consumers League, 426, 440
National Retail Federation, 3, 380, 391, 395
natural fibers, 405
  See also bamboo; cotton
needs, 82–86
  for achievement, 145–46, 440
  advertising creating, 387
  for affiliation, 145, 440
  for cognition (NC), 143, 440
  conflicting, 85*t*
  false, 94–95
  Maslow's hierarchy of, 84, 85, 194
  for power, 146, 147*f*, 441
  primary, 85
  theories of, 84–86
  vs. wants, 82–83, 86, 176
need satisfaction, 82, 441
negative factors, in motivation, 86
negative stimulus (punishment), 69
negativism, 141–42
Neiman Marcus (retailer), 227, 230, 302,
    306, 317
  handbags, 309
  window displays, 342–43
neuroeconomics, 81, 289
neurosis, 142, 441
"The New Gatekeepers" (Louis), 202
*The New Mainstream: How the Buying
    Habits of Ethnic Groups Are Creat-
    ing a New American Identity*
    (Garcia), 357, 359
New York Times, 266, 363
Nickelodeon/Youth Intelligence Tween
    Report, 261
Nielsen, Arthur C., 252
Nielsen studies, 227, 252, 254
Nilsson, Mats, 395
Nitowski, Matt, 171
non-business entity, 329, 441
nonprofit organizations, 107, 329–32, 391,
    441
  cause-related marketing and, 47–48,
    330–32
  celebrities and, 339–41
  fashion and, 337–38
  fashion companies and, 342–43
  for-profit companies and, 50, 327, 341
  hospitals, 337–38

sweatshops and, 389
nontraditional family, 174, 441
nonverbal communication, 357
Nordstrom (retailer), 125, 227, 309, 418
  customer service by, 30, 306
  fair trade and, 392
  recycling by, 393
normative beliefs, 121, 122*t*, 441
normative social influence, 194–95, 441
norms, subjective, 122*t*, 444
Norm Thompson (catalog retailer), 310
nostalgia, 89–90
NPD Group (research firm), 151, 165, 166,
    306
  on accessories market, 258
NPD Group (research firm) *(con't.)*
  on back-to-school spending, 256
  on branding, 150
  on luxury market, 37
NRF Foundation, 315
nuclear family, 172, 441

obedience, 189, 441
object, semiotics and, 148
objectionable ads, 387–89
objectives, in research, 253–54, 260, 441
O'Brian, Thomas, 110–11
observational research, 258–59
obsolescence (rejection) phase, 303, 441
occupation, demographics and, 232–33
older people, memory and, 74
  See also seniors
Olsen, Jerry C., 189
Olson twins, 143*f*, 144
online life, 264, 360
online shopping, 235, 308–10, 369
  cell phones used for, 45, 92–93, 312
  comparison shopping, 251–52, 286
  "cookies" to facilitate, 259, 386
  customer service in, 315, 316
  fiber content information in, 417
  by seniors, 227–28
  by young people, 180–81
online surveys, 368
opinion leader, 143–44, 206–7, 441
optimal stimulation level (OSL), 144–45, 441
organic fabrics, 378, 392, 394–95
organizational hierarchy, 328, 441

organizations, 325–43, 441
    business world and fashion, 334–35
    cause-related marketing, 47–48, 330–32
    family as, 326
    fashion combinations with, 334–43
    for-profit, 50, 327, 341, 437
    market forces and, 332–34
    non-business *vs.* profit organizations, 328
    nonprofit, 47–48, 107, 327, 334, 337–41,
        372–32, 389
    outside forces and, 332–33
    types of, 327
organized retail theft (ORT), 380, 441
OSL. *See* optimal stimulation level
outlet stores, 311–12

Pantone Inc., 358
Patent and Trademark Office, U.S., 424
Paulsen, Lisa, 40
Pavlov, Ivan, 69, 125
peak phase, fashion cycle, 302, 441
Peclers Paris, 358
peer group, 116, 192, 206, 301, 313
people (employees), 45, 46, 335
    salespeople, 61–62
People for the Ethical Treatment of Animals
      (PETA), 126, 389, 390
per capita personal income, 224, 226*f*, 441
perceived cost, 31, 441
perceived risk, 279, 442
perception, 45, 62, 442
    organizational elements, 66–67
    selective, 66, 443
    subliminal, 64, 444
perceptual mapping, 117, 442
perfumes, 60–61
    personalized, 92, 93–94
personal care products, 390, 412
    See also cosmetics; grooming products
personal characteristics, 66
personal income, per capita, 224
personality, 131–54
    attitude and, 113–14
    brand, 149–53
    color and, 151–53
    defined, 132, 442
    effect of, on fashion consumer, 132
    ice cream flavors and, 149*t*

    major theories of, 132–47
    of products, 147–53
    psychoanalytic theory of, 132–34, 138
    psychographics and, 238–41
    self-concept theory of, 136–41
    semiotics and, 147–48
    socio-cultural theories of, 134–36
    trait theories, 141–47
personalized products, 32–35
    fragrance, 92, 93–94
personalized service, 315
persuasion, techniques of, 107
PETA. *See* People for the Ethical Treatment
      of Animals
Petersen, Richard L., 289
Peterson, Tom, 330
Pew Internet and American Life Project, 264
Phat Farm (clothing company), 192
philanthropy, 48, 383
PhotoStamps, 32–33
Pier One (retailer), 120, 121, 332
pilferage, 379
Pininfarina (design firm), 37*f*, 38
place, 45, 46
planning, 36
pleasure, need satisfaction and, 82
plus-size customers, 308*f*, 316
point-of-purchase materials, 109
Polo. *See* Ralph Lauren Polo
Popcorn, Faith, 139
population. *See* demographics, population
    and
pop-up store, 91, 92*f*
Porter, Michael, 41, 332
positioning, 20–21, 44–45, 442
    intensity and, 90
    repositioning, 333
Positioning: The Battle for Your Mind (Ries
    and Trout), 21, 44–45
positive attitude, 104, 118, 123
    See also attitude
positive factors, in motivation, 86
post-purchase dissonance, 89, 287, 442
Potential Rating Index. *See* PRIZM NE
power, need for, 146, 147*f*, 441
premium products, 15–17
    See also luxury brands
price, 45, 46, 381, 423

sales lost to theft and, 380

price discrimination, 284

price fixing, 422–23

pricing strategies, 7

primary data, 35

primary (direct) influences, 200

primary functions, of family, 174

primary needs, 85

primary research, 254, 255

print advertising, 109

privacy, protecting consumer's, 385–87, 423

private brand, 91–92

PRIZM NE (Potential Rating Index by ZIP Code–New Evolution), 242, 243*t*, 442

problem awareness, 276–78, 442

problem solving, 20, 65–66, 108
    See also cognitive learning

process/procedures, 45, 46

Procter & Gamble, 165

product
    life cycle, 339, 442
    personalization, 30–33, 92, 93–94
    requiring accessory products, 96
    seeding of, 262

product, place, promotion, price (4Ps), 45, 46

product development, 7

product differentiation, 21, 442

product evaluation, 260

product labels. *See* labeling regulations

product mix, 316

product placement, 179, 207, 265–66

products, personalities of, 147–53
    brand and, 149–53
    color and, 151–53

product seeding, 262

professional selling, 7

profit motive, 328, 442

programming, social, 194

Promostyl, 358

promotion, 45, 46

Pryor, Mike, 275

psychoanalytic theory, 132–34, 138, 442

psychogenic needs, 85

psychographics, 192, 238–41
    defined, 238, 442
    focus groups and, 238–39

VALS, 240–41

psychology, 7, 81, 442
    cognitive, 282
    gestalt, 67–68, 289, 437

psycho-social approach, 176

public relations, 7

Puff Daddy. *See* Combs, Sean Jean

purchasers, 178–79, 181*t*
    age of. *See* age, purchasing behavior and

purchasing decisions
    in households, 176–81
    post-purchase evaluation, 89

purchasing power, 224, 442

pyramid model, of leadership, 328*f*

qualitative research, 239, 256, 259, 260–61, 333, 442

quality, 30, 58

quantative research, 239, 255–56, 260–61, 333, 443

quantifying, 36, 442

questionnaires, 256. *See also* surveys

quota, 361, 443

radio frequency ID, 47, 386–87

Ralph Lauren Polo, 55–57, 118, 336, 390

rational motives, 88–89, 313

rational perspective, 289, 443

reality principle, 133

reasoned action, theory of, 121–23

reason to buy, 91. *See also* incentive

recall, 410, 443

recognition, of problems. *See* problem awareness

Recreational Equipment Inc. (REI), 393

Red Cross, 329, 340

reference groups, 170, 199, 201, 443
    examples of, 200*t*

regional consumption behaviors, 352

regional economic conditions, 224–25

rejection phase (fashion cycle), 303

Reliability Reports (Better Business Bureau), 426

"rent or buy" decision, 281–85

repair/reuse, 237

repetition
    attitude change and, 125
    used in ads, 106

repositioning, 333, 443
research process, 253–61
    analyzing and reporting data, 261
    cognitive research, 143
    focus groups, 239, 259–60
    methodologies, 255–57
    objectives in, 253–54, 260
    observation in, 258–59
    primary research, 35, 254, 255
    qualitative and quantitative, 239,
            255–56, 259, 260–61, 333
    secondary research, 35, 36, 254–55
    types of research, 253–54
    See also consumer information; surveys
resources, in VALS framework, 241
    See also education; income
response, to stimulus, 276, 443
Retail Forward (consultants), 317, 367–68
retailing/retailers, 305–18
    brick-and-mortar stores, 306–8, 309
    catalog sales, 310
    department stores, 229*t*, 306, 311*t*, 368,
        369
    discount, 104, 229*t,* 231, 307, 311*t*
    environmental concerns of, 391–93
    experience, 136–37
    experimental, 92
    fashion, 305–18
    influence of social presence in, 198–96
    in-store marketing, 266
    loyalty programs of, 385–86
    modest income market, 233
    multi-channel, 310, 317–18
    online (*See* online shopping)
    philanthropy of, 383
    physical surroundings, 313–14
    pop-up store, 91, 92*f*
    shoplifting and, 379–80
    specialty stores, 229*t,* 307–8, 311*t*, 368
    store credit cards, 251, 259, 386
    store design and layout, 313–14
    teen market, 224–25
    WWD customer survey and, 306, 307, 311*t*
retrieval, of memories, 74, 443
Return Exchange (conpany), 381
reward card. *See* frequent-shopper cards
rewards, conditioning and, 69–71
Ries, Al, 21, 44–45

rise phase, in fashion cycle, 301–2, 443
risk
    consumer confidence and, 223
    perceived, 279, 442
Roberts, Sam, 215
role
    defined, 177, 443
    in household, 177–78
routine decision making, 292
Rowden, Ian, 167
Rudner, Rita, 306
Ruehl (retailer), 313, 361
ruggedness, 150
rules of thumb (heuristics), 286, 292–93
rumors, on Internet, 202, 204

safety issues,
    in childrens' products, 405–6, 408, 410
    in cosmetics, 411, 413
    See also Consumer Product Safety
        Commission; Food and Drug
        Administration
Saks Fifth Avenue (retailer), 227, 302, 306,
    392
    Web site, 309
salesperson, enthusiasm of, 61–62
    See also selling, professional
sales promotion, 8
Sam's Club, 4, 231, 314, 383
sapeurs, in Paris, 4
satisfaction. *See* customer satisfaction
SBC Communications, 332
scanners, 46–47, 65–66
schema, 68
Schor, Juliet B., 192
Schultz, Howard, 83
Schweitzer, Albert, 49
Sean Jean line, 114–15, 343, 418
Sears (retailer), 119, 136, 306
secondary data, 35, 255*f,* 443
secondary (indirect) influencers, 200
secondary needs, 85–86
secondary research, 254–55, 443
security
    consumer theft and, 380
    family and, 174
segment. *See* market segment
segmentation. *See* market segmentation

Sehgal, Vikram, 181
selective perception, 66, 443
self, extended, 138
self-concept theory, 136–41, 443
    extended self, 138
self-esteem, 138–38, 443
self-expression, 240
self-image, 443
    as actual self, 137
    ideal social, 137–38
    social, 137
    women and, 50, 139–38, 387
self-sufficiency, 135
self-worth, 135, 138–39
seller's market, 30, 443
selling, professional, 7
selling advantage, 35f
selling concept, 48, 443
semantic memory, 74
semiotics, 147–48, 443
seniors (55-plus generation), 163, 169–70, 220
    memory and, 74
    online shopping by, 227–28
    See also baby boomers
sensory memory, 72, 443
sensory stimuli, 57, 59–62
    attention to, 65, 66
    characteristics of, 66
    levels of, 63
    virtual, 62–63
sensory technology, 63
service. *See* customer service
sex, in fashion promotion, 125, 387–88
shoe designers, 235
shoplifting, 379–80
shopping
    changing trends in, 310
    environments, 312–16
    magazines, 264–65
    with scanners, 46–47
    social aspect of, 310
    See also retailing/retailers; *specific environment*
short-term memory, 72–73, 443
Silverstein, Michael, 171, 230
similarity, 68
Simmons, Russell, 192, 343
sincerity, 149

single household stage, 173t, 176
skincare products, for men, 353
Skinner, B. F., 69
smell, sense of, 60–61
Smith, Adam, 30
SnapFashun, 358
Snoeren, Rolf, 148, 231
Snyder, Kamlyn, 165
social aspect, of shopping, 310
social class, 190, 443
social factors, in motivation, 86
social impact theory, 197–98, 444
social influence, 187–208, 444
    conformity and, 189, 194
    consumer socialization process, 207
    different types of, 188–90
    on fashion and design, 190
    on fashion diffusion, 191–96
    forces influencing behavior, 187–88
    impact of groups, 199–201
    informational, 195–96
    interactive, 197–98
    membership influences, 201–2
    normative, 194–95
    opinion leaders as, 206–7
    reference groups, 170, 199, 200t, 201
    in retail context, 196–98
    types of, 194–96
    urban legends and, 204–6
socialization, 174, 444
social presence, in retail context, 196–98
social proofing, 195
social responsibility, 392–97
    cause-related marketing and, 395–97
    defined, 378, 444
    environmental concerns, 237, 341, 393–95
    on individual level, 378–79
social self-image, 137
societal customs and traditions, 133
societal marketing concept, 49, 341, 444
sociocultural theories, 134–36
sociology, 7, 81, 444
Solomon, Michael, 287
Somerset, Kate, 172
Song, Eunyoung, 65f
Sony Corporation, 63
    PlayStation Portable, 11–12

sophistication, 150
soy, in fabrics, 394
Spain, 365
Spandex, 105, 416
spa services for men, 229–30
specialty stores, 229*t*, 307–8, 311*t*, 368
spirit of the times. *See* zeitgeist
SRI (research organization), 240, 241
stability, need for, 86
stakeholder, 43, 49, 444
Standard for Flammability of Children's
        Sleepwear, 408, 444
Starbucks (coffee chain), 16, 83–85
star power. *See* celebrities
Stewart, Martha, 34, 65, 144
Stihl (tool manufacturer), 17
stimulation, need for, 144–45
stimulus, 68, 444
        attention and, 65, 66, 276
        behavioral learning and, 69–70, 71
        brand and, 58*f*
        motivation and, 82, 86
        sensory, 57, 58–63, 65, 66
Stop Counterfeiting in Manufactured Goods
        Act, 424
store credit cards, 251, 259, 386
store design and layout, 313–14
        See also retailing/retailers
STP formula, 42–45
        See also segmentation; target market;
                positioning
strategic marketing plan, 36, 444
strategy, 41, 444
Strategy Targeting Organized Piracy
        (STOP), 424, 444
street art, 11–12
street vendors, counterfeit goods and, 377,
        383*f*
subcultural groups, 350–52, 353*f*, 356
        shopping habits of, 351–52
        See also Hispanic market
subculture, 190, 444
subjective norms, 121, 122*t*, 444
subliminal perception, 64, 444
superego, 133, 134, 138
        defined, 132, 444
superiority, feelings of, 134
supply chain, 45, 445

management/distribution, 8
surplus, role of, 95
surveys, of customers, 252, 256, 368
        Women's Wear Daily, 306, 307, 311*t*
sweatshops, 390–91, 445
symbols
        brand, 73
        cultural, 355, 357
        semiotics and, 147–48
        in care labeling, 420

target market, 13, 18, 445
        brand personality and, 151
        specialty stores and, 307
target marketing, 43–44, 445
Target (retailer), 57, 104–5, 107, 300, 317,
        410
        cheap chic at, 304, 307
        counterfeit goods and, 383
        design and designers at, 104, 106,
                110–11
        hip TV advertising by, 265
        Mizrahi at, 111, 126, 307
        pop-up store of, 91
        "vertical" fashion show of, 266
tariffs, 361, 445
taste, sense of, 62
technology, buying decisions and, 290–91
teenagers (adolescents), 168–69, 235
        alcohol and, 95, 388
        cell phone use by, 165–66, 264
        "girlcott" protest, 388–89
        growing influence of, 180–81
        peers and, 116
        proper nutrition for, 339
        spending patterns of, 224–25
telephones. *See* cell phones
television, 192, 204, 263, 265
        advertising campaigns on, 35, 36–38
        commercials, 109
        GLBT market and, 231
        product placement on, 265–66
television shopping, 312
Textile Fiber Products Identification Act,
        415–16, 445
textile products labeling, 415–18
textiles, hand of, 57–58
        See also fabric

text messaging, 262, 264

theft, 379–80

theories

 balance, 119–20, 431

 of cognitive dissonance, 124–25, 445

 of fashion diffusion, 191–94

 of learning, 69–72

 of personality, 132–47

 of reasoned action, 121–23, 445

 social impact, 197–98

threshold level, 282

Tiffany & Company, 4, 151, 230, 240

 packaging of, 57

Timberland (manufacturer), 393

Time magazine, 12, 14*f*

timepiece, cell phone as, 165

TiVo (home entertainment service), 265, 291

TLA Entertainment (home-video chain), 281–85

Topshop (retailer), 304, 362

TORA. *See* theory of reasoned action

touch, sense of, 57–58

trade, balance of, 363, 431

trade associations, 254, 255*f*

trade deficit, 361, 362, 445

Trademark Counterfeiting Act (2004), 424

trade publications, 254, 255*f*

trade surplus, 361, 363, 445

traditional family life cycle, 174*t*, 176, 445

traits, 141, 445

trait theories, 141–47

travel apparel market, 227

Treasure Hunt: Inside the Mind of the New Consumer (Silverstein), 230, 317

trend

 defined, 14–15, 445

 forecasting services, 357, 358–59*t*, 445

 global, 360

Trendstop, 358

trickle-across theory, 192

trickle-down theory, 191

trickle-up theory, 192

Trout, Jack, 20, 44–45

Trump, Donald, 34, 120, 123, 144

trunk show, 263, 445

trust (monopoly), 415, 445

truth-in-advertising laws, 387, 421–22, 445

Truth in Lending Act, 423

Turner, Patricia A., 204–6

turnover, in personnel, 335

twenty-first-century family life cycle, 175*t*, 445

unconscious, 132

unconscious motive, 85, 446

Underhill, Paco, 314

Unfairness Policy Statement, 422

UNICEF. *See under* United Nations

uniform industry, 233

Unilever (manufacturer), 351

Uniqlo (retailer), 366

uniquely ME! program, 138

uniqueness, need for, 143

United Kingdom, 361, 368, 369

United Nations, 236

 UNICEF, 340, 341*f*, 342, 395

United States, 214, 369

 changing demographics of, 215–23

 consumerism in, 236

 fashion goods imports of, 361

 Hispanic market in, 222–23, 254, 351

 immigrant population in, 219, 220, 222

 materialism in, 236–37

 subcultural groups in, 350–52

 sweatshops in, 388

 trade deficit of, 361, 362

 urban growth in, 216, 218*t*

United States government. *See* government

United Way, 329

unsought goods, 90, 446

up-branding, 15–17

 See also luxury brands

upper class, 191

upscale look, 335–36

upward flow (trickle-up) theory, 192, 446

urban areas, U.S., 216, 218*t*

urban legends, 204–6

urban uptowners, 242, 243*t*

users, 179, 181*t*. *See also* consumers

utilitarian function, 112, 302

utility, expected, 282

utilitarian influences, 200, 446

VALS framework, 240–41, 446

value, 36, 48, 237, 446

 vs. cost, 30–32

value-expressive function, 112, 113
value-expressive influences, 201, 446
values, and consumption, 234–38
value system, 354–56, 446
    See also ethics
variety, need for, 86, 240
verbalizers, 143
vertical desire, 192
Victoria's Secret (retailer), 123, 308, 387*f*, 410
    college students and, 10, 351
videogames, 267
    advergames, 164, 179
video rental or buy decision, 281–85
viral marketing, 11, 446
vision, 57
visualizers, 143
Voluntary Cosmetic Registration Program, 413

Wall Street Journal, 149, 190, 334
Wal-Mart (retailer), 126, 214, 284, 317, 364
    cheap chic at, 307
    environmental concerns of, 393, 394*f*
    hurricane relief and, 396
    Sam's Club and, 4, 231, 314, 383
    sweatshops and, 391
wants, 446
    vs. needs, 82–83, 86, 176
wealth, distribution of, 225*t*, 233
    See also mass affluent; income
Wealth of Nations (Smith), 30
Weber's Law, 64, 446
web logs. *See* blogosphere
Web sites, 103, 108*f*, 190, 267
    children and, 207
    Consumer Action, 426
    for gays and lesbians, 231–32
    shoe design, 235
    social networking, 13–14, 166–67
    tracking "cookies" on, 259
    See also Internet; online shopping
Western Europe, 236
    See also Europe; *specific country*
What Flavor Is Your Personality (Hirsch), 149
Wheeler, M. Cass, 330–31
Wheeler-Lea Amendment (1958), 415
"Where Americans Shop" (*WWD* study),

306
Who We Are Now: The Changing Face of America in the Twenty-First Century (Roberts), 215
Why Customers Do What They Do (Cohen), 150
Why We Buy (Underhill), 314
window displays, 313, 343
Winfrey, Oprah, 144, 204, 392
women, 395
    automobile advertising and, 228
    birthrate and, 219
    career-age, 58–59
    growing incomes of, 230
    maternity wear for, 164, 219
    self-image of, 47, 139–38
    shopping destinations of, 229*t*
    tools designed for, 173
"Women's Fashion Accessories" (NPD report), 258
Women's Wear Daily (WWD), 148, 254
    shopping survey by, 306, 307, 311*t*
Wooden, Ruth A., 331–32
Woods, Tiger, 120, 144, 263*f*, 264
Wool Products Labeling Act, 416–17, 446
word-of-mouth (WOM), 9–11, 13*f*, 141, 267–68
    See also buzz
world trade, 362
    See also globalization
Worth Global Style Network, 358
Wymore, Cindy, 275

young people. *See* children; teenagers

Zara (retailer), 304, 365
zeitgeist, 6, 332, 333, 334, 335, 446
ZIP codes, 312
    market segments and, 242, 243*t*